SO-ACB-887

ROBERT MANNING
STROZIER LIBRARY

MAY 25 1994

Tallahassee, Florida

Jaguar Books on Latin America

William H. Beezley and
Colin MacLachlan
Editors

Addressing subjects as diverse as the region itself, the Jaguar Books on Latin America guide the reader through the myriad political systems, economies, and societies that comprise today's Latin America. Each volume in the series is edited by an eminent scholar in the field and gathers the most influential primary and secondary documents on a topic of central importance to the region's history and development. Together the Jaguar Books stand as a library of sources for teaching, as well as a useful reference for all those interested in Latin American culture, history, and current affairs.

The Indian
in Latin American History

The Indian in Latin American History

Resistance, Resilience, and Acculturation

John E. Kicza
Editor

Jaguar Books on Latin America
Number 1

A Scholarly Resources Inc. Imprint
Wilmington, Delaware

The paper used in this publication meets the minimum requirements of the American National Standard for permanence of paper for printed library materials, Z39.48, 1984.

©1993 by Scholarly Resources Inc.
All rights reserved
First published 1993
Printed and bound in the United States of America

Scholarly Resources Inc.
104 Greenhill Avenue
Wilmington, DE 19805-1897

Library of Congress Cataloging-in-Publication Data

The Indian in Latin American history : resistance, resilience, and
    acculturation / John E. Kicza, editor.
       p.   cm. — (Jaguar books on Latin America ; 1)
    Includes bibliographical references.
    ISBN 0-8420-2421-2. — ISBN 0-8420-2425-5 (pbk.)
    1. Indians—History. 2. Latin America—History. 3. Indians—Ethnic
identity. 4. Indians—Cultural assimilation. 5. Acculturation—Latin
America. 6. Latin America—Politics and government. I. Kicza, John E.,
1947–   . II. Series.
E65.I45   1993
980—dc20
                                              93-16324
                                                CIP

E
65
I45
1993

The following articles were reprinted by permission of the original publishers or authors, who retain all rights:

Thomas C. Paterson, "The Inca Empire and Its Subject Peoples," from *The Inca Empire: The Formation and Disintegration of a Pre-Capitalist State* (Providence, RI, 1991), 98–116. Reprinted by permission of Berg Publishers.

Steve J. Stern, "The Rise and Fall of Indian-White Alliances: A Regional View of 'Conquest' History," from *Hispanic American Historical Review* 61, no. 3:461–91. © 1981 by Duke University Press. Reprinted by permission.

Nancy M. Farriss, "Maya Society under Colonial Rule: The Collective Enterprise of Survival," from *Maya Society under Colonial Rule: The Collective Enterprise of Survival* (Princeton, 1984), 12–25. © 1984 by Princeton University Press. Reprinted by permission.

Robert Charles Padden, "Cultural Adaptation and Militant Autonomy among the Araucanians of Chile," from *Southwestern Journal of Anthropology* 13, no. 1 (Spring 1957): 103–21. Reprinted by permission of the *Journal of Anthropological Research*.

Ronald Spores, "Spanish Penetration and Cultural Change in Early Colonial Mexico," from *The Mixtecs in Ancient and Colonial Times* (Norman, OK, 1984), 97–121. © 1984 by the University of Oklahoma Press.

William B. Taylor, "Patterns and Variety in Mexican Village Uprisings," from *Drinking, Homicide and Rebellion in Colonial Mexican Villages* (Stanford, 1979), 113–51, by the permission of Stanford University Press. © 1979 by the Board of Trustees of the Leland Stanford Junior University.

Evelyn Hu-DeHart, "Yaqui Resistance to Mexican Expansion," from *Yaqui Resistance and Survival: The Struggle for Land and Autonomy, 1821–1910* (Madison, WI, 1984), 94–117. Reprinted by permission of the University of Wisconsin Press.

Erick D. Langer, "Andean Rituals of Revolt: The Chayanta Rebellion of 1927," *Ethnohistory* 37, no. 3 (Summer 1990): 227–53. © 1990 by American Society of Ethnohistory. Reprinted by permission of Duke University Press.

Frans J. Schryer, "Ethnicity and Class Conflict in Rural Mexico," from *Ethnicity and Class Conflict in Rural Mexico*, 245–56. © 1990 by Princeton University Press. Reprinted by permission.

Evon Z. Vogt, "The Maintenance of Mayan Distinctiveness." Chapter 9 from *The Zinacantecos of Mexico: A Modern Maya Way of Life*, second edition, by Evon Z. Vogt. © 1990 by Holt, Rinehart and Winston, Inc. Reprinted by permission.

Contents

Introduction

John E. Kicza

The history of Latin America does not begin in 1492. Some tens of millions
of peoples organized into distinct polities and ethnic groups had already
lived in this vast region for thousands of years before Europeans reached the
hemisphere. Nor are we dependent just on archaeology and oral traditions
for our knowledge of the history and culture of many of these societies. The
more elaborate among them—most notably, the Maya and the Aztecs—had
developed writing and mnemonic systems that recorded aspects of their
pasts and their beliefs. Further, soon after the arrival of the Europeans, some
members of these cultures learned to write their language using the Spanish
alphabet. They then composed versions both of their histories and of
contemporary events in their societies, sometimes with very little Spanish
intervention.

The native peoples of the Americas have displayed remarkable cultural
resilience in the face of demographic catastrophes; loss of lands and local
political autonomy; recurrent infusions of outside technologies, animals,
foods, and procedures over the centuries; and disrespectful treatment of
their values and ways of life by the governments and citizens of those
nations into which they have been merged. To the extent possible, Indian
peoples have been selective about what aspects of the outside world they
incorporate into their cultures. The indigenous communities have not been
without resources. They have used their internal unity, under dedicated
local leaders in many cases, to incorporate the changes forced upon them on
the best terms that they could muster. Nor were they cowed or passive
before the impositions of colonial and national governments. Both individual
Indians and Indian corporations commonly initiated petitions and lawsuits
to demand remedies for perceived injustices. Local rebellions by native
peoples were endemic in large parts of Latin America over the centuries;
some indigenous communities had well-earned reputations for insurrection.
Occasionally, these rebellions became widespread and threatened major
regions and even national governments. Through a combination of selective
adaptation and peaceful (or sometimes violent) resistance, the native peoples

of Latin America, even those subjugated by the Europeans, have been making their own histories for five hundred years.

Latin American Indians have been so successful in drawing upon their own resources and capacities that today their numbers are growing and they constitute a majority of the population in countries such as Guatemala and Bolivia and a substantial plurality in Mexico, Ecuador, and Peru. Even in countries where they do not make up a large part of the population—Brazil, Colombia, and Chile, for example—native peoples have been able to assert their rights and claims and make the national societies come to grips with the issues of native autonomy and control over land and other resources.

Clear evidence of human habitation in the Americas dates from at least 25,000 B.C., and some findings hint at a human presence in this continent perhaps twenty thousand years earlier. Whatever the actual date of humanity's arrival in this part of the world, undoubtedly the next great transforming development was the emergence of agriculture in the centuries before 1,500 B.C. Indications are that native peoples of Mexico, Guatemala, Colombia, and Peru commenced the cultivation of crops—instead of continuing their practice of hunting and gathering—autonomously and at roughly the same time. By 1,500 B.C. villages of full-time farmers were proliferating. Maize, beans, and squash constituted the primary crops cultivated, but potatoes and manioc dominated some major agricultural zones in South America.

The intensive, permanent cultivation of crops had immense consequences for the native peoples' way of life. It promoted a vast increase in the population and required practitioners to remain settled in communities surrounded by their fields. This sedentary existence facilitated occupational differentiation, as farmers routinely produced food surpluses that they were willing to trade for the finished goods fashioned by local artisans. Social distinctions also emerged. With time, ruling classes, sometimes complete with royal families, appeared, as did a priesthood. In fact, religious practice became more elaborate, and large ceremonial complexes were constructed for the first time. Hundreds of ethnic groups worshipped similar sets of gods, though each group gave its local versions distinct names and, understandably, saw its own gods as the rightful and effective ones, unlike those of the other peoples.

These hundreds of ethnic groups practicing agriculture eventually formed themselves into political entities, organized as provinces in which a head town—where the ruling dynasty resided—controlled a complex of subject villages; in turn, in each village there was a set of families who governed local society. It was from among these sedentary agricultural societies, with their labor surpluses, local craft specializations, and large armies, that empires developed. These entities could be found in Mesoamerica (the sedentary zone of Central America, roughly the southern two-thirds of Mexico, all of Guatemala, and most of El Salvador, Honduras, and Nicaragua) and in the Andean highlands in the modern nations of Ecuador, Peru, and Bolivia at least a millennium and a half before the arrival of Europeans in the hemisphere. No other true empires would appear in indigenous America, for the hundreds of other ethnic groups, totaling in the millions of people, did not practice fully sedentary agriculture and hence lacked the attributes needed for the long-term conquest of other societies (although warfare was common among these peoples).

Mesoamerica and the Andean zone witnessed the rise and fall of a series of empires over the centuries. The conquerors typically demanded labor service from the subjugated peoples and, in the case of Mesoamerica, formal tribute payments also. The Incas and the Aztecs were the last examples—though certainly dramatically successful ones—of such polities, and in most aspects they replicated the institutions and practices of their predecessors. Characteristically, all of these empires permitted the inhabitants of their subjugated provinces to retain their own languages, sets of gods, local rulers, and separate ethnic identities, as Thomas Patterson illustrates in Chapter 1. These long-surviving empires did not destroy the ethnic distinctiveness of the subordinated peoples, who were quick to rebel whenever they saw any chance of success.

Many other peoples practiced some agriculture, but their environments were sufficiently unaccommodating that they had to move their settlements within a certain zone every few years and perhaps supplement their crops with substantial amounts of other foods. Most of the Maya of the Yucatán Peninsula and Guatemala practiced this slash-and-burn, or swidden, agriculture. Such agriculture dictated lower population densities and made enduring empires harder to attain—these peoples were more difficult to organize into large polities and had fewer surplus resources that they could transfer to an imperial power. Besides living in the southern zone of Mesoamerica, substantial numbers of semisedentary peoples resided on the major Caribbean islands and in highland Colombia, Brazil, Paraguay, and Chile.

Hunting-and-gathering peoples who practiced no agriculture remained in the desert, mountain, and tropical areas of Latin America. Organized into many small ethnic groups, they actually totaled far fewer persons than did either the sedentary or semisedentary societies. Without agriculture but with a need to migrate over considerable distances in order to gain sufficient resources to survive, these bands had to remain rather small in order to function effectively. Understandably, there was little political or craft differentiation among these peoples; the primary distinction in labor roles was based on gender. The artistic achievement of these peoples was rudimentary, and they used natural sites rather than constructed arenas as their religious centers. There were no empires among such societies, but they were especially adept fighters, utilizing ambushes and rapid retreats and advances as tactics and bows and arrows, sometimes poisoned, as weapons.

The best estimates indicate that the total native population of the Americas approached 75 million people on the eve of the Europeans' arrival. Of these native peoples, around 8 million lived in North America, more than 22 million in Mexico, some 8 million in Central America, another 8 million in the Caribbean, about 17 million along the Andes, and perhaps 12 million in lowland South America. The vast numbers in Mexico and the Andes resulted, of course, from the dominance of agriculture and densely settled permanent villages in these areas.

It is only to non-natives that these peoples can be classified into a collective population termed "Indian." They were as distinct from each other in language and ethnic identity as their counterparts were in Europe—and often as contentious. In fact, the major differences between native Americans and the peoples of Europe, Africa, and Asia (for the peoples of these three continents shared broadly similar characteristics) were largely accidents of history and geography. The native Americans lacked metal tools and weapons, did not have draft animals, and did not use the wheel in manual labor. They also were insulated from most of the epidemic diseases that regularly ravaged the Old World.

The Americans routinely refined gold, silver, and copper, which they shaped into ornaments. However, they had not developed industrial metals, especially iron, which are harder and thus appropriate for making tools. As a consequence, they largely relied on hard, sharp stones as tools and weapons. Flint and obsidian functioned as projectile points and were placed along the edges of swords and clubs. Overall, their lack of industrial metals led to a certain technological stagnation among these peoples. The tools of the Aztecs and the Incas varied little from those of peoples who preceded them by a millennium and a half.

The Western Hemisphere lacked horses, oxen, and other suitable beasts of burden. It also did not have cattle, pigs, goats, or chickens. The plains of North America were, of course, the home of millions of buffalo, which provided abundant meat, hides, and other necessities of life, but buffalo are totally unsuitable as beasts of burden. Llamas constituted the only useful animals of size in South America, and, although they yielded some meat and could bear some weight, they could not pull plows or wagons. Without draft animals, native Americans had little use for the wheel. They certainly knew of it and incorporated it into small implements, but they could not use it in sizable undertakings without large animals to provide power.

In most respects the Spanish resembled other European colonists of the Americas. Unlike the others, however, the Spanish rarely just established trading bases in new lands; instead, they sought to settle the lands fully and permanently. This process entailed the significant immigration of people (commonly an appreciable minority of the immigrants were women) and importation of animals, the establishment of cities, the setting up of rural enterprises to supply the urban sector, the incorporation of the local native peoples into a dependent labor force, and a rigorous effort to locate and work deposits of precious metals. These people went to the Americas not out of some compelling need for adventure but rather to make a better life for themselves and their descendants. Hardly any of them possessed a strong curiosity about Indian thought and culture. They wished merely for the native peoples to be peaceful, to provide them with unskilled labor, and to convert to Christianity. The actual conversion effort was left largely to members of religious orders with the support of wealthier colonists who financed a good bit of the process. Precious metals were pursued because they constituted the commodity that could be exported most profitably to Europe and thereby underwrite the long-term prosperity of a colony. (Eventually, in some areas in the Americas, commodities such as sugar, tobacco, dyewoods, and furs would also support elaborate colonial societies.)

The defeat of the great imperial armies of the Aztecs and the Incas by small Spanish expeditions seems quite beyond belief until systematically examined. Of course, the Spanish forces did not have to fight all of the millions of peoples who made up these massive empires. In fact, most of the subordinated peoples already within these empires welcomed the Spanish as potential liberators from the demands of their traditional oppressors. Thus Hernán Cortés and Francisco Pizarro were able to get many ethnic groups to agree either to remain outside the fight or even, sometimes, to support the invaders. The Spanish also benefited immensely from their technological superiority over the Indians. Firearms and cannon were not too important, for they were slow to fire, inaccurate, and inappropriate for the battles in open country that characterized warfare between the Spaniards and the sedentary empires. Far more decisive were the metal weapons and armor and the small contingent of horses that each expedition usually had with it. Lacking armor, the native armies could not defend themselves against the crossbow fire, swords, and lances of the Spanish. The Spanish cavalry was virtually unstoppable, able to disperse or outflank any formation assembled against it.

The technological advantage of the Spanish was maximized by the style of warfare practiced by the imperial societies. Making only minimal use of bows and arrows, imperial soldiers preferred close engagement with their opponents. They were equipped with wooden clubs commonly edged with obsidian chips, and they typically fought in the open rather than from cover, stressing capture over the killing of their opponents. The imperial armies presented themselves in tight formations in which only the front rank could actually fight, and they remained under strict hierarchies. When commanders were killed or captured, their forces would fall out of action.

Finally, the Spanish, as did all the European colonists, unwittingly brought with them virulent epidemic diseases with which the American peoples had no experience and against which they had no resistance. Smallpox, measles, and typhus seem to have had the worst impact. These diseases were so contagious that smallpox was already sweeping through the Aztec capital when Cortés had it under siege. Both an Aztec and an Incan emperor died from this disease even though no European was in their vicinity at the time.

After the defeat of their empires, the Indians tried to explain these catastrophic defeats to themselves. Because they were very religious peoples who believed that the gods determined all outcomes, they asserted that their defeats had been prefigured by omens and that they had viewed the Spaniards as returning gods. However, the evidence indicates that this perspective developed after the fact and did not affect the course of the actual conquests.

The Spanish never saw it as in their interest to destroy the structure of native society. Rather, they sought to use the structure that was already in place to govern effectively, to mobilize cheap Indian labor, to funnel resources into the Hispanic sector of the society, and to Christianize the population. Steve Stern (Chapter 2) describes the Spanish reliance on indigenous systems and traditional relationships in the decades just after the conquest of Peru and how the elaboration of a large-scale market economy and the declining native population brought an end to this practice.

Against native peoples who were not fully sedentary and organized into empires, the Spaniards' technological advantages faded. Nancy Farriss (Chapter 3) shows some of the difficulties the Spaniards faced against the loosely confederated Maya in the Yucatán Peninsula. The Spaniards had to fight nearly every individual settlement in this region—a difficult tropical environment in which Spanish mobility was restricted and that the Maya could utilize to their advantage. Mayan settlements could withdraw into the countryside in the face of Spanish advances, and, when beleaguered, Mayan fighters could retreat into difficult country to fight another day.

Robert Padden, in Chapter 4, analyzes one of the most dramatic cases of successful resistance by native peoples. The Araucanians of southern Chile remained independent of outside control until they finally were defeated by the Chilean army around 1880. Mobility, flexibility, and adaptation explain how they were able to retain their autonomy prior to their defeat. The Araucanians adopted the horse and even changed their settlement and eating patterns to enhance their ability to resist. Over the decades they studied the Spanish way of fighting and developed suitable responses. But in the late nineteenth century, the introduction of the repeating rifle and of such developments as barbed wire and the telegraph gave the Chileans the means to subdue the Araucanians. (The Araucanians who controlled southern Argentina also were defeated at this time by an Argentine army utilizing the same advances.)

The Spanish faced immense difficulties in overcoming the hunting-and-gathering peoples located in northern Mexico, at the Amazon head-waters, in eastern Bolivia, and elsewhere. Often the colonists abandoned their efforts to subdue these native groups, which fought them so effectively using bows and arrows and hit-and-run tactics. These Indians held little promise as a usable labor force and generally controlled no resources that the Spanish considered lucrative. It was in this setting that the Spanish would establish missions in an effort gradually to convert the natives and to attract them to a European style of life. In northern Mexico, however, the Spaniards discovered major silver deposits and thus had to protect the region's mining towns and shipping routes from attack. During the second half of the sixteenth century their attempts either to subjugate the local peoples or to run them off were notably unsuccessful. The Spanish viceroys finally resorted to offering the local groups annual shipments of supplies to be provided by the colonial government if they would agree to cease their raids, settle in permanent villages, and accept missionaries among them. The natives generally accepted such offers because the alternative was continued warfare in which the native societies suffered losses and disloca-tion even when they prevailed in a particular campaign. Consequently, much of the north was opened to colonization.

Until roughly 1650 the factor that most transformed Indian life in Latin America was the collapse of the population brought about overwhelmingly by the new epidemic diseases that arrived with the colonists. As these diseases were most virulent in temperate settings where there was heavy population density, central Mexico suffered as badly as, if not worse than, any other region. In a little over a century, successive waves of epidemics reduced the native population by about 95 percent, from more than 20 million people to fewer than 1.5 million. The indigenous community in the Spanish Caribbean literally had been eliminated by 1550. Central America and the Andean region were also badly hit. It must be stressed that the Spanish neither encouraged nor understood the catastrophe. They sought to utilize local native populations, not to eradicate them.

The primary consequence of this enormous die-off was to skew the native–colonist population ratios so greatly that the surviving Indians were more fully acculturated to the European way of life (as described by Ronald Spores in Chapter 5) and could be more closely regulated by Spanish priests and administrators and that great expanses of agricultural land that had become depopulated were thus available for cultivation by colonists. Without this demographic catastrophe, modern Latin America would more closely resemble Africa or India, where the European impact, although certainly significant, was not as transforming of native cultural, social, and political patterns as it was in the Western Hemisphere.

The introduction of Old World animals and tools affected the indigenous way of life as well. Horses, oxen, cattle, pigs, and chickens were brought to the Americas in great numbers. Overall, Indian villagers did not incorporate draft animals into their agricultural practices in a systematic fashion, but pigs and chickens became staples in their diets. Tools, pans, and knives of metal became integral parts of native existence. Firearms, however, seem to have been used rarely by Indians, even in hunting.

The Christianization of the Indians is a controversial and poorly understood development. An appreciation that there was always a shortage of Catholic priests available to work in native communities and that the Indians often were inclined to adopt major components of the religion of their conquerors—even before the arrival of the Europeans—helps to explain much of what transpired. A Spanish cleric typically set up his parish in the head town of an Indian province. He would be able to visit the many villages within the province only two or three times each year. Church marriages, baptisms, and the like thus had to wait for such occasions. Of course, the priest could teach religious doctrine, say Mass, and hear confessions only at these times also. Understandably, then, the form of Catholicism that emerged stressed community values and public celebrations, which did not require a priest's continued presence. Individual towns adopted patron saints and shrines that they promoted in their festivities. Neighborhoods and other community groups organized themselves into religious brotherhoods (*cofradías*) to sustain such activities and to provide benefits to the membership. Over time, assumption of the burden of sponsoring community religious celebrations became the primary avenue by which an individual could rise in respect and responsibility within the society, and the men who sacrificed their interests to those of the community through such endeavors became eligible to hold the highest civic offices. This set of practices has become termed the *cargo system*.

Spanish priests commonly located their churches and chapels upon sites that the Indians already considered sacred. For their part, the Indians often merged the Catholic church's spectrum of saints with their own enduring pantheon of gods. The result of such practices was a certain combining of systems of belief, called syncretism, that has lasted in many areas to the present day.

It would be misleading, however, to argue that Spanish priests—or colonial officials, for that matter—acted as the primary agents of change in native culture. Rather, that honor goes to the colonists themselves, who, by their continuing interaction with the Indians, generally in the most informal and unstructured ways, engendered new practices and relationships. For despite laws against it, Indians interacted incessantly with Spaniards in colonial towns, mining camps, and rural estates. Sometimes natives would fulfill a labor shift at such a location, during which time they would be exposed to European material culture and customs, and then would return to their home community. Other natives, however, remained and became permanent members of Spanish colonial society. Nor did Spaniards and, later, the persons of mixed blood (mestizos) who resulted from the matings between Spaniards and Indians, stay out of Indian communities. Few of these individuals chose to live in such communities in the colonial period (though later a scattering would reside interspersed in Indian villages with regularity), but they passed through as peddlers, labor recruiters, and the like.

Early in the colonial period, Indian communities were expected to supply a portion of their adult male populations—generally around one sixth—on a rotating basis to work in the Spanish sector of the economy. Such labor gangs were organized by the villages' headmen (caciques), and they remained under the immediate supervision of their own leaders during their period of labor. But the fruit of the natives' efforts, of course, directly assisted the Spanish sector of the society. With time, as the colonial economies became more elaborate, this form of temporary unskilled labor became less useful, and, characteristically, it endured only in the more backward parts of Latin America. Instead, Spanish entrepreneurs attracted particularly skilled and industrious Indians as permanent workers in their enterprises by offering them improved terms of employment. Many natives accepted such offers because of the considerable deterioration that had taken place in their own communities from population decline and Spanish demands for labor service and tribute payments. Working for individual Spaniards provided them with a degree of security and protection from the worst of these demands. Over the long term, then, a considerable number of Indians came to reside permanently in Spanish colonial society, and their children were born to this, rather than to the traditional village way of life. As the Indians interbred with Spaniards and blacks in the cities and on rural estates, a large community of persons of mixed blood emerged with whom urban Indians interacted on a regular basis.

The eighteenth century was a time of considerable economic growth in Latin America. Previously peripheral regions were incorporated into the world market economy for the first time and prospered as a result. In already heavily settled and economically developed regions, such as Mexico and Peru, market-oriented estates proliferated throughout the countryside, occupying virtually all of the land suitable for cultivation and grazing. Indian communities were increasingly restricted to just the lands they traditionally controlled, lands that the colonial governments had recognized as theirs and now helped to protect. Both Indian communities and their individual members now enjoyed little opportunity to expand their land holdings.

This situation might not have been harmful except for the sizable growth in the indigenous population that took place during the same era. Whereas the native population in the Americas would never again approach what it had been upon the arrival of the Europeans, it did increase rapidly as the natives built up resistance to the several epidemic diseases that periodically had ravaged their population over the previous two centuries. For example, indications are that Mexico's native population roughly doubled, to a total of about 3.7 million over the hundred years before 1810. But the Spanish and mixed-blood populations were growing as well and at nearly comparable rates at this time. Heightened competition for the limited resources in these societies resulted.

As Indian communities experienced little improvement in productivity, they had to send out their members, either temporarily or permanently, to be laborers in the Spanish sector of the economy. Some natives thus lost their connections with their communities of birth and became permanent dwellers in cities or on rural estates. Others returned to their villages, using their external earnings to help their communities survive economically. (This pattern has endured to the present day, and one may inquire whether modern Indian communities could survive without the continuing outmigration of their young combined with an influx of part of the money that is earned.)

As demonstrated by William Taylor (Chapter 6), village uprisings increased greatly in frequency in both Mexico and Peru during this period. However, these uprisings typically addressed local grievances and, therefore, rarely developed into regional or crossethnic revolts against the government. Nonetheless, in 1780, an Andean cacique named José Gabriel de Condorcanqui, who himself lived and operated regularly within the Spanish sector of the society, initiated a revolt that was joined by great numbers of people in the highlands. He gave himself the name Tupac Amaru II, claiming descent from the last autonomous Inca ruler, Tupac Amaru, who was executed in 1572. His movement dominated the highlands around Cuzco for some months, even attracting active support from people of mixed blood and from lower-class Spaniards, until a military expedition dispatched from Lima defeated the insurgents. Tupac Amaru, his wife (a Spaniard who functioned as one of his primary lieutenants), and other commanders were captured and executed. But the Andean highlands remained in an unsettled state for another half century, with periodic regional revolts breaking out throughout Peru and Bolivia.

Members of Indian communities had surprisingly little involvement in the Latin American independence movements from 1808 to 1825. By and large, the leaders of these movements belonged to local elites, and their complaints simply did not address the place of native peoples in their societies, except for arguing that equality before the law should prevail in the new nations and that ethnic designations should be eliminated. Furthermore, neither the patriots nor the royalists saw a need to mobilize the Indian masses in their warfare against each other.

Although the vast number of Indians who lived in traditional villages under the authority of their ethnic leaders stayed out of the independence struggle (if anything, they seem to have favored the status quo), in Mexico that substantial minority of Indians who had left their communities to live permanently in the Spanish sector of the society strongly backed the initial uprising against the colonial order. This uprising was led by Father Miguel Hidalgo and began in the prosperous agricultural and mining region north of Mexico City. Tens of thousands of lower-class Spaniards, people of mixed blood, and acculturated Indians joined Hidalgo's army as it captured important regional centers and advanced on Mexico City. To the extent that we can determine the intentions of those Indians who participated, it seems that they resented the discrimination they endured under the prevailing social and political order as well as the requirement that they continue to pay tribute to the government even though most of them had long abandoned their association with native communities. When Hidalgo's army was crushed in a battle that took place about six months after the start of the insurrection, most of the priest's supporters tried to resume their civilian lives, but a substantial minority organized themselves into small regional gangs—often not very different from bandits—and remained active for years.

The new national governments, usually dominated by liberals, thought that Indians should lose both the special protections afforded and the obligations placed upon them during the colonial period and become full and equal citizens. They also believed that Indian lands should no longer be held in common but instead should be distributed to individual members of the communities who then would either work their private plots or sell them, as they saw fit. But these early governments were so weak and politically unstable that none could organize an effective campaign to achieve these ends. They were desperate for revenue, and some nations therefore retained the Indian tribute system for several decades after independence, renaming the impost an "indigenous contribution" in an effort to distinguish it from its colonial precedent. Residents of many Indian communities in Central America and in the Andean republics were expected to contribute several days of free labor each year to maintain local roads.

Village uprisings occurred in the early national period much as they had in the late colonial, but now the Indian communities were commonly on the offensive rather than seeking to protect themselves from threatening initiatives. Encountering politically divided elites, failing national economies, and ineffective governments, many Indian communities undertook to take lands away from nearby haciendas. In Mexico, in the late 1840s, several of these movements turned into widespread regional revolts in which the Indians organized into interethnic coalitions and acted jointly to drive all non-Indians (and thus the national government) from their provinces.

The most notable and enduring of these insurrections took place in the Yucatán and was called the "Caste War." Casualties ran into the thousands, and many thousands more fled the region. The non-Indian population had to abandon virtually the entire countryside and cluster in several cities, and the Yucatán's market economy simply collapsed. Within a couple of years, the Mexican government was able to take the offensive against the insurgents, but vast parts of the peninsula remained firmly under rebel control. A belief that a divine cross located in a remote cave spoke to their leaders, directing them to continue the revolt, helped to maintain unity among the insurgents. The rebel commanders demanded heavy labor and military service from their followers but fought among themselves, with assassinations sometimes the result. The insurrection also benefited from the rebels' ability to purchase arms from traders in British Honduras. Finally, in the first years of the twentieth century, the development of henequen plantations in the Yucatán, the fortification of the boundary with British Honduras, and the continuous deteriorating conditions in "Chan Santa Cruz," the territory controlled by the rebels, killed off the organized vestiges of the uprising. Until after World War II, however, extensive parts of the Yucatán backcountry remained in the hands of indigenous villages, which were still autonomous and sought to rekindle the revolt.

Some governments in heavily Indian countries did seek to protect their native populations in the mid-nineteenth century. Perhaps the greatest success was in Guatemala, where for more than twenty-five years starting in 1838, the conservative dictator José Rafael Carrera insulated the communal holdings of native villages from liberal demands that the collectives be broken up into small individual holdings. Carrera's government also enacted an "Indian Code" so that natives did not fall under the jurisdiction of the national legal system. Although Carrera promoted the use of indigenous languages, he still argued, nonetheless, that native peoples should eventually assimilate themselves into the larger Guatemalan nation and culture and that this should be a benign and gradual process.

The half century after about 1870 was perhaps the worst period since the initial conquest era for the Indian peoples of Latin America. Stimulated by a vastly heightened demand in the industrialized world for the commodities and minerals that they held in such abundance as well as by a tremendous influx of foreign capital and by the rapid development of railroad and utility systems and port facilities, Latin American countries installed governments oriented toward capitalist development and friendly to the large-scale projects attractive to individual investors. An atmosphere of disdain toward native peoples and their cultures proliferated throughout the hemisphere. Newly created national armies moved aggressively against those indigenous societies that sought to protect their lands and their traditional political autonomy. Evelyn Hu-DeHart (Chapter 7) recounts a central episode from one of the most enduring resistance movements, that of the Yaquis of northwestern Mexico. This unrelenting attack on native resources, culture, and autonomy continued in most countries well into the twentieth century.

The Mexican Revolution, which took place between 1910 and 1920, marks the first distinct break in this onslaught. The struggle to regain communally owned lands that had been alienated from indigenous villages over the previous half century played a major role within this movement. By the end of the violent stage of the revolution, its leaders had committed themselves to restoring these lands. In the early 1920s, vast amounts of land in central Mexico and in the Yucatán were returned to the native communities that had lost them. Establishing collectives became a central part of the revolutionary program, and their number and extent expanded each decade through the 1970s.

Land reform was not, however, without its opponents and drawbacks. Both the Indian and non-Indian populations of Mexico had increased rapidly after the revolution to the extent that the number of landless rural dwellers continued to grow in absolute terms while a vast amount of land was being distributed to millions of people. The recipients of this land often did not produce surpluses sufficient to feed Mexico's massive urban population or to be sold abroad for badly needed foreign earnings. Nor was the government's protection of native lands totally successful. Local businesspeople, often with official connections, circumvented regulations in order to gain control of communal lands or became favored suppliers and marketers to the native communities.

Beginning in the late 1930s, the Mexican government has sought to protect the diverse Indian languages and cultures of the country. Traditional caciques and village councils have had some of their authority restored. Teachers now often endeavor to provide native children with a bilingual education rather than to eradicate indigenous languages. Powerful government institutes work to preserve Indian cultures and to develop handicraft practices that may earn the natives money in the larger national economy.

Conditions for the native peoples in much of Latin America outside Mexico stayed worse longer. In countries such as Guatemala and Peru, Indian villages were required by statute to provide laborers for public works projects or large agricultural enterprises. Such laws generally were not changed until the World War II period. Even in recent times, native peoples are under duress—often with the compliance of government agencies or armed forces—to labor on plantations far from their homes. They typically are paid very low wages and may in fact owe money by the time that their obligation is over; these debts may be used to compel workers to return the following year. Wives and children often accompany the men during these periods. They live in squalid temporary housing where they are susceptible to dangerous diseases, and sometimes they too have to labor in the fields.

The native peoples of Bolivia, largely Aymara speaking, lost most of their lands early in the twentieth century to Hispanic Bolivians, who used their privileged position in the economy and in the political system to their advantage. Most of these Aymara then became retainers on the large—and typically unproductive—estates that resulted. As Erick Langer demonstrates in Chapter 8, the indigenous populations were not passive before these offensives against them. In their resistance, they revealed their retention of ancient native rituals and beliefs and also their sensitivity to the expectations and procedures of the national Bolivian society in which they lived.

In 1952, appreciating the opportunity afforded them by the overthrow of the government by a reformist coalition, Indian communities throughout Bolivia rose up, expelled estate owners, and reclaimed their traditional lands. Given the total collapse of the Bolivian military and government structures, the amount of violence involved was rather limited. The nascent reform government, recognizing the benefits to be gained from supporting the land seizures, passed a law the following year officially validating the land redistribution. Since that time, although Bolivia remains one of the most impoverished countries in Latin America, most rural villages have experienced an improvement in their quality of life. The villagers have been able to grow crops for urban markets, retain authority over their internal affairs, and benefit from the extension of education and public health services into their communities. They also are connected to the larger political system and to developments at the national level to an unprecedented extent.

Despite some concerted efforts at improvement over the last twenty-five years, conditions for the Indian peoples of Peru continue to be worse than perhaps they are in any other nation of Latin America. Until the late 1960s, the Indians' land and labor situation closely resembled that of the Bolivian native communities before the 1952 land reform. But even more than the Indians of Bolivia, the Indians of Peru were seen as belonging to an inferior culture apart from mainstream life; this attitude and Indian isolation were reinforced because the majority of Indians dwelled in the Andean highlands, whereas the Spanish, internationally oriented sector of Peruvian society predominated in the coastal regions. By the early 1960s, Indian communities and Indian workers on the backward estates that dominated the highlands had begun to protest and, sometimes, to revolt. The military who repressed these movements became sensitized to the plight of these people and to the primitiveness prevalent in this vast region of the country.

The opportunity for systematic change appeared in 1968, when a reformist military regime seized power in Peru. The following year it implemented a large-scale agrarian reform that affected the majority of estates in both the highland and coastal zones. Many permanent workers became members of the collectives that took over these lands. However, the cultural and economic isolation of these regions was not broken. By the mid-1970s, when the country entered a deep and persistent recession, the utility and appropriateness of these collectives were called into question.

In the early 1980s a radical and ruthless terrorist movement, the Shining Path, began to attack exposed highland communities. By the end of the decade they effectively controlled extensive regions and even could attack in cities along the coast. Cocaine production had begun to expand dramatically in this otherwise depressed economic climate, and many communities could survive only by growing coca leaf for the international drug trade.

As this introduction and the readings that follow make clear, most native peoples of Latin America had continued contact with the Spanish sectors of their societies and in response made tremendous modifications in their cultures—often voluntarily, but sometimes forced. In fact, over time, though sometimes haltingly, the Spanish (or Western, if you will) sphere of Latin American society has tended to expand, and the portion of the economy and society that has remained Indian has shrunk. Thus the Indian population residing within modern national societies (which excludes only that small percentage of the overall Indian population that still lives along or beyond the frontiers of effective settlement by Latin Americans of European descent, such as the peoples of the upper Amazon) is so much a part of the larger culture—passing routinely from their communities into large cities and economic enterprises and bringing back to their communities new technology and practices—that some scholars question the utility of categorizing any of these traditional villages as "Indian" any longer. Some of the flexibility in and political volatility of Indian identity in contemporary Mexico is related by Frans Schryer (Chapter 9). As vast numbers of indigenous people have become well integrated into the market economies and dynamic cultures of their national societies, they have lost, willingly or not, most of the attributes that had distinguished them from peoples of European or mixed ancestry.

As Evon Vogt describes in Chapter 10, even where native identity is more firmly set—as it is in the southern Mexican municipality of Zinacantan—powerful forces threaten the cohesion and cultural integrity of the Indian society. Most indigenous communities are so poor that they must send many of their youths to find work out in the larger society. Sometimes these emigrants are expected to send part of their earnings back to their home communities to help support those who remain. As these communities promote their own internal economic growth and diversification, they typically find it difficult to maintain their ethnic distinctiveness. Permitting a significant number of outsiders to marry into or to own property or establish businesses in the community also often threatens the community's distinct cultural heritage over the long term.

Thus many Indian communities in modern Latin America find themselves caught in a dilemma. If they continue their traditional agricultural, landholding, and marriage practices, their internal economies will stagnate, and they will have to export many of their young people or relegate them to increasing poverty. If they encourage integration into the national market economies, however, over time their populations are likely to lose their ethnic uniformity and their societies their cultural integrity. Either choice is unpleasant, but in the modern world the need to make such a choice seems unavoidable.

1

The Inca Empire and
Its Subject Peoples

Thomas C. Patterson

This selection depicts important aspects of life among the most advanced sedentary agricultural peoples of the Andes on the eve of the arrival of the Spaniards. The ayllu (kin-based community) served as the fundamental unit of social and labor mobilization. Ethnic identity and loyalty remained central, and ethnic lords were the primary mediators between their own groups and the outside world. To most Andean peoples, the Incas were alien invaders who exploited their local resources. Inca efforts to create a dominant state apparatus to manipulate and, in some cases, to relocate conquered ethnic groups were resisted. The Incas sought to reformulate local myths and traditions to make them more compatible with their imperial rule. Many of the subjugated groups would view the Spaniards initially as potential allies against this resented imperial power.

L and and human labor power were the two main sources of wealth in the central Andes, both before and after the Inca conquest. In many areas, agricultural land was owned by kin-based communities, even though it was held by individual households. While there was continuity in family holdings, there were also periodic reallotments of agricultural land to bring its distribution into accord with the changing needs of the various constituent households. Llama and alpaca herds were also owned, controlled, shared, or contested with other, similar groups. The animals were sheared for their wool, sacrificed, and occasionally eaten; llamas, the larger of the two camelid species, also served as beasts of burden.[1]

Labor-intensive tasks—like agriculture, house building, or the construction and repair of irrigation systems—were carried out by the community as a whole. The beneficiaries of these efforts were "expected to furnish the seeds or cuttings, to feed the workers and to provide them with maize beer."[2] There were technical divisions of labor that reflected age and gender differences: for example, teenagers typically watched over herds pastured in the puna, the high alpine grasslands; men plowed; and women planted seeds, spun thread, and made beer.[3] There was also some degree of craft specialization, as certain households or ayllus (kindreds) were renowned as silversmiths, potters, or dancers.[4] In many instances, they seem to have practiced their particular skills on a part-time or seasonal basis—after planting or harvesting, before the rainy season in the case of the potters, or when dancers were required for ceremonies or other special occasions. Their artisan activities were grafted onto food production; the goods they produced or the services they performed benefited the entire community.

While traditional land tenure practices undoubtedly continued after local communities were encapsulated and incorporated into the imperial state, the Incas immediately imposed liens on the various sources of their wealth. The state expropriated portions of the producers' agricultural fields, pastures, unworked lands, and herds belonging to the communities. These were set aside for the benefit of the state, the imperial sun cult, and the royal corporations.[5]

The Incas also appropriated labor power from the conquered communities. Their demands took several distinct forms, each of which had its own implications for the encapsulated groups. First, the community members were required to cultivate the fields and tend the herds expropriated by the state for itself and the imperial cult. They planted, cared for, and harvested these fields before they worked on their own lands. The produce from these fields and the wool from these herds were destined for separate storehouses in the provincial capital.[6]

Second, the state also demanded other forms of labor service, collectively called the *mit'a* obligation. The needs of the state were both varied and extensive: building and repairing roads, maintaining rest stops, serving in the army, mining, and guarding fields are only a few of the tasks mentioned. Each year, the state requested labor time at one of its monthly feasts. After being feted and honored, the *kurakas*, the local chieftains, returned to their communities, ladened with gifts and tasks to perform. The immediate goal of the chieftains, once they arrived in their villages, was to persuade, cajole, or beg the members of the community for their assistance. Once they consented, the lord assigned the chores equitably across the communities to ensure that enough members in each group remained at home to tend its fields and flocks. When their labor obligation was completed, the workers returned to their homes. When the next call for *mit'a* labor was issued by the state, they were exempt; they were replaced by another group of workers, since the burden shifted or rotated each year through the community. Since some communities were composed of artisans, like miners and silverworkers, the state undoubtedly drew repeatedly on their labor resources to perform certain specialized tasks.[7]

The third category consisted of colonists, *mitaq* or *mitimae*, who were resettled with their families and leaders in provinces that were scarcely populated, recently incorporated into the empire, or whose inhabitants had rebelled against the state. The colonists were under the authority of the provincial officials in the new location. They were required to retain their own garb and customs; to provide the implements, seeds, and other goods they needed for their livelihood; and to defend frontiers and pacify rebel areas. The resettlement policies of the state were extensive. In some provinces, the colonists apparently outnumbered the original inhabitants, many of whom had been resettled among peoples whose loyalty to the state was not suspect.[8] The lands settled by the *mitimae* and the fields they planted had been confiscated by the state from peoples who either resisted its attempts to impose its will or rebelled against its domination.[9] They were detached from their kin and separated from their traditional means of production. Their capacity to produce a livelihood in their new homes was intimately linked with the continued generosity and intervention of the imperial state.

Finally, the state permanently removed certain categories of individuals from their natal communities, thereby depriving the groups of their productive and reproductive capacities. These were the *aclla*, chosen women, and yana, retainers. The former were the prepubescent girls selected each year by state officials, who were sequestered in the provincial capitals.[10] The latter, described by one chronicler as rebels left out of the census who were spared from death by the queen, worked on royal estates, in the households of local chieftains, and in the shrines of the state cult and other important *wak' as*. They apparently served the rulers, their wives, and families in various capacities that even included chieftainships in Chachapoyas and Collique.[11] The practice of removing *aclla* and yana from their communities gave the state a measure of control over the demographic and social reproduction of their natal communities. The autonomy of the communities and their ability to control their own destinies were diminished, as their fortunes became inextricably intertwined with those of the state.

The thrust of Inca imperial expansion was to drain the encapsulated communities and polities of their means of production and to obscure the fact that the social relations of production and reproduction were being dramatically transformed in the process. While the Inca state attempted to intervene in the everyday lives of their members to ensure compliance with its demands, its capacity to do so effectively and successfully was hampered in significant ways by the virtual impossibility of rapid communication over the long distances separating the imperial capital from the provincial centers. This capacity was also limited by the political structures the state put together in the provincial areas. Although the governors were close allies and kinsmen of the ruler and members of the dominant class, layers of provincial administration immediately below them built on the existing local social and political hierarchies, incorporating them into the decimal organization of the state.

The position of the local chieftains, the *kurakas*, in these rapidly erected administrative and social structures was fraught with conflict. On the one hand, there were opportunities for both the chieftains and the communities they represented to benefit materially by supporting the Inca state. On the other hand, the *kurakas* simultaneously represented the interests of their subjects and served as provincial representatives of the state, conveying its requests for labor service to their subjects. Their ability to meet the demands of the state were only as good as their ability to persuade their subjects to provide labor service. To be persuasive, they had to be generous and hospitable. Their requests could not exceed those customarily expected by their subjects and kin. Chieftains whose demands were unreasonable or excessive risked being deposed or murdered by their subjects.[12] Ultimately, the state's claims were backed up by the threat of judicial or military force. The failure of a *kuraka* to respond to the state's request for labor service was a serious matter. It was the first step toward open rebellion, and he could lose his position or even his life.[13]

The state sought to retain the loyalty of the *kurakas* and to influence their actions in various ways. It held one lord hostage under the pretext that he fomented a rebellion; he was ultimately replaced by his son, who was loyal to the Incas.[14] The Inca ruler married the daughters of local chieftains incorporated into the state apparatus of the empire, and accepted these secondary wives into his household.[15] The sons of local chieftains and rulers, especially those responsible for large numbers of people, were taken to Cuzco, where they learned Quechua, Inca traditions, and the behavior expected from a loyal official of the state and a member of the emerging dominant class.[16] High-ranking *kurakas* were forced to maintain a residence in the imperial capital and live there four months each year; this also involved resettling retainers or subjects to act as servants.[17] The Incas brought provincial *wak' as* to Cuzco for long stays.[18] The presence of the provincial *wak' as* and the sons and heirs of the ethnic lords in Cuzco "made both past and future leaders of their communities hostages to the good behavior of their people, despite the honors with which both *wak' as* and young people were loaded."[19] Gifts of land and servants from the state also ensured the continued loyalty of *kurakas*, shrines, and communities that promoted its well-being.[20]

The Inca state demanded obedience from its subjects and employed various institutions and practices to ensure that it received their compliance and submission: the army, loyal *mitima* colonists, and a group of inspectors or overseers called *tokoyrikoq*, a term that can be translated as "those who see all."[21] They were sent to the provinces to check local conditions, to ensure that tax obligations were being met, and to determine that rebellions were not being fomented by dissatisfied chieftains or provincial governors. The *tokoyrikoq* were "faithful men whom the Inca could trust"; they may have been members of a royal corporation or personal retainers of the emperor, possibly even yana raised in the royal household.[22]

The legal code of the state was repressive, especially toward the lower classes—the members of encapsulated communities. Acquiescence rather than agreement was the desired goal. It attempted to achieve compliance through intimidation and the fear of retaliation for crimes against the state and its ruling class. The penalties were severe. For instance, the penalty for failing to perform work satisfactorily, lying to a census taker, moving the boundary markers delimiting state fields, traveling without permission, or not wearing clothing that allowed officials to identify an individual's natal community involved corporal punishment; the guilty were beaten with a stone or flogged. Individuals who failed to meet their labor obligations to the state not only were tortured for the first offense but also had their labor assessments increased; those who committed this offense a second time were threatened with execution. Foot-dragging, misrepresentation, deception, false compliance, evasion, desertion, traveling without permission, pilfering, and sabotage—which James Scott has called the "weapons of the weak"[23]—were also punishable crimes under the imperial legal code. Death was the penalty for those who stole from the state, the imperial cult, or the fields of the Incas as well as for those who spoke against the Inca, had intercourse with the *aclla*, or committed treason. Rebellious communities were deprived of their lands and herds, and their leaders were taken to Cuzco where they were publicly humiliated by the emperor himself, before they were tortured, skinned, and executed. The emperor then had drinking mugs made from their skulls and drumheads from their skin.[24]

The state also used more subtle methods to gain the acquiescence of subjects. It attempted to recast the myths and practices of the encapsulated communities, which prescribed proper behavior, perpetuated socially acceptable explanations of everyday life, and maintained cohesion by asserting the power of local *wak'as* and ancestors. These attempts extended the traditional networks of mutual rights and obligations to include new groups. However, the mechanisms for transmitting this new ideology were weak, because its interpretation remained in the hands of traditional intellectuals, the spokespersons of local shrines, rather than in the hands of state functionaries or members of the emerging dominant class. The priests who preserved and transmitted the traditional lore of their communities and interpreted the local *wak' as* belonged to the groups that maintained and served those shrines and that provided labor service to the state.[25] The relation of these traditional intellectuals to the state and the emerging dominant class of the empire varied. Some, like the caretakers and priests of Pachacamac or Pariacaca, saw their shrines derive significant benefits from their relations with the state; others saw the traditional lore of their communities suppressed.[26] Thus, the caretakers and spokespersons of the local *wak' as* were never completely assimilated into or supportive of either the developing class or state structures.

The new ideological forms and practices of the state created new relations of exploitation. They linked together the Incas, the *kurakas* who had allied themselves with the crown and the state, and state functionaries— groups that benefited materially from the labor service of the peasants and artisans. This was not, however, a homogeneous social category characterized by tranquil and harmonious social relations; instead, the relations among the various factions were wracked by competition, conflict, rivalries, and conspiracies. What united them was their exploitation of the peasants and their dependence on them for labor service. This placed their interests and those of the state in opposition to the interests of the peasants. As long as the potential for dispute within the dominant class was minimized, and its demands, along with those of the state, were not too excessive or abusive, the potential for rebellion could be contained. When disputes surfaced or demands were excessive, however, the resentment and hostility of the encapsulated communities could erupt into open dissent or even revolt.

In spite of the state's desire to ensure the loyalty of the *kurakas* as well as the acquiescence of their subjects, it ultimately failed to create the kind of society it wanted. While the settings in which the subject peoples conducted their lives were only partly of their own creation, they were not totally without some degree of power or control over their own lives. If the subject communities had acceded to the wishes of the state, then the inspectors and the terror of the harsh legal code would have been unnecessary. That the state found both inspectors and the terror of law necessary indicates how seriously it took threats posed by even petty acts of insubordination.

Everyday forms of passive resistance, regardless of the motivation of those who committed these acts of insubordination, require almost no coordination or planning, since they rely on implicit understandings and informal networks. Passive resistance can also take a variety of forms. Scott has suggested that one way that subjugated classes attempt to penetrate, neutralize, and negate the hegemony of the dominant classes and the state is by using the values and rationale of the earlier social order to press their claims and to disparage those of their opponents.[27] However, they have no monopoly on these techniques, since both states and emerging ruling classes also rework and give new meanings to established institutions and practices to support their new forms of extortion by promoting the illusion of historical continuity. This is why tradition, the past, and heritage are so often contested terrains.

Archaeological evidence from the Ica Valley on the south coast of Peru provides insight into one instance where tradition was decomposed and reconstituted after its inhabitants fell under the sway of the Inca rulers. The local *kurakas* identified with the state and the emerging dominant class and benefited from the association, while their commoner peasant kin created and maintained an oppositional identity rooted in tradition and history. The use of Inca pottery vessels or pottery made locally in the Inca style and to Inca specifications was restricted to the higher levels of the local nobility; this was also true for pottery vessels that combined features of local and Inca styles. These three types of pottery vessels are found exclusively in distinctive structured tombs near Old Ica, the elite residential center of the valley, both before and after it was incorporated into the imperial state. Pottery fragments decorated in these styles are also found scattered on the surface of Old Ica and in nearby refuse deposits. The peasants, however, used only pottery vessels decorated with the traditional local designs rather than ones imitating the Inca style. They also looted tombs for antique pottery vessels of types that were manufactured and used in the valley when it was free of Inca domination; these vessels were used as sources of artistic inspiration, and fragments of them have been found in refuse deposits around the peasant villages and hamlets. They were not only collected and imitated, but used with some regularity during the period of Inca political control. When Inca control collapsed in the mid-1530s, the peasants reasserted the dominance of the local artistic tradition, purging it of all traces of Inca influence. This involved an artistic revival of the old styles—the ones preferred by the peasants, not those adopted by the nobility during the period of foreign domination.[28]

While acts like this may have had only a marginal impact on the state's capacity to extract labor, even such "protests within compliance" or "working the system to minimize disadvantage" issued challenges that were more than merely symbolic.[29] They mitigated or denied the claims of the state and its dominant class. What is ultimately threatening and dangerous about the "weapons of the weak" is that, under the right conditions, they can be transformed into a rallying point for more open defiance of authority or even direct confrontation against it. Such conditions did develop with some regularity in the Inca state, and not all opposition to its policies and practices was passive.

Border wars were a persistent feature of imperial expansion into new territories; rebellions erupted unexpectedly; and civil wars seem to have been an integral part of everyday life, especially after the death of an emperor. Clearly, not all of the communities on the margins of the state or even those already incorporated into it recognized the value of *pax incaica*, acknowledged the superiority of Inca beliefs and norms, viewed imperial demands in the same way as those of their traditional leaders, or were even particularly intimidated by the force the state could muster or the severity of its legal code. The consequence of the border wars and revolts engendered by imperial expansion and conquests, the civil wars produced by disputes over succession to the throne, and the rebellions and uprisings resulting from the desire of subject populations to reassert their autonomy was that the Inca state was engaged almost continuously in armed struggle from its inception in 1438 through the Spanish invasion in 1532 to its collapse in the 1570s.[30] Revolts in the frontier regions and rebellions in the core areas of the state were often sparked by rumors of the emperor's death and the civil disruption caused by the successional disputes that inevitably followed such an event. As a result, the state frequently had to reconquer people that had already been incorporated into the empire.[31]

Border Wars and Imperial Expansion

Through military conquest and negotiated incorporation, the Incas brought different kinds of societies into the imperial state. These included class-stratified kingdoms, such as Chimor or the Lupaqa; kin-based communities with unstable or ambiguously defined social hierarchies such as the peoples of Huarochirí; and kin-based communities such as the Pastos, which showed no evidence for any overarching political authority before their encapsulation by the imperial state.[32] The Inca state was clearly more interested in some peoples and areas than others. Rich, well-populated countries were particularly intriguing because of their human and natural resources. It was considerably more cautious with groups, like the Chiriguana, who were "poor and warlike."[33] While its policies toward subject peoples may have been uniform in theory, they varied in practice, depending on the economic and political importance of a given region, the circumstances under which it had been incorporated into the realm, and, particularly, its existing organization at the time of incorporation.[34]

The Incas frequently intervened in frontier areas because local social and political dynamics created changes in existing arrangements, which they viewed as affecting their interests. The initial goal of the state was usually to establish cordial relations with at least one local group in order to gain and secure a foothold in the region.

Imperial expansion created continually shifting frontier areas and border societies. However, there was nothing automatic about the processes of encapsulation and incorporation that occurred on the frontiers of the Inca state. Communities confronted the expanding empire in various ways. Some abandoned their villages and fields, retreating to more remote, inaccessible locations where they reestablished their lives away from the immediate threat posed by the state. Other communities, finding it beneficial or desirable to establish or confirm relations with the Incas, received the imperial envoys, presented them with gifts, and negotiated their incorporation into the empire.[35] Some, like the Kingdom of Chimor, Huarco, or the inhabitants of Chachapoyas, waged war on the imperial armies sent to pacify them and were subdued only after a series of military campaigns spread over a number of years.[36] Others, like the Pastos in northern Ecuador, were more tentative in their response; they exchanged gifts with the state—cane tubes filled with lice for llamas—but continued to maintain close ties with their neighbors and kin who resided outside the frontier and still retained their autonomy and independence.[37]

From the perspective of the communities being encapsulated, the Inca state appeared in different forms at various stages in the process. During the initial stage, gift-bearing strangers—"spies and harbingers" to use [Pedro] Cieza de León's words[38]—began to appear on the frontier and establish contact with them; they came with llamas laden with food and other goods. These entourages of outsiders represented the state and, in some instances during and after the 1470s, represented its allies as well. For example, Topa 'Inka helped the caretakers of Pachacamac, the great oracle on the central coast, establish branch oracles in Mala and Chincha before those regions were incorporated into the state, and merchants from the coastal kingdoms of Chincha were active on the northern frontiers of the empire in the 1520s.[39] Besides their gifts, the strangers brought news about the aims of the Inca state. Some stayed to trade, talk further with the local people, and establish more intimate contact with their representatives or with the individuals who put themselves forward as important and influential personages; others from the entourage eventually left with information about local conditions and the prestations they had received for their gifts.

While the local peoples exchanged gifts and food with the outsiders, they retained firm control over their means of production, their labor power, and the goods they produced. But interpersonal relations were not quite the same as they had been earlier. In some instances, political authority came to reside more firmly in the hands of privileged members, chieftains, or self-proclaimed powerful individuals, who were able to gain increased control over the movement of goods created outside the subsistence sector through raiding and trade or through their enhanced ability to create and cement alliances with other peoples. Sometimes this consolidation of authority was accomplished subtly within the terms of the customary rights and obligations that prevailed in the community; their ability to make alliances and their control over exchange rested on their legitimacy, the authority they possessed in the eyes of their kin and subjects. In other instances, individuals who had gained prominence and followings through activities that were disconnected from customary practices of the community were able to propel themselves into positions of influence with the foreigners. Their capacity to make arrangements rested on both their relations with the foreigners and their ability to retain the loyalty of their followers in a milieu where some of the old constraints on action had been removed and new avenues for mobility were being paved.[40]

Soon, more strangers arrived. Some were refugees fleeing from the imperial army and the threat of Inca domination; others were deserters from the army, who were unable to return to their natal communities because of the death sentences that hung over their heads. Still another group of outsiders came from the region itself; they were transient merchants, the *mindaláes* or "those with the tattooed faces" in northern Ecuador, who brought food, raw materials, and finished goods from the region and beyond to trade with the local peoples, the new arrivals, and the remaining members of the imperial entourage.[41] The traders' presence benefited the local chieftains and persons of influence as well as the imperial state. In some instances, local leaders or individuals of renown were able to gain or consolidate control over the distribution of goods in circumstances where the local social structures and relations were slowly being distorted, deformed, and modified by the growing interference of the state. The presence of the *mindalá* traders also permitted the imperial state to acquire goods from people who were not under its direct control, and to spread its ideology and language to the independent communities beyond the frontier.

After a while, more strangers arrived from the empire. This time, its envoys came at the head of a column of soldiers, and a moment of decision had arrived for the inhabitants of the region. Should they accept the offers of the gift-bearing strangers and all that implied? Should they resist the invaders and fight them from *purcaras*, the hilltop fortresses and strongholds, that had been prepared earlier? Or should they attempt to avoid the threat altogether by retreating to remote, relatively inaccessible areas or by fleeing across the frontier to lands and peoples whose lives were still unaffected by imperial control?

If they chose to resist, as the Huarco of coastal Peru did, then the state established garrisons, provisioned from the nearest provincial capital, to pacify the region.[42] Once resistance was crushed or the inhabitants acquiesced, acknowledging the balance of forces that prevailed, governors and *mitimae* colonists moved in and settled on lands expropriated from the indigenous peoples by the state. At first, the officials and colonists were also sustained by provisions from the provincial capital, but after the first harvests, they began to establish their self-sufficiency. They often fortified their settlements to ensure their own safety, and they brought whole hamlets and isolated homesteads down from the mountains and resettled their inhabitants in villages where they could be watched more easily.[43] The state did not want to deal with a potential enemy in relatively unknown terrain, where it would be almost impossible to prevent or defend against ambushes, hit-and-run attacks, or the destruction of isolated farmsteads initiated by rebel bands living in remote fortresses.

Pacification and incorporation into the imperial state meant that the local communities had to provide labor. Their members had to cultivate the fields expropriated by the empire and the imperial cult, and, during their *mit'a* obligation, they had to manufacture finished goods, according to imperial specifications, from raw material provided by the state.[44] The authority of the local leaders or persons of influence no longer rested solely on their abilities to distribute goods acquired from the *mindalá* traders, but rather on their connections with the imperial state and their abilities to provide the labor power required to produce the goods and services it demanded. Incorporation into the state diminished the autonomy of the local communities and their leaders, the importance of their contacts with other communities, and the role of local traders as the middlemen of frontier trade. Inca domination would be complete when the encapsulated communities became easily recognized, self-sufficient dependencies of the imperial state. The autonomy of these communities was even further diminished as they began to participate in state-sponsored institutions and practices, like the rituals associated with agricultural production or the *aclla*, which linked their reproduction with that of the empire.

At the same time, the connections between the frontier merchants and the communities and chieftains they once served were severed as the Inca state restructured the traditional economies and became the main source of goods produced by distant peoples. The fate of the merchants now depended on their rather tenuous linkages with and dependency on the state in the borderlands and on their ability to forge new connections with other communities on the margins of or beyond the imperial boundaries.

Unrest or rebellions in the borderlands usually broke out when the state suffered setbacks in its domestic or foreign policies or when it attempted to impose new forms of surplus extraction. For instance, after Huarco successfully resisted Inca efforts to incorporate it into the imperial state in the late 1470s, other groups rebelled. The state was forced not only to continue its struggle with Huraco, which ultimately lasted three years, but also to suppress the unrest or revolts that appeared among other peoples. The state reproached these groups for the resistance they displayed and urged them to remain loyal friends or else they would be visited by a cruel war. At the same time, it enlarged the garrison located in the foothills on the edge of Huarco.[45]

The best-known rebellion was the one that occurred in northern Ecuador during Wayna Qhapaq's reign. While the imperial armies were completing the conquest of Chachapoyas to the south, the peoples on the northern frontier of the state—the Quitos, the Pastos, the Carangues, the Cayambia, and the Huancavelicas—revolted, killing the governors, the spies, and the tax collectors that had been left there to oversee their activities. The revolt probably began around 1510. It is not clear whether the revolt was precipitated by unrest in other parts of the empire, like Chachapoyas, or whether the state precipitated the uprising by attempting to transform what the native peoples viewed as gift exchange and what the state construed as tribute payments into regular *mit'a* labor obligations.

In either event the rebel tribes built fortresses and awaited the arrival of the imperial army, which included recruits from all quarters of the empire. When it entered the border areas, the army's goal was to conquer the Pastos. As the Incas and their allies approached, the Pastos men retreated. Old people, women, and children, guarded by a few warriors, remained to meet the imperial army. They were easily defeated, and, as the army began to celebrate its easy victory, the soldiers became careless. Guards were not posted, as the soldiers drank and partied late into the night. Suddenly, under the cover of darkness, the Pastos warriors counterattacked, and the invading army, composed largely of Colla from the Lake Titicaca Basin, was slaughtered. The survivors escaped and made their way back to the encampments of their allies. Since an easy victory had eluded them, the Inca armies were forced to reenter the Pastos territory for the second time. On this occasion, the soldiers burned their fields and villages and killed rich and poor, men and women, young and old. After the Pastos were finally subdued, the emperor appointed a governor and saw that colonists were settled in the area, before turning his attention to the other groups that had participated in the revolt.[46]

The Inca army encountered stiff resistance when it attacked the other rebel groups, and casualties were heavy on both sides. As the war raged on, the imperial army initiated another scorched-earth policy, destroying the rebels' crops and villages and devastating a large area. Some of the rebels escaped to the fortified strongholds of the Carangues, where they were received as allies. The emperor himself led the army against one of the Carangue fortresses. The battle that ensued was fierce, and, during one of the rebels' counterattacks, the emperor was toppled from his litter and almost killed. He and his kin were humiliated by this turn of events. As the emperor walked back to the encampment, he let his kin and the troops know just how angry he was at the disrespect and lack of support he had received. This marked the beginning of a mutiny and a series of battles that would be waged over a period of several years.

Shortly after their defeat at the hands of the Carangues, several of the Inca nobles planned a mutiny. Their complaints were that the emperor was contemptuous of them, that he failed to provide them with adequate provisions, and that they were suffering from exposure. The mutineers, together with the troops they led, resolved to travel to Tumipampa, the provincial capital in southern Ecuador (Wayna Qhapaq's birthplace), to seize the *wak' as* that watched over and ensured the good fortunes of the army. When they arrived at the shrine, the emperor demanded to know their intentions. They told the emperor that they were going to take the *wak' as* back to Cuzco; this would restore its dignity, as well as their own. Wayna Qhapaq then called upon the priests and priestesses of the state cult to intervene and take back the *wak' as* they had already appropriated. Ultimately, the emperor and his mutinous kin talked and resolved their differences. That night, the emperor sponsored an elaborate series of parties that lasted many days, in which loot, gifts, and *aclla* women were given to the soldiers.

Once the old army was placated and reinforced by new recruits, it undertook another assault on the Carangue fortresses. Once again, the soldiers carried out a scorched-earth policy, and eventually they torched the fortresses themselves, killing or capturing everyone who was inside. Some of the Carangues escaped and fled toward a lake where they attempted to hide in the reeds from the army pursuing them. A massacre ensued as the soldiers murdered thousands of men and adolescent boys.[47] Only a few successfully eluded the invading army.

One of the survivors was a Carangue named Pinto who escaped into the rugged, forest-covered mountains to the east. Here he met bands of roving Cañari rebels and exiles, who had not been pacified earlier by Wayna Qhapaq and who had successfully resisted incorporation into the empire. While the Inca state was establishing garrisons and colonists in the area it had just conquered, Pinto and the Cañari rebels who had joined him were fomenting discontent for the state along the frontier. Given the decade-long revolt that was just coming to an end, the state was clearly not concerned at this point in time with bandits or groups plundering the countryside, but it focused on the real possibility that the rebels might make alliances with restless elements in the borderlands. Troops were dispatched to locate the rebel band and to eliminate the threat it posed. The army eventually found the rebel strongholds and starved them into submission. Wayna Qhapaq offered Pinto gifts if he would recognize and submit to Inca rule; the rebel leader refused and was executed.[48]

The Inca state's relation with the Chiriguana, who inhabited the mountain slopes east of Sucre, Bolivia, may help to explain this concern over the threat posed by Pinto and the renegade Cañaris.[49] The Inca army first invaded the lands of the Chiriguana during the reign of Topa 'Inka; it broke off the invasion of the country because of a lack of provisions and stiff resistance, what chroniclers described as "the savagery of its inhabitants."[50] After fortresses were built and garrisons were established along the frontier to protect its gains, the state turned its attention to potentially more productive expeditions and conquests in other regions. The Chiriguana once again attracted the attention of the Inca state in the early 1520s, while it was suppressing the frontier revolt in northern Ecuador and after it had expropriated extensive agricultural fields in the Cochabamba Valley, roughly one hundred twenty miles northwest of Sucre.[51] Wayna Qhapaq repaired the forts built during his father's reign and used Chiriguana troops in his campaigns against the Carangues.[52] Philip Means concluded from this that, while some Chiriguana seem to have been subject to the *mit'a* labor obligations of the state, a larger number, who resided outside the frontier, began to raid and plunder the Charcas borderlands east of Sucre.[53]

It is possible to discern two broad, loosely organized confederations on the eastern edge of the empire adjacent to Charcas. One consisted of the Chiriguana and their Guarani-speaking allies, some of whom lived as far away as the Paraguay River, roughly four hundred miles to the east. Their relations with the Inca state varied—depending on the time, the place, and the existing labor forces—from sullen acquiescence to open hostility. Their relations with the Chanes and their allies, who were apparently on good terms with the Inca state, were also antagonistic and frequently erupted into raids for plunder and captives. When the Chiriguana raided along the imperial frontier, they took captives, metal utensils, and gold and silver jewelry, which quickly found its way as far east as the Paraguay River. However, groups like the Caracaras or the Candires, who were nominally under Inca control, also exchanged metal objects or precious metal with the lowland people—a practice that was frowned upon by the state, which attempted to control or restrict the distribution of metals.[54] The Chanes and their allies obtained metals through a group called the Payzunos in exchange for bows, arrows, and, by the early 1540s (if not before), slaves.

The Chiriguana resurfaced as a thorn in the side of the empire, especially after the state's military resources had been diverted to deal with the border insurrection in the northern provinces. The construction of the fortresses a generation earlier had indicated to the Chiriguana that the state intended to remain permanently in the borderlands, to secure the frontier, and to bring its inhabitants under the imperial rule. However, the state's policies for dealing with border populations were always narrowly developed: negotiation, intimidation, and the use of force covered the range of available options. When the troops were removed from the southern provinces, the state's capacity for controlling the movement of goods and people across the frontier was diminished. When the Chiriguana began to raid and plunder the borderlands under the Inca control, the state could not respond merely by requesting that they desist; to do so would have alienated other frontier peoples, like the Chanes, who apparently had cordial ties with the Incas that counterbalanced their antagonistic relations with the Chiriguana.

The state's attempt to make the Chiriguana an economically self-sufficient, culturally distinctive enclave, like subject populations in the core area of the empire, was unsuccessful. The inhabitants of the state-administered areas continually constructed and reproduced close relations with Guarani-speaking communities in the hinterland, beyond the frontier. This had a number of implications. It meant that different political-economic relations prevailed in the administered and nonadministered sections of the Chiriguana social formation. The state appropriated surplus labor and possibly expropriated land from the inhabitants of the administered areas, while their kin, who resided outside the imperial boundaries and retained their independence, had the ability to continue traditional use-rights and customary practices. It suggests that the Chiriguana, residing in the backcountry, probably received some of the goods that were distributed by the state to their kin on the other side of the border. This also meant they could raid communities in one area and exchange their spoils in another.

Class and state formation in frontier areas created contradictions and opportunities not only for the empire, but also for the indigenous peoples of those areas. These new conditions led to the constitution of new alliances, the merging of formerly independent communities into new groups, and even the appearance of border states where none had existed before, as people recognized their shared position in the emerging system of production and examined the implications of such infringements on their traditional use-rights and practices. This does not mean that all frontier communities automatically opposed the state either passively or actively; in a number of them, both the peasants and their leaders benefited materially, though differentially, from their new dependent relationship with the empire. Even though the frontier policies of the Incas were narrow, they succeeded, in many instances, in transforming customary use-rights, in separating traditional leaders from their kin and subjects, in linking the fortunes of subject groups with those of the state, and in recasting old enmities so that communities remained pitted against one another and their neighbors.

Notes

1. John V. Murra, "The Economic Organization of the Inka State," *Research in Economic Anthropology, Supplement 1* (Greenwich, 1980), 29–30, 51.

2. Ibid., 30–31.

3. Ibid., 50; John H. Rowe, "The Age Grades of the Inca Census," *Miscellanea Paul Rivet, octogenario dictata*, XXXI Congreso Internacional de Americanistas (Universidad Nacional Autónoma de México, 1958), tomo II, 512–513.

4. Francisco de Avila, *Dioses y hombres de Huarochirí: narración quechua recogida por Francisco de Avila* [1598?], translated by José María Arguedas (Lima, 1966); Karen W. Spalding, *Huarochirí; An Andean Society under Inca and Spanish Rule* (Stanford, 1984), 86.

5. Murra, "The Economic Organization," 37, 52, 54.

6. Ibid., 54; John H. Rowe, "Inca Culture at the Time of the Spanish Conquest," *Handbook of South American Indians*, edited by Julian H. Steward, vol. 2, The Andean Civilizations, Bureau of American Ethnology Bulletin 143 (Washington, 1946), 265–267.

7. John V. Murra, "The *Mit'a* Obligations of Ethnic Groups to the Inka State," *The Inca and Aztec States, 1400–1800: Anthropology and History*, edited by George A. Collier, Renato I. Rosaldo, and John D. Wirth (New York, 1982), 237–262; Rowe, "Inca Culture," 267–269; Spalding, *Huarochirí*, 86.

8. María Rostworowski de Diez Canseco, "Historia del Tawantinsuyu," *Historia Andina 13* (Lima, 1988), 221–224; Rowe, "Inca Culture," 269–270; "Inca Policies and Institutions Relating to the Cultural Unification of the Empire," *The Inca and Aztec States*, 105–107.

9. Murra, "The Economic Organization," 38.

10. Rowe, "Inca Culture," 269; "Inca Policies," 97–105, 107–108; Irene Silverblatt, "Andean Women in Inca Society," *Feminist Studies*, vol. 4, no. 3 (1978), 37–61; *Moon, Sun, and Witches; Gender Ideologies and Class in Inca and Colonial Peru* (Princeton, 1987), 80–108.

11. John V. Murra, "New Data on Retainer and Servile Populations in Tawantinsuyu," *Actas y memorias del XXXVI Congreso Internacional de Americanistas*, Sevilla, 1964, Instituto "Gonzalo Fernández de Oviedo" (Madrid, 1966), tomo 2, 35–45; Rostworowski de Diez Canseco, "Historia del Tawantinsuyu," 196–197, 224–226; Pedro Sarimiento de Gamboa, *Historia de los Incas* [1572], Biblioteca de Autores Españoles (Madrid, 1960), tomo 135, 256.

12. Patricia J. Netherly, *Local Level Lords on the North Coast of Peru* (Ph.D. dissertation in Anthropology, Cornell University, Ithaca, University Microfilms, Ann Arbor, 1977), 178–183.

13. Sally F. Moore, *Power and Property in Inca Peru* (New York, 1958), 66–72, 81–82; John V. Murra, "Social Structural and Economic Themes in Andean Ethnohistory," *Anthropological Quarterly*, vol. 34, no. 2 (Washington, 1961), 47–59; Spalding, *Huarochirí*, 82–83.

14. Miguel Cabello Valboa, *Miscelánea antártica; una historia del Perú antiguo* [1586], Instituto de Etnología, Facultad de Letras, Universidad Nacional Mayor de San Marcos (Lima, 1951), 330–331.

15. Juan de Betanzos, "Suma y narración de los Incas, señores que fueron de estas provincias del Perú . . . [1551]," *Colección de libros y documentos referentes a la historia del Perú*, edited by Horacio H. Urteaga, 2d ser., tomo 8 (Lima, 1924),

148–153; Pedro Cieza de León, *El señorío de los Incas* [1553] (Lima, 1967), 109, 201; Cabello Valboa, *Miscelánea antarticia*, 315.

16. Rowe, "Inca Policies," 95–96.

17. John H. Rowe, "What Kind of Settlement Was Inca Cuzco?," *Nawpa Pacha* 5 (Berkeley, 1967), 62.

18. Bernabé Cobo, *Historia del nuevo mundo* [1653], vol. 2, Biblioteca de Autores Españoles, tomos 91 and 92, Ediciones Atlas (Madrid, 1956), 109–111; Spalding, *Huarochirí*, 94–95.

19. Spalding, *Huarochirí*, 95.

20. Avila, *Dioses y hombres*, 109–111, 114–119, 131–135; Diego Dávila Brizeño, "Descripción y relación de la provincia de los Yauyos toda, anan Yauyos, y lorin Yauyos . . . [1586]," *Relaciones geográficas de las Indias*, edited by Don Marcos Jímenez de la Espada, Biblioteca de Autores Españoles, tomo 183 (Madrid, 1965), 155–165; Rowe, "Inca Culture," 260–261.

21. Rowe, "Inca Culture," 264.

22. Cieza de León, *El señorío de los Incas*, 42–44; Diego Goncalez Holguin, *Vocabulario de la lengua general de todo el Peru llamada lengua quechua o del Inca* [1608], Ediciones del Instituto de Historia, Universidad Nacional Mayor de San Marcos (Lima, 1952), 38; Martín de Murúa, *Historia del origen y genealogía real de los reyes Incas del Perú* [1590], edited by Constantino Bayle, Biblioteca "Missionalia Hispanica," vol. 2, Consejo Superior de Investigaciones Cientificas, Instituto Santo Toribio de Mogrovejo (Madrid, 1946), 206.

23. James C. Scott, *Weapons of the Weak: Everyday Forms of Peasant Resistance* (New Haven and London, 1985), xvi.

24. Cieza de León, *El señorío de los Incas*, 179–182; Cobo, *Historia del nuevo mundo*, 83; Sarimiento de Gamboa, *Historia de los Incas*, 254–256; Moore, *Power and Property*, 165–174.

25. Spalding, *Huarochirí*, 63–66.

26. Cabello Valboa, *Miscelánea antártica*, 319; Thomas C. Patterson, "Pachacamac—An Andean Oracle under Inca Rule," *Recent Studies in Andean Prehistory and Protohistory*, papers from the Second Annual Northeast Conference on Andean Archaeology and Ethnohistory, edited by D. Peter Kvietok and Daniel H. Sandweiss, Latin American Studies Program, Cornell University (Ithaca, 1985), 159–176; "Ideology, Class Formation, and Resistance in the Inca State," *Critique of Anthropology*, vol. 6, no. 1 (Amsterdam, 1986), 75–85.

27. Scott, *Weapons of the Weak*, 336.

28. Dorothy Menzel, "The Inca Occupation of the South Coast of Peru," *Southwestern Journal of Anthropology*, vol. 15, no. 2 (Albuquerque, 1959), 125–142; "Archaism and Revival on the South Coast of Peru," *Man and Culture: Selected Papers of the Fifth International Congress of Anthropological and Ethnological Sciences*, Philadelphia, September 1–9, 1956, edited by Anthony F. C. Wallace (Philadelphia, 1960), 596–600; *Pottery Style and Society in Ancient Peru: Art as a Mirror of History in the Ica Valley, 1350–1570* (Berkeley, Los Angeles, and London, 1976); Patterson, "Ideology, Class Formation, and Resistance," 75–85.

29. Scott, *Weapons of the Weak*.

30. This claim must be tempered to some extent by the fact that warfare probably had a distinctly seasonal character. It follows John Rowe's (1945) chronology of events based on the comparison and correlation of various documentary sources.

From 1438 to roughly 1462, the Incas were either at war with the Chancas or allied with them as they conquered northward and ultimately established a garrison at Cajamarca. During the 1460s, the Inca state subordinated southern Ecuador and waged a prolonged war with the Kingdom of Chimor that probably ended about 1470 (Rowe, 1948:40). They subjugated the south coast of Peru in the early 1470s and then waged a three-year struggle with Huarco (Cañete) later in the decade (Menzel, 1959). The great Colla rebellion that erupted in the 1480s took twelve years to suppress (Avila, 1966:131). The civil strife following Topa 'Inka's death around 1493 lasted several years. Wayna Qhapaq's forces did not secure the areas around Quito until about 1500 (Frank Salomon, *Native Lords of Quito in the Age of the Incas: The Political Economy of North Andean Chiefdoms* [Cambridge, England, 1986], 146). This implies that the state's incursions further north occurred during the first quarter of the sixteenth century and were still taking place when the Chiriguana attacked the Bolivian frontier in the mid-1520s and at the time of Wayna Qhapaq's death in 1527 (Philip A. Means, "A Note on the Guarani Invasions of the Inca Empire," *The Geographical Review*, vol. 4, no. 6 [New York, 1917], 482–484; Erland von Nordenskiöld, "The Guarani Invasion of the Inca Empire in the Sixteenth Century: An Historical Indian Migration," *The Geographical Review*, vol. 4, no. 1 [New York, 1917], 103–121; Charles E. Nowell, "Aleixo García and the White King," *The Hispanic American Historical Review*, vol. 26, no. 4 [Durham, 1946], 450–466). The civil war and rebellions that accompanied the successional dispute between Washkar and 'Ataw Wallpa erupted almost immediately thereafter and continued until 1538, when the Spaniards defeated the last of the Inca armies in Bolivia. At that point, Andean resistance to the Spaniards became localized. However, in 1537, a civil war broke out among the Spaniards, which lasted until 1554. The Spaniards subsequently sent a series of military expeditions against Vitcos, the major pocket of Inca resistance, which was finally defeated in 1572.

31. John V. Murra, "La guerre et les rébellions dans l'expansion de l'état Inka," *Annales: Economies, Sociétés, Civilisations*, tome 33, no. 5–6 (Paris, 1978), 930.

32. Thomas C. Patterson, "Tribes, Chiefdoms, and Kingdoms in the Inca Empire," *Power Relations and State Formation*, edited by Thomas C. Patterson and Christine W. Gailey (Washington, 1987), 117–127; Franklin Pease, "The Formation of Tawantinsuyu: Mechanisms of Colonization and Relationship with Ethnic Groups," *The Inca and Aztec States*, 173–198.

33. Cabello Valboa, *Miscelánea antártica*, 383–384.

34. Craig Morris and Donald E. Thompson, *Huánuco Pampa: An Inca City and Its Hinterland* (London and New York, 1985), 24.

35. Cieza de León, *El señorío de los Incas*, 177.

36. Cieza de León, *El señorío de los Incas*, 162–164, 216; Inca Garcilaso de la Vega, *Comentarios reales de los Incas* [1609], vol. 1, Biblioteca de Autores Españoles, tomos 133–135 (Madrid, 1960), 291–303; María Rostworowski de Diez Canseco, "Guarco y Lunahuaná, dos señoríos prehispánicos, costa surcentral del Perú," *Revista del Museo Nacional*, tomo 44 (Lima, 1980), 187–188; John H. Rowe, "The Kingdom of Chimor," *Acta Americana*, tomo 6, no. 1–2 (Mexico, 1948), 26–59.

37. Pedro Cieza de León, *La crónica del Perú* [1553], Biblioteca de Autores Españoles, tomo 26 (Madrid: Ediciones Atlas, 1947), 385–386.

38. Cieza de León, *El señorío de los Incas*, 177.

39. Patterson, "Pachacamac," 159–176; María Rostworowski de Diez Canseco, "Mercaderes del valle de Chincha en la época prehispánica: Un documento y unos

comentarios," *Revista Española de Antropología Americana*, tomo 5 (Madrid, 1970), 135–177; "Pescadores, artesanos y mercaderes costeños en el Perú prehispanico," *Revista del Museo Nacional*, tomo 41 (Lima, 1975), 311–351; Frank Salomon, "Pochteca and Mindalá: A Comparison of Long-Distance Traders in Ecuador and Mesoamerica," *Journal of the Steward Anthropological Society*, vol. 9, no. 2 (Urbana, 1978), 231–246.

40. Thomas C. Patterson, "La creación de cultura en las formaciones sociales pre-estatles y no-estatales, *Gens: Boletín de la Sociedad Venezolana de Arqueólogos*, vol. 3, no. 1 (Caracas, 1987), 15–25.

41. Patterson, "Tribes, Chiefdoms, and Kingdoms," 121; "Merchant Capital and the Formation of the Inca State," *Dialectical Anthropology*, vol. 12, no. 2 (Dordrecht, 1987), 217–227; Salomon, "Pochteca and Mindalá," 231–246; Salomon, *Native Lords of Quito*.

42. Cieza de León, *El señorío de los Incas*, 194–197; John Hyslop, *Inkawasi, the New Cuzco, Cañete, Lunahuaná, Peru*, British Archaeological Reports, International Series, no. S234 (Oxford, 1985); Rostworowski de Diez Canseco, "Guarco y Lunahuaná," 153–214.

43. Craig Morris, "State Settlements in Tawantinsuyu: A Strategy of Compulsory Urbanism," *Contemporary Archaeology; A Guide to Theory and Contributions*, edited by Mark P. Leone (Carbondale, 1972), 393–401; "The Infrastructure of Inka Control in the Peruvian Central Highlands," *The Inca and Aztec States*, 153–171; Spalding, *Huarochirí*, 99–101.

44. Craig Morris, "Reconstructing Patterns of Non-Agricultural Production in the Inca Economy: Archaeology and Ethnohistory in Institutional Analysis," *The Reconstruction of Complex Societies*, edited by C. Moore (Philadelphia, 1974), 49–60; John R. Rowe, "Standardization of Inca Tapestry Tunics," *The Junius B. Bird Pre-Columbian Textile Conference*, edited by Ann P. Rowe, Elizabeth P. Benson, and Anne-Louise Schaffer, The Textile Museum and Dumbarton Oaks, Trustees for Harvard University (Washington, 1979), 239–264.

45. Cieza de León, *El señorío de los Incas*, 194–197.

46. Cobo, *Historia del nuevo mundo*, 91–93; Sarimiento de Gamboa, *Historia de los Incas*, 261–263.

47. Cieza de León, *La crónica del Perú*, 390.

48. Cabello Valboa, *Miscelánea antárticia*, 382–383; Cobo, *Historia del nuevo mundo*, 91–93; Carl O. Sauer, *The Early Spanish Main* (Berkeley and Los Angeles, 1966), 261–263.

49. Brooke Larson, *Colonialism and Agrarian Transformation in Bolivia: Cochabamba, 1550–1900* (Princeton, 1988), 13–50; Means, "A Note on the Guarani Invasions," 483–484; Nordenskiöld, "The Guarani Invasion," 103–121; Nowell, "Aleixo García," 450–466; There are two accounts of the social conditions and relations that existed east of the Inca empire during the first quarter of the sixteenth century. Alexio Garcia, a Portuguese, was the first European to explore the Paraguay River and cross the Chaco. According to Erland von Nordenskiöld (1917:103–106), who based his account on the earlier work of Rui Díaz de Guzman ("Historia argentina del descubrimiento, población y conquista de las provincias del Río de la Plata [1612], *Colección de obras y documentos relativos a la historia antigua y moderna de las provincias del Río de la Plata*, edited by Pedro de Angelis [Buenos Aires, 1910], 11–111), Garcia left Santos on the coast of Brazil in the early 1520s to explore the interior. He and his companions, two to four other Portuguese and some friendly coastal Indians, set out over land. They crossed the Paraná River and

eventually came to the Paraguay River. They were well received by the Guarani-speaking inhabitants of the villages and persuaded several thousand to accompany them on their explorations to the west. They fought their way across the Gran Chaco, the plain that lies between the river and the Andes Mountains. After many days, they reached the mountains between Mizque and Tomina. They attacked and plundered villages under Inca control and killed everyone they found. When the Charcas counterattacked, they retired to the lowlands, laden with the cloth, utensils, and gold, silver, and copper objects they had stolen. Garcia was killed, but more Indians followed him to the territories where he had been, and settled on the frontier near Tarija.

Alvar Nuñez Cabeza de Vaca (*Comentarios de Alvar Nuñez Cabeza de Vaca, adelantado y governador del Río de la Plata* [1555] [Madrid, 1946], 555–556, 572–573, 579–580, 582–583) provides an overview of the conditions and complex social relations that prevailed east of Charcas in the early 1540s. The Chiriguana were Guarani-speaking peoples who maintained cordial relations with communities that spoke closely related dialects and lived on both sides of the Paraguay River, four hundred miles to the east. They had antagonistic relations with the Caracaras and Candires (groups that were under Inca control or that lived in the borderlands of Charcas), with the Chanes who resided along the imperial frontier to the south, and with the Chimenos, Tarapecocies, and Sacocies—tribes that inhabited areas to the south or east. The Guarani had attacked the villages of the Chanes, Tarapecocies, Sacocies, and Orejones for war captives, metal objects, and other kinds of plunder; some refugees from these raids had banded together and resided in a multiethnic settlement called Puerto de los Reyes on the Paraguay River. The Tarapecocies claimed that a group called the Payzunos who lived to the west gave them precious metals that its members had obtained from the Chanes, Chimenos, Caracaras, and Candires in exchange for bows, arrows, and slaves.

50. Garcilaso de la Vega, *Comentarios reales*, 270; Sarimiento de Gamboa, *Historia de los Incas*, 263.

51. Nathan Wachtel, "The *Mitimaes* of the Cochabamba Valley: The Colonization Policy of Huayna Capac," *The Inca and Aztec States*, 199–235.

52. Garcilaso de la Vega, *Comentarios reales*, 271–273; Fernando Montesinos, *Memorias antiguas historiales y politicas del Perú* [1644], *Colección de libros y documentos referentes a la historia del Perú*, edited by Horacio H. Urteaga, 2d ser., tomo 6, Librería e Imprenta Gil (Lima, 1930), 104–105; Sarmiento de Gamboa, *Historia de los Incas*, 263–264.

53. Means, "A Note on the Guarani Invasions," 482–484.

54. Moore, *Power and Property*, 40, 55–56, 116.

2

Early Spanish-Indian Accommodation in the Andes

Steve J. Stern

The Spanish conquest did not immediately transform social relationships and labor systems for many of the native peoples. Steve J. Stern demonstrates that for nearly a half century after their conquest in the Andes, the Spanish depended heavily on traditional indigenous labor delivery systems and on kurakas *(native lords) for their effective operation. In many ways, Spanish demands on the natives closely resembled those that the Incas had made on the peoples of the region of Huamanga.*

Initially, indigenous religious beliefs helped facilitate Spanish control, for the natives saw the lack of disruption in these early years as an indication that their gods looked benignly on the overthrow of the Incas. By the 1560s, however, when population decline and heightened labor demands placed great stress on indigenous communities, the natives responded with a religiously sanctioned revolt, the Taki Onqoy, that demanded restoration of the pre-Hispanic order.

The colonial history of Latin America usually begins with the drama of conquest, and this is, by and large, appropriate. Yet anyone who has read Bernal Díaz del Castillo knows that beneath the broad outline of conquest exploits lies a more subtle history of Indian-white alliances. The assistance of powerful regional kingdoms like Tlaxcala in Mexico, or that of the Huanca people in Peru, proved critical to the Spanish conquest of the Aztec and Inca empires. Such alliances expressed the internal contradictions and discontents that plagued Aztec and Inca rule and the failure of these empires to eradicate the independent military potential of resentful ethnic kingdoms. Yet we also know that mutually beneficial alliances between Spaniards and restive Indian peoples could prove short-lived. Spanish-Tlaxcalan relations soured after a "positive" early phase, and in 1564 the

Huancas joined their former Inca enemies in a plot to throw off Spanish rule.[1]

This article explores the early history of Indian-Spanish relations in Huamanga, a highland region in the heartland of the former Inca empire.[2] The story focuses not on a major ethnic kingdom that emerged as a strategic power in its own right, but on the diverse region of Huamanga, which comprised numerous rival ethnic or tribal groups, whose desires to secure political autonomy and economic resources frequently pitted them against one another and against the Incas. To understand better how the societies of Huamanga responded to the presence of the Spaniards who founded the city of the same name in 1539–40, we turn briefly to pre-Columbian history and social structure.[3]

Among Huamanga's local peoples, relations of kinship and reciprocity defined boundaries of social identity and economic cooperation. An ethnic group viewed itself as a "family" of ayllu lineages, related to one another by descent from a common ancestor-god. Within such "families," exchanges of labor created bonds of mutual obligation by which households and ayllus gained access to resources and labor assistance. Such cooperation enabled kin units, as coproprietors of the ethnic domain, to work ecologically diverse lands and resources scattered "vertically" in the Andean highland environment. As an economic institution, therefore, reciprocal labor exchange among "relatives" was a fundamental social relationship, governing production and distribution of goods. As an ideology, moreover, reciprocity defined relations between ayllu or ethnic *kurakas* (chiefs) and commoners. For the ethnic "family" as a whole, and for each of its many internal subdivisions, a *kuraka* symbolized the collective identity and interest of "his" people. In exchange for service as a guardian of local norms and interests, *kurakas* at the higher levels of social organization acquired special rights to labor services. A *kuraka* was expected, among other duties, to protect the group's domain against rivals, redistribute and enforce rights to land and other resources, organize work and ritual, and "generously" redistribute accumulated goods in the form of "gifts" from personal and community stores. In exchange, "his" people worked his fields, herded his animals, wove his cloth, and tended to household needs such as water and fuel. The exchange had to appear "balanced" to enjoy legitimacy.

Two consequences of this social and economic organization had important implications for the early colonial period. First, traditions of kinship and reciprocity imposed constraints on native "leadership." Only by building and maintaining a long-term exchange of mutual obligations, expectations, and loyalties did a *kuraka* acquire the prestige or "influence" that made ayllus or households responsive to his formal "request" for labor services. *Kurakas* who failed to fulfill the expectations of kin, or who consistently violated local norms, risked an erosion of prestige that undermined their authority. Second, the local mode of production tended to divide producers into competing, self-sufficient groups. The division of provincial society into autarkic, ethnically distinct networks of producer-relatives whose scattered properties often overlapped or were interspersed among the claims of other such networks, fostered fierce conflicts over lands and "strategic" ecological zones (coca fields, for example). Even within the bounds of an ethnic "family," decentralized networks of kinship and reciprocity bred competition between distinct kin groupings for self-sufficiency, prestige, and wealth. The very nature of local social and economic structure, therefore, tended to generate endemic rivalries between kindreds and ethnic groups.

The Incas conquered Huamanga around 1460. Their empire converted communities and ethnic groups into a peasantry whose surplus labors sustained an expansive state, but left intact traditional relations of production that assured local self-sufficiency. Despite the sophistication of Inca statecraft, loyalties remained fragile; local peoples proudly retained oral traditions of resistance to the invading Incas. To consolidate control over the region, the Incas implemented their standard policy of settling ethnic *mitmaq* (outsiders) in strategic zones of Huamanga. Inca domination thus left Huamanga a legacy of intensified ethnic fragmentation together with anti-Inca politics and attitudes and usurpations of local peoples' resources and labor, but without undermining the internal organization of local production and social identification. The disintegration of the Inca empire after 1532 brought a resurgence of small-scale community and ethnic societies whose economic vitality drew on centuries of local tradition and experience.

The confrontation of these peoples and the Spanish conquistadores gave rise to a complex pattern of alliances—negotiated primarily between encomenderos and Indian *kurakas*—in the new, post-Incaic era. As we shall see, both sides had good reasons to develop mutually acceptable relationships, but fundamental contradictions limited such relations to a transitory adaptation, and doomed the post-Incaic alliances to failure.

The Rise of Uneasy Alliances

The Europeans wanted riches and lordship. After the distribution of precious metals brought to Cajamarca to ransom the Inca Atahualpa, Francisco Pizarro and his fellow conquistadores set out southward to subjugate, plunder, and rule over an Andean colony. The European thirst for precious metals and the looting of religious shrines created the folk legend that Spaniards ate gold and silver for food.[4] Pizarro distributed encomiendas of

Indian peoples to his conquistador allies. The encomendero was charged with serving the crown's military and political needs in the colony, and attending to the material and spiritual well-being of the Indians "entrusted" to his care. In exchange, he was free to command tribute and labor from them. As the personal representative of the crown in the field, the encomendero could use his authority over "his" people to enrich himself, but he also carried the burden of forging colonial relationships with the new Indian subjects.[5]

Military security quickly became a top priority, particularly after the puppet Inca emperor, Manco Inca, soured on his European friends and escaped to the *montaña* northwest of Cuzco in 1536. From his hidden jungle fortress, Manco organized raids that disrupted European commercial routes and harrassed Indian societies allied to the Europeans. The resistance of Manco's "neo-Inca state" became so troublesome that Pizarro resolved to consolidate European control and expansion along the highland route between Jauja and Cuzco. The few Europeans who had set up a frontier town in Quinua (Huanta) held out precariously against Manco and the local groups who supported the Inca's cause. Pizarro sent Vasco de Guevara, a veteran of Nicaragua and Chile, and twenty-five Spaniards to the area in 1539, hoping to establish the Europeans more firmly in the region of Huamanga.[6]

In the interests of security, the more than twenty encomenderos centered in Huamanga decided in 1540 to move south from Quinua to a more defensible site.[7] The move was carried out under the leadership of Vasco de Guevara. Huamanga overlooked a strategic area west of the neo-Incas, and the conquistadores repeatedly sought to stabilize a European population in the new city to counter the threat of neo-Inca raids and local rebellions.[8] Those who settled in Huamanga saw the local Indian communities as a source of labor and plunder. Spanish settlers required Indian labor and tribute for the most basic necessities—food; transport of water, wood, and merchandise; construction of houses and public works such as churches, roads, and bridges.[9] Furthermore, the loyalty of the local Indians was essential to the Europeans if they were to resist Inca encroachments. The cabildo, a municipal council controlled by the European encomendero elite, sought to curb abuse of the natives in 1541 because it "would give the Indians reason to turn against us, killing Spaniards as they used to do."[10]

Fortunately for the conquistadores, local Andean societies had good reason to ally themselves with Europeans. The military prowess of the Spaniards, skilled masters of horse and sword, impressed the *kurakas* who accompanied Atahualpa in Cajamarca in 1532. As is well known, peasant societies are remarkably sensitive to changes in power balances important to their survival, and the Lucanas peoples of Andamarcas and Laramati quickly recognized the Spaniards as new masters. The *kurakas* of the Lucanas Laramati peoples proclaimed themselves "friends of the Spaniards" when the victorious entourage passed through Vilcashuamán en route to its historic entry into Cuzco. Once the Spaniards broke the Inca siege of Cuzco in 1537, such proclamations acquired additional credibility.[11]

Besides having a healthy respect for Spanish military skills, local societies of Huamanga saw positive benefits in an alliance with the Europeans. These local societies could finally break the yoke of Inca rule, and advance ethnic interests in a new, post-Incaic era. Some of the *mitmaq* populations settled in the northern Huamanga by the Incas returned to their home communities. The Europeans were not the only people who plundered the Andean sierra in the early years. Local communities sacked warehouses once dedicated to the discredited Incas and major huacas (deities) associated with the state, and a mushrooming population of yanaconas—individuals who left ayllu society to become dependent retainers of the Europeans— joined their masters in the hunt for precious metals.[12]

Given these circumstances, the conquistadores got the help they needed, despite tenuous loyalties and occasional conflicts between Europeans and their native allies. Early in 1541, Indians from northeast Huanta, who bore the brunt of Manco Inca's assaults, came to Huamanga to warn of the Incas' plans to overrun the Spanish city. The cabildo sent Francisco de Cárdenas to lead an expedition of twenty Spaniards and "two thousand Indian friends" to forestall the attack and "to protect the natives."[13] Through the early 1550s, the continual turbulence of civil war among the Spaniards and fights with the neo-Incas put local societies and their *kurakas* in a difficult position.[14] Given the claims all sides made for logistic and military support, native peoples could not choose neutrality. They had to decide what kind of alliance would most benefit ethnic or communal interests. Robbed of the option of neutrality, local societies participated heavily in the early wars, which "[left] the Indians destroyed." While some Indians of Huamanga joined forces with the neo-Incas, most groups—including Incas settled in Huamanga—fought on the side of the Spanish crown. The strategic highway connecting Lima (founded in 1535), Huamanga, and Cuzco threw the burden of fighting upon the societies of the northern districts through which it passed—Huanta, Vilcashuamán, and Andahuaylas. In addition, Huanta and Andahuaylas bordered on the area controlled by the neo-Incas. A *kuraka* "guarding a pass out of fear of the Inca" sent urgent notice in 1544 that Manco Inca, with the help of dissident Spaniards, was planning an attack that threatened the encomienda Indians of Pedro Díaz de Rojas. But even the societies far to the south did not escape involvement. When

Francisco Hernández Girón rebelled against the crown in the early 1550s, he raided the rich herds of the Soras and Lucanas peoples for supplies. The raids provoked Indian elites into supporting the royal campaign. [15]

The encomenderos knew that they needed favorable working relationships with "their" *kurakas*; the shrewdest sought to cement alliances with favors and gifts. Encomenderos and other Spaniards frequently came before the cabildo in Huamanga's first decade to ask for *mercedes* (land grants) for estancias or farms. Percipient encomenderos encouraged the cabildo to grant *mercedes* to their *kurakas* as well. The *kurakas* of Juan de Berrio received ten *fanegadas* (nearly thirty hectares) in the fertile Valley of Viñaca west of the city of Huamanga; one *kuraka* sponsored by Berrio received title to twenty *fanegadas*. Francisco de Balboa asked the cabildo to grant sixteen *fanegadas* in the rich Chupas plains south of Huamanga to his chief *kuraka* (*kuraka principal*).[16] Diego Gavilán claimed twenty *fanegadas* for himself in the Chigua Valley, and then had the cabildo grant the rest of the valley to his *kuraka*.[17] One of the most successful encomenderos, Diego Maldonado, showered gifts upon the *kurakas* of his Andahuaylas encomienda. The native elite received a black slave, mules, horses, livestock, and fine Inca and Spanish cloths. In a later dispute, a *kuraka* pointed out that such gifts were given "because [Maldonado] owed it to them for the services they would render him."[18]

Communities and ethnic groups hoped that alliances with Europeans would help them gain the upper hand in their own native rivalries. In 1557, for example, the Lucanas Laramati peoples complained that neighboring groups were intruding upon valuable hunting lands. With the help of their encomendero, Pedro de Avendaño, secretary of the viceroy and a resident of Lima, they obtained a viceregal ban on hunting directed against the Lucanas Andamarcas, Yauyos, Huancas, Parinacochas, and coastal peoples who surrounded the core settlement area of the Lucanas Laramati.[19] The Chancas of Andahuaylas, traditionally bitter rivals of the Incas, used European power against their enemies. When the neo-Incas kidnapped the Chanca guardians of coca fields in Mayomarca (between Huanta and Andahuaylas), ethnic groups from Huamanga threatened to take over the treasured fields. The Chancas solved their difficulty by persuading their encomendero to lead a military expedition to Mayomarca, which secured their control.[20] Collaboration with Europeans, despite the tolls of war, tribute, and labor, brought its advantages.

A closer look at the Chancas of Andahuaylas shows how astute encomenderos cultivated working relationships with native elites and societies. Diego Maldonado, one of the richest and most successful encomenderos, preferred negotiating agreements with the *kurakas* to resorting to brute force. Through one such agreement, Maldonado persuaded some natives who had lived in distant valleys and punas to resettle in a valley nearer the royal highway to Cuzco. Maldonado also avoided usurping treasured Chanca resources. Instead, he carved out lands and herds for his hacienda from the vast holdings once dedicated to the support of the Inca state. Initially, at least, Maldonado settled personal yanaconas on his lands rather than demand encomienda labor. When Indians complained that his expansive herds damaged their crops, he (or his administrator) inspected the claims and distributed corn, potatoes, *ají* (hot peppers), and other products as compensation for damages incurred. Maldonado also negotiated agreements with the *kurakas*, specifying the tribute obligations of his encomienda. Maldonado customarily set aside a third of the tribute in foodstuffs for redistribution, and in lean agricultural years donated food and relieved his encomienda of various tribute obligations. He contributed the labor of African slaves and yanaconas to the construction of an *obraje* jointly owned by his Indians and a Spanish entrepreneur, and distributed European novelties such as scissors and glass cups. He preferred agreements to unsystematized plunder, and thus in a sense integrated himself into native society as a generous, "redistributive" patron, though Maldonado's son later exaggerated when he stated that his father's gifts were responsible for the *kurakas'* impressive wealth. Indian workers on his fields received, besides the customary payments, "gifts" of corn, coca, salt, *ají*, meat, sheep, and wool. During the twenty-two-day harvest of coca leaves, Maldonado would regale workers with eight baskets of coca.[21] In his will, he donated thousands of cattle to his Indians. During his lifetime, Maldonado sometimes acted as if he were a shrewd ethnographer applying Andean rules of "generosity" to create dependencies and "reciprocal" exchange obligations.

Alliance did not, of course, imply that life was free of conflict or abuse. Behind the negotiations often lay violence and the respective power and needs of both sides. At one point, Indians killed an African slave of Maldonado's, and the encomendero sometimes jailed the Chanca elites. A record of fines collected by Huamanga officials from 1559 on documents the rough, violent episodes that marred many relationships. Among the encomenderos themselves, gambling and fighting seemed to be a way of life. The Indians were subject to whippings, looting, and rape by Spaniards, blacks, mestizos, and mulattoes. Labor conditions were crude and harsh. Construction of Huamanga in its original site cost the lives of many workers.[22]

As conquerors and aspiring commanders of the labor of their Indians, encomenderos saw themselves as agents personally responsible for basic public tasks. To construct a church, they assessed themselves a labor draft of 510 Indian workers. Later, they assumed responsibility for supplying Indians to carry water to urban Huamanga's households. In general, encomenderos and masters of yanaconas tended to treat their wards as personal property. For the native workers, such a relationship imposed harsh demands. For example, a lively business flourished around the rental of Indian workers and sale of Indian subjects.[23] Rental of Indian labor encouraged its exploiters, like some conquistadores bent on returning to Spain after a few years' plunder, to ignore the long-run survival of workers. The buyer of Indians who sought to squeeze out the most work in a short time period, as one observer put it, "enters like a hungry wolf."[24]

The abuses should not blind us, however, to facts that were so obvious to the native peoples themselves. Cooperation or alliance with the conquerors of the Incas offered at least the possibility of protection against extreme violence. Significantly, the majority of fines collected for personal abuse of Indians was not imposed on members of Huamanga's small circle of elite families, but on lesser Spanish, mixed-blood, and native residents. If alliance did not create an idyllic era, it nevertheless offered the advantages sketched above—continued freedom from Inca (or neo-Inca) rule, special privileges for the *kuraka* friends of the conquistadores, and valuable help in the endemic rivalries among local communities and ethnic groups.

Early relations, then, displayed an uneasy mixture of force, negotiation, and alliance. The parties to the post-Incaic alliances probed one another for weaknesses, testing the limits of the new relationship. In the early years, each encomendero—accompanied by soldiers if necessary—"asked his cacique [*kuraka*] for what he thought necessary, and [the chief] bargained about what he could give." Ill-treatment and extortion varied "according to the care and greed of each [encomendero], and the skill that he had with his Indians."[25]

Sheer ignorance of the true resources available to local societies handicapped the conquistadores. The first inspection of the Huamanga region, in 1549, turned up only 12,179 native males between the ages of fifteen and fifty; several years later, when population should have declined, Damián de la Bandera counted 12,771 tributaries. Despite his considerable skills and knowledge, Bandera had little choice but to rely on *kurakas* for much of his information.[26] Felipe Guaman Poma de Ayala wrote a scathing indictment of the European colonials around 1600. Significantly, this bitter Indian critic from Huamanga praised the first generation of encomenderos. The conquistadores "used to sit down to eat and gave all the clothes and textiles the [Indian] notables wanted, and if the crops froze or were lost, they pardoned the poor Indians [their tribute]." Francisco de Cárdenas, who had led two thousand Indians against the neo-Incas in 1541, left his Indians thousands of sheep on their punas in Chocorvos and Vilcashuamán. Don Pedro de Córdova, said Poma de Ayala, helped protect his Lucanas Laramati peoples from abusive priests and officials.[27] The Lucanas Laramati, who had always sought to be "friends of the Spaniards," granted Córdova a huge ranching estate "for the many releases of taxes and tributes which, as encomendero, he made and pardoned them."[28] The parties of the post-Incaic alliances understood very well that they needed one another.

The Early Commercial Economy

By securing cooperative relations with native elites and societies, an aspiring ruling class of encomenderos laid a foundation for the colonial economy and society in Huamanga. By the 1550s, Spanish-Indian relations entered a second phase as a corregidor and other appointed officials began to assume responsibility for many judicial and administrative tasks. The colonial state, centered in Lima, thereby began to intervene in a restricted way to limit the regional autonomy of Huamanga's leading families. Colonial officials, however, tended to enter into alliances with powerful local Spaniards, and, in the early years, the cabildo, dominated by encomenderos, had moved quickly to establish rules and guidelines for a colonial society.[29] The cabildo, almost immediately, had taken on the task of assigning *solares* (town lots) for homes, shops, gardens, and small farms, and of granting *mercedes* for farm and pasture lands.[30] During the years 1540 to 1543, the cabildo granted forty-two *mercedes* for estancias (grazing sites) and farm lands to twenty residents.[31] In 1546, the city appropriated common lands "that are around this town that are neither worked nor populated by Indians." It appears that eighteen notables of Huamanga received an average of eighty hectares each.[32] Twelve years later, the cabildo distributed thousands of hectares in the irrigated Chaquibamba plains to more than sixty *vecinos* and other residents.[33]

Leading citizens acquired lands and pastures for their own personal gain. Encomienda tributes already supplied Huamanga with food, cloth, artisan products, and precious metals.[34] An encomendero who owned a fine home in the city and a productive encomienda had little reason to yearn for a huge estate to satisfy status pretensions. Commercial agriculture, however, offered lucrative possibilities. Lima, Cuzco, and the booming silver town of Potosí created markets for foodstuffs, cloth, wine, sugar, coca, tallow, hides, and artisanal items. Huamanga itself served as an economic pole attracting rural products. Corn and potatoes, for example, sold for twice the price in Huamanga that they fetched in faraway rural Lucanas.[35] Through cabildo *mercedes*, sales by *kurakas*, negotiations, or force, encomenderos and lesser European residents began to claim lands. Rather than consolidate holdings in a single large estate, the Europeans commonly carved out multiple holdings—often small- or middle-size—on lands whose fertility, suitability for marketable products such as coca or wine, or location near the city or major commercial routes (that is, the main highway in Huanta and

Vilcashuamán) promised material reward. Herds of cattle, sheep, and goats; irrigated patches of wheat, corn, vegetables, and alfalfa; groves of fruit trees and carefully kept vineyards; and water-powered flour mills began to dot the valleys of Huatata, Yucay, and Viñaca near the city of Huamanga. Along the eastern edges of Huanta, aggressive entrepreneurs set up coca plantations.[36]

Commercial capital, understood as buying or producing cheaply to sell dearly, thus structured early patterns of investment and initiative.[37] The Europeans cast their entrepreneurial eyes not only toward agriculture, but also toward mining, manufactures, and trade itself. Already in 1541, Pedro Díaz de Rojas had uncovered rich gold mines in the coca *montaña* of Mayomarca (eastern Huanta). The gold mines attracted fortune seekers fired with passion and dreams of glory; in 1545, the cabildo sent a leading citizen to restore order and authority to the violent, rough-and-tumble life of the mines.[38] The discovery of major gold and silver deposits in Atunsulla (Angaraes) in 1560, and of mercury in Huancavelica in 1563, made Huamanga a major mining region in its own right. The royal accountant in Huamanga joined encomenderos rushing to Atunsulla to extract minerals worth tens of thousands of pesos. On January 1, 1564, the encomendero Amador de Cabrera registered the fabulous mercury deposits of Huancavelica. Mercury soon circulated as a regional medium of exchange, along with gold and silver.[39] With the discovery of major mines, Huamanga's entrepreneurs began to build textile workshops and *obrajes*. Within fifteen years of Cabrera's discovery, encomenderos had established at least three major rural *obrajes* to supply the growing mining and commercial centers of Huamanga. In neighboring Andahuaylas, another *obraje* had been supplying the Cuzco market since the 1550s.[40] Huamanga's encomenderos had established trading networks with Lima very early, and the Vilcashuamán tambo (inn) on the Inca highway from Huamanga to Cuzco rapidly emerged as a major trading center.[41]

The Indians, rather than isolate themselves from these economic developments, usually sought to take advantage of new trends and opportunities. Individually and collectively, Indians searched for money and commercial advantage. To be sure, native societies had to find ways to acquire money if they were to pay tributes owed to the encomenderos. The early documentation, however, offers evidence that belies the conclusion that native societies participated reluctantly in the commercial economy just to gather money needed for tribute. On the contrary, communities displayed an open, aggressive—even enthusiastic—attitude that rivaled the boldness of Diego Maldonado's amateur ethnography in Andahuaylas. Long before the Spaniards gained control of Atunsulla around 1560, communities well over a hundred kilometers away had sent *mitmaq* representatives to mine "the hill of gold" abandoned by the Incas. The Lucanas Indians worked local gold and silver mines for their own benefit, but complained bitterly about demands that they work Spanish mines in faraway sites. *Kurakas* in Andahuaylas sent natives to set up ethnic outposts in the distant silver mines of Potosí.[42] Unhampered by Inca claims on coca fields, local societies expanded coca production and sales. One group used coca to pay "the tribute [they owed], and with what remained after paying tribute, they sustained themselves." Another group used the coca left after tribute to buy sheep and swine.[43] By the 1550s, the Chancas and Adrián de Vargas, a Spanish entrepreneur, agreed to build an *obraje* half-owned by the Indians, who sold some of the finished textiles to their encomendero in Cuzco.[44]

Individually, too, natives reacted innovatively to the new colonial economy. By 1547, Indian workers and traders captured an impressive share of the Mayomarca gold dust in exchange for their services and products.[45] Native merchants flocked to supply the dynamic mines and commercial centers of Huamanga, and artisans left ayllus to find opportunities elsewhere.[46] Silversmiths joined encomenderos in Huamanga, where their skills yielded handsome rewards. Stone masons earned money in colonial construction, and skilled native artisans became indispensable specialists in the Huancavelica mines.[47] The brisk commerce in coca led Indian entrepreneurs, especially the *kurakas*, to join Spaniards in setting up private coca farms or plantations.[48] Andean ethnic "families" had always been plagued by internal tension and stratification; now, colonial society offered new possibilities to dissatisfied individuals willing to abandon or loosen ties with ayllu society. Some looked for alternatives in the city of Huamanga. In the mines, the loyalties of ayllu Indians sent to work distant ore deposits on behalf of their ethnic groups sometimes abated.[49]

The *kurakas*, in fact, were in some ways better equipped than the Spaniards to take advantage of new opportunities. The Europeans needed their cooperation to stabilize the early colony and to exact tribute and labor from ayllu society. The native elite, moreover, enjoyed special privileges precisely because their "kinfolk" recognized them as guardians of the collective welfare of their ayllus and communities. The long-run "reciprocal" exchange between peasant households and *kurakas* gave elites, as privileged leaders, the means to initiate rewarding activities in the colonial economy. One knowledgeable observer called the privately owned coca farms "their particular trade." The *kurakas'* power, complained the corregidor of Huamanga, allowed them "to rent [the natives] like beasts and to pocket the money themselves."[50] It was true that a *kuraka* who consistently violated his kinfolk's sense of a fair reciprocal exchange ran the risk of encouraging emigration or disloyalty. In extreme cases, Indians even turned to colonial authorities or patrons to denounce a *kuraka* or to challenge his authority. In

1559, Huamanga's officials fined one such chief 250 pesos for "certain torments and deaths of Indians."[51] In less extreme cases, however, or when native societies found alliance with European colonials beneficial to their interests, the *kurakas'* economic initiatives did not necessarily erode their traditional prestige or "influence" among ethnic "relatives."

Thus the Indians, impelled by the hunt for money and commercial profit, joined in the creation of a colonial economy. The native-white alliances did not only enhance the ability of Huamanga's colonials to create an impressive array of commercial production and relationships; they reinforced the natives' "open" attitude toward the newcomers, which focused on taking advantages of new opportunities rather than withdrawing sullenly from contact.[52] The goals of Indians and Spaniards were different and ultimately in contradiction, but joint participation in the commercial economy was, nevertheless, quite real. The Indians embraced the entry of commercial capital on the Andean stage; only later would they discover that the embrace was deadly. The encomenderos saw that alliance with local elites and societies could lay a foundation for colonial extraction; only later would they discover that the foundation was unstable and that it could crumble under pressure.

Labor and Tribute under the Alliances

The problem was that, under the terms of the early alliances, the colonial economy continued to depend for goods and labor almost wholly upon an Andean social system, managed and controlled by Andean social actors, relationships, and traditions. A colonial state apparatus had only partially rooted itself in Huamanga. Despite the presence of outside colonial officials and formal tribute lists by the 1550s, the colonials could not rely on the state to organize a new economic system that would funnel them native goods and labor. On the contrary, the natives went "over the heads" of local colonials to appeal for favorable rulings from metropolitan-oriented officials in Lima and Spain. The "state" in Huamanga in actuality remained the personal responsibility of about twenty-five encomenderos and a handful of cooperating officials who, as the king's representatives, sought to rule over the area.[53] Under such conditions, it was difficult to reorder the native economy.

Instead, it seemed more feasible to base colonial extraction upon long-standing Andean traditions. The more formal lists by officials in the 1550s and 1560s specified a large variety of items far more impressive than the short lists after 1570. Aside from the gold and silver, food, animals, and cloth of the post-1570 lists, the early tributes included items such as wooden plates and vases, washtubs, chairs, footwear, horse and saddle gear, large sacks and ropes, cushions and rugs, whips, and so forth.[54] The diversity not only attests to the capacity of native societies to incorporate new products and skills into their economic life, but it also dramatizes the dependence of Europeans upon indigenous communities, governed by Andean-style labor relations, for items that would later be supplied by a more hispanized artisan and handicrafts economy. The documents also hint that early encomenderos—to obtain their tributes—had to respect at least some of the traditional rules governing Andean labor and "taxes." Households continued to retain exclusive rights to crops produced on ayllu lands for local use; to pay tribute, households and ayllus contributed labor time on other lands specifically designated to satisfy outside claimants.[55] Traditionally, such practices protected ayllus and households from having to pay a tribute in goods from subsistence crops or from reserves in years when crops fared poorly. A shrewd observer of Andean life commented that Indians would rather go as a community to work fifteen days on other fields than give up for tribute a few potatoes grown by the family for its own use.[56] Poma de Ayala's praise of Huamanga's early encomenderos for lightening the Indians' tribute burdens in bad years perhaps reflected the encomenderos' inability or unwillingness to overturn such cherished rules. In Andahuaylas, Diego Maldonado supplied the wool needed to make textiles the Indians "owed" him.[57] Such practices respected the rule that peasants supplied labor to claimants rather than raw materials or local subsistence products. Ethnic groups and communities distributed tribute obligations—including money tributes—by ayllu, in accordance with traditional practices.[58]

To obtain labor for public works, transport, and agriculture, the colonials had to pursue a similar policy. To replace worn fibrous cable bridges, the cabildo of Huamanga ordered "that all the caciques [*kurakas*] and Indians of the this province come together [to say] who are obligated to make bridges . . . from old times, and their [European] masters are ordered to donate the Indians [thereby designated]."[59] To "rent" Indians to transport wares or to work lands, a European often had to make the arrangement with *kurakas* rather than hire the laborers directly. A contract as late as 1577 shows that the prominent Cárdenas family could not independently hire the workers they needed on their estancia in Chocorvos. Instead, a *kuraka* loaned twenty-seven kinsmen to the family and received the 162 pesos owed them after six months of labor. (Presumably the chief then distributed six pesos to each worker.)[60]

We should not exaggerate, of course, the dependence of the Europeans. They had alternatives and used them when they felt it necessary. Aside from an impressive population of yanaconas, they could draw on the services of slaves, mestizos, and other mixed-blood dependents, or exploit individual natives directly by extortion or agreement. For ambitious enterprises, however, these alternatives could only supplement rather than replace the labor of ayllu-based encomienda Indians. In the case of the Cárdenas estancia, the twenty-seven encomienda herders far outnumbered the "five *yanaconas* and four Indian cowboys" on the spread.[61] Furthermore, even if an encomendero wished to deal directly with individual natives to work various farms and estates, his ability to do so stemmed from a general spirit of cooperation with native societies as a whole, led by their chiefs. The Maldonados of Andahuaylas secured workers to tend to various herds, grow wheat and barley, harvest coca leaf, and so forth. Such relations sometimes carried the flavor of a direct interchange with native individuals, who earned food and money for their labors. Often, however, the Indians worked not to receive money, but to discharge collective tribute accounts settled upon with the *kurakas*. Even in the cases where encomienda Indians received individual payments in coin or in kind, Maldonado's access to their labors was facilitated by the *kurakas*' early approval, as spokesmen for communities and ethnic groups, of such relations. In the first year, *kurakas* had given Diego Maldonado llamas and Indian workers to transport items to Potosí and Lima. A tribute list in 1552 probably systematized earlier rules on the numbers of workers *kurakas* could spare to help out on Maldonado's farms, orchards, and ranches, and in domestic service.[62] As we saw earlier, Maldonado's success was related directly to a shrewd amateur ethnography. He rewarded cooperation with "gifts" and favors, negotiated agreements with the *kurakas*, and tended to respect traditional Andean prerogatives.

It is perhaps not surprising that the majority of the agricultural and artisanal surplus, and a considerable amount of the precious metal tributes, funneled to the Europeans rested heavily on the *kurakas*' ability to mobilize the labor of kinfolk in accordance with traditional Andean norms and expectations. More dramatic, however, is that even in the most dynamic sectors of the colonial economy—mining and textile manufactures—the Europeans could not transcend their reliance upon the *kurakas*. The mines and *obrajes* were strategic nerve centers crucial to the growth of a thriving commercial economy. Yet the voluntary flow of individuals or families to work the mines was not enough to assure an adequate and regular labor force. In 1562 a special commission struggled unsuccessfully to reform Huamanga's mines and stabilize a labor force. Still, as late as 1569, Amador de Cabrera negotiated with the *kurakas* of his encomienda to contract Indians he needed to work the mines of Huancavelica. The corregidor complained that Huamanga's rich mine deposits were languishing "because of a lack of Indian workers."[63]

Well into the 1570s—a transitional decade—European entrepreneurs depended upon the *kurakas* to supply workers for *obrajes*. In 1567, Hernán Guillén de Mendoza reached an agreement with the Tanquihuas Indians of his encomienda to rotate a force of sixty Indians for his *obraje* "Cacamarca" in Vilcashuamán. Ten years later, in Castrovirreyna, the *kurakas* of the Cárdenas family agreed to provide forty adults and fifty children to run a new *obraje*. Only an agreement among the chiefs of the various lineages—tied to one another and to their people by the long-standing expectations and interchanges of local kinship and reciprocity—could commit ayllu Indians to labor in the *obraje*. One Huamanga contract recorded the formal approval of seven different chiefs; a similar contract from another region recorded the unanimous agreement of sixteen *kurakas* and *principales* (notables). Significantly, the *kurakas* of Cárdenas sent a minor chief to oversee production in the new *obraje*. In the 1570s, though not in later years, Antonio de Oré appointed prominent encomienda Indians instead of Europeans or mestizos to manage his *obraje* in Canaria (Vilcashuamán). The native elites oversaw labor relations with the *obraje* and adapted traditional Andean techniques to the manufacture of textiles.[64]

Excluded from the traditional web of reciprocities among "kinfolk," which mobilized labor and circulated goods in Andean ethnic "families," and unable to reorganize the native economy or control directly the basic elements of production, the colonials had little choice but to rely upon their alliance with the *kurakas*. Even if Europeans aspired to take on the precarious task of reordering internally the native economy, the limits of their position would force them to rely upon the *kurakas*' ability to persuade their kin to participate in this change. By cultivating working relationships with the managers of autonomous native economies, Huamanga's colonials could, at least, receive a portion of the wealth and labor available in dynamic local economies without having to try to organize a powerful state apparatus or reorder local society. Whether the alliance was more voluntary or forced in character, the chiefs would use their traditional prestige to mobilize a flow of labor and tribute to the colonial economy. Combined with an impressive show of Spanish military skill in Cajamarca and elsewhere, and some willingness to help local societies promote ethnic interests, such a strategy seemed sensible at first. It is no accident that the early decades produced figures like Juan Polo de Ondegardo and Domingo de Santo Tomás. Experienced and shrewd colonials, they urged the crown to base its exploitation of native economies upon a respect for the traditional relationships and prerogatives of Andean society. To the greatest extent consistent with crown interests, royal policy should siphon off surplus goods and labor from ongoing native economies rather than reorganize or control them directly.[65]

Extracting a surplus by allying with the chiefs of autonomous and rather wealthy economic systems was for the conquistadores a realistic path of least resistance, but it soon led to a dead end. The *kurakas* controlled the basic processes of production and reproduction that sustained the colonials' economic, social, and political positions. If the *kurakas* were not at all "inferior" to the Europeans, but in fact directed the social relations and dynamic economies crucial to the survival of colonial enterprise, why should they accept a subordinate position in colonial society? On the contrary, their indispensable position tended to reinforce their posture as collaborating allies rather than dependent inferiors. The colonials remained foreign, extraneous elements superimposed upon an autonomous economy in which they served little purpose. Such a limitation did not augur well for an aspiring ruling class's hegemony, or for its long-run capacity to dominate a society and capture the wealth it produced. As soon as the specific advantages of the *kurakas*' alliance with the Spaniards began to run out—because the Europeans demanded too much or because Andean kinfolk reacted against the alliance—the early colonial system would enter a crisis. The dependence of Europeans upon native elites for access to exploitable labor in agriculture, transport, public works, manufactures, and mining exposed the artificial character of foreign hegemony. The economy erected by the post-Incaic alliances was deeply vulnerable to changes in the natives' cooperative policies. Disillusion with the Europeans could spell disaster.

Contradiction and Breakdown

To understand why disillusion set in, we should remember that the native-white alliances had always been uneasy and contradictory. The encomenderos cultivated working relations with local chiefs and societies in order to rule over the Andes and to extract as much wealth as possible. The natives accepted an alliance with the victorious foreigners as a way to advance local interests and to limit colonial demands and abuses. The contradictions of the post-Incaic alliances thus bore within them the seeds of severe disillusion. The violence and arrogance endemic in early relations warned of the limitations of such alliances for both sides.

In many ways, Huamanga's native societies had fared relatively well by allying with the Europeans. Their adaptations freed them of onerous bonds with the Incas, found them allies in ever-present struggles with rival native groups, and offered them the opportunity to accumulate wealth in the form of precious metals. The combined effects of epidemic disease, war, and emigration of yanaconas took their toll upon the several hundred thousand natives of Huamanga, but the decline was not as irrevocably devastating as that in other Andean areas. The Lucanas peoples, who in 1572 numbered about twenty-five thousand claimed in the 1580s that their population had even increased since the turbulent reign of the Inca Huayna Capac (1493–1525).[66] For Huamanga as a whole, a high birth rate, the relative immunity of people in high-altitude areas to disease, shrewd politics, and good luck helped cut net population decline to an average rate of perhaps 0.5 percent a year, or some 20 percent over the 1532 to 1570 period.[67] Such a loss posed hardships for a labor-intensive system of agriculture, but was not by itself disastrous. Indeed, the rich herding economies of the high punas of Lucanas, Chocorvos, and Vilcashuamán served as a kind of "insurance" against a decline of labor available for agriculture.[68] Successful adaptation to colonial conditions had enabled Huamanga's Indians to maintain traditional relationships and economic productivity. Inspections of southern Huamanga in the 1560s turned up many local huacas, presumably supported by retaining rights to lands, animals, and ayllu labor.[69] Several years later, Viceroy Francisco de Toledo was so impressed with the wealth of the Lucanas Laramati peoples that he nearly tripled their tribute assessment.[70] Huamanga's *kurakas* joined other Andean chiefs in offering King Philip II a dazzling bribe to end the encomienda system—one hundred thousand ducats more than any offer by the Spanish encomenderos, who wished the system continued.[71]

Nevertheless, the alliance with the Europeans had created ominous trends. First, even though Huamanga's rural societies weathered the effects of epidemic, war, emigration, and population decline relatively well, these were disturbing events. Economically, unpredictable drops in the population available for local tasks augured poorly for the long-run dynamism of ayllu-based society. A certain expected level of available human energy was a prerequisite for the maintenance of the traditional economic prerogatives, relationships, and exchanges that tied producers together. Ideologically, Andean societies tended to interpret misfortune—especially disease or early death—as the result of poorly functioning, "imbalanced" social relationships within the community of kin groups and gods (many of them ancestor-gods). Disease was often considered the work of neglected or angry deities. War and epidemic disease raised the specter of fundamentally awry relationships, which could bring about a major catastrophe far more devastating than earlier trends.[72]

Second, colonial relationships created humiliations and dependencies that undercut the ethnic freedom gained by liberation from Inca hegemony. Aside from the individual abuses and extortions that natives confronted everywhere, local societies found themselves relying upon colonial authority to defend their interests. Using an alliance with Europeans to protect against encroachments by outside ethnic groups was one matter, but dependence upon Europeans to settle internal disputes or to correct colonial abuses was quite another. Unfortunately, such a dependence grew increasingly frequent. Given the internal strife that plagued decentralized ethnic "families," it was difficult to avoid turning to Europeans as a source of power in local disputes over land rights, tribute-labor obligations, and chieftainships. By the 1550s,

Huamanga's Indians commonly traveled as far away as Lima to redress local grievances.[73]

Finally, the new relationships generated demands for labor that might go beyond what local societies were willing to offer in exchange for the benefit of alliance with the colonials. The number of Spaniards, of course, increased over the years. Moreover, the demands of any particular set of colonials did not necessarily remain static. Consider, for example, relations with Catholic priests. The *doctrineros* (rural priests) theoretically lived among ayllu Indians to indoctrinate them on behalf of the encomenderos; in practice, many were "priest-entrepreneurs" who sought to use their positions to promote commercial interests.[74] At first, many communities probably accepted the necessity of an alliance with the priests. To ally with the Europeans without cooperating with their gods was senseless from the Indians' point of view. The powerful Christian deities had defeated the major Andean gods at Cajamarca, and, like the native gods, could improve or damage the material well-being of the living. Since the Catholic priests mediated relations with the pantheon of Christian divinities (including saints) who affected everyday welfare, Indians did not rebuff the priests or their demands lightly. By the 1550s, churches and crosses—however modest—dotted rural areas, and their priests demanded considerable labor services, including those for transport, construction, ranching, and household service. By 1564, the rural priests' ability to extract unpaid native labor inspired jealousy among the urban encomenderos.[75] But as the priests' demands escalated, would native societies judge them far too excessive for the supposed advantages that favorable relations with Christian gods offered them?

The *kurakas*, as guardians and representatives of the community, could not ignore such evaluations of the relative advantages and disadvantages of cooperation with colonials. The *kurakas* who mobilized labor for European enterprise did not, in the long run, enjoy complete freedom to will the activities of their peoples. The chiefs bolstered their privileges and "influence" by fulfilling obligations to guard the communitarian unity and welfare. The traditional interchanges of reciprocities that enabled chiefs to mobilize the labors of kinfolk created expectations that might be difficult to reconcile with a unilateral flow of goods, labor, and advantages to European society. Traditional reciprocities also placed limitations upon the kinds of requests a *kuraka* could make of his ayllus and households. Production of textiles for the Europeans through a "putting-out" system similar to accepted Andean practices was one matter. As we shall see, sending workers to distant mines was quite another. Natives would be reluctant to comply, and once at the mines might never return to the domain of local society.

Evidence shows that labor demands became a matter provoking resentment among Indians, even when the labor was sought for activities superficially similar to traditional Andean practices. If labor demands were originally the price for the relative advantages of working relationships with the encomendero elite, the advantages could dwindle over time, and the price could rise unacceptably high. In local society, for example, canal cleaning had normally been an occasion for celebration on the agricultural and ceremonial calendars. In ritual led by the native elite, a community of "relatives" reaffirmed the importance of such tasks for the collective welfare of the group. But the same activity carried an onerous flavor if viewed as uncompensated labor to the exclusive benefit of others. The Huachos and Chocorvos Indians complained in 1557 that they were forced to sweep clean the great canal "with which the citizens [of Huamanga] irrigate their [farms]." The Indians did not benefit from or need the water.[76] Under such conditions, *kurakas* could not transfer the celebratory aspect of Andean work to colonial canal cleaning even if they had so wished. A *kuraka* who felt compelled to satisfy colonial labor demands could not assume that his call for labor would be accepted as justified.

In the 1560s, the contradictions inherent in the post-Incaic alliances sharpened. The growing dependency of Indians upon Europeans to settle disputes;[77] the economic shortages or hardships imposed by colonial extraction, emigration, or population decline;[78] the tendency of encomenderos, local priests, and officials to demand increasing shares of ayllu goods and labor—all these eventually would have provoked a reassessment of native policies toward the colonials. What made the need for a reevaluation urgent, however, was the above-mentioned discovery in the 1560s of gold and silver at Atunsulla and mercury at Huancavelica. The discoveries fired Spanish dreams of a thriving regional economy whose mines would stimulate a boom in trade, textile manufactures, artisanal crafts, construction, agriculture, and ranching. The only obstacle or bottleneck would be labor. If European demands escalated far beyond the supply of individual laborers, or of contingents sent by *kurakas*, how would the colonials stabilize an adequate labor force?

By 1562, the labor problem merited an official inquiry by the distinguished jurist Juan Polo de Ondegardo. Polo investigated Indian complaints, set out to reform and regulate labor practices, and ordered native societies to turn over a rotating force of 700 weekly laborers for the Atunsulla mines. The labor regime imposed by the miners had been harsh. Miners sought to maximize their exploitation of native laborers. Natives personally hauled loads of fuel, salt, and other supplies from distant areas; in the mines themselves, laborers had to meet brutally taxing production quotas; after fulfilling their labor obligation, they faced a struggle to obtain their wages.[79] Small wonder that the Indians asked a noted defender, Fray Domingo de Santo Tomás, to inspect the mines. Santo Tomás found that "until now the Indians have been paid so poorly, and treated worse . . . that even if they went voluntarily, [these abuses] would wipe out [their willingness]." Hopeful that Polo's reforms—boosted by higher salaries—could attract enough voluntary labor, Santo Tomás warned that the Indians and *kurakas* would resist attempts to force natives to work under the abusive conditions of the past, "even if they knew they would have to spend all their lives in jail." Santo Tomás found the Indians restless about demands for mine labor. The Soras and Lucanas peoples, farther away than other groups from Atunsulla, were particularly vexed about working under abusive conditions current in distant mines.[80]

Polo's reforms changed little. The supply of native laborers forced or coaxed individually or through the *kurakas* remained irregular and insufficient. The corregidor of Huamanga complained in 1569 that work on the region's fabulous deposits faltered because of the labor shortage.[81]

The mines made obvious the limitations of previous relationships to both sides. For the Europeans driven by the international expansion of commercial capital, alliances with native societies meant little if they could not supply a dependable labor force for a growing mining economy. For the Indians—*kurakas* as well as their kinfolk—collaboration with the colonials offered few benefits if the Europeans insisted upon draining ayllu resources in a drive to develop a massive mining economy beyond the control of local society. The Europeans wanted favors that the *kurakas* could not or would not give them. Yet the colonials still lacked the organized state institutions and force that could compel the chiefs to turn over large contingents to the mines.

At this very moment, contradictions between metropolis and colony encouraged the Indians to rethink the necessity of cooperation with encomenderos. In Spain, the rulers had long debated whether to abolish the encomienda system and convert the Indians into direct vassals. By 1560, the crown had received impressive bribe offers from both encomenderos and the native *kurakas*, but had not reached a decision. A commission sent to report on the merits of the encomienda issue dispatched Polo (proencomienda) and Santo Tomás (antiencomienda) to conduct an inquiry. The pair toured the Andean highlands in 1562. In Huamanga as elsewhere, they organized meetings of natives to participate in a public debate of the encomienda issue. The Indians sided with Santo Tomás.[82] Royal interests and moral sensibilities, honed by frictions between encomenderos and the church, created a spectacular debate. In the very years when mine discoveries made the basic antagonisms between natives and whites ever more weighty and ominous, the crown's distinguished representatives advertised political instability, divisions among the elite, and a receptivity to the idea that the encomenderos were dispensable to crown and native alike.

If growing disillusion with labor demands prompted sabotaging or discarding colonial relationships, the apparent vulnerability of such relationships to reform imposed by the metropolis could only give further impetus to such urges. Soon after 1560, native discontent expressed itself in the number of broken alliances. In 1563, *kurakas* in seven different Huamanga encomiendas refused to send Indians to the city plaza for corvée duty. The mines continued to suffer from an irregular labor supply. Many of Huamanga's peoples, especially the Soras and Lucanas, confirmed Santo Tomás's warnings by openly rejecting calls for laborers to work the mines. Indian shepherds cost their encomendero, Diego Maldonado, a claimed seven thousand sheep through robbery or neglect. Encomenderos blamed priests for the natives' growing tendency to ignore previously accepted obligations; one observer placed the blame on popular rumors that the Spaniards would kill natives for medicinal ointments in their bodies.[83] In an economy where the Europeans depended greatly upon alliances with native elites to gain access to exploitable labor, the spread of such disillusion and resistance poisoned enterprise. In a society where the neo-Incas maintained a military force in the *montaña* between Cuzco and Huamanga, and the colonials had not yet organized an impressive state apparatus, growing hostility posed strategic dangers as well. The corregidor of Huamanga warned the acting viceroy, Governor-General Lope García de Castro, that a rebellion might break out. In neighboring Jauja and in Andahuaylas, alarming discoveries of stored arms confirmed that Indian-white relations were in jeopardy.[84]

Demands for mine labor on a new scale, the encomenderos' political vulnerability, and the neo-Incas' probable willingness to lead a revolt created a conjuncture that compelled second thoughts about the post-Incaic alliances. From the beginning, the inherent contradictions of the early alliances had created the likelihood of disenchantment. Despite the relative success of their adaptation to colonial conditions, Huamanga's native peoples confronted trends that threatened to undermine local autonomy, relationships, and production. Demographic decline and instability, humiliation and dependence, growing demands for labor—all tended to expose the erosive consequences of an alliance among partners whose fundamental interests clashed. The discovery of major gold, silver, and mercury mines brought such contradictions to a head. The Indians' severe disaffection expressed itself in a radical millenarian upheaval, "Taki Onqoy," which inflamed Huamanga. The sect preached pan-Andean unity, proclaimed an end to all contact with Hispanic society, and pressured *kurakas* to cut off cooperation with colonials. The movement had exceptional appeal to peoples ethnically divided against themselves, and deeply disillusioned by the consequences of cooperation with the Hispanic world. By the end of the decade, *kurakas* stubbornly refused to send Indians to the mines, and colonial relationships entered a crisis stage.[85]

Conclusion

The rise and fall of Indian-white alliances in Huamanga yield broad implications for the study of early colonial history. First, the activities of local Andean peoples had a decisive impact upon the particular texture of early relations and institutions "imposed" by Hispanic society (encomienda, tribute, labor drafts, Christianization, and the like). Yet a deeper understanding of the interests and motives behind native activity is elusive unless informed by an awareness of preconquest history and social structure. In this perspective, the line between pre-Columbian and colonial history becomes, in many respects, artificial and misleading. Second, the *kurakas'* importance as strategic mediators singled out for special favors by Spanish allies, and the impact of Andean ethnic rivalries upon native-white relations, indicate that divisions and tensions internal to local Andean societies played key roles in European success and failure, and the colonial process in general. We would be well advised, therefore, not to homogenize the "Indians" into a seamless social category, thereby ignoring internal contradictions that shaped events. Third, the crisis of the 1560s and its link to the mining economy illuminate the fundamental contradictions of purpose and interest that marred early native-white alliances, and doomed them to failure. Indeed, the demise of the alliances meant that only a more effective, direct control of local native life and institutions, backed by a revitalized state, would truly serve Hispanic interests, and develop the mining economy. It is in this sense that massive reorganization of the Andean colony, like that led by Viceroy Francisco de Toledo (1569–1581), was a historic necessity. Early alliances and cooperation represented not a "golden era" of native-white relations, but a transitory phase whose contradictions would eventually assert themselves with increasing force.

Finally, the Indian-white alliances might lead us to reassess the old distinction between sedentary native societies ruled by the Aztecs and Incas, and more independent or mobile peoples who had escaped subjugation by pre-Columbian empires. We normally observe that Europeans experienced little trouble dominating a sedentary peasantry already accustomed to rule from above, but encountered much more difficulty conquering stateless peoples undefeated by the Aztecs and Incas.[86] There is merit in the distinction, and we may certainly contrast the options and "moral economy" of peasants and those of free and independent "savages."[87] But the contrast misleads us in certain respects. It underestimates the degree to which stateless Indian people forged early alliances with Europeans, and the dynamics that drove such relations to disaster.[88] It overestimates the power of "habits of obedience" among peasantries exploited by the Aztecs and Incas. We presume that such habits generated a passive posture toward the Europeans, who simply filled the void left by Aztecs and Incas. By this line of reasoning, colonizers commanded surplus labor and products of peasants not because the latter (and their chiefs) had reason to comply, but because tradition dictated obedience. If the birth, evolution, and final demise of Huamanga's post-Incaic alliances tell us anything, however, it is that sedentary peasantries actively assessed their alternatives and made choices within the confines of their interests and power, and that, like many human beings, they could even change their minds.

Notes

1. For the history of these peoples' relations with Spanish conquistadores, see Charles Gibson, *Tlaxcala in the Sixteenth Century*, 2d ed. (Stanford, 1967); Waldemar Espinoza Soriano, *La destrucción del imperio de los Incas: La rivalidad política y señorial de los curacazgos andinos* (Lima, 1973); Manuel de Odriozola, ed., *Documentos históricos del Perú en las épocas del coloniaje después de la conquista y de la independencia hasta la presente*, 10 vols. (Lima, 1863–77), III: 3–9.

2. The Huamanga region corresponded roughly to the contemporary Peruvian departments of Ayacucho and Huancavelica. Huamanga's "core" districts included the *corregimientos* of Angaraes (Huancavelica), Huanta, Vilcashuamán, Chocorvos (Castrovirreyna), and Lucanas. Parinacochas and Andahuaylas were "swing" districts in many respects, oriented both to Huamanga and to Cuzco, and I cite data or patterns from these *corregimientos* when they accord with evidence from the "core" districts. For a convenient map of *corregimiento* districts, see Guillermo Lohmann Villena, *El corregidor de indios en el Perú bajo los Austrias* (Madrid, 1957), 200.

3. My understanding of pre-Columbian social and economic structure relies heavily on the pioneering studies of John V. Murra, *Formaciones económicas y políticas del mundo andino* (Lima, 1975). The following three paragraphs draw upon the much more extended discussion of Huamanga before Spanish conquest in this author's "The Challenge of Conquest: The Indian Peoples of Huamanga, Peru, and the Foundation of a Colonial Society, 1532–1640" (Ph.D. diss., Yale University, 1979), 5–53. The largest ethnic groups of Huamanga probably number no more than thirty thousand individuals or five thousand to six thousand domestic units. Even within these groups, social identification, economic claims, and political authority were significantly varied along lines of kinship and ethnicity.

4. Felipe Guaman Poma de Ayala. *Nueva corónica y buen gobierno (codex péruvien illustré)* (Paris, 1936), 369–370.

5. For early encomienda grants by Pizarro, see U.S. Library of Congress, Harkness Collection (hereinafter HC), Stella R. Clemence, ed., *Documents from Early Peru: The Pizarros and the Almagros, 1531–1578* (Washington, DC, 1936), 154, 170. On

the Peruvian encomienda, see Enrique Torres Saldamando, *Apuntes históricos sobre las encomiendas en el Perú* (Lima, 1967); Manuel Belaúnde Guinassi, *La encomienda en el Perú* (Lima, 1945); Manuel Vicente Villarán, *Apuntes sobre la realidad social de los indígenas ante las leyes de Indias* (Lima, 1964), 25–100; James Lockhart, *Spanish Peru, 1532–1560: A Colonial Society* (Madison, 1968), 11–33, and passim.

6. See Vasco de Guevara, as quoted by Marcos Jiménez de la Espada, ed., *Relaciones geográficas de Indias—Perú* (hereinafter cited as *RGI*), reprinted in *Biblioteca de autores españoles*, tomo 183 (Madrid, 1965), 181–182 n.2; James Lockhart, *The Men of Cajamarca: A Social and Biographical Study of the First Conquerors of Peru* (Austin, 1972), 424. For Inca *mitmaq* who fought against the Spanish, see "Autos criminales que siguieron Juan Tucabamba y Pedro Cachi, indios . . . 1567," Archivo General de la Nación, Lima (hereinafter cited as AGN), Derecho Indígena (hereinafter cited as DI), leg. 1, cuad. 9, fol. 5.

7. Raúl Rivera Serna, transcriber, *Libro del cabildo de la Ciudad de San Juan de la Frontera de Huamanga, 1539–1547* (Lima, 1966), 28–33.

8. See ibid., 47, 64–65, 68, 71, 91, 95, 100, 121, 128–129, 137, 165, 194.

9. See ibid., 21–22, 30, 31, 46–47, 54, 62, 64, 112, 189; Viceroy Francisco de Toledo to Corregidor of Huamanga, Valley of Yucay, May 26, 1571, HC, doc. 985; Don Pedro de la Gasca to ?, Jauja, Dec. 27, 1547, Biblioteca Nacional del Perú (hereinafter BNP), ms. A127.

10. Serna, *Libro del cabildo*, 64.

11. Luis de Monzón et al., "Description . . . de los Rucanas Antamarcas," *RGI*, 238; Monzón et al., Descripción . . . de Atunrucana y Laramati," *RGI*, 226–227; Roberto Levillier, ed., *Gobernantes del Perú*, 14 vols. (Madrid, 1921–26), II: 103–104, 153, 183, 192. On the sensitivity of peasants to power balances, see, for example, Frances Fitzgerald, *Fire in the Lake: The Vietnamese and the Americans in Vietnam* (New York, 1973), 28–32, 397–398.

12. Serna, *Libro del cabildo*, 47, 69, 100; Juan Polo de Ondegardo, "Informe . . . al Licenciado Briviesca de Muñatones," *Revista Histórica*, 13 (1940), 156. Some of the yanacona retainers of Europeans may have been yana retainers alienated from ayllu society before the Spanish conquest. On the preconquest yana, see Murra, *Formaciones*, 225–242; on yanaconas as an auxiliary arm of conquest, see Nathan Wachtel, *Sociedad e ideología: Ensayos de historia y antropología andinas* (Lima, 1973), 149–158; John Hemming, *The Conquest of the Incas* (New York, 1970), 136, 171, 180, 184, 186, 305–306, 362.

13. Serna, *Libro del cabildo*, 63.

14. For a concise history of the Peruvian civil wars, see Lockhart, *Spanish Peru*, 3–5; for the role of Huamanga in colonial politics, see Serna, *Libro del cabildo*, 71–72, 73–79, 85–88, 93–96, 98–99, 141, 142–145, 146–150, 152, 159–164, 168–174, 199; Domingo de Santo Tomás to King, Lima, May 20, 1555, in Emilio Lissón Chaves, ed., *La iglesia de España en el Perú*, 4 vols. (Seville, 1943–46), II:57.

15. Report by La Gasca, Lima, Sept. 25, 1548, BNP, ms. A127; Archivo Departamental de Ayacucho, Ayacucho (hereinafter cited as ADA), Protocolos Notariales (hereinafter cited as PN), Navarrette 1627, fols. 473–474; "Autos que siguieron don Melchor y don Salvador Ataurimachi . . . 1643," AGN, DI, leg. 6, cuad. 109, fols. 2r, 5v; Damián de la Bandera, "Relación general . . . de Guamanga," *RGI*, 178; "Provisión de los indios Cañaris de Vilcas . . . 1612," BNP, ms. B44, fol. 8r; Serna, *Libro del cabildo*, 121, 142, for quotations; Poma de Ayala, *Nueva corónica*, 431–433.

16. Serna, *Libro del cabildo*, 45, 50–51, 130. For other cases, see idem, 38, 45, 48, 61, 120, 124, 132. One *fanegada* is approximately 2.9 hectares.

17. Ibid., 61, 97, 100, 120; "Autos que sigue el Común de Indios . . . de Chiara . . . 1806," AGN, Tierras de Comunidades, leg. 3, cuad. 19, fols. 40v, 42r; "Libro de Cabildo . . . 1557," BNP, ms. A203, fol. 65v.

18. "Autos . . . contra Juan Arias Maldonado . . . 1573," AGN, DI, leg. 2, cuad. 17, fols. 195, 226.

19. Viceroy Marqués de Cañete to Indians of several repartimientos, Lima, Sept. 27, 1557, HC, doc. 1013. The Yauyos and Huancas mentioned in this document refer to those who lived in southern Huamanga (Chocorvos and Vilcashuamán) rather than the societies of the central sierra north of Huamanga.

20. "Autos . . . contra Juan Arias Maldonado . . . 1573," AGN, DI, leg. 2, cuad. 17, fols. 178r, 197r, 219v–220r.

21. Ibid., esp. fols. 179, 191–195 (son's exaggeration: 195v), 208–209, 226.

22. Ibid., fols. 195r, 208v, 215v; "Libros de penas de cámara . . . de Huamanga . . . 1559," BNP, ms. A336, passim; cf. Serna, *Libro del cabildo*, 30, 122.

23. Serna, *Libro del cabildo*, 21–22, 31, 64, 112; cf. Marie Helmer, "Notas sobre la encomienda peruana en el siglo XVI," *Revista del Instituto de Historia del Derecho*, 10 (1959), 124–143.

24. José María Vargas, *Fray Domingo de Santo Tomás, defensor y apóstol de los indios del Perú: Su vida y escritos* (Quito, 1937), "Escritos" section, 10.

25. Polo, "Informe . . . al Licenciado Briviesca de Muñatones," 157. Polo's observations were probably based upon patterns in the greater Cuzco region. For similar data from Huamanga, see Monzón et al., "Descripción . . . de los Rucanas Antamarcas," 238.

26. See Bandera, "Relación general," 176; "Autos criminales que siguieron Juan Tucabamba y Pedro Cachi indios . . . 1567," AGN, DI, leg. 1, cuad. 9, fols. 20–22.

27. Poma de Ayala, *Nueva corónica*, 559.

28. Monzón et al., "Descripción . . . de Atunrucana y Laramati," p. 227; "Testimonio . . . y confirmación de la Hacienda de LOCCHAS . . . 1625," AGN, Títulos de propiedad, cuad. 747, fols. 4v (quotation), 16.

29. For juridical, economic, public works, and other cabildo policies and regulations, see Serna, *Libro del cabildo*, 21–22, 42–43, 46–47, 54, 62, 112, 126, 132, 145, 184, 185, 196.

30. Ibid., 35, 36, 38, 39–41, 43–46, 48, 51, 53, 54–59, 65, 72, 97, 121, 154.

31. Ibid., 40, 43, 46, 48, 52, 54, 56–61, 63, 73, 93, 120–122, 126–127, 130, 133, 153–155.

32. Ibid., 179 for quotation; 180–181, 182–183, for distribution.

33. "Libro de Cabildo . . . 1557," BNP, ms. A203, fols. 24–25.

34. For the incredible variety of items in pre-1570 tribute lists, see "Autos . . . contra Juan Arias Maldonado . . . 1573," AGN, DI, leg. 2, cuad. 17, fols. 179–180, 184–186; "Testimonio . . . que siguió doña María Carrillo . . . sobre . . . la mitad del repartimiento de ANDAMARCA . . . 1576," AGN, DI, leg. 1, cuad. 8, fols. 109–112.

35. "Testimonio . . . que siguió doña María Carrillo . . . sobre . . . la mitad del repartimiento de ANDAMARCA . . . 1576," AGN, DI, leg. 1, cuad. 8, fol. 110v, for prices in 1563.

36. In addition to notes 31–33 and 28, see Serna, *Libro del cabildo*, 62; Pedro de Cieza de León, *Parte primera de la crónica del Perú*, in *Biblioteca de autores españoles*, tomo 26 (Madrid, 1853), chap. 87; Juan López de Velasco, *Geografía y*

descripción universal de las Indias, edited by Marcos Jiménez de la Espada (Madrid, 1971), 241; "Sobre la medición . . . de unas tierras en Yucay . . . 1578," BNP, ms. Z305; "Testimonio de los títulos . . . de Guatata, Churucana y Pacuaro . . . 1626," BNP, ms. B75, fols. 23v, 46r; "Copia de los títulos de las tierras de CHINCHE-PAMPA . . . 1568," AGN, Títulos de propiedad, cuad. 8; untitled *expediente* concerning Huanta lands disputed among various Europeans and Indians, 1678, ADA, Corregimiento, Causas Ordinarias, leg. 2 (provisional classification in 1977), esp. fol. 935; land registration of Monastery of Santa Clara, 1642, Registro de Propiedad Inmueble de Ayacucho, tomo 21, partida XXXIII, 330; "Libro de Cabildo . . . 1557," BNP, ms. A203, fol. 33v.

37. This definition of commercial capital refers to a profit mechanism based on: (1) "underpaying" producers by acquiring labor power or commodity goods for free (tribute) or at less than their market value, and (2) exploiting a position as intermediary at between high-priced and low-priced markets. On the distinction between industrial capital or capitalist production, and commercial capital in precapitalist settings, see Karl Marx, *Capital*, edited by Frederick Engels, 3 vols. (New York, 1967), esp. III, chaps. 20, 36, 47. As Marx pointed out, it is important to distinguish between the dynamics of commercial capital within a capitalist economy and the commercial capital that predates the dominance of capitalist production. In the text, I refer to the later form of commercial capital.

38. Serna, *Libro del cabildo*, 50, 123, 142, 166; see Levillier, *Gobernantes*, 1, 190. On the social atmosphere of mining centers, see the fines collected in Atunsulla in the 1560s, as recorded in "Libro de penas de cámara . . . 1559," BNP, ms. A336.

39. See "Don Diego de Salazar pide que se le ampare . . . 1622," AGN, Minería, leg. 2, Ayacucho 1622, fols. 55, 169–172, 192; Fernando Montesinos, *Anales del Perú*, edited by Víctor M. Maúrtua, 2 vols. (Madrid, 1906), I, 278; *expediente* concerning mines of Amador de Cabrera, AGN, Minería, leg. 13, Huancavelica 1585–91, exp. 1, fol. 49; *expediente* regarding property and debts of Amador de Cabrera, AGN, Minería, leg. 11, Huancavelica 1562–72, fols. 254–255.

40. "Causa de cuentas dada por Dn. Diego Guillén de Mendoza . . . 1616," BNP, ms. Z313, fols. 164–165; ADA, PN, Romo 1557, fols. 202–204; "Para que el corregidor de Vilcashuamán . . . hara [haga] averiguaciones . . . 1600," BNP, ms. B1485, fols. 62r, 247r; "Autos . . . contra Juan Arias Maldonado . . . 1573," AGN, DI, leg. 2, cuad. 17, fols. 193v–194r.

41. See Lockhart, *Spanish Peru*, 23; Lockhart, *The Men of Cajamarca*, 297; López de Velasco, *Geografía*, 241.

42. "Don Diego de Salazar pide que se le ampare . . . 1622," AGN, Minería, leg. 2, Ayacucho 1622, fol. 79r; Santo Tomás to Royal Council of the Exchequer in Lima, Andahuaylas, Apr. 6, 1562, Archivo General de las Indias, Seville (hereinafter cited as AGI), V, Lima 313; "Autos . . . contra Juan Arias Maldonado . . . 1573," AGN, DI, leg. 2, cuad. 17, fols. 192v–193r.

43. Bandera, "Relación general," 177; "Autos criminales que siguieron Juan Tucabamba y Pedro Cachi, indios . . . 1567," AGN, DI, leg. 1, cuad. 9, fols. 1r (quotation), 3v.

44. "Autos . . . contra Juan Arias Maldonado . . . 1573," AGN, DI, leg. 2, cuad. 17, fols. 192–194.

45. Serna, *Libro del cabildo*, 112, 193; "Autos . . . contra Juan Arias Maldonado . . . 1573," AGN, DI, leg. 2, cuad. 17, fol. 192v; Polo, "Informe . . . al Licenciado Briviesca de Muñatones," 189.

46. See Viceroy Toledo to Regimiento of Huamanga, Yucay Valley, June 10, 1571, HC, doc. 983; Juan Polo de Ondegardo, "Ordenanzas de las minas de Guamanga," in *Colección de libros y documentos referentes a la historia del Perú*, 4 vols. (Lima, 1916), IV: 142; López de Velasco, *Geografía*, 241.

47. Bandera, "Relación general," 177; "Registro de escrituras públicas . . . 1592," BNP, ms. Z306, fols. 490, 491; ADA, PN, Padilla 1602/1613, fol. 339v; Marqués de Cañete to Garci Díez de San Miguel, Lima, Aug. 21, 1559, HC, doc. 1014; *expediente* regarding property and debts of Amador de Cabrera, AGN, Minería, leg. 11, Huancavelica 1562–72, fol. 258.

48. Polo, "Informe . . . al Licenciado Briviesca de Muñatones," 189.

49. ADA, PN, Peña 1596, fol. 311r; "Autos . . . contra Juan Arias Maldonado . . . 1573," AGN, DI, leg. 2, cuad. 17, fol. 193r.

50. Ibid.; Bandera, "Relación general," 180, for quotations.

51. "Libro de penas de cámara . . . 1559," BNP, ms. A336, entry for Oct. 13, 1559.

52. The "open" strategy of native society had religious and cultural dimensions as well, but space constraints limit my discussion to socioeconomic patterns. For the religious and cultural sides of the Indian-Spanish alliances, see Stern, "The Challenge of Conquest," 77–79.

53. The encomendero population was not completely stable in the first years after Huamanga's founding in 1539, but usually hovered around twenty-five.

54. For tribute lists in the 1550s and 1560s, see "Testimonio . . . que siguió doña María Carrillo . . . sobre . . . la mitad del repartimiento de ANDAMARCA . . . 1576," AGN, DI, leg. 1, cuad. 8, fols. 109–112; "Autos . . . contra Juan Arias Maldonado . . . 1573," AGN, DI, leg. 2, cuad. 17, fols. 184–188.

55. Bandera, "Relación general," 179.

56. Polo, "Informe . . . al Licenciado Briviesca de Muñatones," 169.

57. "Autos . . . contra Juan Arias Maldonado . . . 1573," AGN, DI, leg. 2, cuad. 17, fol. 185r. For similar practices elsewhere, see Karen Spalding, "*Kurakas* and Commerce: A Chapter in the Evolution of Andean Society," *Hispanic American Historical Review (HAHR)* 53 (Nov. 1973), 586–588.

58. For clear examples from 1570 to 1572 in Andahuaylas and Parinacochas, see "Autos . . . contra Juan Arias Maldonado . . . 1573," AGN, DI, leg. 2, cuad. 17, fols. 181–183; "Libro común de sumas . . . por el tesorero Miguel Sánchez. Cuzco, 1572–1573," Yale University, Sterling Library, Department of Manuscripts, Latin America Collection, vol. 5, fol. 62v. Cf. "En la residencia secreta . . . a Dn. Francisco de Cepeda, Corregidor de Parinacochas . . . 1597," BNP, ms. A236, fols. 20r, 22r.

59. Serna, *Libro del cabildo*, 40.

60. Bandera, "Relación general," 180; ADA, PN, Romo 1577, fols. 331–332. Cf. three contracts recorded in Cuzco in 1560, in *Revista del Archivo Histórico* 4 (Cuzco, 1953), 25, 31, 32.

61. ADA, PN, Romo 1577, fol. 332v.

62. For the data above, see "Autos . . . contra Juan Arias Maldonado . . . 1573," AGN, DI, leg. 2, cuad. 17, fols. 179, 186–187, 191–192, 207, 213r, 216–217.

63. Guillermo Lohmann Villena, *Las minas de Huancavelica en los siglos XVI y XVII* (Seville, 1949), 28, 91–92; Polo, "Ordenanzas de las minas de Guamanga," 139–151; Vargas, *Fray Domingo*, "Escritos" section, 57–62; *expediente* regarding property and debts of Amador de Cabrera, AGN, Minería, leg. 11, Huancavelica

1562–72, fol. 62r; "Libro 50 del Cabildo . . . 1568," BNP, ms. A603, fol. 23v (quotation). See Levillier, *Gobernantes*, II: 573, 578.

64. "Causa de cuentas dada por Dn. Diego Guillén de Mendoza . . . 1616," BNP, ms. Z313, fols. 164–165; ADA, PN, Romo 1577, fols. 202–204, esp. 203; "Concierto en el asiento de Colcabamba . . . 1571," BNP, ms. A455; "Para que el corregidor de Vilcashuamán . . . hara [haga] averiguaciones . . . 1600," BNP, ms. B1485, fol. 61r; Miriám Salas Olivari, "El obraje de Chincheros. Del obraje a las comunidades indígenas, siglo XVI" (Bachelor's thesis, Pontífica Universidad Católica del Perú, 1976), 109–110 (courtesy of Scarlett O'Phelan).

65. Santo Tomás, an opponent of the encomienda, was the more extreme proponent of this view. On these two personalities, see Murra, *Formaciones*, 285–286, 306–311; Patricia J. Bard, "Domingo de Santo Tomás, a Spanish Friar in 16th Century Peru" (M.A. thesis, Columbia University, 1967).

66. Monzón et al., "Descripción . . . de los Rucanas Antamarcas," 238; Monzón et al., "Descripción . . . de Atunrucana y Laramati," 227.

67. See Noble David Cook, "The Indian Population of Peru, 1570–1620" (Ph.D. diss., University of Texas at Austin, 1973), 238; see John H. Rowe, "Inca Culture at the Time of the Spanish Conquest," in Julian H. Steward, ed., *Handbook of South American Indians*, 7 vols. (Washington, DC, 1946–59), II:184. It should be noted that the first major sixteenth-century epidemic in the Andean zone struck in the 1520s, *before* the European conquest in 1532.

68. On the importance of livestock herds as a kind of insurance resource in Huamanga and elsewhere, see Bandera, "Relación general," 177; Murra, *Formaciones*, 202–203.

69. See the "Relación de Amancebados, Hechiceros y Huacas" included in Luis Millones, ed., *Las informaciones de Cristóbal de Albornoz: Documentos para el estudio del Taki Onqoy* (Cuernavaca, 1971).

70. Noble David Cook, ed., *Tasa de la visita general de Francisco de Toledo (1570–1575)* (Lima, 1975), 261.

71. Hemming, *Conquest*, 386–387.

72. On the importance, in Andean culture, of "balanced" relationships with the gods for the material welfare and health of the living, see Stern, "The Challenge of Conquest," 30–35. For the tendency to interpret disease and misfortune as the work of offended deities, see Poma de Ayala, *Nueva corónica*, 109, 137, 158, 286; Francisco de Avila, *Dioses y hombres de Huarochirí*, translated by José María Argüedas (Lima, 1966), 47, 49, 149, 151.

73. Marqués de Cañete to various Corregidors, Lima, Nov. 9, 1556, HC, doc. 1012.

74. See Lockhart, *Spanish Peru*, 52–55.

75. Marqués de Cañete to various Corregidors, Lima, May 25, 1557, HC, doc. 1009; Bandera, "Relación general," 176; García de Castro to Priests of Huamanga, Lima, Dec. 16, 1564, HC, doc. 1008.

76. Marqués de Cañete to Corregidor of Huamanga, Lima, Feb. 21, 1556, HC, doc. 1017.

77. For examples from the 1560s, see Vargas, *Fray Domingo*, "Escritos" section, 59; "Autos . . . contra Juan Arias Maldonado . . . 1573," AGN, DI, leg. 2, cuad. 17, fol. 208r.

78. "Autos . . . contra Juan Arias Maldonado . . . 1573," AGN, DI, leg. 2, cuad. 17, fols. 194v, 209r; Montesinos, *Anales del Perú*, I:243, II:18.

79. See Polo, "Ordenanzas de las minas de Guamanga," 139–151.

80. Santo Tomás to Don Alonso Manuel de Anaya, Huamanga, Mar. 23, 1562, Santo Tomás to Council of Indies, Andahuaylas, Apr. 5, 1562, Santo Tomás to Royal Council of the Exchequer in Lima, Andahuaylas, Apr. 6, 1562, AGI, V, Lima, 313 (also available in Vargas, *Fray Domingo*, "Escritos" section, 55–62).

81. "Libro 50 del Cabildo . . . 1568," BNP, ms. A603, fol. 23v.

82. Archbishop Gerónimo de Loayza to King, Lima, Nov. 30, 1562, AGI, V, Lima 300; Santo Tomás to Anaya, Huamanga, Mar. 23, 1562, AGI, V, Lima, 313. See Hemming, *Conquest*, 385–390, for an overview of the encomienda perpetuity issue.

83. All the evidence cited above is from the period 1563 to 1571. "Libro de penas de cámara . . . 1559," BNP, ms. A336, entry for May 3, 1563; Viceroy Toledo to Judge of Huamanga's mines, Yucay Valley, June 10, 1571, HC, doc. 984; Lohmann, *Las minas*, 93 n.3; "Autos . . . contra Juan Arias Maldonado . . . 1573," AGN, DI, leg. 2, cuad. 17, fol. 196r; Lohmann, *El corregidor*, 28; Cristóbal de Molina, *Relación de las fábulas y ritos de los incas*, in Francisco A. Loayza, ed., *Las crónicas de los Molinas* [*sic*] (Lima, 1943), 79.

84. Molina, *Relación de las fábulas*, 82; Cristóbal de Albornoz, "Instrucción para descubrir todas las guacas del Pirú y sus camayos y haciendas," edited by Pierre Duviols, *Journal de la Société des Américanistes* 56–1 (1967), 36.

85. A detailed presentation of this movement's history in Huamanga lies beyond the scope of this article. For an extended discussion, see Stern, "The Challenge of Conquest," 101–143; see Juan M. Ossio, ed., *Ideología mesiánica del mundo andino* (Lima, 1973), especially the essays by Luis Millones and Nathan Wachtel on 85–142.

It should be noted that the crisis of the Indian-Spanish alliances did not lead to a *total* breakdown of native-white cooperation or alliance. The rupture was most severe on the issue of mine labor, and some evidence suggests ambivalent attitudes of *kurakas* in the 1560s. Nonetheless, events of the 1560s plunged earlier relations and expectations into crisis. See Guillermo Lohmann Villena, "Juan de Matienzo, autor del 'Gobierno del Perú' (su personalidad y su obra)," *Anuario de Estudios Americanos* 22 (1965), 767–886; Stern, "The Challenge of Conquest," 124–130, 140–145.

86. See, for example, Eric R. Wolf and Edward C. Hansen, *The Human Condition in Latin America* (New York, 1972), 29–30, 57–59. For a sixteenth-century version of this observation, see Cieza de León, *Parte primera*, chap. 13.

87. See, for example, James C. Scott, *The Moral Economy of the Peasant: Rebellion and Subsistence in Southeast Asia* (New Haven, 1976); Philip Wayne Powell, *Soldiers, Indians and Silver: North America's First Frontier War* (Tempe, 1975; orig. pub. 1952), 32–54; R. C. Padden, "Cultural Change and Military Resistance in Araucanian Chile, 1550–1730," *Southwestern Journal of Anthropology* 13 (Spring 1957), 103–121.

88. For examples in Brazil, Paraguay, and North America, see Alexander Marchant, *From Barter to Slavery: The Economic Relations of Portuguese and Indians in the Settlement of Brazil, 1500–1580* (Baltimore, 1942); Stuart B. Schwartz, "Indian Labor and New World Plantations: European Demands and Indian Responses in Northeastern Brazil," *American Historical Review* 83 (Feb. 1978), 43–79; Elman R. Service, *Spanish-Guaraní Relations in Early Colonial Paraguay* (Ann Arbor, 1954), esp. 18–22, 33; Gary B. Nash, *Red, White, and Black: The Peoples of Early America* (Englewood Cliffs, NJ, 1974), passim.

3

Persistent Maya Resistance and Cultural Retention in Yucatán

Nancy M. Farriss

When the Spanish encountered peoples such as the Maya, who practiced slash-and-burn agriculture, had no indigenous imperial structures, and lacked immediately marketable commodities (especially precious metals), they did not pursue systematic conquest with the same fervor as they did in central Mexico or in the Andes nor did they colonize in the same numbers. The trajectory of cultural change among the Maya, then, was completely different from that found in these two important central regions. The international market economy on the periphery did not penetrate as directly, and Spanish settlers were not able to install draft labor systems to draw indigenous workers into the colonial economy with the same success. The presence of the church was commensurately reduced, and the Christianization of the natives was understandably diminished in scope and character. The existence of a frontier enabled some natives to evade the colonial system and constituted a continuing threat and alternative to Spanish rule.

A case for the comparatively mild effects of Spanish colonization in Yucatán rests ultimately on the entire record of the colonial regime. Throughout most of the colonial period, Yucatán's position on the periphery of the Spanish empire preserved for the Maya a degree of isolation and autonomy that the Aztecs and other groups in the economic and political core had lost within decades of the conquest. But differences are apparent from the start, in the first confrontations between Indians and Spaniards in what is present-day Mexico. The conquest of Yucatán was a lengthy affair. The prolonged warfare produced much material devastation. Yet by the same token it represented a less abrupt and therefore a less traumatic break with the past than the rapid overthrow of the Aztec empire. Indeed, for large areas of Yucatán it is difficult to say exactly when the conquest ended and colonial rule began.

Yucatán was discovered in 1517 during a voyage of exploration out of Cuba. This first encounter with the more sophisticated Indians of the American mainland, who wore clothes, had stone buildings, and above all possessed gold, stimulated Spanish plans to colonize the new territory. But Yucatán itself was bypassed. A second voyage had received a friendlier reception and hints of more substantial wealth to the west. A third expedition, organized by Hernán Cortés in 1519, touched only briefly at Yucatán on the way to Veracruz and ultimately to Cortés's rendezvous with Moctezuma at Tenochtitlan.[1]

Only in 1527, after campaigns throughout the Mesoamerican highlands and into Honduras, did the Spanish turn their attention to Yucatán, under the leadership of one of Cortés's lieutenants, Francisco de Montejo. It took two full decades to conquer Yucatán, in contrast with a bare two years to subdue the Aztecs. The Maya had no overarching imperial structure that could be toppled with one swift blow to the center. Yucatán was divided into at least sixteen autonomous provinces with varying degrees of internal unity. Each of the provinces, and sometimes the subunits within them, had to be negotiated with, and failing that, conquered separately.

At times Yucatán must scarcely have seemed worth the trouble of conquest. Discontent with lack of gold thinned Montejo's ranks. The dense bush and potholed terrain of Yucatán proved difficult for horses and ill-suited to the pitched battles that favored Spanish weapons and tactics. Resistance was fierce in some areas and worst of all, the Maya refused to stay conquered.

The conquest of Yucatán is generally considered to have ended with the suppression in 1547 of the Great Revolt, a large-scale uprising by the Maya of the entire central and eastern regions. The Spanish hold over the peninsula was never again seriously challenged, but it was incomplete and remained so throughout the colonial period. In a low-key and sporadic way, the conquest was to continue for centuries.

The initial thrust had stopped at the southern borders of the provinces of Mani and Cochuah. Beyond them lay a vast, barely explored region stretching through the Montaña district and the Petén to the settled foothills of Guatemala and Chiapas, a region bypassed and largely ignored after Cortés's brief swing through the heart of the area on his march from central Mexico to Honduras in 1525.[2] An isolated missionary outpost was founded in the Montaña district but lasted only from 1604 to 1614. In the east along the Caribbean coast the Spanish had subdued the provinces of Ecab, Uaymil, and Chetumal but failed to occupy them permanently, except for the fortified settlement of Bacalar at the base of the peninsula. For the first century and a half after the colony was established, the Spanish actually lost ground, pulling back from territory that they still nominally claimed but lacked the means and the incentive to control.

The colonists had settled in the most hospitable part of the peninsula, the northwest, where the Indians were more numerous and the drier climate proved more attractive to Europeans. Spanish influence remained concentrated in this region for the same related combination of factors. The rain forests of the Montaña and the Petén, once the teeming heartland of Classic Maya civilization, had already suffered a severe population decline (although exactly how severe is still debated) long before the Spanish arrived. The depopulation of the eastern and southwestern coastal provinces was their unwitting handiwork. Except for Uaymil and Chetumal, these provinces had all submitted to Spanish rule with little or no resistance, so that losses through warfare and disruptions in food production were minimal in most areas. Climate and strategic location, which had been the basis of their prosperity, now contributed to their decline. The moist climate, with heavier rainfall and more surface water, produced good crop yields but was also particularly congenial to many of the Old World pathogens introduced by the Spanish and their African slaves.

Equally devastating in its effects, though perhaps more difficult to measure, was the collapse of the Maya economy, which had been based largely on long-distance trade. At the time of contact vigorous commercial centers nearly ringed the peninsula from Chauaca in the north, down through Cozumel and Tulum on the Caribbean to Nito on the Bay of Honduras, and across the base to the gulf coast. All were controlled by or affiliated with the "Putun," or Chontal Maya, in southwestern Campeche, who have been called the "Phoenicians of the New World."[3] Strategically located, they funneled goods between the peninsula and the highlands of Mexico and Central America. Even before the actual conquest of Yucatán, their traditional trade networks had been disrupted by the overthrow of the Aztec empire in central Mexico and of other trading partners in Guatemala and Honduras.[4]

By the time the Spanish turned their attention back from the northwestern part of the peninsula to these peripheral regions that had been so quickly and easily won (again, with the exception of Uaymil and Chetumal, which were virtually destroyed in a late, fierce campaign), they found them already in severe decline. What once had been flourishing zones were reduced to a few scattered settlements well before the end of the sixteenth century. By the latter part of the seventeenth century these regions had been officially abandoned. Their strategic location had contributed to their further decline, for they were exposed to attack by French, Dutch, and English pirates who had been attracted to the Caribbean by Spanish wealth and had already begun to harass ships and settlements along Yucatán's coasts by the 1560s. Faced with the impossibility of defending the peninsula's long, exposed shoreline, except for the major port of Campeche (itself sacked several times), the Spanish decided to move the remnant Maya populations well inland and abandon the coasts to the "Lutheran corsairs."[5]

In the mid-seventeenth century the colonial frontier had contracted to a line curving from below Champoton up to the Puuc hills, across to Peto and Tihosuco, and then angling northeast to the Caribbean along a line now marking the boundary between the states of Yucatán and Quintana Roo. The territory beyond that frontier was officially referred to as *despoblado*, or uninhabited. In fact, it became the home of large numbers of refugees who fled colonial rule to form independent settlements of their own or to join their unconquered cousins, who held out in small pockets in the east and controlled all the territory to the south. They were never left totally in peace. Every so often a wave of evangelistic fervor would sweep through the local Franciscans, and a missionary or two would be dispatched into the bush to make or renew contact with any unconverted or apostate Maya they could locate. The Indians generally received them peacefully. On occasion they became exasperated into discourtesy and even threats, but only three unescorted missionaries are on record as having won the "crown of martyrdom" in the entire unpacified area.[6] The Maya were aware that resistance would provoke armed reprisals and they found it more prudent to feign submission, and then relocate their settlements or simply revert to former habits once the friars had left.[7]

Military expeditions were also undertaken sporadically by the Spanish to round up fugitives by force and resettle them in the pacified areas, and these raids seem to have cleared out a large part of the eastern region.[8] The Spanish could not, however, mount guard along the entire frontier, and as long as the large and accessible territory to the south remained unsubdued, the conquest of the rest of the peninsula could not be considered complete.

The existence of totally independent Maya politics, the largest and most powerful of them the Itza kingdom centered at Lake Petén, blurred the boundary between pre-Columbian and colonial, pagan and Christian, unconquered and conquered. The effect was analogous in kind if not in degree to that of the Inca state in exile that held out on the borders of the kingdom of Peru for decades after the initial overthrow. In Yucatán as in Peru, there was no clean break with the past on either side of the frontier, which the Maya found highly permeable in both directions. Refugees, raiding parties, delegations from the Itzá and other groups, and, above all, traders moved back and forth in steady if often clandestine contact. We have no way of measuring the volume of the illicit trade, about which the Spanish had some notion but could not stop. Interregional commerce had been brisk in pre-Columbian times; it became reinforced by the new demand among both pagan and apostate Maya for the steel axes and other tools introduced by the Spanish. Trade in salt, which the west and north coasts of the peninsula had presumably long supplied to the interior, continued after conquest. It is more than likely that part of the honey and wax the Spanish collected in tribute from the pacified Maya for export to central Mexico came originally from the unconquered interior.[9]

The unconquered zones were an escape hatch for some of the colonized Maya; they were a cultural and political as well as an economic factor in the lives of all of them. Contact between separated kinsmen was not entirely broken, for news traveled rapidly with the trade goods. Even for the great majority of Maya who did not flee there, the zones of refuge were an ever-present and familiar (if only by hearsay) option rather than a frightening unknown. Masses of them chose this option during the latter part of the seventeenth century. They swelled the unconquered settlements in the south that seemed to be coalescing under a native "king." These groups became increasingly bold, raiding pacified border towns and making the not wholly bombastic claim of sovereignty over them.[10] Long at a standstill, the conquest now seemed to be going into reverse.

Despite some inconclusive forays into the Petén from Spanish settlements in Tabasco, Chiapas, and Yucatán, the interior remained largely outside Spanish control until 1697, when a combined expedition from Yucatán and Guatemala conquered the Itzá kingdom.[11] Another series of expeditions in the early 1700s finally expelled the English from the Laguna de Términos, where a military outpost was established to protect Spanish settlements along the gulf en route toward Tabasco.[12] A new mission was founded in the interior west of Bacalar, and thin archipelagos of pacified villages grew up along the trails linking Yucatán with Bacalar and a new outpost at Lake Petén. The much acclaimed conquest of the Petén did not, however, destroy the zones of refuge. The groups of fugitives and unpacified Maya merely moved further into the bush, harassed by occasional raids but never totally reduced to Spanish rule.[13] Deep in the interior, the Lacandon Maya, survivors of this population, have never, strictly speaking, been conquered to this day.

When did the conquest of Yucatán actually end? In 1547, with the suppression of the Great Revolt? In 1697, with the conquest of the Petén? Some might consider the nineteenth-century Caste War as the final fix. Drawn into the factional strife of postindependence Yucatán and regaining a long dormant taste for military victory, the Maya launched their own struggle in 1847 to rid themselves of what they still regarded as foreign domination. For a brief time it looked as if they might succeed. From the east around Valladolid, Tihosuco, and Sotuta (the same regions that had united in the Great Revolt three hundred years earlier), the rebellion spread south to Bacalar and, much more menacingly, began to close in on Mérida. The city and the whites who had taken refuge there were saved only by the "grace of God," the Maya term for maize. Reaching within attacking distance of Mérida just as the rainy season was approaching, the Maya troops— farmers all—retreated to their villages and their maize fields. First things first: the maize had to be planted, tended, and harvested, and only then could they return to finish the war. But they had lost their chance. The *dzuls* (foreigners) were not, after all, to be driven out of Yucatán. On the other hand, the Maya never admitted defeat, either. They only retreated east again and established a rebel state around a Maya-Christian cult of a Speaking Cross, acquiring the name of *cruzob* Maya from the *Santa Cruz* or Holy Cross they worshipped. They actually managed to push the old colonial frontier back to its mid-seventeenth-century position, where it was to remain, with minor advances and retreats, for the next fifty years.[14]

In 1901, Chan Santa Cruz, the *cruzob* capital, fell to federal troops from central Mexico. Does this defeat mark the end of the Caste War and, along with it, the conquest of Yucatán? Or did both the war and the conquest continue for another sixty years or so? During this time the *cruzob* Maya still controlled the district into which they had retreated and which encompassed a large portion of the present state of Quintana Roo in eastern Yucatán. But perhaps the conquest was not complete until 1969, with the death of the chief of the *cruzob* town of Chumpom and the last of the Caste War leaders. His successors decided after much deliberation not to carry out their threat to attack the highway crew that pushed its way into the formerly isolated territory. Federal troops had been sent to guard the crew and the Maya had been unsuccessful in obtaining modern carbines to replace their antiquated firearms. The road was completed and the *cruzob* Maya, like it or not, are now being incorporated into the fabric of national society. Some of them hold jobs with the national archaeological institute as custodians of the pre-Columbian sites in their areas; others have already been tapped for military service in the army that their grandfathers held off for so long.

Maya Perceptions of the Conquest

The Yucatec Maya have left several accounts of the sixteenth-century Spanish conquest, accounts that differ markedly in tone and perspective from the Aztec versions. Their narratives of the arrival and military campaigns of the Spanish are spare and matter-of-fact.[15] And while there is a certain poignancy in the later chronicles that record the evil times ushered in by the conquest, they lack the immediacy and grief-stricken anguish of the Aztec elegies for a world that had been suddenly and irrevocably shattered.[16] The contrast reflects, in part, different experiences: swift and total military defeat with the leveling of a mighty city to a heap of rubble, as opposed to a drawn-out series of skirmishes and battles carried on for the most part outside the population centers. It also reflects different perceptions of the significance of defeat and foreign domination.

The Spanish conquest was a particularly rude shock to the Aztecs because of their own mystique of invincibility based on a long, virtually unbroken record of military success. Foreign domination was an unfamiliar experience in the central highlands, where the pattern was conquest from within. The Aztecs, and the Toltecs before them, were outsiders originally, but they had arrived as humble migrants who gradually assimilated into and then dominated the local scene before expanding outward.

If the Mexican highlands were the dynamic center of expansion within Mesoamerica, Yucatán was a favored target, and the Maya had a long history of conquest to prepare them psychologically and cognitively for the arrival of the Spanish. The well-known "Toltec" invasion, which brought the cult of the Feathered Serpent (Quetzalcoatl-Kukulcan) and other distinctively highland influences to the peninsula in the late tenth century, was once thought to be unique. It is now seen by scholars as simply one of a series of more or less warlike intrusions into the lowlands, ranging in time from at least the early centuries of the Christian era down to the Spanish conquest itself.[17] The Spanish invasion could take its place in that series with a little stretch of the imagination.

These intrusions were not always or necessarily full-scale invasions directly from the highlands. The lowland Maya engaged in much local warfare among themselves. Border conflicts and civil strife provided ideal opportunity for small groups of foreign adventurers, either Mexican or Mexicanized intermediaries, to gain a foothold. Rather than replace the local contenders entirely, the foreigners joined in the fray, jockeying for position by strategic alliances and eventually merging with the local rulers through intermarriage. The struggle for control of the late Postclassic center of Mayapán, abandoned in 1441, provides one of the better-known examples, involving at least three different foreign groups of varying antiquity in the peninsula. The Cocom lineage, identified with the former rulers of Chichén Itzá, was overthrown by the more recently established Xiu, despite the aid of Mexican troops, and these latest arrivals were then able to establish themselves as local rulers in the Ah Canul province.[18]

The record of these past invasions was well preserved in the Maya's written chronicles and oral traditions.[19] The memory was kept fresh by the expansionist activities of the Chontal Maya traders and by the continued presence of Mexican troops in their trading enclave at Xicalango on the shores of the Laguna de Términos (the source of the earlier Cocom allies). At the time of the Cortés expedition the Aztecs are reported to have assembled a large force in Xicalango under Moctezuma's brother for yet another major invasion, a plan that was thwarted only by the collapse of the Aztec empire at the center.[20]

Whether or not the Maya were expecting this particular invasion, Spanish actions followed patterns familiar enough to suggest that history was repeating itself. And since the Maya's entire view of time was based on the conviction that each of their twenty-year *katun* periods repeated itself with the same recurring events at 256-year intervals (with no doubt some ex post facto juggling to make the proper fit), the suggestion must have had compelling force. The Spanish arrived in small numbers, invading the peninsula both via the east coast into the interior around Chichén Itzá as the Itzá had done perhaps eight centuries before, and then via Tabasco into Campeche, the route of more recent penetrations. They quickly adopted the local stiffened cotton quilting for armor instead of steel cuirasses. In their second invasion they even brought central Mexican (Aztec and Tlaxcalan) troops, whose participation in the conquest meant in a sense that Moctezuma's original scheme was not totally aborted. These auxiliaries, like their predecessors, settled in Yucatán as conquerors. They retained throughout the colonial period the special privileges granted them by the Spanish for their services, and they followed precedent by merging genetically and culturally with the conquered Maya.[21] Thus it was not only due to the Maya's cyclical view of time, in which history and prophecy are intertwined in recurring patterns, that the major pre-Columbian invasions (called "descents" by the Maya) are often hard to distinguish from the Spanish in the native chronicles.

The Maya did not confuse the fair-skinned bearded Spaniards with Mexicans, whom they knew well as trading partners as well as potential conquerors. But neither did they take them for gods. The Spaniards must have been a strange and frightening sight with their "thunder sticks," their horses, and their fierce hunting dogs. But the Maya were not troubled by the same perceptual problems that initially paralyzed the Aztecs, who were at first unsure whether the newcomers were gods, emissaries of gods, or mere men and therefore vacillated in their reactions to them.[22] We find no supernatural overtones in the Maya's responses. They seem to have accepted the Spanish simply as some kind of human strangers and to have acted on purely pragmatic political grounds in dealing with them, according to how they calculated their best interests.[23]

In view of the fragmented political structure of the lowland Maya, it is not surprising that their interests were narrowly conceived, often in terms of possible advantages to be gained against neighboring groups. Interprovincial rivalries, sometimes based on centuries-old traditions of enmity, prevented the Maya from uniting against the intruders. Foreign conquerors throughout history have profited from this kind of provincialism that, with hindsight, seems so myopic. The Maya leaders, like many others in similar circumstances, sought to place the newcomers into the existing framework of the region's politics, without realizing that the new element would destroy the framework and thus render obsolete the basis of their calculations.

Some of the Maya lords chose a policy of active cooperation, joining the invaders in the conquest of neighboring provinces. Such alliances seem to have been a traditional expedient in local warfare. Many of the Maya lords were of foreign origin themselves and at least some had gained ascendancy through similar means. In theory, all the lowland Maya dynasties traced descent from one or another earlier group of conquerors as part of their claim to rulership, no matter how remote the ancestral ties. Some were, however, of more recent stock, and it is among these comparative newcomers, such as the Chontal Maya on the gulf and east coasts, the Pech, Chel, and Canul dynasties, and most notably the Xiu rulers of Mani province, that the Spanish found the friendliest receptions.[24]

In the interior of the peninsula, among the Cupul, the Cochuah, and the Cocom (of Sotuta), the Spanish met with unrelenting resistance from beginning to end—and beyond. For these same provinces joined forces again in the Great Revolt of 1546–47. The antecedents of the Cochuah have not been recorded, but it is perhaps no coincidence that the most unequivocal enemies of the Spanish were the Cupul and the Cocom, the two most ancient ruling lineages in Yucatán, who traced their ancestry back to the Itzá invaders who had established their capital at Chichén Itzá.[25] They were presumably more thoroughly Mayanized, certainly more isolated from foreign influences, and possibly for that reason more hostile to outsiders, especially Mexican outsiders.

Only in retrospect does the policy of resistance seem the more astute choice or at least the more farsighted one. We cannot credit Nachi Cocom, the lord of Sotuta, with any clearer insights into the consequences of Spanish victory than his neighbor and enemy, Tutul Xiu of Mani, who chose to ally himself with the Spaniards. All the Maya rulers drew on more or less the same historical traditions, and all of them must have been dealing in their calculations, based on the region's past experience, with questions of political power not cultural survival. They merely reached different conclusions about how best to preserve or enhance their own power.

However unwelcome domination by foreigners had been in the past, leaving a legacy of resentment that can be detected in the later chronicles, it does not seem to have been coupled in the minds of the Maya with devastating culture shock. Mexicans, after all, were part of the larger Mesoamerican civilization that had come to share many basic features through centuries of interaction. Some of the influences trickled in through the peaceful vehicle of long-distance trade; some were imposed by force. Foreigners had left traces of their impact in the style of public monuments, in Nahuatl words incorporated into the vocabulary, in new deities added to the local pantheon, and in other innovations.[26] There is evidence that the old guard continued to find some of these innovations very distasteful.[27] But the Yucatec Maya had shown a capacity again and again to absorb alien influences without being overwhelmed by them.

Immediate impressions of the Spanish were in this context reassuring, giving the Maya little hint that anything drastically different was in store for them. Aside from bringing familiar Mexican auxiliaries with them, with their familiar central Mexican *atl-atls*, or spear throwers, and aside from following the usual invasion routes, the Montejos (father, son, and nephew all confusingly bearing the same name of Francisco) pursued prudent and— again—familiar policies in their dealings with the Maya lords. They always sought to negotiate a peaceful agreement first, often sending ahead native emissaries. They offered, and initially honored, highly reasonable terms that left the local power structure intact under Spanish overlordship.[28] None of the native rulers was deposed. Even the implacable Nachi Cocom retained his position, as did the other leaders of the Great Revolt, despite the fact that they, having once taken an oath of fealty to the crown, were all in Spanish eyes guilty of treason.

The terms of submission to Spanish authority included, along with the loss of autonomy and the exaction of tribute (a galling but predictable price of conquest), the acceptance of Christianity. It is unlikely that this acceptance implied for the Maya lords any radical break with the past. The introduction of new religious cults by a conquering group—cults that would coexist along with the old—was a Mesoamerican tradition. That Christianity was an exclusive religion, one that demanded the total extinction of the Maya's own beliefs and deities, would not have been immediately apparent. Montejo, though by all accounts a devout Christian, was no religious zealot. Neither he nor the chaplains who accompanied his forces were given to dramatic scenes of idol smashing of the sort indulged in by Cortés. This was in part because Maya idolatries, which did not involve human sacrifice on any large scale, outraged Spanish sensibilities considerably less than the gory spectacles of the Aztecs. But only in part, for Cortés had already started his iconoclastic activities on the Maya island of Cozumel.

Evangelization was a decidedly low-key affair in Yucatán during the initial stages of contact. Several local lords, we are told, sought baptism, although it is hard to say what significance they attached to this ceremony, since none of the few clergymen who accompanied the Spanish forces ever learned the Maya language, and all confined themselves almost exclusively to their duties as military chaplains.[29] The old cults persisted virtually unchallenged in practice. No churches were built for the Indians and no organized program of conversion was undertaken until a handful of Franciscan missionaries arrived at the end of 1544 or early in 1545.[30]

The conquest itself brought much suffering, as any protracted military struggle will do. Reprisals and systematic devastation were, however, limited to the Uaymil and Chetumal districts under the desperate and semi-independent campaign of the Pachecos, although other provinces also resisted as stubbornly. Montejo had rivals and enemies within his own ranks, and if he had countenanced or committed similar acts of cruelty and indiscriminate slaughter (which also characterized Spanish campaigns in the Caribbean islands, in Panama, and in Mexico under Cortés's successor, Nuño de Guzmán), his accusers would have mentioned them in the detailed inquiry into his conduct ordered by the crown. The one major accusation against him that involved the Indians, as opposed to acts deemed detrimental to the interests of the crown or his follow Spaniards, was the shipment of prisoners of war to central Mexico for sale as slaves.[31] Whether consciously or not, Montejo had merely followed local tradition. Slaves had been one of Yucatán's principal exports in pre-Columbian times, and slave taking a major incentive for the endemic border warfare in the region. Montejo's local allies were induced to aid in suppressing the Great Revolt (and most likely to aid in the original conquest) with the promise that they could continue their custom of enslaving the prisoners they captured.[32] Far more objectionable and portentous from the Maya rulers' point of view than Montejo's slave trading must have been the crown's subsequent order emancipating all slaves in the recently conquered territory, whether owned by Indians or Spaniards.

During the first decades of confrontation with the Spanish, then, the Maya had little cause to believe that this latest incursion would not take its place in the same recurrent pattern of earlier conquests. Logically, this small band of warriors, vastly outnumbered and far from their home base, would be assimilated into the local elite like their Mexican predecessors. A few adjustments would have to be made: some loss of autonomy, new gods added to the local pantheon, extra tribute. Disagreeable, perhaps, but hardly intolerable. If some of the Maya lords expected a replay of previous episodes of foreign hegemony, the prohibition against slavery, which represented an important source of their wealth, was simply one of the many unpleasant surprises in store for them as the new overlords set about turning the conquered territory into a colony organized according to entirely alien principles.

Perhaps the Maya never perceived or acknowledged the full significance of the Spanish conquest. Along with the sense of grievance and loss, their later accounts of the conquest reveal that they retained from the pre-Columbian past their cyclical view of time, which under the circumstances must have been a great source of comfort. According to this view, all human history repeats itself in the same orderly fashion as the recurrent movement of the heavenly bodies. All things good and bad, have their appointed time to end and to be repeated in an endless cycle, in which past is prophecy and prophecy is the past.[33] The persistence of this sustaining cosmology (when it was lost, if ever, is uncertain) is symptomatic of the resilience of Maya culture.[34] Some of the resilience rested on a history of accommodation already sketched out. Much, however, was due to the circumstances of colonial rule itself. Conquest, which was less immediately catastrophic for the Maya than for the Aztecs—less literally world shattering as an event— was also to prove less destructive in its long-term implications.

Notes

Abbreviations for works frequently used:

AA	Archivo del Arzobispado (Secretaría), Mérida.
AGI	Archivo General de las Indias, Seville.
AGN	Archivo General de la Nación, Mexico, D. F.
BN	Biblioteca Nacional, Mexico, D. F.
DHY	*Documentos para la historia de Yucatán.* 3 vols. France V. Scholes et al., eds. Mérida: 1936–1938.
RY	"Relaciones de Yucatán." In *Colección de documentos inéditos relativos al descubrimiento, conquista y organización de las antiguas posesiones de Ultramar.* 25 vols. Madrid: 1885–1932, vols. 11, 13.

1. Robert S. Chamberlain, *The Conquest and Colonization of Yucatán, 1517–1550* (Washington, 1948), provides an impeccably documented summary of the main events from discovery to the establishment of royal government in 1551.

2. The journey, which actually lasted from October 1524 to April 1526, is recounted in Hernán Cortés, *Cartas de relación* (1522–1525), edited by Manuel Alcalá (Mexico, 1963), (fifth letter), 185–208; and Bernal Díaz del Castillo, *Verdadera historia de la conquista de la Nueva España* (1554?–1568), edited by Joaquín Ramiro Cabañas, 2 vols. (Mexico, 1968), 2:188–217.

3. J. Eric S. Thompson, *Maya History and Religion* (Norman, 1970), 7. The basic study of the late Postclassic "Putun" and their commercial and political networks is France V. Scholes and Ralph L. Roys, *The Maya Chontal Indians of Acalan-Tixchel: A Contribution to the History and Ethnography of the Yucatán Peninsula* (1948), 2d ed. (Norman, 1968), 15–87. See also Anne Chapman, "Port of Trade Enclaves in Aztec and Maya Civilizations," in *Trade and Market in Early Empires*, edited by Karl Polanyi, C. M. Arensberg, and H. W. Pearson (New York, 1957), 114–153; Thompson, *Maya History*, 3–47, 124–158; Jeremy A. Sabloff and William L. Rathje, "The Rise of a Maya Merchant Class," *Scientific American* 233 (1975),

72–82; and Arthur G. Miller, *On the Edge of the Sea: Mural Painting at Tancah-Tulum, Quintana Roo, Mexico* (Washington, 1982), chap. 4.

4. Cortés, *Cartas*, 185–186, 206.

5. On the postconquest decline and eventual abandonment of the east coast, see Ralph L. Roys, France V. Scholes, and Eleanor B. Adams, "Report and Census of the Indians of Cozumel, 1570," *Contributions to American Anthropology and History* (Washington, 1940), 6:1–30; and Arthur G. Miller and Nancy M. Farriss, "Religious Syncretism in Colonial Yucatán: The Archaeological and Ethnohistorical Evidence from Tancah, Quintana Roo," in *Maya Archaeology and Ethnohistory*, edited by Norman Hammond and Gordon R. Willey (Austin, 1979), 224–229. On southwestern Campeche, see Scholes and Roys, *Maya Chontal*, 159–167, 229–315. On the effects of pirate raids, see, for example, AGI, Justicia 1029, Probanza sobre los daños . . . corsarios luteranos, 1565; Patronato 75, no. 1, ramo 1, Probanza Diego Sarmiento de Figueroa, April 4, 1578; Mexico 359, Governor to Crown, Nov. 28, 1565, April 2, 1579, and Nov. 15, 1600; Mexico 360, Governor to Crown, July 10, 1638; and a number of *expedientes* from the 1670s and 1680s in AGI, Escribanía de cámara 307-A and 307-B.

6. Two Dominicans in the southern Petén in 1555 (Juan de Villagutierre Sotomayor, *Historia de la conquista de la provincia de el Itzá* [1701] [Guatemala, 1933], 49–54) and a Franciscan in Tayasal in 1628 (Diego López de Cogolludo, *Historia de Yucatán* [1654] [hereafter cited as Cogolludo] [Madrid, 1688], Lib. 10, cap. 2). Five others were killed while they were accompanying Spanish military expeditions, which appear to have supplied the provocation: one in Saclum in 1624 (Cogolludo, Lib. 10, cap. 3) and four in or near Tayasal in 1696 (Villagutierre Sotomayor, 284–294, 314–315, 352, 375). An unverified martyrdom is reported by Pedro Sánchez de Aguilar, *Informe contra idolorum cultores del obispado de Yucatán dirigido al Rey N. Señor en su Real Consejo de las Indias* (c. 1613), 3d ed. (Mérida, 1937), 120–121, who alleged that the Indians of Cozumel had deliberately drowned their curate in a boating "accident."

7. AGI, Mexico 359, 367, 369, and 3048, and Indiferente 1387 contain many letters and reports, 1564–1585, referring to the sporadic missionary activity on Cozumel and the east coast, some of them published or summarized in Roys, Scholes, and Adams, "Report and Census"; Miller and Farriss, "Religious Syncretism"; France V. Scholes and Eleanor B. Adams, *Don Diego Quijada, Alcalde Mayor de Yucatán, 1561–1565*, 2 vols. (Mexico 1938), 2:79–83; and *DHY*, 2:70–94. See, especially, Mexico 369, Relación del viaje de Fray Gregorio de Fuente-Ovejuna y Fray Hernando de Sopuerta, Aug. 15, 1573. Missionary activity, sometimes in conjunction with military *entradas*, was more intense along the southern frontier. France V. Scholes and J. Eric S. Thompson, "The Francisco Pérez 'Probanza,' of 1654–1656, and the 'Matrícula' of Tipu (Belize)," in *Anthropology and History in Yucatán*, edited by Grant D. Jones (Austin, 1977), 43–68, summarizes information on the Bacalar-Tipu region, 1618–1655. See also Cogolludo, Lib. 8, caps. 5–10, 12–13 (including Tayasal), Lib. 11, caps. 12–17; AGI, Mexico 360, Governor to Crown, July 10 and Nov. 30, 1638; and Mexico 369, Bishop to Crown, June 1, 1606, and Memorial Bishop of Yucatán, 1643. Scholes and Roys, *Maya-Chontal*, 251–290, contains material on the Montaña and Tichel-Popola-Sahcabchen regions to the 1660s. Villagutierre, *Historia*, 119–128, 156–158, 200–208, 233–243, 252–257, 262–264, 303–311, summarizes activities converging on Tayasal, 1575–1700. On the Montaña region, 1604–1624, see also Cogolludo, Lib. 8, cap. 9, Lib. 10, caps. 2–3 (including Tayasal); Francisco de

Cárdenas Valencia, *Relación historial eclesiástica de la provincia de Yucatán de la Nueva España escrita en el año de 1639* (Mexico, 1937), 74; AGI, Mexico 359, Cuaderno de documentos, 1604, Governor to Crown, June 21 and Sept. 19, 1608, and Certificate Francisco de Sanabria, June 22, 1608; Mexico 369, Governor to Crown, Dec. 22, 1604, Bishop to Crown, Sept. 29, 1604 and Dec. 12, 1605; Mexico 294, Testimonio del requerimiento, 1604, and testimonio de varias cartas, 1604–1605; Escribanía de cámara 308-A, no. 1, pieza 3, Probanza Fray Gerónimo de Porraz, 1624.

8. For raids into the *despoblado* of the east coast, see Cogolludo, Lib. 7, caps. 13 and 15 (1592 and 1596), and Lib. 8, cap. 8 (1602); AGI, Patronato 56, no. 2, ramo 4, Probanza Juan de Contreras, 1596; Mexico 294, Probanzas Andrés Fernández de Castro, n.d. (1601), and Antonio de Arroyo, 1604; Mexico 130, Información . . . Br. Juan Alonso de Lara, 1611; Mexico 140, Probanza Capt. D. Juan Chan, 1622; and Escribanía de cámara 308-A, no. 1, pieza 6, Testimonio de información a favor de la religión franciscana, 1644.

9. Cogolludo, Lib. 8, cap. 9. See also Grant D. Jones, "Agriculture and Trade in the Colonial Period Central Maya Lowlands," *Maya Subsistence: Studies in Memory of Dennis E. Puleston*, edited by Kent V. Flannery (New York, 1982), 275–293, and, among the many references in the contemporary documents to the "comercio oculto," AGI, Mexico 359, Franciscan Provincial to Audiencia of Mexico, May 5, 1606.

10. On *sublevaciones* in the central Montaña region in the period 1614 to 1624 (including the Saclum massacre of 1624), see Cogolludo, Lib. 10, cap. 3; AGI, Escribanía de cámara 305-B, ramo 6, Antonio de Salas to Governor, Oct. 16, 1624, and ramo 7, Méritos y servicios Diego de Vargas Mayorga, Nov. 12, 1624; Mexico 359, Royal cédula to Governor, Nov. 18, 1624; and Escribanía de cámara 308-A, no. 1, pieza 3, Probanza Fr. Gerónimo de Porraz, 1624. Documentation on the heightened unrest in the 1660s and 1670s is voluminous, most of it contained in the *residencia* of Governor Rodrigo Flores de Aldana: see especially AGI, Escribanía de cámara 317-A, cuad. 4, Autos contra Antonio González, 1670; Escribanía de cámara 317-5. cuad. 8, Autos hechos por Pedro García Ricalde, 1668; and Escribanía de cámara 317-C, Papeles y recaudos presentados por . . . Flores de Aldana, 1664–1674. Franciscan reports are in AGI, Escribanía de cámara 308-A, no. 1, piezas 13–15, 1664–1680; and BN, Archivo Franciscano 55, nos. 1142 and 1143, letters from Fray Cristóbal Sánchez to the Provincial, 1672–1673.

11. The actual battle for the Itzá stronghold in Tayasal, recounted in Villagutierre, *Historia*, 366–373, was brief, culminating a two-year campaign of encirclement and intense diplomatic pressure.

12. See María Angeles Eugenio Martínez, *La defensa de Tabasco, 1600–1717* (Seville, 1971), 72–158, on expeditions against the English, 1680–1717. On the construction of the fort, 1718–1765, see AGN, Real caja 54, Informe Antonio Bonilla, April 29, 1772.

13. Raids by and against both pagan and apostate Maya were reported into the nineteenth century: AGI, Mexico 1018, Sobre conversiones del Itzá y Petén, 1703–1704; Mexico 898, Josef de Zaldívar to Crown, Dec. 14, 1742; AGN, Historia 534, no. 4, Sobre aprehensión de indios caribes en los ríos de Usumacinta, 1784; AA, Asuntos pendientes 2, Expedte. sobre . . . la misión de Chichanha, 1782; Oficios y decretos 3, Franciscan Provincial to Bishop, Sept. 9, 1786; Oficios y decretos 4, Joseph Nicolás de Lara to Bishop Feb. 19, 1782, and Juan José Arias Roxo to Bishop, April 10, 1785; Documentos del Petén Itzá. Exp. sobre residencia de un

religioso en el pueblo de San Antonio, 1799; Domingo Faxardo to Provisor, Oct. 21, 1800, and Faxardo to Bishop, May 14, 1813.

14. Nelson Reed, *The Caste War of Yucatán* (Stanford, 1964), is an excellent summary account of the war and the *cruzob* Maya up to 1915. Moisés González Navarro, *Raza y tierra: La guerra de castas y el henequén* (Mexico, 1970), links the war to the socioeconomic background of nineteenth-century Yucatán.

15. The earliest extant accounts are probably two almost parallel texts written by members of the Pech lineage of Ceh Pech province in the mid-sixteenth century: "Chronicle of Chac-Xuleb-Chen [Chicxulub]," Maya text and English translation, in Daniel G. Brinton, *The Maya Chronicles* (1882, reprint, New York, 1969), 187–259, and Juan Martínez Hernández, ed. *Crónica de Yaxkukul* (Mérida, 1926), Maya text and Spanish translation. Alfredo Barrera Vázquez, ed. *Códice de Calkini* (Campeche, 1957), Maya facsimile and Spanish translation, written in the latter part of the century, is a history of the Ah Canul province, including an account of the conquest period, 25–31, 41–57. Gaspar Antonio Chi, of the Xiu lineage of Mani province, has accounts of the conquest in RY 1:42–45, and AGI, Mexico 104, Probanza de Gaspar Antonio Chi, 1580. See also AGI, Guatemala 111, Probanza de don Francisco, cacique of Xicalango, 1552; and the Acalan Chontal account, composed c. 1610 from oral traditions or earlier documents, in Scholes and Roys, *Maya Chontal*, 367–382. It should be noted that all these accounts were written by Maya lords (or their descendants) who had allied themselves early with the Montejos and were concerned to record (and sometimes exaggerate) the friendly reception they gave the Spanish in contrast with the Chilam Balam books, cited below, which were intended solely for a Maya audience and reflect purely Maya concerns.

16. From internal evidence the extant texts of the Chilam Balam books seem to date from the seventeenth century. They were copied and recopied later but without major modification. They thus represent midcolonial perceptions of the pre-Columbian and the conquest pasts. In addition to the straightforward historical accounts of the conquest, in, for example, Ralph L. Roys, *The Book of Chilam Balam of Chumayel*, 2d ed. (Norman, 1967), 119–120, 145–146, the sections known as *katun* prophecies contain many references, some of them explicit, more commonly veiled in the characteristically metaphorical language of Maya sacred texts, to the conquest and the afflictions and miseries that followed: Roys, *Chumayel*, 144–163; Eugene R. Craine and Reginald C. Reindorp, eds., *The Codex Pérez and the Book of Chilam Balam of Mani* (Norman, 1979), 157–171. Ralph L. Roys, ed., "The Maya Katun Prophecies of the Books of Chilam Balam. Series I," *Contributions to American Anthropology and History* (Washington, 1960), 12:1–60, contains a composite translation of the Series I prophecies from the Chilam Balam books of Tizimin, Mani, Chumayel, and Kaua, with notes and commentary; Miguel León-Portilla, ed., *Visión de los vencidos: Relaciones indígenas de la conquista* (Mexico, 1959), contains Spanish translations from a variety of Nahuatl sources, prose and verse, many of them previously unpublished. Not surprisingly, the Tlaxcalan version, excerpted here, is closer in its pragmatic tone and self-serving interpretations to the accounts produced by the Spaniards' Maya allies, cited in note 15. Nathan Wachtel, *The Vision of the Vanquished: The Spanish Conquest of Peru through Indian Eyes* (New York, 1977), 13–32, compares Maya, highland Mexican, and Andean perceptions of the Spaniards and the conquest, based on these same texts. It may not be fortuitous that the Peruvian and highland Mesoamerican "Dances of the Conquest" (analyzed in Wachtel, 33–58) have no counterpart among the lowland Maya. Perhaps, having assimilated the fact of conquest into their cyclical conception

of time, the lowland Maya have had no need to reenact it in search of psychic resolution.

17. Gordon R. Willey, "External Influences on Lowland Maya: 1940 and 1975 Perspectives," _Social Process in Maya Prehistory_, edited by Norman Hammond (London, 1977), 57–75, summarizes the archaeological literature on the entire Maya lowlands from 1940 to 1975. Many references to foreign intrusions (usually lumped together under the label "Itzá") into the northern lowlands are contained in the oral traditions recorded in Landa, _Relación_, 16–17, 20–26, 32–35; RY, for example, 1:121–122, 161, 213, 254–255, and 2:159–161; Sánchez de Aguilar, _Informe_, 140; and a fragment from the "Valladolid Lawsuit" (1618), in Brinton, _Maya Chronicles_, 114–116, in addition to the chronicles and _katun_ prophecies of the books of Chilam Balam. For recent attempts to sort out the obscure chronology of these references and correlate them with archaeological evidence, see J. Eric Thompson, _Maya History_, 5–25; Joseph W. Ball, "A Coordinate Approach to Northern Maya Prehistory: A.D. 700–1200," _American Antiquity_ 39 (1974), 85–93; Arthur G. Miller, "Captains of the Itzá: Unpublished Mural Evidence from Chichén Itzá," _Social Process in Maya Prehistory_, edited by Norman Hammond (London, 1977), 197–225, and "The Little Descent: Manifest Destiny from the East," _Actes du XLII Congrés des Américanistes, Paris 1976_ (Paris, 1979), 8:221–236.

18. Barrera Vázquez, _Códice de Calkiní_, and Diego de Landa, _Landa's Relación de las cosas de Yucatán_, translated and edited by Alfred M. Tozzer (Cambridge, 1941), 32–39. See also Ralph L. Roys, "Literary Sources for the History of Mayapán," _Mayapán, Yucatán, Mexico_, by Harry E. D. Pollock et al. (Washington, 1962), 24–86.

19. See the chronicles and oral traditions (recorded by the Spanish) cited in notes 16 and 17.

20. RY 2:221–222, Relación of Giraldo Díaz del Alpuche, who married doña Isabel, daughter of an unnamed brother of Moctezuma in charge of the invading force. The Mexican garrison apparently remained at Xicalango (RY 1:352, 364), where Díaz del Alpuche presumably learned the story and teamed up with doña Isabel in 1537 en route to Campeche from Tabasco on Montejo's second _entrada_.

21. Antonio de Ciudad Real, _Relación de las cosas que sucedieron al R. P. Comisario General Fray Alonso Ponce . . ._ (1588), _Colección de documentos inéditos para la historia de España_, vols. 57 and 58 (Madrid, 1872), 2:400–401, 413. A 1605 document mentions that there were "criollos mexicanos" in Mérida who could still speak Nahuatl (AGI, Mexico 369, Memoriales de los indios de los pueblos de Usumacinta), but by the eighteenth century only the patents of _hidalguía_ distinguished them from the Maya: AGI, Mexico 898, Diego de Anguas to Crown, July 12, 1735. See also the parish censuses, 1784–85, in AA, Visitas pastorales 5, for Sisal de Valladolid, and Vistas pastorales 6, from Chunhuhub.

22. In addition to the native chronicles of the conquest already cited, Spanish accounts of the initial contact with both groups also attest to the differing reactions. See Henry R. Wagner, _Discovery of Yucatán, by Francisco Hernández de Córdoba_ (Berkeley, 1942), and _The Discovery of New Spain in 1518, by Juan de Grijalva_, edited by Henry R. Wagner (Berkeley, 1942), for texts (in translation) relating the early voyages of exploration. For a comparative view, see Díaz del Castillo, _Verdadera Historia_, who participated in all the voyages (except the Grijalva voyage of 1518, according to Wagner) as well as the conquest of Mexico. On Maya reactions to the first Montejo _entrada_ in 1527, see Gonzalo Fernández de Oviedo y Valdés, _Historia general y natural de las Indias_ (1535–1547), 4 vols. (Madrid,

1851–1855) Lib. 32, caps. 2–3; and, among the various conquerors' accounts, the Probanza of Blas González, 1567, in AGI, Patronato 68, no. 1, ramo 2.

23. The Xiu later claimed (RY 1:44–45) that they had submitted to the Spanish because of prophecies of their arrival (without any suggestion that the Spaniards themselves might be gods), but their cooperation seems rather to have been stimulated by the recent flare-up of their old conflict with the Cocom of Sotuta province: RY 1:288–289; Landa, *Relación*, 54; AGI, Mexico 104, Probanza Gaspar Antonio Chi, 1580, all recounting the Cocom massacre of Xiu nobles on a pilgrimage to Chichén Itzá. A later, more self-serving Xiu version of the incident, with the victims portrayed as peace emissaries of the Spanish, is given in *Codex Pérez*, 187–188; Cárdenas Valencia, *Relación*, 100–101; and Diego López de Cogolludo, *Historia de Yucatán* (1654), Lib. 3, cap. 6 (Madrid, 1688).

24. See Scholes and Roys, *Maya Chontal*, 88–128, on the Acalan Chontal. For the east coast, see Oviedo y Valdés, *Historia*, Lib. 32, cap. 2; AGI, Patronato 68, no. 1, ramo 2, Probanza Blas González, 1567; RY 2:110–111. Ralph L. Roys, *The Political Geography of the Yucatán Maya* (Washington, 1957), summarizes the background of the Canul (11–13), the Pech (41), the Xiu (61–64), and the Chel (81) dynasties.

25. "Valladolid Lawsuit," in Brinton, *Maya Chronicles*, 114–116; and Landa, *Relación*, 23, n. 126 (quoting from Torquemada on the Cocom). Corroborative evidence is equivocal but the Cupul are elsewhere identified with early invaders from the east coast (RY 2:161–162), and the Cocom claimed to be a more ancient lineage than the Xiu "foreigners": RY 1:161, 288; Landa, *Relación*, 26, 31, 40.

26. Alfred M. Tozzer, *Chichén Itzá and Its Cenote of Sacrifice: A Comparative Study of Contemporaneous Maya and Toltec*, 2 vols. (Cambridge, 1957), is a detailed treatment of "Toltec" influence at Chichén Itzá. For other discussions of "Mexican" cultic influences, see E. Wyllys Andrews IV, *Balankanche: Throne of the Jaguar Priest* (New Orleans, 1970); Miller, *On the Edge of the Sea*; and Harry E. D. Pollock, Ralph L. Roys, Tatiana Proskouriakoff, and A. Ledyard Smith, *Mayapán, Yucatán, Mexico* (Washington, 1962), especially 136–139, 428–431. The frequent assertions that idolatry and human sacrifice were unknown in Yucatán until introduced by Kukulcan (RY 1:52, 78–79, 121–122, 215, 225–226, 242–243, 270–271) presumably refer to new cults and a greater emphasis on human sacrifice.

27. The Chilam Balam books contain many expressions of disapproval directed against the Itzá ("insolent," "impudent," "rogues," "rascals," "vulgar foreigners," "lewd," and "dissolute"), who were held responsible for the decline in Maya learning and religion. See the *tun* prophecies in Roys, "The Prophecies for the Maya Tuns," especially 173; and *Codex Pérez*, 98–116, especially 104–105, 108. A major complaint was the introduction of sexual licence—a cult of eroticism that may have included homosexuality (*crimen nefando*); Roys, *Chumayel*, 151; RY 1:149, 216, 256.

28. AGI, Patronato 80, no. 1, ramo 1, Instrucción dada por el Adelantado n.d. (1543), in Probanza of Alonso Sánchez de Aguilar. See also AGI, Justicia 300, Residencia Adelantado Francisco Montejo, 1549, for much detailed testimony on the Montejos' policies.

29. Juan de Caraveo (probanza in AGI, Indiferente 1294, no. 11, 1533) accompanied the first *entrada*. Francisco Hernández, who accompanied the second, distinguished himself principally for his role in supervising the branding of slaves, for which services he was awarded an encomienda by Montejo (AGI, Justicia 300, Residencia Montejo, 1549; Mexico 364, Cabildo Merida to Crown, July 14, 1543).

A third cleric, Francisco Niño de Villagómez (probanza in Indiferente 1209, 1547), did not arrive until the very end of the conquest.

30. Cogolludo, Lib. 2, cap. 5, Lib. 5, caps. 1 and 5, Lib. 8. As a Franciscan, Cogolludo was hardly an unbiased source, but he was generally favorable to Montejo. The evidence for the dating of this and an earlier abortive mission to Champoton in c. 1534 is analyzed in Gómez Canedo, "Fray Lorenzo de Bienvenida."

31. AGI, Justicia 300, Residencia Montejo, 1549. Justicia 244, no. 3, contains a summary of the twenty-nine charges brought in the *residencia*. See also AGI, Justicia 126, Juan Ote Durán con el Adelantado, 1537. The colonists' main grievance was in fact the suppression of the slave trade: AGI, Mexico 364, Cabildo Merida to Crown, June 14, 1543; RY 1:229, 234.

32. *Cartas de Indias* (Madrid, 1877), 70–80, Fray Lorenzo de Bienvenida to Crown, Feb. 10, 1548, quoting Montejo, "No querrán ir los amigos, si no les damos licencia de hacer esclavos."

33. See Miguel León-Portilla, *Tiempo y realidad en el pensamiento maya* (Mexico, 1968), for a discussion of the ancient Maya's conception of time.

34. Although the ancient *tzolkin*, or ritual calendar of 260 days, may have died out among the Yucatec Maya (see Robert Redfield and Alfonso Villa Rojas, *Chan Kom: A Maya Village* [Washington, 1934], 367) awareness of the prophecies of Chilam Balam, with the notion of recurring events, was still widespread in the mid-nineteenth century: Justo Sierra O'Reilly, *Los indios de Yucatán* (1848–1851), edited by Carlos R. Menéndez, 2 vols. (Merida, 1954–1957), 1:87.

4

Cultural Adaptation and Militant Autonomy among the Araucanians of Chile

Robert Charles Padden

Some indigenous peoples stopped Spanish colonial expansion in its tracks. The most acclaimed and best studied of these cases of successful resistance is that of the Araucanians of Chile. The Araucanians maintained control over the southern third of this territory until the last quarter of the nineteenth century, as often as not taking the offensive against the Spanish and even seizing parts of southern Argentina during the colonial period.

To continue as a politically autonomous people, however, the Araucanians had to make profound changes in their way of life, even in their diet and in their settlement patterns, as Robert C. Padden illustrates in his examination of this phenomenon. A number of Spanish deserters, including clerics, lived among the natives, and there was continuous contact between the Spanish and Araucanians during this entire period.

The term "Araucanian culture" suggests a definition and unity which are more applicable to present-day aborigines of Chile than to the culture which the Spaniards encountered in the sixteenth century. While the great majority of Chilean Indians were closely related in race, language, and culture, there were minor variations among them.[1] Those differences, however, were infrequently heeded by the Spanish invaders. Thinking in geographical rather than ethnological terms, and measuring culture with reference to military proficiency, the Spanish chroniclers postulated three spatial bands of culture, the first extending from the Aconcagua to the Nuble River; the second from the Nuble to the Imperial River; the third from there to the Gulf of Reloncavi.[2] Within these regions the Indians were of a single Mapuche culture, as they so identified themselves. Peoples living to the north of any given Mapuche group, although still within it, were identified as Picunche, those to the south as Huilliche.[3] The Spaniards applied these denominations to their conception of cultural distribution, thus making them appear to be raciocultural entities, which, of course, they were not.[4]

The only outstanding difference among these three groups, as the Spaniards saw them, was the ability of the central band to resist effective Spanish settlement, not only through the sixteenth century, but, as it developed, into the late decades of the nineteenth century. The Araucanian culture in which the present paper is interested is limited to the widest Spanish designation, that is, those Indians between the Nuble and Imperial rivers, and more precisely, the area which today comprises the province of Arauco. This tiny province, some sixty miles long and twenty wide, was the focal point of Araucanian resistance.

The Spanish conquest of Araucanian Chile began in 1550 when Pedro de Valdivia and his followers built a fort and founded the town of Concepción on the northern bank of the Biobío River. From this point they moved south, inflicting military defeats on the Araucanians and dividing them in encomienda. Within three years the Spaniards had ranged below the Calle-Calle River, founding towns and reducing most of the Indians to servitude. The Indians were restive under this imposition of Spanish dominion, but offered no openly unified resistance. On the heels of this initial pacification Valdivia brought in experienced prospectors and miners from Santiago to search out the gold deposits that were believed to exist. The gold seekers enjoyed incredible success: several strikes were made which yielded nuggets the size of almonds. "*Desde agora*," quoth Valdivia, "*comienzo a ser señor.*"[5]

But the Araucanians were not of like mind. Rapid development of the mines and discoveries of new ones portended undisguised slavery. Under such apprehension the Indians of Tucapel contrived a cunning trap for Valdivia into which he fell, and he was then killed and eaten.[6] This signal event inspired a general uprising which lasted for four years, ending with the death of the Indian leader Lautaro in the battle of Peteroa in 1557.[7] Although the general rebellion was ended at this time, the War of Arauco was begun. The Indians of Arauco, Tucapel, Catiray, and Purén (the present province of Arauco and its peripheries) stubbornly resisted effective Spanish settlement. This phase of the struggle lasted until 1598, when the Indians captured and ate Governor Martín García de Loyola.[8] There followed a spontaneous rebellion of subjugated Indians from the Maule River to Osorno in the south: every Spanish town worthy of the designation was wiped out below the Biobío, with the exception of Castro on the Isle of Chiloé.[9] Thus by 1600 the Spaniards, in spite of heavy expenditures of blood and treasure, faced a triumphant foe across the Biobío.

This impasse which marked the turn of the century suggests the central problem in understanding Araucanian culture. What faculty or genius did the Araucanians possess which enabled them to succeed so brilliantly where other indigenous American cultures had failed? How was it possible for the Araucanian warriors to boast rightfully, after some fifty years of warfare, that the Spaniards knew almost as much about the military art as they did?[10] Historians have been prone to avail themselves of superficially reasonable explanations: most cite the numerical superiority of the Indians; some blame the forest because it hampered the functions of the Spanish cavalry; others stress the overly long lines of supply from Peru, coupled with a chronic lack of viceregal interest. These factors are joined to a common belief that the Araucanians simply adopted the Spanish forms and techniques of war, making up in numbers what they lacked in skill. Chilean historians, especially since the nineteenth century when their homeland fought for independence from Spain, have quite happily viewed the historical record as a proof of Araucanian hence mestizo thence Chilean bravery and love of freedom. The point is that it is not merely a question of military science, topography, relative numerical strength, or racial declension. These may be significant particulars, but a war of survival between two ethnic groups implies a conflict of total cultures.

At once we are at a serious disadvantage because we have no such conception of early Araucanian culture, however well we may feel that we know the Spanish. By means of archaeological evidence and brief narratives of exploration we are able to piece together a rather crude notion of what Araucanian culture was like before the Spaniards came, but nothing more. Largely because the area under discussion became almost at once a zone of perpetual conflict, the work of the religious orders did not develop as it did elsewhere in the Indies, and we keenly feel the lack of Mendicant chronicles. Consequently, most of our information concerning Araucanian life during the first century of conquest is derived from chronicles and histories of the war in which brief glimpses of Indian life all too infrequently appear. There are added limitations. Wherein the Indians were concerned, the chroniclers were seldom efficient observers. In matters of simple fact they tend to be trustworthy, but when the fact becomes interpretive they almost invariably fail to grasp the human thought and action that lay behind it. Rather than as men, they thought of the Indians as wild savages who blindly resisted the sweet yoke of Christianity and Spanish dominion. For this reason they seldom inquired into the possibility of Indian method; rather, Indian resistance was madness. Another weakness inherent in the chronicles is the factor of cultural change. At any given moment the chroniclers made their notations in the belief that what they saw was and had been thus from the beginning of time. Only when contemporaries gave information which contradicted their own observations did they give evidence of change, but without attempting to explain it.

It is seldom wise to take an interpretive fact, as disclosed by one of the chroniclers, at its face value. When we are told, for instance, that the Spaniards lost a given battle because the Indians outnumbered them it is entirely unlikely that the chronicler is telling us the whole truth. We have every reason to doubt him because we already know that the Spaniards, with or without Indian allies, had an enormous talent for winning military victories with inferior numbers. At no time was it normal for Spanish forces to outnumber the enemy anywhere in the Indies. Why, then, did the Indians win not only the battle in question, but a majority of the engagements? The suggestions are several: perhaps the Indians, in their own right, had become superior strategists; perhaps they had improved their own weapons to a point which offset the Spanish advantages of gunpowder and horse; perhaps they had developed a creed for life which made resistance both possible and meaningful. Our questioning of an apparently reliable fact leads us to recognition of a neglected factor, the potentiality of early Araucanian culture. By following these suggestions through and corroborating them with associated evidence, we may well come to an understanding of that particular battle which is far superior to that entertained by the chronicler. More importantly, when the battle is multiplied by 1,000 and the conditions of Spanish defeat remain relatively constant, significant conclusions concerning Araucanian culture are inescapable.

By the passing of the first generation of conquistadores the war had become institutionalized, and observers began to think and write about it historically. In the seventeenth and eighteenth centuries several histories of Chile and its Araucanian War were written which contained a relative abundance of passages describing Indian life. These writers, like their predecessors in the sixteenth century, did not take into account the factor of cultural change, and their judgments were almost entirely based upon the present in which they observed and wrote. Nor did they, with few exceptions, have the opportunity of consulting the major chronicles of the sixteenth century. Most of those manuscripts were sent to Spain for publication, but a good many of them were intentionally or innocently shuttled off to a dark repository to await the dawn of modern historiography on Chilean historians.

There are thus three categories of documentary materials from which to draw an image of Araucanian culture: the chronicles of first contact, the chronicles and documents of the first century of conquest, and the histories of the later colonial period. In past reconstructions scholars have tended to assign cultural forms found in later and better documented periods to earlier periods wherein documentation is not generously provided. With disregard for the depth of time, elements have been taken from documentary sources of the entire colonial period and placed side by side in a synchronic mosaic. At best, this type of reconstruction is an abstraction of culture, and like any abstraction, it is essentially unreal. Nowhere does it give a hint of the potentiality of Araucanian culture: on the contrary, such description lends itself to demonstration of a culture which, by the lessons of historical anthropology, should never have survived the first Spanish onslaught. Such reconstruction follows from a basic assumption of cultural constancy. In some phases of material culture this technique is doubtless warranted and valid, especially in the presence of sufficient archaeological documentation. However this may be, the idea of constancy stands in opposition to the idea of change, and from what can be made of the documents, the strength with which the Araucanians resisted Spanish domination was derived not from a constancy of their cultural forms but from the ability to change them. It seems valid, therefore, to view the sources of the later colonial period as indications of what Araucanian culture *became* under the stress of the long Spanish war rather than as evidence of what it was before the conquest.

The chronicles of the first century of conflict, when viewed from this position and subjected to critical analysis, provide considerable insight into the design of change. The term "culture" in the present case does not refer to fine art and letters and the numerous connotations usually associated with the term. Such development was not a concomitant of war, nor, it seems clear, did the Araucanians tend in the direction of refined sensibility. Araucanian cultural development occurred only in those arts which had a survival value, and was canalized by the hostile forces which threatened the total culture. Spanish pressure was exerted in three areas—military, political, and religious. The Araucanians, under the stimulus of this external pressure, turned inward upon themselves and developed their own corresponding forms to a point of equal resistive strength. The Spanish challenge in terms of relative force of impact was first military, secondly political, and lastly religious. Araucanian reaction and response to the challenge followed the same gradient.

The founding of Concepción by Valdivia in 1550 marked the real beginning of Araucanian resistance. Located just across the Biobío, out of Araucanian territory proper, it served as a strategic base of operations and key position of Spanish strength. Before its foundation the Spaniards posed a transient threat, but after it began to serve as a springboard for trans-Biobío conquest and settlement, the Indians better understood the consequences involved. With alarming speed the Spanish moved southward, through the provinces of Arauco, Catiray, Tucapel, Purén, and Marigueño, coming to a temporary halt at the Calle-Calle River. This entire area, bordered on the west by the sea and on the east by the camino real (the easiest passage through the central valley), was divided in encomienda, Arauco, Tucapel, and Purén being retained by Valdivia as the basis of a princely estate.[11] These provinces, especially Arauco, were highly prized by the Spaniards as the most heavily populated of the whole kingdom, and as possessing an abundance of food stuffs, fine lands, and a most provident climate.[12]

Within this area the Indians lived in small, decentralized kinship groups, with no apparent intergroup relationship of an institutional nature. The sources of the sixteenth century are so meager as to preclude the possibility of clear understanding of the sociopolitical divisions within the individual group. The local clusters of dwellings, in early chronicles called *levos*, in later ones *reguas*, composed a larger unit known as the *allaregua* (or *aillarewe*). Each *allaregua* was composed of nine or less *levos*. [Miguel de] Olaverría, writing in 1594, describes this area as consisting of only five *allareguas*, but the context in which he mentions them suggests that this semicentralization was of relatively recent origin.[13] There is no factual basis for postulating anything but a crude kinship relationship, markedly particularized by geographical isolation, at the time of the Spanish arrival.

These people, albeit ready warriors, were soundly defeated by Spanish arms and remained so for almost four years. Subsequent events, the revolt against Governor Valdivia in December 1553, and the continuing War of Arauco, indicate quite clearly that this short peace was a period of Araucanian maturation. Through military action, service in encomienda, and free intercourse in the Spanish towns (Concepción, Imperial, Valdivia, and Villa Rica) they observed and learned much about Spanish military organization and strategy, government, social custom, mores, and religious concepts. The lessons they learned were adequately demonstrated in subsequent resistance against the invaders.

This initial period of communication with Spanish culture was constantly amplified throughout the following century. Military action was usually confined to the summer months. During harvest time and winter both Indians and Spaniards tended to refrain from active combat, holding what had been gained and preparing for summer campaigns. Through peaceful Indians, those serving the Spanish, the rebels kept themselves fully informed of all Spanish activity. Never lacking information, the Indians always had a precise idea of Spanish strength or weakness. There was seldom a rigid military perimeter; in those areas where the invader could maintain a fort and military supremacy the Indians were reduced to servitude. With a weakening of Spanish strength, rebellion inevitably occurred, so that the distinction as a peaceful or warlike Indian depended largely upon the state of affairs of the moment. Because the Indians so frequently changed roles, they were never out of personal contact with the Spanish.

The Indians received some aid and encouragement from Spanish deserters. There is no telling how many deserted to enemy ranks in the course of the sixteenth century, but in the year 1600 alone it is known that there were over sixty desertions.[14] A good many of these renegades were still living among the Indians in 1607.[15] In fear of peace and subsequent retribution, the traitors taught the Indians many things that would have been difficult for them to learn themselves, such as the proper use of firearms, the building of forges and ironmongering, and even the techniques of political administration. The Spaniards were greatly perturbed when a mestizo powder maker went over to the other side. With volcanic sulphur, saltpeter, and charcoal in abundance, the Indians could make deadly use of the large stores of field pieces and firearms which they had captured. As luck would have it, the deserter repented and returned to the Spanish fold, whereupon he was forgiven and permitted to return to Peru. There were also clerical renegades who apostatized and urged the Indians on in their own religious beliefs and practices.[16]

It is most important to understand that the motive for Araucanian observation of Spanish cultural forms was not to emulate them and thereby raise the level of their own, but to discover Spanish weaknesses and to mobilize Araucanian strength for forceful opposition. A fundamental weakness of Spanish occupation was its dire need of peace. Exploitation of this weakness became a cornerstone of Araucanian strategy throughout the sixteenth century and beyond. Spanish forces, both civilian and military, were too few and too widely dispersed, and the line of supply from Peru was much too long. Effective occupation and permanent settlement depended upon a guaranteed supply of Indian labor. This, of course, was in turn dependent upon total pacification, which would allow the colonists to concentrate on development of mining and agriculture rather than military defense. As experience in Mexico and Peru had shown, a mere handful of soldiers, colonists, and friars could work great wonders if the Indians would but submit. When they first settled Santiago the Spaniards proved that they could provide their living with their own hands, but full barns and producing mines were impossible to realize without Indian labor.[17] Because of this, the Spaniards always hungered for peace, and through past experience in the Indies, expected it to follow each victory over the Indians.[18] This was the great error of the Spaniards in the sixteenth century. Whenever the Indians found it advantageous to themselves to live in peace—whether because of famine or disease or military weakness—they willingly surrendered themselves to service in the encomienda, there to repair their fortunes and to watch. The Spaniards, hopeful that this was indeed the dawn of a new day, almost invariably sought immediate expansion of their mining and agricultural activities. With a quickening of economic activity, military vigilance declined to a point which invited rebellion. The Araucanians honored such invitations without fail.[19]

Spanish military strategy was also based upon the gnawing hunger for peace. From past experience the invaders knew that peace would follow the defeat and usurpation of a central authority. In the absence of a central Araucanian authority the only alternative was to instill fear by demonstration of military supremacy, and so the Spaniards constantly sought a definitive battle which, when won, would convince the Araucanians of the futility of resistance. Some civilians differed, advising an Indian policy founded upon kind treatment and remission of personal service, but their voices were seldom heard. Recognizing the Spaniards' willingness to do battle, the Araucanians always chose their own battle sites where the terrain could be used to advantage, where the horse, as a military instrument, could be rendered less effective, and where their own strategies could be best effected. With monotonous regularity the Spaniards, always seeking the big victory, sent an army to defeat a rumored gathering of Indians, which rumor was usually broadcast by the Indians themselves. Upon arrival the Spaniards found themselves outmanned and outmaneuvered, and so were frequently forced to flee for their lives, leaving baggage trains in the hands of the enemy.[20]

It was military planning of this kind that led to the capture and death of Valdivia. Historians generally recognize the death trap into which he fell as the handiwork of Lautaro, the most famous former groom in all history. Lautaro has since become one of Chile's great national heroes, symbolizing all that was best in Araucanian culture. Be that as it may, there is considerable reason to believe that Lautaro hailed from the vicinity of Santiago, and was therefore an Araucanian by nothing more than association.[21] His relations with Araucanians are not clear historically beyond the fact that he led their resistance, aided by other chiefs, until his death in 1557. He was extremely well versed in military strategy, and his deployment of squadrons in place of mass attack and the use of encirclement were valued contributions to Araucanian knowledge, but the fact that many other military techniques were developed after he had passed from the scene would indicate that there were countless Araucanians of equal ability.

Generally speaking, the Araucanians retained their own weapons in the war against the Spanish. Bows and arrows, long lances, spears, long clubs with weighted heads, and slings were the weapons most often used.[22] Strategy was much more important than weapons. As noted above, the Indians never fought in a place that was not of their own choosing if they could avoid it. The horse was their greatest problem and one around which their strategy revolved. They chose battle sites wherein the horse would be difficult to manage; they made use of snares on long poles with which to pull the rider from his horse; they dug pitfalls and trenches, placing sharp stakes upon which rider and mount would be impaled; in all of this their chief aim was to get the Spaniard off his mount.[23]

Through the spoils of war and peacetime thievery the Indians acquired a vast supply of horses. By 1594 it was not uncommon for them to put several hundred horsemen in the field. It is to be noted, however, that they used the horse as an auxiliary rather than as an instrument of war. Riding as far as thirty miles a night they raided settlements and ranches under the cover of darkness, leaving death and destruction in their wake.[24] But acquisition of this new mobility did not alter their basic strategy for fighting Spanish forces. Throughout the sixteenth century they continued to lure Spanish troops into carefully prepared ambuscades, themselves remaining on foot. To have done otherwise would have undone their whole strategy. As the Spanish horsemen approached the main Indian force, their lines of retreat were closed by concentric rings of warriors. If the Spanish were fortunate enough to defeat the enemy they found no difficulty in retracing their steps. If, on the other hand, the Indians proved too strong for them, they could retreat only with great difficulty. Once having forced the Spaniards into retreat, the Indians followed them on foot. When the horses tired sufficiently, their riders could be struck down. A Spanish horseman afoot, because of the weight and bulk of his equipment and his inability to dodge through the forest undergrowth, did not have a chance for his life.[25]

The idea of Indians running down horses is not as incredible as it at first seems. In the heat of summer, when most of the fighting took place, the Spanish mounts tired quickly, especially after the long trip to the Indian ambuscade. Besides this, the Araucanians were accustomed to hunting wild game by literally chasing it to death. This required a tireless trot, at which they were proficient. Profiting by the lessons of their own strategy, the Araucanians devised an extremely light saddle in order to increase the endurance of their mounts on long rides. When they used captured Spanish saddles they first cut them down so as to make them considerably lighter.[26]

Shortly after the turn of the century, by 1611 to be exact, the Indians developed a cavalry that in terms of mobility was superior to the Spanish. They likewise possessed the best horses in the whole of Chile. These advantages were demonstrated in more daring raids on Spanish towns and a willingness to meet the Spanish cavalry on its own ground.[27] From this time forward the war passed into a new phase in which Araucanian offensive power became an increasingly significant factor. The source of that power, of course, lay in mastery of the horse. In little more than a generation the animal from which the Indians had once fled in terror had been incorporated into their culture, transforming it into a factor of defiant military power, dedicated to the eradication of Spanish culture. The Spaniards were not only dismayed to recognize this development of Araucanian military strength, but were piqued as well at the sight of barbarous savages riding horses with an air of equality. In answer to Spanish resentment the Indians pledged never to quit their war for freedom and their horses to enter serfdom on foot.[28]

The existence of a skilled and effective military force bespeaks the presence of a comparable political organization under whose genius it is formed and directed. In the development of Araucanian political organization the chronicles indicate two major forces at work: the geographical particularism in which the Araucanians traditionally lived and a counterforce provoked by the presence of the enemy and inclining towards Araucanian unity. Throughout the first century of conquest ancient localism clashed with incipient nationalism. This conflict produced a political ambivalence which in itself contributed heavily to the cause of Araucanian independence. Centralization of politico-military authority was achieved to a point where successful resistance was possible, but did not develop to a state where the Spaniards could defeat and usurp it.

The center of anti-Spanish unity was founded in what the Spanish termed "*el estado*." This was a geographical expression signifying the area that Valdivia held in personal encomienda.[29] It was these Indians, particularly those of Arauco, Tucapel, and Purén, who planned and carried out the revolt of 1553, and who assumed leadership of the resistance movement. After the first few years of bitter warfare the Spaniards began to imbue the term "estado" with political connotations, hence Don Alonso de Ercilla's image of "*el estado indómito*" was much more than a flight of poetic fancy.[30]

It is virtually certain that the Indians, in pre-Hispanic days, were in the habit of seeking transient familial and friendship alliances in the conduct of war between localities. Upon their first major defeat by Valdivia, following which he recrossed the Biobío and founded Concepción, the more intelligent Indian leaders voiced a wide call to arms.[31] The resulting alliance was effective in that it led to the downfall of Valdivia, but it had no permanent character. With each new Spanish thrust the caciques of the *estado* had to re-form alliances and seek wider support for their efforts. In 1556, for example, Lautaro and the chiefs established relations with the Indians of Santiago, attempting to incite them to rebellion.[32] Temporary alliances were both frequent and effective. In search of allies the chiefs used glass beads, dogs, and various types of Spanish plunder to effect negotiations.[33] There also developed a type of Indian mercenary who supplied his own weapons and served for a specified length of time at a prearranged scale of pay.[34]

It seems quite clear that there was no pan-Araucanian sentiment to which the *estado* could appeal. When local chiefs were asked for troops they not uncommonly rejected the request. If they acceded to the demand, they chose the bravest man for a leader and dispatched the force under his command. Service was performed in the *estado*'s forces for no more consideration than lodging and hospitable treatment. In the event of mortality the close relatives of the fallen warrior were compensated by the residents of the province in whose defense he had died.[35]

Some of the localities simply did not want to fight the Spaniards, preferring to make the best of conditions under Spanish rule. The Indians around Angol, for instance, joined the Spaniards in war against the *estado* for a number of years. While the *estado* leaders accused them of subverting the general Indian cause, the Angol tribes retaliated with accusations of plunder and theft.[36] The *estado*, with its own crops destroyed by warfare, never hesitated to raid the stores of those who were not immediately allied to the cause. Araucanians who refused to fight were subjected to violent reprisal.[37] Even in the province of Arauco all was not unanimity. An old chief was forced to flee with his family and take refuge in the Spanish fort in Arauco because he would not support the war, thereby giving evidence of pro-Spanish sympathies.[38] It is difficult to guess how many others there might have been.

By 1594, according to Olaverría, the *estado* claimed suzerainty over all of the *allareguas* from the Biobío to the Imperial River, and was held in dread by all of the Indians as far south as Osorno. The *estado* was so feared and respected, he said, that Indians in the extreme south would break the peace when the chiefs of the *estado* so desired.[39] Nevertheless, the chiefs never succeeded in gaining effective suzerainty, even for purposes of war. Authority continued to be local, rather than central, and cooperation was most often found in the realm of diplomacy.

With the turn of the century a more precise political and military division was created by the Araucanians. The region between the Biobío and Toltén rivers was divided into three longitudinal strips called *butanmapos*: they were the sub-Andean range, the central valley, and the coastal strip (including the *estado*). Each *butanmapo* had clearly defined limits and jurisdictions; each had, at least in time of war, a principal chief, or *toque*. It was customary for the chiefs to debate plans for war in a parliamentary junta in which the three territories were represented. Strategy was agreed upon by common consent.[40] The relationship between the local chiefs and territorial *toques* is not clear, but it seems likely that military power was held both to qualify and to assure authority. When disagreement occurred between *toques*, war between territories could and did sometimes develop.[41]

Gerónimo Pietas, writing around 1729, describes a further development of this general schema. At this time the territorial strips had been increased to four in number. These provinces were still called *butanmapos*, but they extended farther north and south than did the older territories. This extension of Araucania is mute testimony to the growth of Araucanian strength and confidence. In Pietas's description each *butanmapo* had a hierarchy of three superior chiefs: a *toqui-guilmen* (commander), a *guinca-guilmen* (field commander), and a *pelqui-guilmen* (diplomatic courier). While these officers assumed absolute authority in their positions within the province, they were inferior to a *toque-general* who apparently wielded a measure of authority over the whole of Araucania. He further describes a conventionalization of diplomacy involving three forms for the calling of war. A general war could be called for only by the *toque-general*, and at his discretion. When he desired to begin hostilities word was passed to all chiefs through a group of subchiefs called *cones*. Only the *toque-general* could dispatch the *cones*, and in the event of hostilities between the provinces, the fact of being called to council by a *con* was a guarantee of safe conduct. All chiefs attended the councils, wherein strategy was planned and forces drawn up.

War could also be called for by a regional *toque*. As messenger he sent his *pelqui-guilmen* to the other *butanmapos*, asking their aid and support, which they might or might not give. In the third instance war could be initiated simply by attacking the Spaniards. In this event the warring chieftain used force of arms to enlist the support of the local Indians for his designs. [42] As incomplete as this description is, it does give evidence of a relatively sophisticated politico-military organization which stands in sharp contrast against that of the first generation of *estado* caciques.

Development of religious beliefs among the Araucanians is a most difficult postulation because we know so very little about their pre-Hispanic religious ideas. The chroniclers generally agree that the spirits of Araucanian ancestors formed an important cult, each kinship group having an ultimate progenitor whose spirit was called *Pillán*. This spirit was believed to be immanent, and so could be propitiated. Before going into battle the Indians sometimes sought divination from oracles, and once having gained a victory in a given locality through the intercession of supernatural forces, they believed that they could not lose a subsequent battle in that particular place. [43] Given the immediate religious background of the chroniclers of the sixteenth century, one in which religious and nationalistic sentiment were perfectly united, and the omnipresent tradition of the *reconquista*, one must always wonder if the early chroniclers reported what the Indians actually believed, or if they instead reflected the paths of their own cognition.

As the Spaniards made war in the name of an omnipotent God, the Araucanians appear to have rationalized a deity for their own defense. There were innumerable *Pilláns* hovering over every locality, and in the absence of concerted missionary effort they doubtless remained. In describing an Araucanian ceremonial that he witnessed in 1629, [Francisco Nuñez de

Pineda y] Bascuñan depicts an interesting bit of symbolism which suggests the evolution of a super-*Pillán*. The occasion of ceremony was the execution of a Spanish captive. Involved in the execution was a lance with three knives fixed to its end, representing the three *butanmapos*. After the captive's brains had been dashed out, his captor took from the lance that knife which represented his personal region of Araucania and used it to cut out the victim's heart. He sucked its blood, took tobacco smoke and blew it to the heavens, then passed the heart around to the other chiefs for similar usage, after which it was divided and eaten.[44] The three knives symbolized Araucania, and the sucking of blood was a form of thanksgiving to the *Pillán* for victory. This ceremony closely approaches the abstraction of Home, Country, and God.

Later in his captivity Bascuñan had occasion to spend several days in the company of one of the small sons of a chief. One afternoon he asked the child if he would like to learn how to pray. The boy answered affirmatively; he had already learned something of prayers from a Spanish captive. With little instruction the child recited the Pater Noster in Spanish, but without understanding what it was he was reciting. Bascuñan, speaking Araucanian fluently, decided to teach him in the Araucanian tongue. The child was delighted to understand the recitation. The trenchant Bascuñan then asked him if he understood the idea behind the prayer. Yes indeed, was the reply. God could be none other than a great *Pillán*, superior to other *Pilláns*.[45] Bascuñan registered satisfied delight. The question is, should he have been so delighted?

In order to maintain a spirit of unqualified resistance the leaders of the *estado*, who manipulated majority opinion, instituted indoctrinational forms for boys and youths. Beginning at six years of age boys were taught the use of military weapons. By observing him the boy's tutors would decide which weapon he was most proficient with, and then he would be trained as a specialist in the use of that weapon. At the same time he was arduously trained in running and swimming.[46] Another type of training begun at this early age was the torture of Spanish captives. The boys were given knives and living Spaniards, then instructed in the arts of slow dissection, roasting, and eating.[47] They were further required to memorize certain verses which recounted Spanish offenses since the beginning of the war, and were made to recite them at the command of their elders. In this way a boy became a man with a clearly fixed purpose in life. As a youth the Araucanian would speak thus of his lance: "This is my master: it does not order me to dig for gold, or carry food or firewood, nor to herd cattle, or to follow it about. And since the master sustains my liberty, it is with him that I wish to pass."[48]

There was seldom talk of peace in the *estado*. Even a chief, if he dared speak of peace in war council, could be cut down on the spot by the nearest soldier. Apparently it was quite common for the warriors to kill any Indian who spoke of peace, or who was suspected of having the word in his mouth. [Alonso González de] Nájera describes a rigorous "inquisition" by the warriors to suppress the minority who wanted to farm rather than fight. Christianity was also forbidden. In the course of time many Indians were introduced to its tenets through close contact with the Spanish, especially the Indians who lived around the Spanish settlements. After the disaster of 1598, of course, the towns were no more. Many of the Indians had become reconciled to Spanish occupation and were genuinely converted to Christianity. Now they were exposed to the mercy of the *estado*'s inquisitors. From what we know, it did not go well with them.[49] Standing in opposition to Christianity was an apparently well-defined Araucanian concept, to wit: the Indian way of life is the only one; those who die in war against the Spanish go to another land where they enjoy more women and luxuries than they ever had in this life; there is nothing to fear in death.[50]

Araucanian opposition to Spanish intrusion was not confined to the field of battle. At all times they waged psychological warfare with consummate skill. While they always celebrated a victory over the Spaniards, and let the settlers know of their celebration, they never disclosed the identity of the fort or community that had fallen.[51] With great finesse they obstructed Spanish intelligence, keeping the enemy in a state of worried ignorance. It is relatively certain that human flesh was not eaten by the Araucanians in pre-Hispanic times except in times of dire necessity.[52] With the advent of the Spanish invasion, however, the eating of Spaniards became institutionalized. Time and time again the chroniclers tell of Spaniards being eaten, in whole and in part, and sometimes, their horses with them. Since there does not appear to have been a tradition to support this practice, nor any magical or superstitious belief connected with the act, it seems reasonable to assume that it was developed for its propaganda value. This would represent an intended clash of values. Discovering the abhorrence with which the Christians viewed cannibalism, the Araucanians appear to have developed it as a cultural opposite, a symbol of resistance. The great chief of Arauco, Caupolican, in hurling a challenge at Governor García Hurtado de Mendoza, boasted that he had eaten the previous governor (Valdivia) and would do the same with him.[53] In some cases, even the well-picked bones of Spaniards were consumed in wine after being burned and powdered, the idea being that no memory of the Spaniards should remain.[54]

Another Araucanian device was the making of flutes from Spanish shinbones, most often extracted while the victim was still alive. On occasion the victim was forced to play his threnody on his own shinbone.[55] After the Indians developed their own cavalry they used the shinbones in lieu of trumpets. Nájera describes the sound they made as one which was doleful and morose, producing depression in those who heard it.[56] One can but imagine the effect on the settlers produced by a night-riding horde, sweeping over the countryside, accompanied by its unearthly music.

The Araucanians had still other ways to indicate their scorn for Spanish culture. On occasion they cut [tree] limbs and made crosses upon which to crucify their captives before roasting and eating them.[57] In their treatment of captive Spanish women the Indians made calculated mockery of the enemy's institutions. The conquerors' ladies were highly prized by the chiefs, who used them as concubinary slaves. In 1605 a new Spanish governor, Don Alonso García, came down from Lima with one thousand troops. With this show of force he opened negotiations with the caciques of the *estado* for return of female captives, offering Indian hostages in exchange. The chiefs of Arauco decided to part with some of their prizes, and at the appointed time produced the prisoners. Before waiting husbands and fathers the women appeared, calloused, lousy, naked below the waist, and more often than not, visibly pregnant.[58] Now we know that the Araucanians had the same ideas of physical propriety as did the Spaniards. Both made the same distinction as to public and private parts of the anatomy.[59] It was by intention alone that the chiefs of Arauco forced their unfortunate victims to appear thus before their menfolk. The chiefs of Purén, although they liked the Spanish no better, provided coverings with which their captives could hide their shame.[60]

The foregoing brief review of Araucanian culture in its history has embraced the outward manifestations of change rather than its internal mutations. Two principal aims have directed the study: one intended to restore the chronology which is so basic to cultural history; the other to divert study of the problem of Araucanian resistance from narrow analysis of Spanish strength and weakness. It is apparent that understanding is to be found in the sphere of Araucanian cultural experience. In plowing the furrow it is inevitable that questions tentatively answered should suggest a multitude of new ones laying deeper beneath the surface.[61] With more intensified study, surface appearances which now seem to be certainties will doubtless be proved to be more apparent than real. Even so, we can better understand why an observation made by an historian in the middle of the eighteenth century could, with small exception, have been made in the sixteenth:

> In a short time the Spanish conquered the three powerful empires of the American hemisphere, those of Peru, Mexico, and Bogotá, but the hundred and ninety years that have elapsed since the beginning of this conquest have not sufficed to end it with the subjugation of the Araucanians. Nor has the vast expenditure of fifty million pesos and more than 25,000 recruits, nor the effusion of blood that has been spilled done so, even though in the past century the King declared this war to be equal to those

of Spain, Flanders, and Italy. Today the Araucanians possess the fairest portion of Chile, from the Biobío River to the Straits of Chiloé, a hundred and fifty leagues stretching between the Cordillera and the sea. In the whole of this area the Spanish hold nothing but the fortified towns of Arauco and Valdivia: the Indians live in independence and enjoyment of their coveted liberty.[62]

Notes

1. For discussion of Chilean prehistory see Francisco Antonio Encina, *Historia de Chile desde la prehistoria hasta 1891* (19 vols., Santiago, 1940–51), vol. I, chaps. 2, 3; Ricardo E. Latcham, *La prehistoria chilena* (Santiago, 1928), 147–154, passim.

2. Miguel de Olaverría, "Informe de don Miguel de Olaverría sobre el reyno de Chile, sus indios y sus guerras" (in Claudio Gay, *Historia física y política de Chile*, Paris, Santiago, 1844–71). This work comprises twenty-eight volumes, two of which are document collections, numbered I and II, hence, Gay, II:19–20. Olaverría was an old soldier in Chile when he wrote his chronicle in 1594. His work is both dependable and readable. Also see "Viaje de García Hurtado de Mendoza al sur de Valdivia y fundación de Osorno" (Gay, I:224–225).

3. Encina, I:72–74; cf. Latcham, *La prehistoria*, 152–154.

4. The term *Picunche* did not come into vogue until the seventeenth century. Writers of the eighteenth and nineteenth centuries accepted and compounded these delineations. In addition to these three areas the Spaniards further differentiated between the Picunche, who extended somewhat south of the Maule River, and the Promaucaes, who lived between the Nuble River and the Biobío, including the site of Concepción. The Promaucaes were extremely warlike, but since they lived north of the Biobío they were not Araucanians in the proper sense, nor did they make up any part of the *estado* (see note 29).

5. Alonso de Góngora Marmolejo, "Historia de Chile desde su descubrimiento hasta el año de 1575" (in *Colección de historiadores de Chile y documentos relativos a la historia nacional*, 49 vols., Santiago, 1861–1942), II:33–34 (this collection will hereafter be cited as CHC). Marmolejo came to Chile with Valdivia in 1549, hence he wrote with considerable experience and authority. His work is fundamental to the study of Araucanian culture.

6. Idem, 37–39. Marmolejo's account of Valdivia's death is based on an eyewitness account, hence it is more acceptable than are the many others that are based on rumors and hearsay.

7. For a survey of the first general uprising see Encina, vol. I, chaps. 8 and 9.

8. Idem, vol. II, chap. 23; also see Gregorio Serrano, "Relación de lo subcedido en Chile desde veinte de diciembre de noventa y ocho hasta primero de mayo de noventa y nueve" (CHC, XLV:227–233).

9. Alonso González de Nájera, "Desengaño y reparo de la guerra de Chile" (CHC, XVI:10–14, 63–65, passim). The author was in Chile from 1601 to 1607. Experienced in military science, he made a brave attempt to analyze Araucanian resistance. His work is invaluable for Araucanian study.

10. Idem, 93–94.

11. Olaverría, 20.

12. Marmolejo, 25; Pedro de Valdivia to King, Sept. 25, 1551 (Gay, I:139–142).

13. Olaverría, 21.

14. Encina, II:306.

15. Nájera, 117.

16. Idem, 69, 73–75, 117–122, 143–148. In spite of Spanish fears, firearms did not play a significant role in Indian strategy until late in the seventeenth century.

17. It should be kept in mind that conquest and settlement were private financial ventures, and very expensive ones. See Governor García Hurtado de Mendoza's complaint in Marmolejo, 90.

18. This was Valdivia's experience in Santiago; the Indians tired of "running like beasts" and submitted to reduction (Valdivia to King, Sept. 4, 1545, Gay, I:61).

19. This technique of dissembling was practiced widely, both in Spanish towns and on the frontiers. The Indians were so skilled that the Spanish were never able to tell whether they really meant to keep the peace or not. Either way, there was nothing the Spanish could do but accept, driven as they were by the economic imperative of their way of life. The Indians seem to have understood this perfectly. The granting of terminal peace in critical areas as a part of wider strategy became common. Revolts were well planned: the chiefs had the white women divided among themselves in advance; the gold that had been dug for the whites during peace was thrown into the nearest river, or used to ransom Indian hostages; bloody revenge was visited upon the erstwhile masters. See Marmolejo, 58–59, 125; Nájera, 46–47, 65.

20. For typical accounts see Marmolejo, 35ff., 85, 101, 171–176, 186–187. In the matter of Indian strategy and resistance the Spaniards could not see the forest for the trees. They laid responsibility for their failures on everything but the Indians. A widely prevalent idea, as expressed by Martín Ruiz de Gamboa (Gay, II:123), held that more polished *peninsular* gentlemen were needed to fight the Indians, ignorant creoles being unfit for the task. Discrimination against Creoles was a constant source of dissension in Spanish ranks. In 1557, García Hurtado de Mendoza arrived in Chile as governor with many *peninsulares* in his train. The abandon with which he handed out encomiendas to his peninsular friends enraged the luckless creoles. In his reply to their complaints he suggested that no more than a handful of the Chileans knew the identity of their fathers, and then insultingly inquired, "En qué se andan aquí estos hijos de putas?" (Marmolejo, 80). Nájera (36–37) took a more realistic view. He stated that Creoles were born in war and carried the brunt of the fighting, and did it well. Because the chroniclers ignored their deeds, he added, they were unappreciated in Spain. He considered the disparity between Creole and *peninsular* to be utterly inane.

21. Marmolejo simply states that among those who plotted Valdivia's downfall was a yanacona named Alonso, who had been Valdivia's servant (36). This brief notice is the only valid evidence of Lautaro's origin. Among the chroniclers in Chile the term *yanacona* invariably meant a friendly and allied Indian from the north. Chilean historians are prone to begin with the premise that he was an Araucanian, but have difficulty in explaining how he could have become so *españolado* in the brief period between Valdivia's first contact with the Araucanians and his death. It seems much more likely that Lautaro was taken by Valdivia in Santiago when he was a boy. See Benjamin Vicuña Mackenna, *Lautaro* (Santiago, 1876), for the standard nationalistic version.

22. Olavarría, 33–34; Nájera, 95–98. For a plausible account of Araucanian reaction to the Spanish danger after 1550 see Ricardo Latcham, "La capacidad

guerrera de los Araucanos: Sus armas y métodos militares" (*Revista Chilena de Historia y Geografía*, vol. 15, no. 19, 1915, 122–193). While this study is valuable for purely military affairs, it does not attempt to explore or interpret the force behind Araucanian military organization beyond the factor of Indian bravery. Another weakness is the author's uncritical use of Pedro Mariño de Lovera's *Crónica del reino de Chile* (CHC, vol. VI). Lovera was another soldier who came to Chile in 1551, served there for a number of years, and then retired to Lima to write a history of Chile. Ostensibly because it was not well written, the manuscript was turned over to a Jesuit, Bartolomé de Escobar, for rewriting. As a true courtier, he shifted emphasis to flatter his patron, García Hurtado de Mendoza, and otherwise took liberties which rendered the history worthless. After his revision it was probably revised by Hurtado himself. A copy was subsequently disseminated in Spain by Hurtado in suit for royal reward for services rendered. In like vein, Hurtado was ired at publication of Ercilla's *La Araucana*, which he felt slighted his person. In retaliation he commissioned Pedro de Oña to write his dull *Arauco Domado*, an epic in which Hurtado emerged as the conqueror of Arauco. As Nájera remarked, Oña merely made himself a fool in describing Arauco as subdued when in fact Arauco was more victorious and impregnable than ever before (36–37). See Diego Barros Arana, *Historia jeneral de Chile* (16 vols., Santiago, 1884–1902, II:282–288).

23. Marmolejo, 44–49, 85, 62–63. John M. Cooper, "The Araucanians" (in *Handbook of South American Indians*, Julian H. Steward, ed., Bulletin, Bureau of American Ethnology, no. 143, 1946, II:697), is in error when he concludes that the Indians mastered European military tactics and strategy, making them their own.

24. Olaverría, 34.

25. Marmolejo, 40–43, 47–49. These are but representative of many such descriptions.

26. Nájera, 42, 110–116. Cooper (II:704) gives the impression that Indian saddles and riding gear were nothing more than crude imitations of Spanish models.

27. Nájera, 107–110; "Informe de Juan de Xaraquemada," May 1, 1611 (Gay, II:239); Xaraquemada to King, Jan. 29, 1611, and Jan. 28, 1612 (idem, 247, 255–257); Alonso García Ramón to King, 1613 (idem, 267).

28. Nájera, p. 116. Whenever the Indians found it necessary or advisable to grant a temporary peace, the Spaniards first insisted that they turn in their horses and move about on foot, as subject persons were expected to do. The Indians invariably turned in their *rocinantes*, keeping their good stock hidden for use after the next rebellion (idem, 128).

29. Olaverría, 20. The area included the Indian localities of Talcamavida, Laucamilla, Catiray, Marigueño, Angol, Arauco, Andalicán, Tucapel, and Purén. After the *estado* had been recognized as a political entity the term was applied to all or part of it. In essence, the term *estado* came to mean the center of Indian resistance, whether it embraced all of the above-named provinces or merely one of them.

30. Alonso de Ercilla y Zúñiga, ed., José Toribio Medina, *La Araucana* (5 vols., Santiago, 1910). Historians and anthropologists seem to be under a strange compulsion to use this poem as a prime documentary source. This is not to say that in select instances the practice is not warranted, but the wide use to which it has been put must certainly be held in question. Everyone knows that there is much truth in it, although seldom is it possible to determine precisely where it resides.

31. Marmolejo, 22–23. It took nearly three years to organize the first rebellion. It is sometimes implied that the Araucanians were introduced to cooperative military effort on a large scale through attempted invasions by the Incas. This seems most unlikely because the Incas were held at the Maule River, and the Indians occupying this area, as nearly as can be ascertained, were the warlike Promaucaes, who were not Araucanians. Nor could the Inca invasions have had anything to do with the formation of the *estado*, since, as we have seen it was created by the imposition of Spanish dominion, without which it could have had no meaning.

32. Idem, 61–62.

33. Idem, 105, 133.

34. Juan de Herrera, "Relación de las cosas de Chile" (CHC, II:251).

35. Olaverría, 23.

36. Marmolejo, 126–127.

37. Idem, 83. The Indians around the settlements who were friendly toward the Spanish were sorely vexed by the depredations of the *estado*'s warriors. Crops were burned or stolen, and women and children were carried off to be used as drudges. See Alonso García Ramón to the King, 1613 (Gay, II:270, 279); "Informe de Juan de Xaraquemada" (idem, 241–242; Nájera, 60). Through acts of terror the *estado* sometimes forced friendly Indians to rebel against the Spanish. Through maladministration the Spanish sometimes achieved the same end. Plundering of Indian stores and raping of their women brought alienation and revolt. See Francisco Nuñez de Pineda y Bascuñan, *Cautiverio feliz* (CHC, III:51–52).

38. Marmolejo, 110–113.

39. Olaverría, 22.

40. Bascuñan, 39–41. Latcham (*La prehistoria chilena*, 153–154) considers this to be an ancient Mapuche military organization, even though it is first reported almost a century after the Spaniards arrived. From what we know of the ancient Mapuche, this would appear to be an unduly sophisticated organization.

41. Idem, 94–99, 144–148; "Relación de Luis de Valdivia," 1611 (Gay, II:281–282).

42. Gerónimo Pietas, "Noticias sobre las costumbres de los Araucanos" (Gay, II:489–493).

43. Marmolejo, 172; Nájera, 48; also see Latcham, *La prehistoria chilena*, 193–194. Cooper (742–752) makes a noble attempt to unravel the confused threads of early Araucanian religious belief.

44. Bascuñan, 39–43. The author was a captain in the Spanish infantry and the son of Alvaro Núñez de Pineda, *maestro de campo general*, one of Chile's distinguished soldiers. In 1629 the Araucanians crossed the Biobío and fell on Chillán. They captured Bascuñan and took him back to their stronghold. His captivity was one of those storybook affairs, almost too romantic and dramatic to be real. He was befriended by Maulican, a powerful chieftain of the *estado*, and likewise the son of a famous warrior. When the other chiefs learned of Bascuñan's identity they demanded his head to use as a trophy to incite peaceful Indians to war. By chicanery and ruse Maulican saved him and, after some months of comfortable captivity, returned him to his own people. His account of the adventure is invaluable, although it is somewhat tiresome to read. He was a creole and educated in Chile. He apparently felt compelled to show that a creole scholar could hold his own with a *peninsular*, hence his excessive quotation from and reference to classical authors.

45. Bascuñan, 155–156. Also see Córdoba y Figueroa, *Historia de Chile* (CHC, II:26).

46. Olaverría, 23.

47. Nájera, 60.

48. Idem, 61, 105.

49. Idem, 60, 70, 100, 119, 163; "Tratado de la importancia y utilidad que ay en dar por esclavos a los indios rebelados de Chile," 1599 (in José Toribio Medina, *Biblioteca hispano-chilena, 1523–1817*, 3 vols., Santiago, 1897–99), II:13.

50. Oliverría, 40.

51. Nájera, 75–76, 98, 100.

52. See Cooper, 732, and José Toribio Medina, *Las aborígines de Chile* (Santiago, 1952), 220–221. Marmolejo (57) states that in the spring of 1556 the Indians were visited by a terrible plague (called *chavalongo*). In the aftermath of famine the Indians turned to cannibalism as a means of survival.

53. García Hurtado de Mendoza, "Relación" (Gay, I:183–184).

54. Nájera, 54.

55. Idem, 53–54, 54–57.

56. Idem, 115.

57. Idem, 58.

58. Nájera, 67–71, 118. The author also stated that over five hundred Spanish women had been taken captive and at the time of writing some two hundred remained in captivity (37–38).

59. Idem, pp. 46–47.

60. Idem, p. 69.

61. One such problem is suggested by the sources. In pre-Hispanic days the Araucarians were sedentary farmers of predominantly vegetarian habits. Frequent mention is made in the documents of a growing cattle economy, especially in Spanish sheep and goats. Inasmuch as warfare disrupted agricultural planting in the valleys, the Araucanians moved their fields to impenetrable sierras. It may be that lower yields in the mountains created a greater need for animal foodstuffs to supplement lowered agricultural production. See, for example, Julián de Bastida to Don García Hurtado de Mendoza, Nov. 15, 1563 (CHC, XXIX:498); Olaverría, 36–38; Marmolejo, 76–77; Nájera, 23. The implications suggested in a shift of basic economy are highly significant and require further investigation.

62. Córdoba y Figueroa, *Historia de Chile* (CHC, II:29). His statistics seem to be far from the mark. In 1664 the casualty figures, as Latcham reports them, were twenty-nine thousand Spaniards and sixty thousand Indian allies ("La capacidad guerrera de los Araucanos," 58).

5

Spanish Penetration and Cultural Change in Early Colonial Mexico

Ronald Spores

Many peoples in Mexico and Peru never experienced a military conquest by the Spanish but instead yielded peacefully to the newcomers. The Mixtecs of southcentral Mexico were among these. As Ronald Spores demonstrates, relatively few Spaniards and blacks settled in this region in the early decades of the colonial period, largely because the area was not well integrated into the emerging market economy. The native social hierarchy, family structure, and settlement patterns were hardly modified. The local Spanish administrative districts, church parishes, and distribution of Indian laborers were all based on long-existing indigenous traditions.

Nevertheless, social change and resistance are certainly visible in this region. Many caciques became the owners of large estates during the colonial period. They accommodated themselves smoothly to the Spanish social and economic systems even though this meant estranging themselves at least somewhat from the interests of and their identification with their own people—a development that took place oftentimes in the Andes as well. As will be discussed in Chapter 6, rebellions were commonplace and continued through the centuries.

The Mixteca was visited by Spanish exploratory and military parties early in the colonial period: by Gonzalo de Umbría in early 1520, Francisco de Orozco in 1521, and Pedro de Alvarado in 1522.[1] After relatively minor resistance the area was pacified, and between 1525 and 1530 dozens of encomiendas were assigned to Spanish conquistadores.[2] By 1531–32, Spanish corregidores had been installed at Teposcolula, Coixtlahuaca, Tejupan, Yanhuitlan, Tamazola, Tilantongo, and Teozacoalco.[3] Secular and Dominican priests established contacts in the area around 1530 but made little concerted effort at conversion until 1538.[4] Few Europeans had visited the Mixteca before this time, and the effective Spanish occupation of the region did not occur until the late 1530s. From this time forward, however, the Mixteca and its people came fully into the Spanish colonial realm with consequent changes in native technology, economy, social organization, government, and ideology.

 Spanish political, religious, and economic institutions provided the principal mechanisms guiding the evolution of Mixtec society during colonial times. Critical to the Spanish plan for control and exploitation of the region and its people was the establishment of effective provincial government. Eventually three major administrative zones, the provinces of Teposcolula, Nochixtlan, and Teozacoalco, were recognized, but this was accomplished only after a period of trial-and-error experimentation in territorial organization.[5]

In the late 1540s, administrative-judicial *corregimientos* were established in Teposcolula, Coixtlahuaca, Tejupan, Yanhuitlan, Tonaltepec-Soyaltepec, Texacoalco, Amoltepec, Tamazola, and Tilantongo.[6] These communities were in the most populous and productive areas of the Mixteca and hence were regarded as desirable power bases for the Spaniards.

By 1552 the Teposcolula polity had been transformed into a more extensive *alcaldía mayor* with jurisdiction over eighteen major crown and private encomienda communities.[7] In 1554 the *corregimiento* of Tonaltepec-Soyaltepec was converted into the *alcaldía mayor* of Yanhuitlan, with a jurisdiction comprising Yanhuitlan and its numerous subject communities, Nochixtlan, and eleven other communities.[8] Teozacoalco and several neighboring communities in the southern Alta were reassigned in the 1570s from Teposcolula province to the jurisdiction of more proximate Oaxaca.[9]

Around 1595 the *alcadía mayor* of Yanhuitlan was absorbed into the *alcaldía mayor* of Teposcolula.[10] For two centuries the province operated under the name Provincia de Teposcolula y su agregada de Yanhuitlan. A *teniente de alcade mayor* and, when available, *escribanos* were assigned to Yanhuitlan to act on behalf of the alcade mayor of Teposcolula-Yanhuitlan. Separate judicial and notarial registries were maintained in Teposcolula. Criminal and civil cases were heard in Yanhuitlan as well as in Teposcolula, and jails as well as crown offices were maintained in both centers. Similar arrangements were made in such centers as Tlaxiaco, Chalcatongo, Tamazulapan, and Coixtlahuaca.

A major jurisdictional reorganization took place in the 1680s. The *alcaldía mayor* of Nochixtlan was segregated from Teposcolula and given jurisdiction over Tilantongo, Chachoapan, Etlatongo, Huauclilla, Tejutepec, Tiltepec, and Jaltepec. Later, in the mid-eighteenth century, the Ixcuintepec-Peñoles area of the southeastern Alta was added to the province.[11] At the same time Teozacoalco was withdrawn from the jurisdiction of Oaxaca and combined with Tecuicuilco as an aggregated *alcaldía mayor*.[12]

By 1746 the communities of the Mixteca Alta were grouped into four political-administrative units. Largest in territory and population and of greatest economic importance was the aggregated province of Yanhuitlan-Teposcolula, with forty-two communities.[13] Nochixtlan province contained eleven communities.[14] Ixquintepec-Peñoles, a relatively small province in the southeastern Mixteca, contained nine scattered communities.[15] Teozacoalco province, in the southern Mixteca, contained only five communities, some of which contained Chatino as well as Mixtec speakers.[16] This political arrangement remained in force until the late 1780s, when the intendancy form of provincial government was introduced to Oaxaca and the Mixteca. Even after 1786 there was virtually no significant shift in regional political organization, administration, or judicial function.

It was within this geopolitical context that colonial acculturation and the transformation of Mixtec society took place. Political institutions provided the essential framework and the necessary legitimate coercive power to bring about the effective articulation of European ideology, social forms, technology, and economic institutions with their Mixtec counterparts. Our present concern will be with the social system that underlay, and was interrelated with, those developments.

The Social System

The "transformation" of native society under Spanish rule was neither uniform nor pervasive. Family organization, kinship reckoning, marriage, and patterns of socialization underwent little modification. The four-level class system of caciques, *principales, macehuales, and terrazgueros* of pre-Hispanic times persisted but was substantially modified through addition of Spanish bureaucrats, clergy, merchants, and the three or four status groups of "aristocratic," common, itinerant, and indigent Spanish, and criollo and mestizo civilians residing permanently or temporarily in the Mixteca. To this could be added members of the Spanish military and a relatively small group of Africans and part-Africans. The result was a social amalgam of Indians, Europeans, mixed forms, and a contingent of slaves and their pure and intermixed descendants.

It is both an oversimplification and a distortion of reality to conceive of the social system as an ethnic-political diad of colonials and a subservient underclass of natives and Africans. Some Indians—caciques or *principales*—ranked on a par with European bureaucrats or clergy and above certain Spanish civilians, military, and indigenes. Even as regards the *macehual* class, the intent of Spanish policy was to deal evenhandedly with natives and to protect them from abuse. There is no evidence in the thousands of criminal and civil cases processed by the magisterial court in Teposcolula that Indians were treated either more or less fairly than were Spaniards, mestizos, or others. Likewise, offenses and abuses against Indians were dealt with as rigorously as were acts committed against Europeans.

Social Networks

The social mechanisms linking pre-Hispanic Mixtec families into communities, communities into kingdoms, and kingdoms into regional and interregional networks persisted into colonial times, but with modifications. Community endogamy continued to characterize common-class marriage, while intercommunity marriage was customary among the nobility (*principales*). Interkingdom and interregional marriages continued among members of the ruling (cacique) class throughout the colonial period, thereby preserving traditional interpolity and interregional social and political ties.[17]

The marketing complex continued to serve as a basis of social contact for members of the common class, as well as an institution of economic interaction. Colonial documentation indicates substantial movement among communities such as Yanhuitlan, Nochixtlan, Tamazulapan, Coixtlahuaca, Teposcolula, and Tlaxiaco, most actively on market days, but also to visit with relatives, engage in ritual activities, transact business outside the periodic market (that is, in stores or with individuals), or for such services as curing, smithing, and butchering.[18] Relations were not always harmonious, however. Many of the sixteenth-century criminal cases recorded in the Juzgado of Teposcolula involve disputes, thefts, and violent interaction between individuals of different communities coming together on market day or in the transaction of business in administrative centers.[19] However, the incidence of conflict between individuals from different communities was not by any means as great as it was within communities. On the other hand, intergroup conflict was most often between communities.

Specialization

Many full- or part-time specializations were practiced by Indian men and women. Among these were weaving and tailoring, basket making, pottery making, brick making, candle making, cloth making from rabbit fur, metalworking and smithing, woodworking, human and animal transport, butchering, hide preparation and leather working, and cobbling. Trading was the most common occupation, however, with hundreds of Mixtec families selling and bartering goods as itinerant or fixed-locus merchants.

Spaniards specialized in public administration, religion, store keeping, long-distance trade and brokerage, and livestock breeding (*ganadería*).[20]

The few mestizos living in Mixtec communities tended to follow pursuits closely associated with the Indian sector or were involved in shop keeping and trading.

Most of the highly skilled artisans came into the Mixteca from Oaxaca, Mexico, and Puebla de los Angeles on a short-term basis. Such specialists, normally Spaniards, included architects, artists, sculptors, platers, bell makers, master masons, brick makers, and metalworkers. These craftsmen were normally very well paid, well housed, and well fed.[21] They interacted socially with the local Spanish aristocracy during their tenure, and some were regarded as celebrated figures. Many, such as the great religious artist Andrés de Concha, acquired property in the large Mixtec communities but maintained permanent residence in Mexico, Puebla, or Oaxaca.[22]

Indian Family and Household Organization

Several sixteenth-century sources provide useful information on midcentury population, community, and household composition. Most useful among the published sources are the *Suma de visitas* of 1547–48, the *Libro de tasaciones* covering the period 1531 to 1600, the *Relación del Obispado de Oaxaca* of the 1570s, and the *Relaciones geográficas* of 1579 to 1581.[23] Of these general sources the *Suma de visitas* provides the earliest extensive coverage of the Mixteca Alta, giving limited geographical, demographic, economic, and social data for a number of communities around 1547–48 (see Table 5.1).

The average household (*casa*) size in 1547–48 ranged from 3.2 persons in Teposcolula and Tilantongo to 6 persons in Achiutla and a perplexing 8.6 persons in Yucuañe. Figures for eleven major towns in the Mixteca yield a combined average for the area of 4.84 individuals per household. The addition of the "under three years of age" component would likely place the true average at just over 5 individuals a household. No appreciable differences in household size are noted for cabeceras as opposed to *sujetos*. Nor is there a consistent disparity between large and small communities. The 1547–48 figures suggest that, while some households were composed of nuclear families, at least some also consisted of joint or extended families composed of one or two couples, their children, and various combinations of widowed grandparents and/or unmarried adults.

Although the types of data vary from community to community and from time to time, certain conclusions can be drawn concerning basic Hispano-Indian social, demographic, and settlement patterns that were established by 1550. People resided in compact settlements, as they had in pre-Hispanic times, rather than being dispersed about the countryside in isolated homesteads.[24] There were two types of settlements: a single center with more or less contiguous barrios and a *cabecera-sujeto*, multiple-settlement complex. These patterns remained constant even though by 1550 at least three centers, Nochixtlan, Tamazulapan, and Chachoapan, remained in their elevated aboriginal locations above the sites to which they were relocated between 1550 and 1580. As tempting as it would be to work out exact equivalents between stated numbers and tributaries and population, tribute figures and population, and tributaries and the number of composition of families, this is made difficult by lacunae and inconsistencies in the data, changing administrative policies and practices, and myriad associated problems of interpretation and inference.[25]

A census list dating from 1746 provides useful information on the number of families residing in Mixtec communities in later colonial times (Table 5.2).[26] Although the figures are useful for determining the numbers of Indian and non-Indian families, it is difficult to correlate or compare the 1547–48 and 1746 data since (1) the census criteria (*casas, tributarios,* and population in the *Suma,* as opposed to *familias* in *Theatro Americano*) were different, and (2) community composition was variable, making it difficult to determine whether or not the Apoala, Achiutla, or Teozacoalco of 1547 were structured the same in 1746 or precisely how they differed. Two clear differences are the drastic decrease in the number of families and, therefore, total population and the substantial presence of non-Indian families in the provincial cabeceras and larger communities.

Indian Kinship, Marriage, and Inheritance

Colonial kinship, marriage, and residence patterns varied from class to class, but little change in intra- or interclass relations occurred over the years 1550 to 1820. For native commoners there were continuations of bilateral kinship reckoning and patterns of inheritance, community endogamy, ambilocality in postmarital residence selection, and preference for nuclear or limited extended family household organization.[27]

Males and females divided their property among their heirs. Customarily the surviving spouse received the family residence and most of its furnishings. If there was no surviving spouse, the principal residence might go to either a son or a daughter. Additional structures, farmlands, livestock, and personal property were divided among heirs. Male heirs tended to receive more land and livestock than did females and older offspring more than younger, but practice was variable, and in many instances women received inheritances as large as or larger than those received by men. Often larger, or even principal, benefactors were religious foundations or ministers. "Average" families at the time of transmission of estates included a surviving spouse and three children. The number of additional family members—daughters-in-law, sons-in-law, and grandchildren—depended on such factors as age of the testator, reproductive success, and epidemiological circumstances. Although wills often do not make clear the specific place of residence of various heirs, some wills do provide such information, and this, when coupled with census data, establishes general trends and patterns.

As nearly as can be told from available evidence, *principales* rather closely approximated commoners in kinship reckoning, family organization, and residence. Marriage, however, was marked by greater emphasis on local exogamy, *principales* tending overwhelmingly to select mates from their own class and from communities other than their own.[28] In this respect *principales* stood intermediate between commoners, who tended to marry within their communities, and highest-status caciques, who married within the cacique caste and beyond community and even regional boundaries. Although there is no indication that *principal* families were larger or more complex in their basic organization, inheritance was more selective. Major holdings tended to be left to one heir, normally an oldest son, or to a surviving mate to hold in trust until a child reached maturity. As befitted the *principal* class, normally there was more and better property, and landholdings were more extensively distributed through town and countryside.

In the traditional patterns of inheritance for caciques, estates of parents might be joined and passed on to a single heir as a conjoined—but not combined—estate, or parents' estates might be held separate and passed on to either of two children.[29] In a family with several children, lesser or non-*cacicazgo* land and movable property could be left to children other than the principal heir. Although *cacicazgos* could be joined, individual *cacicazgos* were viewed as impartible. Marriage was a requirement for succession to title, but *cacicazgos* were held individually by the contracting parties. Residence was ambilocal, cacique couples maintaining multiple residences and settling at whichever locality they deemed most advantageous. Although the Spanish administrative and judicial system imposed a male bias on the system of inheritance, women as well as men inherited *cacicazgos* throughout the colonial period. From the mid-sixteenth century to the end of the colonial period, cacicas of such places as Nochixtlan, Tejupan, Tlaxiaco, Achiutla, and Teposcolula were among the wealthiest people in Oaxaca.

Spaniards were more inclined to execute formal wills than were Indians. Large estates were often involved, and litigation frequently lasted for decades. The more than two hundred fifty testamentary cases contained in the Archivo del Juzgado de Teposcolula (AJT) reveal that resident Spanish families normally consisted of a man, his wife, and two or three children. Frequently one or both grandparents and a spinster or widowed sister shared a household with a basic nuclear family.[30] There was a strong tendency for mature children to leave the Mixteca and move to Antequera, Puebla, or Mexico City. Strong kinship, social, and economic ties existed between the Spanish families of the Mixteca and their urban counterparts. Their houses were customarily filled with the silken, gilded, and padded trappings of the city, and the inventories of their *tiendas* indicate an active traffic in European luxuries, most of them well beyond the reach of most Indians. The abundant notarized transactions, the loans, the dowries, the apprenticeships, the partnerships, the obligations, the wills, and the endless civil litigation leave no doubt about the firm tie between town and country. The Spaniard of the Mixteca countryside represented more a socioeconomic appendage of the city than a socially integrated component of Mixtec life.

Inheritance tended to follow an order of preference, with widows or widowers being favored, then older sons, older daughters, younger sons and daughters, the church, and satisfaction of debt. There is sufficient variability in patterns of inheritance, however, to make generalization difficult. Long histories of litigation underscore the variability and ambiguity that not infrequently pitted brother against brother and sister, widow against son or the church, kinfolk against affines. The complex story of Spanish society in the colonial countryside must, however, be deferred to other times and contexts.

Although the native population declined precipitously and more or less continuously between 1540 and the first third of the seventeenth century, no perceptible alteration in settlement patterns or social organization is seen between the 1540s and late colonial times. The basic colonial pattern had been established by 1550, and neither population fluctuations nor economic change appear to have had much effect on settlement, family organization or size, kinship reckoning, marriage, postmarital residence, or intergroup relations. Analysis of nineteenth-century data, in fact, suggests strongly that these patterns persisted through colonial times into the Republican period.[31]

Settlement and Social Class

Mixtec communities served as the stage upon which colonial social life was enacted. The small pueblos and the estancias were socially and economically homogeneous settlements occupied almost exclusively by Indians. A large group of commoners and a very few *principales*—perhaps only a single family—constituted the population of the settlements.

It was in the capital centers, the cabeceras, that social diversification and stratification were most evident. Situated in the central precinct, with its plaza, church, administrative offices, and principal places of business, were the highest-status Indians, the cacique and wealthier *principales*, and upper-status Spanish businessmen and administrators and their families.[32] Attached to each of these households were a few Indian servants and African slaves. The friars usually resided in the church or monastery, but many also owned houses in the central precinct of the larger centers.

Lying just beyond the central precinct was a zone populated by a few Spanish or mestizo tradesmen, artisans, and skilled laborers, and a few Indian *principales*. Here also were Indian commoners of relatively advanced social status. Some were attached to business enterprises in the center; others functioned as mediators or brokers between higher-ranking Indians and Spaniards and the Indian common class.

In the outlying barrios resided the mass of Indian commoners. Some of them were engaged in full-time farming in surrounding fields; others performed services for high-status Spaniards, mestizos, or Indians, or were engaged in the production of textiles, clothing, baskets, candles, wood or metal goods, ceramics, and other consumable goods; still others processed plant and animal resources, or carried on commercial activities. Many commoners made their living by a combination of these pursuits.

The result was a hierarchically structured social system of interdependent socioeconomic status groups serving complementary functions, living together but separated by ethnic differences, custom, and preference. Social groups were integrated by economic necessity, common religious concepts and institutions, and allegiances to a common political system centering on the government of New Spain and the Spanish Empire.

Ethnicity and Social Class

Social differences were clearly related to differences in wealth and access to productive resources. The names of wealthy and influential Spanish families—Arana Barbosa, Andrada, Biuas, Duarte, Herrera, Luna y Arellano, Matías, Pérez, Medina, Rodríguez Franco, and Sánchez Mellado—appear repeatedly in the notarial records from the late sixteenth century to the end of the period.[33] They were involved in countless transactions in land, slaves, livestock, mines, raw and processed goods, loans and mortgages, wills and inventories, requests for special licenses and privileges, and arrangements of dowries. Wills, inventories, and recorded transfers of property found in Teposcolula attest to the great wealth and the extensive economic interests and holdings of many Spanish residents of the Mixteca.[34]

The estates of the sixteenth-century Mixtec caciques of Yanhuitlan, Teposcolula, Tlaxiaco, Nochixtlan, and Tejupan were valued at hundreds of thousands of pesos, as befitted their social station, political power, and economic importance. Although the status of the caciques declined after 1600, they continued to possess great wealth and power to the end of the colonial period. Their wealth in goods, lands, privileges, and services was exceeded by no one, even affluent Spaniards.[35] Between 1665 and 1725, Teposcolula caciques Francisco Pimentel y Guzmán and his son and successor, Agustín Carlos Pimentel Guzmán, controlled vast estates. They held farmlands, grazing lands, houses, and livestock valued at hundreds of thousands of pesos; made large donations to religious foundations; and regularly rented and sold lands. The Mixteca cacique families of Guzmán, Mendoza, Pimentel, Velasco, Villagómez, and Arellano operated with greater or lesser success as native landed gentry from the sixteenth century until the middle to late eighteenth century. Other cacique families, although less wealthy and influential than those mentioned above, were well-to-do in comparison with Indians or less-than-affluent Spaniards and mestizos. About three hundred cases in the [Archivo del Juzgado de Teposcolula, Oaxaca] AJT and many hundreds of cases in the Archivo General de la Nación (AGN) reveal a vast, tangled skein of land and property suits, claims to title, inheritance and succession matters, grants of licenses and privileges, loans, and livestock, and trade and other business enterprises.[36]

Estates of common-class Indians contrast markedly with those belonging to Spaniards and caciques. Examination of many wills in Mixteco and in Spanish in the Teposcolula archive reveal individual holdings, as well as patterns of inheritance among *macehuales*.[37] For example, in 1588, María Sihueyo, a relatively wealthy Indian of the barrio of Yuchaychi, of Yanhuitlan, left an estate of 400 pesos, 70 pesos' worth of clothing, 6 mules valued at 120 pesos, large quantities of yarn and cloth, weavers' tools, kitchen wares, 7 turkeys, 4 chickens, and 3 pieces of land (one containing 130 maguey plants and another containing 10 maguey plants).[38] Her will concludes with the statement, "All of this God saw fit to provide me during the time I was on earth."

Domingo Ramos, of Yucuita, drew up a will in 1710.[39] He left his farmlands to one of his sons. An adobe house, a storage chest with key, a bed, a skirt, a quilt, and a sorrel mare went to his wife. Other lands, cloth, 1,060 green feathers, 40 new green feathers, 21 new Castilian plumes, 83 old Castilian plumes, 20 mares, and some silver were divided among a second son and other relatives. Domingo had more than average possessions. Most Indians left only a jacal, a few furnishings and personal items, a small piece of land, and perhaps an animal or two.

Although common Indians were treated fairly before the law, it is undeniable that their economic circumstances were less than ideal. They did not have the privileges or the level of access to resources enjoyed by *principales*, caciques, and Spaniards. They were caught up in a pervasive system of economic and social inequality that had existed in pre-Hispanic times and persisted through the colonial period into the modern era. But this is a condition not peculiar to the Mixteca, Oaxaca, or Mexico; it exists persistently throughout the world.

Black Slaves

An active traffic in African slaves was carried on in the Mixteca throughout the colonial period. Spanish civilians, merchants, officials, and priests, as well as aristocratic Indians, bought, sold, and held slaves. Slaving activity is well documented in the Teposcolula judicial archive. A sampling of seventy-two transactions in slaves, representing only a fraction of the actual traffic in such "goods," extended from 1563 to 1749.[40] Slaves also figured in dowries and inherited estates.[41] During periods for which surviving notarial records are reasonably complete, four to five transactions a year occurred in Teposcolula. Prices for slaves ranged from 50 pesos to 550 pesos, depending on sex, age, physical condition, and deportment.[42] Priests held, bought, or sold slaves about as frequently as did any other occupational group, but businessmen and owners of large estates held the largest numbers.[43]

Little is known of the daily life of black slaves in the Mixteca. They worked as domestic servants in the houses of wealthy Spaniards in Yanhuitlan and Teposcolula, worked lands and tended flocks held by priests, and tended private, communal, and church livestock herds. There is no evidence in the Mixteca Alta of collectivities beyond procreational families, no record of barrios or settlements of blacks, no record of sociopolitical groups. Slaves were attached to European or aristocratic Indian families as an aggregate of individuals disposable at the whim of the owner.

Africans were more numerous in the lowland areas of the Mixteca de la Costa, in Cuicatlan-Teotitlan, and in other warmer areas, where they were utilized in sugar production. Oaxaca City was a major center for traveling trading, and most blacks in the Mixteca came into the area and left it with traders or owners with primary residence in the city.

Blacks and mulattoes (*mulatos*) were accused and convicted of crimes roughly in proportion to their numbers. Runaway slaves, some from as far away as central Mexico, were often apprehended and returned to their owners. Some were manumitted and given their freedom by their owners, particularly during the mid-eighteenth century.[44] Many former slaves were gradually absorbed into colonial society as *pardos*, or mulattoes. Others were conscripted into the Spanish provincial militia. Still others formed separated barrios or communities, particularly along the Pacific coast of Oaxaca. Many migrated to Veracruz and the Acapulco region.

Interethnic Relations

The colonial social system was characterized by a high level of direct interaction between Indians and Spanish administrators, religious, merchants, traders, miners, encomenderos, travelers, and residents. In addition to the alcaldes mayores, corregidores, *jueces*, scribes, fiscal authorities, and friars who could legitimately reside in at least the large native communities, a very few civilians maintained residence adjacent to the civic-ceremonial centers of larger administrative and commercial capitals, most prominently Yanhuitlan, Teposcolula, Tlaxiaco, and Tamazulapan, in the Alta, and Acatlan and Huajuapan, in the Mixteca Baja. Spanish civilians controlled the distribution of European goods in the region and brokered large quantities of locally produced livestock, wool, silk, cochineal, cotton, and grain.[45] Social status corresponded with economic function. Spanish merchants and clergymen served a vital role in the integration of the native economic system into the international system, and, even from the Indian perspective, they became a necessary component of Mixtec society. The radical extension of native economy and the articulation of local regions and societies into the world system would not have occurred without this mediation.

For the most part, the natives of the Mixteca accepted their status as a massive native majority dominated by an exceptionally small (never more than 10 percent) Spanish minority. Despite this typical colonial institution, the popular conception of the docile, self-effacing, meek Indian cowering before the aggressive, overbearing Spaniard is overdrawn. The Indians were often restive and rebellious, fond of quarreling and of fomenting litigation or refusing to labor on public works or to accept shoddy merchandise and short weight. They were often accused of being troublemakers, of uttering insulting statements to Spaniards, and of cuffing, seriously injuring, or killing Europeans.[46] Many examples can be cited from judicial and administrative records.

In 1583, three Indians from the estancia Santiago of Teposcolula were accused of being rebellious and litigious and were cited for refusing to pay assessments and furnish labor services.[47] In 1649, Juan Pérez and Juan Daniel, alcaldes of Achiutla, were accused of being troublemakers and of stirring up the natives of their community.[48] Early in colonial times the crown forbade Indians and mestizos to carry firearms.[49] In 1597, twenty-nine *arcabuces* and other firearms were confiscated from the caciques of Teposcolula, Tilantongo, Yodocono, Jaltepec, and Tecomastlahuaca, but the alcalde mayor of Teposcolula prudently dropped charges of illegal possession.[50] In 1598 several Indians of Tlaxiaco were convicted of having fomented a major disturbance (*alboroto*) when they forcibly liberated certain prisoners from the Teposcolula jail.[51]

Affronts and recalcitrance by Indians occurred throughout the colonial period, but complaints against Spaniards' abuses were more common.[52] Abuses centered around exploitation of natives for labor and tribute, assault, larceny, misappropriation, cohabitation with Indian women, residence in Indian communities without the required permit, and disturbance of the peace. Spaniards were accused and convicted of sale of wine to Indians, interference in local government, destruction of property, trespass, use of false weights in marketing, adulteration of merchandise sold to Indians, and, more rarely, armed robbery, kidnapping, and murder.

Although the impact of Spanish settlement and policy on the Mixteca was great, traditional patterns of social intercourse among native populations were not seriously altered. What was new was the social confrontation with a politically dominant group of foreigners. Surprisingly, however, the bi-ethnic hierarchical structuring characterizing Spanish-Indian relations in much of Spanish America did not develop to any significant degree in the Mixteca. The persistence of and toleration for many traditional Mixtec sociopolitical institutions, the sparse Spanish population, the desire of Mixtecs to participate in the world economy, and the genuine efforts of the Dominicans and most administrators to protect the rights of Indians and frequently to intervene on their behalf promoted successful interethnic adaptation. A reasonably effective administrative-judicial system also provided a means for airing and resolving conflicts that otherwise might have culminated in violence or in the formation of patterns of pervasive opposition between the two groups.

Both Spaniards and Indians stood to gain far more by cooperation than by divisiveness. Economic and ideological exploitation of the Indians would not have been possible if they were dead, totally alienated, or completely unwilling to cooperate with the Spaniards. By the same token, the rewards of Catholic ritual and doctrine and participation in an extensive commercial network would have been impossible for the Indians without intervention by Spaniards. As a result, serious European-Indian intergroup conflict was avoided. Conflicts developed horizontally between adjoining communities, not hierarchically between socially stratified status groups.

The often idealized peasant revolution was never a feature of Mixtec colonial society. Minor uprisings occurred occasionally, but organized political revolts or social movements did not. The organization and, from all indications, the attitude and motivation were lacking. Nativistic or revitalistic movements known to result from disadvantageous colonialism in other areas of the world did not develop in Mixteca. The need to rise and throw off the yoke of colonialism either was not widely felt or was not effectively articulated by a charismatic native spokesman. By the end of the sixteenth century natives had been integrated into colonial society, and from all indications either were accepting the condition of life or were resigned to their fate.

Table 5.1. Census of the Mixteca Alta, 1547–48

Communities	Population	Tributaries	Households	Barrios	Estancias
Nochixtlan[a]	1,030	—	262	—	—
Tamazulapan[b]	3,320	—	—	—	—
Yucuañe[c]	552	—	64	2	—
Mitlatongo[d]	—	526	388	5	—
Jaltepec[e]	—	2,098	845	6	6
Teposcolula[f]	9,387	—	2,934	6	—
Tilantongo[g]	2,366	—	726	—	5
Tejupan[h]	1,016[i]	—	—	6	—
Teozacoalco[j]	—	1,791	1,010	7	23
Tamazola[k]	605	—	—	—	14
Atoyaquillo[l]	—	30	—	6	—
Etlatongo[m]	642	—	105	—	7
Yanhuitlan[n]	12,207	—	—	—	16
Tiltepec[o]	365	—	72	—	—
Chachoapan[p]	540	—	140	—	—
Apoala[q]	(866)	—	352	—	10
Soyaltepec[r]	1,022	—	223	—	6
Achiutla[s]	2,406	—	402	4	—
Tlaxiaco[t]	4,019[u]	—	913	—	31

[a]*PNE*, 1:163. Unless indicated otherwise, all population figures are for individuals over three years of age.

[b]Ibid., 250.

[c]Ibid., 149–50.

[d]Ibid., 159. *Suma de visitas* figures: 355 tributaries and 256 households in cabecera; 171 tributaries and 132 houses in 5 estancias. Married heads of families counted as full tributaries; widows, widowers, and mature adults (*solteros*) counted as half tributaries.

[e]*PNE*, 1:288. *Suma de visitas* figures: 1,217 tributaries and 606 households in cabecera; 881 tributaries and 339 households in 6 estancias.

[f]*PNE*, 1:248. Population decline in Teposcolula after the mid-1560s is noted in the tribute assessments. In 1564 there were 6,833 tributaries; in 1568, 5,026; in 1571, 4,500; in 1603, 2,448. *Libro de tasaciones*, 354–56; *Relación del Obispado de Oaxaca*, 64; AGN, *Libro de congregaciones*, 50r–53v.

[g]*PNE*, 1:249.

[h]Ibid., 249.

[i]Ibid., 4:56. The *Relación geográfica* states that the pueblo held around 12,000 at the time of the conquest. Archaeological data and simple logic compel the conclusion that such

a figure is a gross distortion, a mistake, or a misprint. "Dos mil indios arriba" is far closer to reality than "doze mill."

ʲ*PNE*, 1:283–84. *Suma de visitas* figures: 608 tributaries, 346 households in cabecera; 1,183 tributaries and 670 households in 23 estancias.

ᵏ*PNE*, 1:284. By 1569 epidemic had reduced the number of tributaries to 301. *Libro de tasaciones*, 327–28.

ˡ*PNE*, 1:50.

ᵐIbid., 107.

ⁿIbid., 131. It is assumed that, since the names of *sujetos* (e.g., Yucuita, Tillo, Añañe, Sayultepec, Suchixtlan, Andua, and Sinaxtla) are not mentioned elsewhere in the *Suma de visitas*, the stated population included both the cabecera and the subject estancias.

ᵒ*PNE*, 1:249.

ᵖIbid., 75–76.

ᑫIbid., 49–50. *Suma de visitas* figures include Apazco and Xocotiquipaque. In all, there were 352 houses with 709 *casados*, 314 *solteros*, and 537 *niños*.

ʳ*PNE*, 1:75.

ˢIbid., 31.

ᵗIbid., 282–83. *Suma de visitas* figures: 1,852 hombres, 1,356 married women, 433 girls, and 379 boys twelve years and older. Four of eight clusters of Tlaxiaco estancias had 4.67, 4.95, 5.81, and 6 persons per household. There were 2.15 tributaries per household in three clusters and one tributary for every 2.2 persons.

ᵘ*Relación del Obispado de Oaxaca*, 64. For 1565–1570 the figure 4,500 tributaries is given for Tlaxiaco and its subject settlements (including Chicahuaxtla, Cuquila, Ocotopec, and so on).

Table 5.2. Family Census, Mixteca Alta, 1746

Community	Indian Families	Non-Indian Families
Yanhuitlan	900	35
Teposcolula	717	160
Tlaxiaco	888	104
Tamazulapan	270	(10)
Tejupan	192	(5)
Coixtlahuaca	604	(5)
San Miguel Guautla	78	—
Atoyac	29	—
San Juan Teposcolula	98	—
Ocotepec	216	—
Chicahuaxtla	342	—
Tlaltepec	64	—
Cuquila	76	—
Yolotepec	254	—
Petlaztlahuaca	184	—

San Juan Atoyaquillo	70	—
Atlatlauca	108	—
Chalcatongo	610	—
Tecaltitlan	66	—
Copala	104	—
San Andrés de los Reyes	76	—
Santa Cruz Yuunduza	116	—
Monte León	52	—
Chilapa	128	—
San Miguel Achiutla	260	—
Yucuañe (Malinaltepec)	116	—
Tulancingo	96	—
San Mateo del Peñasco	600	—
Teotongo	74	—
Xipacoya	55	—
Tonacatepec	16	—
Jaltepetongo	39	—
Santiago Ixtatepec	35	—
San Pedro Topiltepec	104	—
Tillo	180	—
Apoala	58	—
Soyaltepec	64	—
Tequicistepec	88	—
San Miguel Chicahua	48	—
San Mateo Coyotepec	22	—
Nochixtlan	134	30
Santa Cruz Mitlatongo	58	—
Jaltepec	112	—
Santiago Mitlatongo	8	—
Tilantongo	102	—
Etlantongo	75	—
Guautla	58	—
Tejutepec	15	—
Tiltepec	109	—
Tamazola	78	—
Chachoapan	68	—
Ixquintepec Peñoles	50	12
San Juan Elotepec	284	—
Santa María Huitepec	80	—

Santiago Huajolotipac	10	—
Santa Catarina Estetla	34	—
Tlazoyaltepec	72	—
San Pedro Chilapa	30	—
San Mateo Tepantepec	66	—
San Pedro Totomachapa	44	—
Teozacoalco	285	12
Teoxomulco	150	—
Amoltepec	96	—
Ixtalutla	48	—
Tezontepec	180	—

Source: Figures are derived from *Theatro Americano* (Madrid, 1960–61), 128–36, 142–43, 169–71, 173–74. Parenthetical figures for non-Indians are approximations based on such statements as "algunas familias de Españoles y Mestizos" (Tejupan), or on documentation in AJT relating to Spanish families in Tamazulapan, Coixtlahuaca, and Tejupan.

Notes

Abbreviations for works frequently cited:

AGN Archivo General de la Nación, Mexico City.
AJT Archivo del Juzgado de Teposcolula, Oaxaca.
ASNV Ronald Spores, *An Archaeological Settlement Survey of the Nochixtlan Valley, Oaxaca*.
IAJT María de los Angeles Romero and Ronald Spores, *Indice del Archivo del Juzgado de Teposcolula, Oaxaca*.
IRI Ronald Spores and Miguel Saldaña, *Documentos para la Etnohistoria del Estado de Oaxaca: Indice del Ramo de Indios, Archivo General de la Nación México*.
IRM Ronald Spores and Miguel Saldaña, *Documentos para la Etnohistoria del Estado de Oaxaca: Indice del Ramo de Mercedes, Archivo General de la Nación, Mexico*.
PNE Francisco del Paso y Troncoso, ed., *Papeles de la Nueva España*.
RMEH *Revista Mexicana de Estudios Históricos*.

 1. Peter Gerhard, *A Guide to the Historical Geography of New Spain* (Cambridge, 1972), 285.
 2. Ibid., 200–201, 285–86.
 3. Ibid., 201, 276, 286.
 4. Ibid., 201–202, 286–87.

5. Ibid., 199–203, 275–77, 283–90.
6. Ibid., 201, 276, 286.
7. Ibid., 286. The communities included Achiutla, Amoltepec, Atoyaquillo, Cenzontepec, Yucuañe, Mitlantongo, Mixtepec, Yodocono, Tamazola, Tamazulapan, Teozacoalco, Teposcolula, Tejupan, Tezoatlan, Tilantongo, Tlaxiaco, Tutla, and Yolotepec.
8. Gerhard, *Guide*, 201, 286. Other communities were Chachoapan, Etlatongo, Tiltepec, Jaltepec, Coixtlahuaca, Chicahua, Iztactepec, Guantla, Tequecistepec, Jaltepetongo, and Jocotipac.
9. Gerhard, *Guide*, 276.
10. This is at variance with the account of Gerhard (*Guide*, 286). Abundant documentation contained in the AJT leaves no doubt about the aggregation of the two *alcaldías mayores* in the mid-1590s. To date, no specific order for the aggregation has been found, and no precise date can be assigned to the event.
11. Gerhard, *Guide*, 201.
12. Ibid., 276. The *alcaldías mayores* of Teposcolula-Yanhuitlan, Nochixtlan, and Teozacoalco-Tecuicuilco remained intact when they were converted in 1786–87 into *subdelegaciones* of the intendancy of Oaxaca.
13. See detailed family census figures in Table 5.2, *Theatro Americano* (Madrid, 1960–61), 128–36, 171–73.
14. Ibid., 169–71.
15. Ibid., 142–43.
16. Ibid., 173–74.
17. Ronald Spores, *The Mixtec Kings and Their People* (Norman, 1967), 100–188; Heinrich Berlin, *Fragmentos desconocidos del Códice de Yanhuitlán* (Mexico City, 1947), 39–41.
18. *IAJT*, 272–87.
19. Ibid., 271–72 ("Argravios" "Averiguaciones"), 277–78 ("Conflictos *entre individuos*").
20. María de los Angeles Romero, "Los intereses españoles en la Mixteca—siglo XVII," *Historia mexicana* 29, no. 2 (1979), 241–61.
21. *IAJT*, index nos. 18, 81, 98, 336, 375, 447, 532, 590.
22. Ibid., index. nos. 375, 532.
23. *PNE*, vols. 1, 4; *El Libro de las tasaciones de pueblos de la Nueva España siglo XVI*; Luis García Pimentel, ed., *Relación de los Obispados de Tlaxcala, Michoacan, Oaxaca y otros lugares en el siglo XVI* (Mexico City, 1904) ; *RMEH*, vols. 1–2; Ignacio Bernal, "Relación de Guautla," *Tlalocan* 4, no. 1 (1962), 3–16.
24. *ASNV*, 187–94.
25. Procedures for, and problems arising from, document-based demographic research are considered in detail in the many referenced works of Woodrow Borah and S. F. Cook. See also William M. Denevan, ed., *The Native Population of the Americas in 1492* (Madison, WI, 1976); Spores, *The Mixtec Kings*, 70–75.
26. *Theatro Americano*.
27. The section relating to Indians is based heavily on about fifty Indian wills contained in AJT, including AJT 25, exps. 1–10, 26; 37, exps. 31, 78, 91; 42, exps. 2, 6, 7, 14.
28. Ronald Spores, "The Zapotec and Mixtec at Spanish Contact," *Handbook of Middle American Indians*, edited by Robert Wauchope and Gordon R. Willey, q.v.
29. Spores, *The Mixtec Kings*, 131–54; Spores, "Marital Alliance in the Political Integration of Mixtec Kingdoms," *American Anthropologist* 76 (1974), 297–311.

30. *IAJT*, 285 ("Testamentos").

31. Ronald Spores, "Multi-Level Government in Nineteenth-Century Oaxaca," in Ronald Spores and Ross Hassig, eds., *Law and Government in Central Mexico: Pre-Columbian Times to the Present*, Vanderbilt University Publication in Anthropology, no. 30 (1984).

32. The disposition of various social classes within the major centers is based on exhaustive search of deeds, bills of sale, transfers, wills, and inventories contained in AJT. See *IAJT*, 274–76 ("Cartas de obligación," "De venta," "De poder," "Arrendamiento y venta de casas"), 285 ("Testamentos").

33. *IAJT*, index nos. 227, 229, 234, 239, 242, 243, 251, 253.

34. Ibid., 274–76, 285; Romero, "Los intereses españoles." Typical eighteenth-century estates left by Spaniards are as follows: Josef Mariano de Yta Salazar, 64,000 pesos; Pedro de Valdenebro y Robles, former alcalde mayor of Teposcolula-Yanhuitlan, 57,652 pesos; Alonso Ruiz Raquel, 78,850 pesos; Luis Cepeda, merchant and resident of Yanhuitlan, 180,677 pesos. AJT 52, exps. 2, 3, 39, 46; AJT 50, exp. 39. Others had more, but still others died insolvent and deep in debt.

35. *IAJT*, 249, 273–74 ("Caciques," "Cacicazgos"), 274–76, 285; AJT 7, exp. 2; AJT 34, exp. 18, fols. 4–5, 21–22; AJT 40, exp. 2; Spores, *The Mixtec Kings*, 155–72, 189–93, 241–44; AGN Tierras 24, exp. 1; AGN Tierras 34, exp. 2; AGN Tierras 400, exp. 1; AGN Tierras 985–86; AGN Civil 516; Fray Francisco de Burgoa, *Geográfica descripción*, 2 vols. (Mexico City, 1934).

36. *IAJT*, 273–74.

37. AJT 50, exp. 50.

38. AJT 32, exp. 15.

39. AJT 30, exp. 7.

40. See *IAJT*, 297, for reference to ninety-one cases involving black slaves in the Mixteca.

41. AJT 29, exp. 23.

42. Exemplary cases: A healthy eighteen-year-old youth was sold for 300 pesos in 1563 (AJT 2, exp. 3); a twenty-three-year-old male married to a free mulata, 500 pesos in 1589 (AJT 30, exp. 1, fol. 23); a healthy ten-year-old boy, 200 pesos in 1589 (AJT 34, exp 18, fols. 13–14); a healthy mature male, 200 pesos in 1603 (AJT 11, exp. 4, fol. 22); a healthy young female, 400 pesos in 1603 (ibid., exp. 4, fol. 44). In 1596, Hernando de Salas, *alguacil mayor* of Antequera, sold a thirty-three-year-old male to Tristán de Luna y Arellano, alcalde mayor of Teposcolula, for 500 pesos. The description on the bill of sale read ". . . a negro slave between *boca* and *ladino* [semiacculturated] called Sebastián from the land of Biafra, thirty years of age, which I sell you [with the assurance that] he is neither a drunk nor a thief, nor a runaway, nor does he have any fault of infirmity, public or concealed, for the price and quantity of five hundred gold pesos" (AJT 29, exp. 4). Also in 1596, Pedro Hernández sold Don Tristán a black woman, Dominga, *"muy ladina,"* twenty-two years of age, for 550 pesos (AJT 26, exp. 34).

43. Surviving records in AJT include nine transaction involving priests during the period 1634 to 1732 (*IAJT*, index nos. 729, 1189, 1297, 1541, 2018, 2145, 2208, 2360, 2632) or approximately 12.5 percent of the total of seventy-two transactions known from Teposcolula for the period 1563 to 1749. Captain Don Joseph de Veytia, a wealthy merchant of Teposcolula, held seven slaves at the time of his death in 1758. (AJT 27, exp. 1).

44. AJT 12, exp. 13; *IAJT*, index nos. 245, 2171, 2350, 2401, 2786.

45. *IAJT*, 273 ("Bienes"), 274–76 ("Cartas . . . ," "Comerciantes y mercaderes"), 285 ("Testamentos," "Tiendas").

46. See, for example, AJT 34, exp. 3.

47. AJT 1, exp. 7.

48. AJT 34, exp. 4.

49. AGN Mercedes 8, fol. 122; *IRM*, no. 956.

50. AJT 1, exp. 46.

51. AJT 4, exps. 52, 57.

52. See *IRM*, 275 ("Agravios, daños y vejaciones"); *IRI*, 319 ("Agravios, abusos, daños, o vejaciones"); *IAJT*, 272 ("Agravios, alborotos"), 277 ("Conflictos entre individuos"); AGN Indios 6, pt. 1, exp. 220; AGN Indios 6, pt. 2, exp. 246; AGN Indios 4, exp. 339; AGN General de Parte 2, exps. 133, 1337.

6

Patterns and Variety in Mexican Village Uprisings

William B. Taylor

In recent years, scholars have become increasingly aware of the commonality of local uprisings in the rural zones of Mesoamerica and the Andes. Contradicting the long-prevailing view of stolid Indian acquiescence to European domination, numerous studies now demonstrate that recurrent resistance to attempts to modify their accepted patterns characterized many native communities throughout Latin America. In certain cases, these local resistance efforts even took the offensive, seeking to regain lands previously alienated or uniting in regional revolts.

In this selection, William Taylor examines both the recurrent patterns in and the internal dynamics of a number of revolts that took place in important regions in late colonial Mexico. His analysis of these uprisings tells us a great deal about the composition of and relationships within the rural villages that participated.

Uprisings have been a popular topic in the study of lower-class life and change in the Latin American countryside. Modern historiography of rural uprisings goes back to the works of nineteenth-century local historians, who used examples of rural violence to inform a literate urban readership of the barbarousness of peasants and vagabonds, and to warn of the horrors awaiting Latin America's pockets of "civilized" city life. The 1920s brought a new surge of interest in the history of rural revolts in Mexico. Studies undertaken then were designed to document a tradition of peasant uprising against injustice that could presage and give added meaning to the great upheaval in Mexico from 1910 to 1920. More recently, Latin American and foreign scholars have been much interested in the study of such major insurrections as the Tupac Amaru rebellion in late-eighteenth-century Peru, the Tzeltal revolt in Chiapas in 1712, the Indian wars of northern Mexico in the eighteenth and nineteenth centuries, and the participation of rural people in national upheavals such as the independence wars of the early nineteenth century. Sociologists and anthropologists as well as historians have shown increasing interest in the history of rural violence as a touchstone to demonstrate and explain the revolutionary potential of the rural segment of modern Latin American countries.[1]

Despite obvious differences, the forebodings of the nineteenth-century local historians, the teleologically inspired studies of the 1920s, and the more analytical, detached research of modern social scientists share a common focus: insurrections or regional revolts, in which whole zones of rural people band together in a violent assault on state authority and privileged classes. In setting out to discuss rural uprisings in colonial Oaxaca and central Mexico, I am not primarily concerned with major insurrections of this sort for the good reason that there were precious few of them. To be sure, plans for insurrection were rumored in both areas, and a few short-lived regional uprisings occurred in the jurisdictions of Tulancingo, Actopan, and Metepec, along with a number of simultaneous uprisings in villages within the same region. But there was nothing comparable to the eighteenth-century Andean insurrections or, closer to home, the regional movements in Chiapas in 1712, in the Sierra Zapoteca of Oaxaca in 1660 and 1696, and in Yucatán during the 1840s and 1850s.

That regional revolts were isolated and infrequent in Oaxaca and central Mexico does not mean that the countryside was at peace with the demands and abuses of Spanish rule, "the peace of the grave" as José Vasconcelos once put it. Nor does it mean that colonial villagers were fatalistic, long-suffering people who were content to leave their fate to God ("sea por Dios") or the *patrón*, rarely taking the law into their own hands. In fact, a great deal of collective violence erupted at the community level.

The numerous violent village outbursts, or local rebellions, are the main subject of this chapter. The distinction between "rebellion" and "insurrection" is crucial to understanding the kind of collective acts described here. Both are violent political acts, but rebellions are localized mass attacks, generally limited to restoring a customary equilibrium. They do not offer new ideas or a vision of a new society. Insurrections, on the other hand, are regional in scope, constitute part of a broader political struggle between various segments of society, and aim at a reorganization of relationships between communities and powerful outsiders.[2] This distinction between rebellion and insurrection may not always be so clear in practice—simultaneous rebellions in a number of villages could have the same consequences as an insurrection—but nearly all of the examples located in my search for rural uprisings qualify as rebellions.

The evidence is a series of 142 judicial investigations of communities in revolt between 1680 and 1811. Of these cases, 91 are from the districts of central Mexico used in this study, 19 from the Mixteca Alta, and the remaining 32 from the Valley of Oaxaca. Rebellions and insurrections of earlier periods and in areas on the fringes of our central and southern Mexican regions are included only when they suggest new developments or shed light on main points. I have grouped my questions about these uprisings into two main sections. First, speaking generally, what happened? How did the movements begin, who participated in them, what did the rebels do and say, how long did the uprisings last, and how did they end? Second, what were the causes and the results of these village rebellions? I should emphasize that I am interested primarily in identifying general patterns. Individual uprisings are discussed when they illustrate a general point especially well or provide a striking exception. Most of the evidence and specific illustrations, however, will be found in the notes.

Peasants in Revolt: General Characteristics

Eighteenth-century rebellions were not random or limitless in variety. They reveal quite a definite structure and sequence of development. Most of the village uprisings in central Mexico, the Mixteca Alta, and the Valley of Oaxaca were alike in repertory of actions, instruments, and dramatis personae. Some features are especially striking. Nearly all were spontaneous, short-lived armed outbursts by members of a single community in reaction to threats from outside; they were "popular" uprisings in which virtually the entire community acted collectively and usually without identifiable leadership. The rebellions were highly aggressive but significantly patterned acts, punctuated by open insults, threat, attacks, and a general release of high emotion; most were directed against agents of the state and local buildings that symbolized outside authority. The rebellious behavior was controlled in the sense that there were few examples of general destruction and pillaging.

The spontaneous, collective quality of these village uprisings is repeated time and again throughout the eighteenth century. At a commonly understood signal, usually the ringing of the church bells or the sounding of a trumpet or drum, the townspeople assembled with whatever weapons were at hand.[3] The weapons—household tools, farm implements, sticks, and rocks—generally confirm the spontaneous eruption of the violence. These humble tools provided variety enough: pickaxes, hatchets, machetes, cattle bones, hoes, iron bars, clubs, cudgels, chains, sharp-tipped spindles, knives, burning sticks of pitch pine, lances, and a unique indigenous weapon, powdered chile peppers, used to blind and immobilize the enemy temporarily. Uprisings that lasted for more than a few hours usually brought into play more specialized weapons, such as bows and arrows, sabers, spears, javelins, and horses. Infrequently, eyewitnesses mention firearms. Only three cases of an old blunderbuss or flintlock pistol being used by villagers are recorded among the 142 risings. This would suggest that firearms were rarely to be found in rural villages, whether because the colonial prohibitions against Indian ownership were rigorously enforced or because villagers could rarely afford to acquire them. Rocks, thrown by hand or hurled with slings, usually were the most damaging weapon used by villagers in revolt. In cases of serious harm to persons and property, the victims frequently spoke of "a deluge of stones" or "a shower of rocks" descending upon them.

Virtually the entire community turned out for local rebellions.[4] Militiamen called in by the Spanish authorities were likely to encounter nasty mobs of hundreds of women brandishing spears and kitchen knives or cradling rocks in their skirts, and young children and old people carrying or throwing whatever they could manage, as well as better-armed groups of adult men. "The whole community" and "multitudes" of armed villagers of all ages are descriptions constantly repeated in the reports and testimony. The place of women is especially striking. Perhaps because men were more often traveling outside the community or working fields several miles from town, more women than men usually took part. In at least one-fourth of the cases, women led the attacks and were visibly more aggressive, insulting, and rebellious in their behavior toward outside authorities.

In 1719, Mariana, a tall scar-faced Indian of Santa Lucía near the city of Oaxaca, led a mob of men and women against a group of royal officials, priests, and militiamen who had come to mark the town's boundaries. After cutting the measuring rope, she took on one of the Spaniards in a hand-to-hand struggle, held up a bleeding arm to spur on her compatriots, and led the rock-throwing barrage that drove the outsiders back to the city.[5] Scenes like this have been repeated often, not just in the eighteenth century, but well into contemporary times. This open, sometimes leading role of women in the Oaxaca and central Mexico rebellions contrasts with the accounts of uprisings and Indian wars in northern Mexico, which consistently refer to adult men doing the fighting. Perhaps the difference stems from clearly defined male specialization in hunting and the use of weapons in the less sedentary native societies of the borderlands and the more active participation of women in the complex social relationships of sedentary peasant villages in central and southern Mexico.

The question of leadership in village uprisings is difficult to document. Colonial authorities were inclined to assume premeditation and leadership by a few local troublemakers, but the evidence from trials and investigations does not lend strong support to this assumption. Alcaldes mayores and higher judges usually were determined to find "*cabecillas*," people who led or incited others and who were singled out for punishment as examples to the rest of the community. This was a convenient way of demonstrating the firm hand of Spanish justice without encouraging the whole community to desert for fear of punishment, but I suspect that colonial Spaniards, whether Creoles or *peninsulares*, could not conceive of a political movement that did not have a leader who planned and directed it.

In spite of the assumption that movements require leaders and of the political advantages of exemplary punishment, surprisingly few of the trial records for community uprisings provide clear evidence of planned leadership. In the formal trials village rebels, in order to escape punishment themselves, sometimes willingly testified against a few of their compatriots in response to leading questions from the prosecutor. Still, of the 142 cases, only 20 offer clear evidence against one or a small group of peasant leaders (usually the village governor and other members of the hereditary nobility). Parish priests led five attacks; five more—all from central Mexico—were inspired by resident non-Indians; and in another twenty cases prosecutors alleged individual leadership but were consistently contradicted by peasant witnesses who insisted that the violence was not organized ahead of time by local leaders. The choice of everyday objects for weapons, the timing of uprisings when some adult men were away, and a lack of clustering by season, festive calendar, or days of the week lend additional weight to the conclusion that these outbursts were generally unplanned.[6]

The behavior of villagers in revolt belies the image widely held by scholars of docile, or "*encogido*," Indian peasants who were too attached to servitude and too alienated from society at any level to take up arms for social reasons. Thunderous shouts, whistles, obscene, mocking insults, and impudent gestures, often accompanied by the beat of a drum or the sour notes of an old trumpet, were standard accompaniments to the rebellions. Role reversal was another distinguishing mark. Village rebels could assume the arrogant manners of their colonial masters. Especially in central Mexico, peasant rebels insulted district officials in the same terms that Spaniards had heaped upon them—"dog," "nigger," and "pig." Priests and alcaldes mayores were forced to humble themselves before the village elders. Outside our regions there are examples of peasants forcing local Spaniards to hear pagan services and making Spanish women marry Indian men with the blessing of native priests.[7] Generally, such changes in roles parallel Octavio Paz's description of Mexican fiestas—an explosive suspension of everyday rules and privileges when the poor could dress like the rich and men like women, without fear of censure. The fiesta, according to Paz, is a kind of symbolic revolution, but as a symbolic act it replaces or exhausts the commitment to overturn the social circumstances that resume at the end of the fiesta. The rebellion is not identical in its result, for it is a political action more than a therapeutic expression of conflict that usually did not return the community to exactly the same position afterward. On the other hand, community rebellions usually did exhaust themselves without spreading their feelings of outrage to other communities and without creating an unflinching opposition to colonial rule. After initial success in driving out the enemy, the rebellions occasionally turned into festive celebrations with music, dancing, singing, and general "*alegría*" replacing the howls of anger.

Although the rebellions seem to have been unplanned and accompanied by a spontaneous and noisy release of emotions, there is pattern and direction in the way the outbursts were played out. Certain landmarks in the village were starting points for organized violence; other places were the usual targets at which the violence was aimed. The village church was usually at the heart of the action. The townspeople often gathered in the churchyard cemetery to hear the news before moving on the enemy. Since rebellions were directed against outside authority including the priesthood, it seems paradoxical that the church, the religious arm of the colonial state, should provide a symbolic dwelling place, a home base from which to assert the community's power. The answer, I think, is that Christianity occupied an ambiguous but very important place in the adjustment of Indian villages to Spanish rule. The church, in pursuing its own purposes—conversion, enrichment, and ministry to the souls of Indian neophytes—nurtured communal responsibilities through *cofradías* and new rituals.[8] Although not always displacing local popular beliefs, Christianity reinforced an Indian inclination to communal organization. The parish priest might be hated and ridiculed by villagers, but the church and its grounds were sacred places, connecting the past to the present and future.[9] Colonial parish churches often were built on the holy places of pre-Hispanic gods, sometimes with the very stones of ancient temples. Village churches were impressive in size and by the eighteenth century venerable in age, many of those in our two regions having been constructed in the sixteenth century. Their grounds often enclosed the cemetery, which further connected the community to its past. The atrium, or courtyard, facing the church (usually walled) was a sanctuary of trees and shade and a meeting place for community business, public ceremonies, and *cofradía* activities—a living arena of community decision making and collective activity.

Few of the rebellions turned into general looting and burning. On the contrary, the violence was almost always focused on a particular person or place. The object of attack typically was a colonial official or a building identified with outside authority, usually the *casas reales* (government offices) or the jail. The jail was the most frequent inanimate victim of the people's wrath, villagers descending upon it to release a native son or daughter and then set it aflame. It was the most concrete and hated symbol of the rule of alien law. As one thoughtful Oaxacan priest tells us, "Because the Indians grow up in the open fields, they view imprisonment as a fate worse than death."[10] Human objects of community violence were local agents of the state: usually the alcalde mayor or his deputy assigned to the town (26 percent); sometimes the parish priest (22 percent) or officials who attempted to collect an unpopular or increased duty (20 percent); and occasionally the schoolmaster (3 percent). If the victims were not state officials, they were likely to be citizens from a rural town, or from the political head town or a subject town, and sometimes abusive native officials or local rivals in a factional dispute.

Restriction of violent action to specific targets was not accompanied by restraints on the intensity of the violence itself. Although most of the armed uprisings were short-lived they were more than just symbolic gestures. Weapons were used to expel the offending parties. Killings and serious injuries were often the result. In at least eighteen cases colonial officials, militiamen, and other outsiders were killed.[11] In many other cases the enemies were seriously injured or fled just in time to escape alive. In one case an alcalde mayor saved his own life by hiding in a roll-up mat in a dark corner of the *casas reales*.[12] Priests seem to have been the one group that was attacked but rarely injured. Unlike their martyred brothers in the northern borderlands or Chiapas and Yucatán during the regional insurrection, priests in central Mexico and Oaxaca were menaced and sometimes injured by flying rocks, but none were killed.

The violence was not often sustained for long. Unless militia forces were sent in, the attacks usually ended in a day or two, although short bursts of collective violence seem to have occurred sporadically in some villages over long periods of time.[13] Occasionally, the local priest or the alcalde mayor persuaded the villagers to lay down their arms, identify the *cabecillas*, and negotiate a settlement. Since priests are often considered to have had great moral suasion in their parishes, it should be noted that the voices of spiritual reason and moral authority counted for little in subduing these village outbursts. There are many more cases of priests shoved aside with cross in hand and words rebuffed than cases of priests swaying the angry mob in the heat of battle. A few rebellions were quelled in midcourse when the crowds were dispersed with firearms, and in one case an alert militiaman halted a rising by cutting the bell ropes.[14] But most village rebellions simply burned themselves out without much interference from the colonial authorities. The violence usually ended with the villagers achieving their immediate goal of driving off the intruders, releasing their fellow townsmen from jail, or extracting a promise from the colonial authorities that their grievances would be acted upon. Especially if the rebellion had resulted in killings or serious injuries, the attackers, and sometimes the entire community, abandoned the town site for refuge in the mountains. Depending on the season, the town might be vacated for several months, but such an exodus rarely led to permanent desertion. Village representatives were usually quick to complain to judicial authorities in the provincial capital and enter into litigation for a formal settlement.

The Spanish response to community uprisings in central and southern Mexico, a calculated blend of punishment and mercy, generally followed the principle of "pacification without destroying the Indians." Since the colonial militias were small and often ill equipped to subdue peasants in revolt, and since the surplus produced by villagers in the form of taxes and labor drafts was an important source of revenue for the crown, or as an Oaxacan priest put it, "La tilma del indio a todos cubre" (the Indian's cloak covers us all), colonial leaders were anxious to end revolts by negotiation and especially to prevent them from spreading. The Spaniards' fear of regional insurrection was apparently quite real. It was common for officials to think of rural uprisings in terms of dread diseases such as epidemic "contagion," "cancer," and festering wounds that would spread and consume the body politic. Such fear was strong in the minds of Mexican officials after the widespread uprisings in southern Peru and Bolivia in the early 1780s. A 1781 rebellion at Izúcar de Matamoros evoked fear of another Tupac Amaru uprising; and late colonial rebellions north of Mexico City made royal officials take precautions against spread to the "wild" Chichimec and Huaxtec Indians.[15] As long as the violence had not spread to neighboring communities, colonial magistrates were inclined to conciliatory verdicts in which village loyalty to the Crown was reaffirmed. Generally, a few local rebels were singled out by the judge as leading troublemakers subject to exemplary punishment (whippings, labor service, exile, and occasionally execution), whereas the community at large received a pardon, tempered with a threat of harsh punishment for future violence.

Sentences for presumed leaders of village revolts in central and southern Mexico ranged from the indignity and pain of the lash to fines, exile from the district (usually for two to six years), and penal servitude. The last, which was quite common in eighteenth-century sentences, took the form of service in an *obraje* for one to six years, in a presidio for up to ten years, or on public works projects for shorter periods. In one extraordinary case the judge ingeniously combined penal service with the improvement of local security by sentencing the leaders to construct a sturdy jail and to clear one league of land surrounding the town in order to destroy the rebels' easy refuge.[16] Fines had the same effect as a sentence to hard labor. Since peasants were rarely able to pay in cash, their fines were often paid by employers who were allowed to claim the labor of the convict up to the value of the fine. The harshest sentences were reserved for individuals who had escaped arrest and were sentenced in absentia. In most cases of conviction the leaders were released before the sentence to service had been completed or were pardoned with a threat of severe punishment if they were involved in an uprising again.[17] Capital punishment or long periods of penal servitude were more common in the rare eighteenth-century regional insurrections, such as the Tzeltal revolt of 1712. Captives taken by the Spaniards in the chronic warfare with Indians in the northern borderlands were most likely to be executed or shipped south as slaves.[18]

Except for an occasional fine and a stern warning, the community as a whole was unlikely to be punished, even in cases where death or serious injuries were inflicted. The murder of a hacienda overseer by the people of Macuilxóchitl (Valley of Oaxaca) in the 1740s can serve as an example. Macuilxóchitl's bitter land dispute with a hacienda of the Bethlemite order had escalated into regular raids against the estate and retaliatory whippings by the overseer. The overseer eventually blundered into the village to vent his anger and was immediately seized by a large group of townspeople and taken to the *casa de comunidad* for trial. With the entire community vociferously present, the elders pronounced the death sentence, and the unfortunate Spaniard was hurried off to the town plaza and hanged. Several elders were arrested, but in the course of the gathering evidence it became clear to the Audiencia that the entire community had passed judgment and carried out the sentence. Without individual culprits the court was at a loss. It exacted a pledge of loyalty from the town and ordered a stone gallows to be erected in the plaza as a permanent symbol of the punishment the community deserved for its crime.[19]

One major exception to this flexible, almost lenient pattern of sentencing was the verdicts handed down by Visitador José de Gálvez following the local rebellions in Michoacán and San Luis Potosí during 1767 to 1769. In the 1767 rebellions, which coincided with the expulsion of the Jesuits from New Spain, the colonial authority's response was swift and severe: in San Nicolás (jurisdiction of San Luis Potosí), eleven Indians were executed, the town secretary's right hand was cut off, and the village was deprived of its political rights; in El Venado (jurisdiction of San Luis Potosí), twelve Indians were executed, seven received two hundred lashes, seventy-two were exiled, and the community lost its usufruct rights to public lands; in San Francisco (jurisdiction of San Luis Potosí), eight were executed, two were whipped, seven were sentenced to life imprisonment, and twenty-six received limited prison sentences; in Pátzcuaro (jurisdiction of Michoacán), two Indians were executed, twenty received life sentences, twenty-four were subjected to two hundred lashes, and twenty-nine were exiled. In uniquely cruel fashion, these sentences amounted to punishment for the sake of punishment as the unbending response of a leading *peninsular* reformer who had little understanding of the delicate divide-and-rule policies that had governed the Mexican countryside for two centuries. Two years later, when a major uprising occurred at San Sebastián Agua del Venado in the jurisdiction of San Luis Potosí, the sentence was again exceptionally severe, but it followed the standard pattern of penal servitude: all three hundred Indian men arrested were sent to presidios for varying periods of service, and eleven received heavy fines—fifty pesos for ten of them, and five hundred pesos for the principal leader, which effectively meant that he would spend the rest of his life in servitude.[20]

Although the Spanish reaction to communities in revolt was usually restrained, it did not mean that the colonial authorities sympathized with or respected the peasants' reasons for resorting to arms. Little of the utopian good will that was an important strand of Spanish motivation in the sixteenth century was evident in these eighteenth-century investigations, even among the clergymen who appeared as witnesses. Occasionally, a hostile outburst was forgiven as overexuberance on a festive occasion or the product of a legitimate grievance, but official explanations of the risings usually seized on solemn abstractions and innate personality traits of Indian peasants, such as their lazy, ignorant, uncouth, vice-ridden, insolent, rebellious nature or their uncivilized way of life, "lacking God, Law, and King."[21] When the colonial officials got down to specifics, they condemned especially the village traditions of government "in which everyone rules." In trying to discover the cause of a major rebellion in Zimatlán (Valley of Oaxaca) in 1772, the parish priest concluded that it resulted from the Indians' "wicked" style of government. Drawing a parallel to Spain's archrival England, he warned that continual uprisings could be expected in Indian villages because "everyone rules," including women and children.[22] Consensus decision making in peasant villages received little sympathy from Spaniards, imbued with the idea of a natural order based on highly stratified hierarchies. Occasionally, colonial authorities saw the root of rebellion in the bad example of a neighboring town or in excessive drinking. In one case we can look beyond the rather restrained language of the Spanish magistrates and find a local Spaniard's feelings about Indian villagers in the wake of a rebellion. The evidence comes in the form of an anonymous note tacked to the door of the magistrate of Tlamatlán, who was investigating the uprising of two small villages against the parish priest. The note read: "The monkey, even dressed in silk, is still a monkey. Whoever speaks of Indians speaks of shit because the Indian is like the monkey. It's as simple as that, because the Indian, like the monkey, utters a thousand stupidities which have neither beginning nor end. This is the truth and no lie. They are also very malicious and devilish."

This is not a very coherent statement of opinion, but it is nevertheless a rare glimpse of feelings that are usually masked from the historian's view, of the hatred and fear of a Spaniard living close to villagers but sharing with them few if any affirmative beliefs.[23] Underlying this anonymous author's hatred and fear is the knowledge that the Indian villagers were certainly capable of mob violence if they sensed an overt threat to their lands or to the psychic territory of their daily and seasonal routine.

For their part, villagers usually acquiesced in the conciliatory spirit of colonial judges, tentatively returning to the village from their mountain refuges. In the end, both villagers and colonial authorities wanted rapid resolution and return to settled village life. The villagers had land to farm, families to feed, and a sense of community that was not easily destroyed at one blow; they were also aware of the costs of lengthy litigation. The crown had taxes to collect and a political system to preserve. Considering the slow pace of much colonial administration in the eighteenth century, the judicial system dealt with most *tumultos* with remarkable speed, completing most investigations in a matter of weeks. The old leader of the little village of Coamelco in the jurisdiction of Meztitlán, which had risen up against the parish priest in 1777, knew from experience when he wrote with obvious resignation that "a poor settlement now is better than a long lawsuit that eventually turns out well."[24]

Few of the eighteenth-century uprisings in central and southern Mexico developed into regional movements with peasant villages banding together in common cause. Those exceptional movements that did submerge purely local interests in an abortive or temporarily successful regional union followed patterns familiar to peasant insurrections at other places and times. They developed as millenarian movements or formed around nonvillage leaders with whom the peasant shared a common enemy. In both cases, they were fragile movements centered on loyalty to particular leaders rather than to principles based on an identity of conditions and desires.

One impressive regional uprising of peasants occurred in the jurisdiction of Tulancingo (state of Hidalgo) in 1769, with several thousand Indian villagers from as far away as Meztitlán and Tenango joining a "New Savior" in the mountain fastnesses of Tututepec. Millenarian appeal—a retreat from the burdens of colonial life into a new theocratic utopia—seems to have been the source of regional support. The New Savior, a charismatic native messiah, was an old Indian who was accompanied by a woman venerated as the Virgin of Guadalupe. Together, they worshiped an idol-studded cross, proclaimed death to the Spaniards, and ruled above a newly created Indian priesthood that was to replace the Catholic hierarchy and end the hated clerical and state taxes. According to these spiritual leaders, the Catholic priests were true devils who should not be obeyed. The One True God of the movement was dedicated to the cornfields and chile fields, clearly an appeal to the popular fertility cults at the heart of peasant religion.[25] By calling for an end to all colonial taxes, for sparing the lives of only those Spaniards who would pay tribute to the Indians, and envisioning a world in which bishops and parish priests would line up to kiss the New Savior's hand, the movement hinted at a classlike war of poor against rich and sanctioned bloody attacks on colonial officials and nonbelievers who blundered into the believers' path.

A second short-lived regional revolt flared in the jurisdiction of Actopan, not far from Tulancingo, in 1756. The immediate cause of this uprising is clearer than the inspiration of the one at Tulancingo, and it followed a rather different, nonmillenarian course. The occasion for violence was a new labor draft in the jurisdiction for the purpose of draining the mines at Pachuca. Villagers complained that the mine labor was dangerous and that they were just beginning to harvest their corn crop. The revolt began on a Wednesday market day in the provincial center of Actopan, with as many as two thousand Indian men and women from nearby towns joined by non-Indians who were also subject to the labor draft. They converged on the plaza, brandishing knives, rocks, and banners, closing off the roads into town, shouting "Death to the Governors," and threatening to destroy the place. In the ensuing three days, eight Spaniards were killed or wounded and there was considerable destruction of property. Priests, some of whom had supported the Indian complaints prior to the uprising, negotiated a settlement: a half-caste *lobo* was singled out for punishment as the leader, the excesses of the common people were pardoned, and the towns agreed to a reduced labor service.[26] This insurrection is more like the sort of working alliance between villagers and lower-class townspeople who shared a common grievance that might be expected to produce strong feelings and violence against Spaniards in general. In this case, the movement joined Indian villagers chafing under new mine labor levies with vagrants and mestizos and mulattoes from the head town of Actopan, who also were being forced into the mines.

A local uprising in 1762 in the town of San Andrés, jurisdiction of Tenango (state of Mexico), exposed plans for another regional movement. The incident for the local revolt was the district lieutenant's search for contraband liquor on the evening of the patron saint's fiesta. In one house he found many men and women getting drunk around a large pot of *tepache*. As he tried to make arrests, the church bells were rung and "a multitude" of people descended on the house. The lieutenant and his militiamen barely escaped with their lives. In the course of the investigation into these events, witnesses testified to the long history of community revolts in Tenango and the neighboring jurisdiction of Metepec: a history of colonial officials driven out of town, of villagers refusing to obey written orders, and of several unsuccessful attempts at regional movements against Spanish authority.[27] Spanish fears of regional revolts, however, were rarely justified when the movement depended upon simultaneous uprisings by villages without a millenarian leader who could connect them to other groups outside the villages.

In Oaxaca, stirrings of regional unrest in the eighteenth century did not reach such proportions, but the revival of the cochineal trade, with coercive methods used to force production in villages of the Mixteca and the Sierra Zapoteca, did give rise to several brief regional uprisings. Townspeople of San Felipe, San Mateo, and San Francisco in the jurisdiction of Teozacualco rebelled simultaneously in 1774 against the district lieutenant for interfering in local affairs, demanding cochineal, and attempting to collect tax on liquor produced for local consumption. Rebellion planned in Achiutla (Mixteca Alta) during 1785 nearly became a regional uprising. Messengers from Achiutla carried the call to arms to surrounding villages. Again, the common enemy was the district lieutenant, who was hated for harsh treatment and abuse in the collection of the tribute tax and cochineal.* In general, however, peasants in eighteenth-century central Mexico and Oaxaca were not engaged in new economic activities that could lead to new perceptions about deprivation.

---

*Additional light might be cast on the low incidence of regional revolts in the settled highlands of Mexico in the eighteenth century by comparison to the other great highland peasant societies in Peru and Bolivia, where regional revolts were more frequent. A cycle of three periods of major uprisings have been identified in eighteenth-century Peru: 1737–1740, 1750, and 1780–1782. These widespread uprisings seem to have been touched off by similar changes in tax levies and land encroachments and the *reparto de efectos* that we have noted in the Mexican regions. One distinctive feature of the three periods of insurrection in Peru and Bolivia absent in the rural unrest in Mexico was messianic leadership by hereditary native nobles who proclaimed a return to the rule of the Incas, with themselves as the legitimate heirs. The bases for such a series of messianic movements would appear to be the survival of a Hispanicized native elite and ethnic ties among Indian peasants reinforced by rivalries among different regions, more movement of peasants outside the villages, and weaker village units. There is some disagreement about the nature of the Tupac Amaru revolt in Cuzco province in 1780. Oscar Cornblit emphasizes the role of local Creoles in launching the revolt and the participation of *forasteros* (uprooted Indians from other regions). Magnus Mörner's careful new work on the rebellion in Cuzco province returns to the importance of the community nobles, who were fighting among themselves for the control of bridges as well as against the abuse of power by local colonial officials. *Forasteros*, according to Mörner, played a minor role in the uprising. It was basically fought by groups of villages attached to a mutually acceptable *curaca*. By contrast, we have noted the general decline of ethnolinguistic units in Mexico and the rarity of collective action by Indian linguistic groups in the late colonial period (AGN *Criminal* 306 exp.1).

No one village rebellion typifies the structure discussed here, but the events at Tlapanoya (tributary to Atotonilco in the jurisdiction of Atitalaquia, modern state of Hidalgo) in July 1690 and at Amanalco (jurisdiction of Metepec, state of Mexico) in February 1792 bring a number of characteristics into play.[28] A brief description of these two uprisings can make our composite picture more vivid.

The Tlapanoya *tumulto* began on a Sunday afternoon when the Indian *gobernador* and two nobles of Atotonilco arrived in the village with an order signed by the alcalde mayor. They were to be given custody of two citizens of Atotonilco who recently had settled in Tlapanoya to avoid the personal services exacted by the *gobernador* and the alcalde mayor. The Tlapanoyans who encountered the messengers refused to obey the order and, after muttering to themselves, declared that they no longer accepted the alcalde mayor as their judge. They began to whistle and call for the villagers— men and women—who assembled in a menacing crowd with clubs, rocks, plows, and other weapons to attack the Atotonilco *gobernador*, who fled for his life. When word of the *tumulto* reached the alcalde mayor, he sent the militia to arrest the officials of Tlapanoya. The townspeople fled to the mountains, but two sons of the *gobernador* of Tlapanoya were captured. The *gobernador* himself was in Mexico City at the time to register a complaint with the Audiencia against the forced labor and cash extortions demanded by the alcalde mayor. During the investigation of the *tumulto* ordered by the Audiencia, the alcalde mayor asserted that the Tlapanoyans were insolent people who refused to perform labor service for the king and who were his enemies because he had arrested seventeen men and twenty-three women of the village for producing illegal alcoholic beverages. The Audiencia was not impressed. It ordered that the village be protected against arbitrary demands of the alcalde mayor and released the arrested Tlapanoyans with a stern warning not to take up arms against the king's representative.

The occasion for the uprising in the Amanalco jurisdiction was an attempt by the parish priest, with the aid of three Indians, to take a census for tax purposes. Three of the villages in the parish refused to allow the census takers in, saying that the priest and his assistants could not be trusted to make a proper accounting. When the priest tried to take the census in San Lucas, the villagers, joined by knife-wielding, rock-throwing men and women from Amanalco and San Miguel, chased the census takers back to the priest's lodgings in Amanalco. Amidst a peal of church bells, shouts and whistles, and general "*alegría*," a "numberless" mob (consisting mainly of women) broke into the church, stormed the jail, and released three of their own number. Waving his blunderbuss, the priest fought off what amounted to a halfhearted assault on his person by the women. *Gente de razón* in the district quickly came to his aid, and in the ensuing hours of confusion one

Indian died and three were seriously injured. The rebellion died down only after the peasants seized and battered Isidro Hernández, one of the three Indians who were in league with the priest. A few peasants were arrested, but most escaped to the mountains; and the priest was relieved of his duties. In his attempt to investigate the uprising, the *subdelegado* of Metepec was frustrated by the welter of name-calling, complaints, and counterclaims lodged by the peasants and the *gente de razón*. He did determine that the priest had overcharged the peasants for his services, obstructed their travel to Mexico City, whipped local people without sufficient reason, and allowed his three assistants, particularly Hernández, to usurp community lands. Hernández was also hated for supposedly perpetrating several deaths by witchcraft. In September, having noted that the peasants had returned in peace and were paying their taxes, the *subdelegado* released the rebels who were still in prison.

In what circumstances were the personal representatives of outside authority attacked? Perhaps the most common occasion for attacks on the royal or divine representative was the collection of new or higher taxes, an apparently universal reason for peasant unrest.[29] An uprising by the villagers of Pozontepec in September 1758, for example, was touched off by the parish priest's attempt to collect a new schedule of higher clerical fees authorized by the crown (subsequent investigation revealed other, perhaps more fundamental, peasant grievances against the priest's behavior in this parish and earlier rumors of rebellion). An argument between the priest and some of the peasants escalated to insults and shoves. That night a general *tumulto* broke out, the priest's house was set on fire, and the priest himself narrowly escaped the flames in his underwear.[30] Of the more than thirty uprisings against parish priests, all but eight were touched off by new clerical fees, with villagers complaining of raised charges for baptism, marriage, burial, and celebration of the Mass, or of withholding of priestly services because the villagers were not performing exceptional services for the cleric.

The collection of secular taxes was an equally important occasion for touching off community violence against tax collectors and local judges. Changes in the tribute schedule frequently ignited community violence, and some state taxes, no matter what the rate, had explosive potential. Particularly galling to villagers in central Mexico were the taxes on pulque commerce and salt production. Late colonial schoolmasters who tried to supplement their incomes as tax collectors on monopoly goods, such as tobacco, also invited violence.[31] In both central Mexico and Oaxaca, the *reparto de efectos*—the alcalde mayor's monopoly on the sale of certain goods within his district, such as horses and mules, which were often forced upon village buyers—touched off still other rebellions.[32]

Rejection of new or unexpected taxes is part of a larger set of circumstances of economic deprivation and economic incursion. Tax increases meant the allocation of additional family and community resources to nonproducers and outsiders, principally the state and the church. As a new demand, however, the tax increase had a greater impact on the local economy than merely that of extracting another increment of the community's production. Since taxes normally were collected in cash in the eighteenth century, higher charges usually forced villagers to look outside their community for additional sources of cash, through the sale of village produce, rental of lands, or wage labor. The effect of a tax increase was to make the village more dependent on cash-bearing employers, buyers, and trading partners, in addition to reducing the community's share of its production. In spite of these unsettling effects of taxation, it is important to note once again that eighteenth-century peasants in revolt rarely were challenging the structure of colonial relationships between themselves and the Spanish state. They were protesting *new* taxes or new levels of old taxes, not the right of the state to tax and the Indian subjects' obligation to pay tribute and other traditional levies.

Other economic threats also occasioned collective violence in peasant villages. Labor demands by local officials, the priest, or neighboring hacendados; forced sale of community stores of an essential product, such as corn, salt, or lime; and government orders to allow traders from a rival town to sell in the local market all led to mass uprisings at the village level in central Mexico and Oaxaca.[33] The most important economic incursion after the changing tax burden and labor demands was boundary encroachments. Like tax rebellions, mass invasions or occupations of land are familiar events to students of peasant uprisings in other areas of the world. Land disputes between villages or between a private landowner and a village are not especially numerous in this sample of village rebellions (30 of 142 cases), but my earlier work on land tenure in the Valley of Oaxaca suggests that control of land was a particularly tender matter because such a close relationship endured between village identity and a specific territory. As the judge in the Santa Lucía case realized, every official boundary inspection involving the borders of a peasant village was provocation enough for a collective outburst. Comprehending this potential rarely enabled the authorities to prevent an uprising. In the case of Santa Lucía, the judge was careful to prepare himself with all the trappings of royal authority—a large retinue of high church and secular officials, militiamen, and public criers who announced the official orders for the survey. Nevertheless, the mere attempt to execute a formal measurement aroused the villagers to take matters into their own hands and send the officials running for their lives with a shower of rocks and curses. New pressures on the land in the eighteenth century—resulting from population growth and the expansion of private estates producing for urban markets—suggest that boundary questions were a chronic occasion for violence in both of our regions, but it is noteworthy that the Oaxaca examples (both from the Mixteca Alta and the Valley of Oaxaca) of boundary wars and attacks on public officials in *vistas de ojos* were especially prolonged and acrimonious. Although their fears were not always justified, valley peasants assumed that a survey would mean a loss of land. As one sympathetic alcalde mayor understood, "What they fear most is losing the peace and tranquillity in which they live, and the lands that each individual and his community peacefully possess."[34] Menacing crowds of Indian peasants usually turned out for these inspections. Occasionally, they would throw rocks at the officials, steal the measuring rope, and mass in front of the inspectors, refusing to let them proceed with the measurement. A frightened alcalde mayor of the Cuatro Villas jurisdiction reported the following scene at a boundary survey east of the city of Oaxaca in 1720:

> When we reached the boundary of a plot of land belonging to Gabriel Martín, a native of the pueblo of Santa Cruz . . . , many Indians from Santa Cruz appeared, joining others who had assembled there. Massing together in a crowd, they sought, in disobedience of the Royal Order and Royal justice, to stop the proceedings, shouting that we would not be allowed to go beyond the said boundary. At the same time, the Indians picked up stones and threw three; they aimed one at Your representative, but it struck one of the Indian officials instead.[35]

There surely were many more cases of specific economic incursions of this type (new taxes, labor drafts, boundary troubles) than there were *tumultos*. One additional ingredient in a number of our examples of rebellion that seems to have been a final—if not always indispensable—precipitating factor was the arrest or corporal punishment of village officers for failing to enforce the decisions of colonial officials. Many uprisings began with the storming of the local jail where the officers were being held, with an attack on the militia detachment that was removing an arrested official to the head town for trial, or with an attack at the scene of an exemplary punishment— usually a whipping—of village leaders for objecting to the new exaction. Whippings were a special form of humiliation to Indians because . . . by law Spaniards could not be whipped.

A second major category of occasions for village uprisings has apparently little to do with material conditions or new economic incursions, but much to do with villagers' sense of autonomy and community. In these cases, of which there are thirty-four examples, villagers testified that they rose up in defense of their liberty or their way of life. Revolts against parish priests provide some well-documented examples of such symbolic affronts.

In 1799 the people of Atlautla staged a violent uprising when they learned that the parish priest had sold their prized altarpiece to a nearby rival town; in a similar incident the priest of Cuauhtitlán provoked violence in 1785 by attempting to refurbish an Indian chapel without consulting the parishioners; other priests courted trouble by repairing village churches with stones from ancient ceremonial structures. In Zimatlán in 1773 the townspeople protested violently against a priest who tried to keep them from speaking their native language, Zapotec; another town, Almoloya (1787), protested the priest's refusal to preach in their language by not attending Mass and, finally, by driving him out of town. Another priest aroused the people of Chacatongo to revolt in 1674 by moving his place of residence to another town within the parish; the priest of Almoloya created a similar complaint among the subject towns in his parish in 1792 by removing their baptismal fonts and requiring them to attend the principal church to receive the sacraments. Other priests angered peasant parishioners by interrupting local celebrations, forbidding processions, and meddling in the selection of village officials.*

Attempts to quarantine villagers in order to prevent the spread of epidemic disease also represented the kind of violation of local independence that could provoke a violent response. Teotitlán del Valle, a peasant community in the Valley of Oaxaca especially hard hit by the smallpox epidemic of late 1792, was singled out for special attention by the Board of Physicians in the city of Oaxaca. At the board's request, the intendant ordered the entire community quarantined and a makeshift infirmary constructed on the outskirts of the town to separate the afflicted from the healthy. Residents of Teotitlán were not permitted to leave the village, even to tend their crops, nor could families visit or send food to their isolated relatives in the infirmary huts. To *teotitleños* this forced community isolation and separation of family members was an intolerable intervention. Their first response, conditioned by three centuries of colonial experience, was to hire a lawyer in the city to petition the viceroy for relief. The leisurely legal process was not, however, a satisfactory means of coping with this kind of real emergency. The peasants soon took the issue into their own hands, storming the infirmary, retrieving sick relatives, and burying the dead in the

---

*In the Papantla revolt of 1768, the alcalde mayor's plan to cut down trees in the community combined material and ideological threats to the local people: "The trees gave the people shade and helped them to persevere; also, they served for tying up their animals and protected their houses from fire; also, the twigs and leaves provided fodder" (AGI *Audiencia de Mexico* 1934). Sentiments of village liberty were also aroused by official attempts to force villagers to move to a new town site or, in one case by efforts to make them stay where they were (AGN *Civil* 1599 exp. 9, 2166 exp. 5).

churchyard. The attack was apparently spontaneous, beginning with a mother attempting to recover her child from the infirmary.[36] It ended, like so many rebellions, with a plan for appeasement designed to avoid permanent confrontation with communities in the region. The intendant in Antequera first ordered the urban militia to patrol the outskirts of Teotitlán (an assignment that lasted more than two weeks) but did not attempt a punitive expedition against the town or dare to punish the townspeople beyond the brief imprisonment of fifteen men and women. Colonial authorities hit upon making a scapegoat of the lawyer as a way out of direct confrontation with the peasants. In spite of the fact that the *teotitleños* had come to him for advice in opposing the quarantine, the lawyer was charged with stirring up innocent Indians and condemned to a stiff prison sentence and a heavy fine. The *teotitleños* emerged from the affair as "extremely peaceful people" who had never been rebellious until they met this city lawyer—a convenient case of Spanish amnesia, judging by the violent land disputes involving Teotitlán with Macuilxóchitl and Tlacolula throughout the eighteenth century.[37]

A third category of conditions leading to collective violence is political relationships, both within individual villages and among villages in the same political jurisdiction. The growth of the rural population in the eighteenth century contributed to new conflict between subject towns and head towns in our regions. Agitation by *sujetos* to acquire cabecera status—and thereby separate themselves from nominal political subordination to another town and the consequent irritating service obligations—was a common occurrence. Attempts to transfer villages from one district to another were also common. These jurisdictional tensions sometimes touched off village uprisings.[38] The Los Reyes–Xocotitlán (jurisdiction of Ixtlahuaca) *tumulto* of October 1767 and the Zozoquiapan (jurisdiction of Meztitlán) *tumulto* of May 1805 provide good examples. The *sujeto* village of Los Reyes rose up against the *gobernador* of the cabecera, Xocotitlán, after he arrested the leading citizen of Los Reyes and his wife for "lack of respect" and failure to turn over all the tribute owed by the village. This incident brought to the surface the villagers' fears that the *gobernador* served only the interests of the cabecera and of the parish priest, who resided in Xocotitlán. The Zozoquiapan *tumulto* occurred when Indian villagers, led by a local noblewoman, Felipa Escudero, refused to accept an order from the Audiencia transferring their community out of the jurisdiction of Meztitlán. The militia was sent in to arrest members of the local cabildo, and the townspeople drove them out. Members of the village who testified in the alcalde mayor's investigation said they were afraid that the transfer would mean the loss of their lands and the disruption of local elections.[39]

Another kind of political problem leading to uprisings was internal factionalism, which seems to have been less directly connected to population growth than were intercommunity disputes. Armed uprisings of commoners against the local nobles and officeholders, especially after a disputed election, and attacks by one barrio on another bring us back to Georg Simmel's premise of the tensions inherent in the relationships between dominant and subordinate groups. What is important to us in a historical study of peasant life is that major violence related to factionalism does not seem to have been more prevalent in the eighteenth century than in the seventeenth. On the other hand, factionalism and the weakening of community bonds is more apparent in the mid-nineteenth century. (We will take up this change briefly in later pages.)

Crowd behavior was also an indicator of the occasions for rebellion. We have already considered the kinds of people who participated in the uprisings, the places and people attacked, and the ambiguous end to most outbursts of this sort. Another aspect of crowd behavior—the words exchanged with royal officials and the shouts that accompanied the attacks—is especially important for a consideration of precipitating causes. In sifting through the evidence, I found that the noise of village rebellions consisted of more than the terrific din of war whoops, profanity, ear-splitting whistles, church bells, horns, and drums. There were also choruses of shouts, articulate enough to find their way into the testimony of two or more eyewitnesses. These spontaneous utterances are as close as we can probably come to identifying the conscious goals of the villagers' actions. Unlike the testimony in formal investigations—which can be useful in other ways—chants and shouts are unguarded, direct declaration of feelings that are rarely expressed at other times or documented in other kinds of written records.

Many of the shouts were scornful insults and threats to the representatives who abused colonial authority, or to other outsiders who posed a threat to the community's peace, such as the owner or administrator of a neighboring estate: "We're going to kill you and drink your blood"; "Kill these dogs"; "Kill these niggers"; "Dirty pig"; "Nigger"; "Cuckold robbers"; "Now you'll see, you devil-dog alcalde mayor and your thieving cronies"; "We'll not leave a Spaniard alive in this town"; "You'll pay for this, you dog-governor"; "Now you'll see, you lying, thieving dog"; "Death to them all"; "The governor has ordered us to kill the Riveras"; "To hell with you, Rivera, you have stolen our lands and we're going to kill you"; "War, war."[40] Righteous indignation directed against outsiders who maligned the villagers, attempted to seize their lands, or imposed new taxes are contained in all of these heated words. But there is more here. "Pig," "dog," "devil-dog," and "nigger" were standard Spanish expletives, often applied to Indians.[41] In calling a *peninsular subdelegado* a "nigger" or the parish priest a "dog," the central Mexico villagers turned the tables on their political masters, repaying them in kind. In two of these examples, Ixmiquilpan in

1642 and Actopan in 1756—both in areas of Hidalgo where peasants were forced into service in the mines of Pachuca and Real del Monte—the sense of outrage against an individual Spaniard spilled over into a general call of "Death to them all"; "We'll not leave a Spaniard alive in this town."[42] This would seem to be a groping toward class war, but both rebellions burned themselves out in a few days, without spreading and without any mass killing of Spaniards. Nevertheless, they are early and interesting examples of a latent potential for insurrection and liberation.

A second type of common exclamation reveals what seem to be vague democratic aspirations and an instinct for self-preservation. They were not directed at anyone in particular; they were declarations of local rights and imperatives, and of strong opposition to any new infringement on local habits: "We alone are sovereign in this town"; "Now we're the masters of this land"; "We have no master"; "This boundary measurement should not be made; the King has no business here"; "We refuse to obey the alcalde mayor or to consider him our judge." One Indian alcalde declared that his staff of authority was equal to that of the king's representative, after which the villagers shouted the same.[43] Villagers regarded themselves as "free" people, but the kind of liberty that seems to have animated the rebellions was confined to the small world of the local village. It did not readily translate into a notion of shared or equal rights with other villages that could serve as the basis for regional revolts.

Community rebellions in central Mexico, the Mixteca Alta, and the Valley of Oaxaca provide little evidence that accommodation was breaking down in the eighteenth century because of new peasant perspectives on legitimacy, elite intransigence, or a significant gain in power by the subordinate villages (all in spite of the major administrative reforms made by the Bourbons at the provincial level). Real or imagined abuse of power by district officials and loss of vitality of the ruling group seem to be the political developments most closely related to village uprisings.

The new economic demands and the cultural conditions we have identified as the two types of occasions of collective violence share a common element. Both were actions taken by the state—by local judges or priests acting either in compliance with colonial orders or on their own initiative. They are the external events that explain the timing, if not the underlying causes, of the rebellions. In Simmel's terms, the legitimacy of the priests or alcaldes mayores suffered a temporary collapse because of what the villagers perceived as an abuse of their power in making new demands on the community. In a few cases it is also possible to speak of the ruling group's loss of vitality as a factor in the descent into violence. Rivalries between the parish priest and the local Spanish judge damaged the unity of state control, confused the existing structure of accommodation, and raised village sensitivity to the abuse of state power. In five cases we find parish priests intervening directly to lead village rebellions against new laws on the administration of *cofradía* finances or against the arbitrary acts of the alcalde mayor or his lieutenant. The growing reliance of alcaldes mayores on lieutenants (appointed deputies who bear a resemblance to the corrupt political bosses of rural Mexico today) to oversee public affairs at the local level also weakened the lines of loyalty between peasant villages and royal officials in the late colonial period.

The vitality of the rural church was also in decline. The parish priest's ability to guide his congregation was no longer as great as we might imagine from early church history in Spanish America. Many dedicated parish priests still commanded the blind faith of their flocks in the last colonial decades, but even more of their brethren had lost the sense of utopian mission and personal sacrifice that had animated the "spiritual conquest" in the sixteenth century and had won the neophytes' loyalty. In spite of their numbers, eighteenth-century *curas* were usually more remote from their peasant parishioners, weakening the ties between religious authority and village life.

Some priests complained that a rural assignment was like living in exile from the civilized world they had known as students.[44] Many others became permanent residents of the parish seat, where most non-Indians resided, making only infrequent visits to remote villages to administer the sacraments. At an urgent summons to the deathbed of a peasant in a village several hours' walk from his home church, one indifferent Oaxacan *cura* declined to go, sending a message that the dying man be given a sprinkling of holy water and a hot brick for his stomach.[45] Many quibbled with their parishioners over church finances, clerical fees, and the provision of food and lodging. All parish priests lost a measure of local prestige and wealth as a result of the Bourbon confiscation of *obras pías* and control of *cofradía* finances in the last decades of Spanish rule. Under these circumstances, it is not surprising that rural priests and peasant villages came into conflict, and that the moral authority of priests eroded—or that both developments could translate into collective violence.

The importance of actions by colonial authorities as occasions for local rebellions exposes the peasants' primary conscious motive for collective violence: the *defense* of relationships that were threatened. The structure of relationships showed geographic variation. Some regions—even in central Mexico—had not allowed a priest or alcalde mayor into their communities for years and paid the tribute tax grudgingly. Others paid existing tax assessments without complaint and served the priest and magistrate regularly. Defensive uprisings against state actions that were perceived as *new* encroachments were common to both kinds of villages, even though the degree of real deprivation caused by the demands of the colonial authorities was relative.

Rebellions often were set off by what appear to be minor changes, but to the rebels more than only a nominal tax increase or the arrest of a common criminal was at stake. Peasant villages were reacting to what they considered an immediate threat to their way of life. As one alcalde mayor put it, they feared "losing the peace and tranquillity in which they have lived," or being "deprived of [their] liberty," or "losing [their] lands and houses."[46] Peasants' beliefs about themselves and their communities also contributed to this climate of distrust and of resistance to change from outside. As the crowd behavior suggests, new colonial rules and restraints on customary behavior were commonly seen by villagers in revolt as threats to the ideal of the independent landholding community. Eighteenth-century peasant rebels who were later called to account and whose testimony was recorded in the formal records of investigation frequently proclaimed their "natural liberty" and inveighed against "the yoke of subjection."[47] Spanish witnesses spoke of the "false pride" of the villagers and their resistance to anything the crown's local representatives attempted to correct. Resistance to change in dealing with colonial officials represented an understandable distrust of powerful outsiders serving their own interests and an affirmation of the community's solidarity and belief in its separateness.

The considerable number of community uprisings in central Mexico and Oaxaca during the eighteenth century shows quite clearly that local villages were capable of popular spontaneous violence. As we have seen, this violence did not develop in a mindless way but had structure and coherence—even if the peasants did not fully control the situation. As a collective response to collective experience, it expressed community solidarity and hope. The spontaneous massing of armed villagers in the two regions bears witness to a long history of community violence and collective action in landholding villages under certain predictable conditions: specific changes in the economic demands of powerful outsiders and other direct encroachments on the community's rights. Defense of village integrity gave these uprisings the appearance of sacred struggles against violators of the community's visible and invisible boundaries. The community's perception of its independent rights was a relative matter, but it is noteworthy that nearly all of the 142 rebellions examined here took place in communities that possessed subsistence landholdings of their own and enjoyed a measure of separation and independence from the demands of colonial authorities through relative isolation, production of a significant surplus, or militant resistance.

The ability of our peasant communities to translate disaffection into political unrest rather than to retreat or fall into masochism is evidence of the strength of localized village identity. On the other hand, the rebels' goals were usually limited to correcting particular abuses; and the strength of *village* rather than regional resistance suggests very little identity of conditions and desires among villages that might bring them together in regional uprisings. Villagers in our two regions did not see themselves as a deprived class able to unite against a common oppressor. For most, the enemies were the neighboring villages as well as the abusive local magistrate or priest, not the higher authorities who were ultimately responsible for the burden of taxes and service. This local political unity and militant myopia made villagers good rebels but poor revolutionaries.[48] Individually, they defended their community borders with some success, but, in doing so, they failed to comprehend the larger forces that threatened their independence. They did not want to take power outside the local district, and, if they had, I suspect that they would not have known what to do with it. Without question villagers accepted the existence of neighboring haciendas and plantations; certain taxes and service; the formalities of a higher system of justice in certain kinds of crimes and disputes; the legitimacy of colonial priests and magistrates until they personally betrayed village trust; and the sanctity of that most remote figure, the king of Spain, and his personal representative in Mexico, the viceroy.

In late-colonial Mexico little village unrest was transformed into war on the rich or on the colonial system. A few of the longer lived village rebellions came close to spilling over into class wars with shouts of "death to the Spaniards" and "Death to the *gente de razón*." Some priests and colonial representatives died in the bloody outbursts, but the exalted threats to annihilate outsiders were never accomplished. There *were* regional uprisings in Chiapas (1712), Yucatán (1761), and the Petén (1775), which became limited race and anticolonial wars. For our regions, only the Tulancingo (Hidalgo) regional revolt of some two thousand peasants in 1769 might qualify as an uprising against the colonial system.

Our examination of peasant uprisings ends rather abruptly with the beginning of Mexico's wars of independence in 1810. Are changing conditions after independence reflected in new patterns of rural collective violence? To answer this question, we need to know much more than we now do about the last 150 years of Mexico's rural history. The secondary works on socioeconomic conditions and rural violence in nineteenth-century Mexico do, however, provide us with enough material to hazard a few guesses about changing conditions and responses that highlight our evidence on the eighteenth century. The postindependence period brought massive impersonal changes to peasant life, comparable in scale to the sixteenth-century political revolution, epidemics, resettlement programs, religious conversion, and labor and tax systems that resulted from Spanish colonization.

These new challenges were in part conscious programs of the state and federal governments; in part, they were the product of Mexico's expanding population and growing role in the world economy as a neocolonial exporter of primary products.

The Indian peasant's legal status in independent Mexico was altered to make him a citizen equal before the law to other Mexicans. Paternalistic colonial laws for the protection of Indian communities were abolished. Non-Indians were no longer forbidden to reside in Indian communities, special Indian courts such as the Juzgado de Indios were disbanded, and the special protection of community property afforded by the colonial judicial system and the Indians' right to legal counsel fell into disuse. We know that these colonial laws were often honored in the breach and that the institutions created to protect Indians as wards of the Crown had serious shortcomings, but the colonial state did assume moral and legal responsibility for the survival of Christian tax-paying rural communities.

The weight of moral and legal authority in the colonial period did not sanction the dismemberment of rural communities and the seizure of their lands. This moral commitment was cold comfort to communities that lost their lands and their means of subsistence, but the survival of peasant villages was placed in greater jeopardy when the state became a moral enemy.

Equality of individual Mexicans before the law in independent Mexico would lead to careful scrutiny of the church and other groups that had had special rights and held corporate property under colonial law. As early as 1833 the state of Mexico, a new political jurisdiction that included most of our central Mexico region, enacted a law against communal property that opened the way to alienation of village lands.[49] The process of dismemberment began in the late 1820s and reached its peak during the reform period, from 1854 to 1876, when the Liberals attempted to integrate Indians into national society by dissolving their communal life. The national laws of the reform period against corporate property were not uniformly enforced, but illegal seizures as well as sale of village lands became more common. Village lands that were set aside for the support of the church or that were rented out were especially vulnerable to sale by the state. Finally, during the Porfirian dictatorship of the late nineteenth century, land survey laws allowed the alienation of more lands for which the peasant occupants could not produce formal titles. This final assault on village integrity affected our regions much less than it did the northern states of Sonora and San Luis Potosí and the semitropical areas of Veracruz and Yucatán.

At the same time that state and federal governments were expropriating corporate property, other pressures were being exerted on village lands: an expanding rural population throughout central and southern Mexico, and the growth of commercial farming in such lucrative export crops as sugarcane, henequen, and coffee. Commercial farming of sugarcane expanded dramatically in Yucatán and Morelos in the nineteenth century, henequen plantations opened in Yucatán, coffee fincas developed in Veracruz, and ranching expanded in the Bajío. These expanding enterprises competed for the peasants' means of livelihood—their farm land, water sources, common pasture lands, woodlands, salt deposits, and equally important, their labor. Whole zones of rural communities that had previously enjoyed a measure of local control and placed a high value on village independence were threatened with displacement and the total subservience of unorganized landless wage laborers. The assault on peasant lands was one of a variety of incursions against rural villages that intensified in the nineteenth century: peasant labor was the object of an expanding system of debt peonage and captive labor on the plantations; and the value placed on modernization by Mexico's ruling Liberals and positivists led to a view of peasant villages as hard lumps of backwardness that had to be separated from their traditional ways if they were to become Mexican.

Central Mexico and Oaxaca were less affected by the changes in land tenure than many other regions because neither had great potential for producing the new export crops, and capital investment in the countryside of both regions was relatively weak. The central valleys of Oaxaca continued in the old pattern of strong landholding villages. Valley peasants were increasingly integrated into the regional economy and the urban marketplace of Oaxaca city, but largely on a voluntary, part-time basis. Other parts of Oaxaca were experiencing competition among peasants, politicians, and entrepreneurs for salt, farmland, grazing land, and the labor needed for weaving cotton textiles, but these new conditions did not resemble the engulfing commercial economies of Yucatán, Morelos, and Chiapas.

In the central Mexico region, pressure on village lands in the nineteenth century usually reinforced the colonial land and labor system rather than transforming land tenure and land use by new kinds of commercial agriculture. Demand for central Mexico's lumber increased in the late nineteenth century (especially for construction materials in the mines and railroad ties) and some commercial crops, such as *zacatón* (a native plant whose root is processed for broomstraw and brushes), blossomed; but the expansion of private lands happened more gradually, was mainly fostered by the Liberal politics of free enterprise, and pitted villages against their old foes, the pulque, ranching, and grain-producing haciendas that had their beginnings in the colonial period.* An estimated 40 percent of the central Mexican

---

*In the eighteenth century some haciendas in the future state of Mexico had added textile workshops to process estate wool. If these weaving activities had been expanded in the nineteenth century, the expansion would have increased competition for local labor and perhaps fueled more land pressure.

villages retained their lands throughout the nineteenth century.[50] Other politically unsettling circumstances of the nineteenth century were the weakness of the national government and the periodic foreign invasions that threw local politics into turmoil and destroyed the legitimacy of central authority enjoyed during the colonial period by the Spanish monarchy.

Accompanying these economic and political changes, which threatened the semi-independent position of rural villages, were more regional revolts and leagues of peasant communities, or community factionalism and resort to political homicide, which were barely evident in the eighteenth century. Nineteenth-century regional peasant movements were especially impressive in places that had waged earlier major insurrections, such as Chiapas (1712 and 1869), Yucatán (1761 and 1847–1855), and Papantla (1743, 1767, 1847–48, and 1891). In each case, however, the level of resistance was greater and the reasons for armed resistance more radical. The Caste War of Yucatán in the late 1840s was, for a time, a war to the death between Indians and whites; the Papantla rebels in 1848 spoke of the traditional grievances of heavy taxes, forced labor, and abuse of community freedoms, but they also called for the abolition of debt peonage and the destruction of haciendas and distribution of their lands to the villages.[51] Regional uprisings over land control were also occurring sporadically in central Mexico and the mountains of Oaxaca. The concentration of these insurrections in the late 1840s, 1860s, and early 1870s is illuminated by the weakness of elites, which was noted by Simmel as one of several changes in elite behavior that can bring on political violence. The Mexican-American War of 1846 to 1848 not only took the federal government's attention away from internal affairs, but also exposed the weakness of the government in defending Mexican territory. During this period, rural insurrections were mounted in Yucatán, the Isthmus of Tehuantepec, the Huaxteca region of Papantla, Veracruz, and the Sierra Gorda region of San Luis Potosí.[52] Also, attacks by leagues of rural villagers were made on neighboring haciendas in central Mexico at this time, which the Mexican historian Jan Bazant identifies as an important break with the past.*

Crises in the national government in the late 1860s and early 1870s were also accompanied by insurrections over land and community rights in Jalisco, Nayarit, Zacatecas, Michoacán, and Chiapas. The legitimacy of the national government was endangered in the 1850s and 1860s, not only by its weakness in the face of civil war and French occupation, but also by its

---

*Bazant, 59. Political homicide and factionalism in communities seem to replace insurrection as a response to these political and economic changes in some areas. Hidalgo's high homicide rate in the nineteenth century may well reflect increased political homicide. A similar change from insurrection to political homicide is recorded by Paul Friedrich for a community in Michoacán.[53]

attack on the church, which had been the state's traditional ally. A number of the rural uprisings after 1855 were led by disaffected parish priests who made common cause with villagers against the "sacrilegious" reform laws.

The catalyst in transforming local disaffection and loss of faith in national rulers into regional political movements was often an ambitious provincial chieftain who articulated the common fears and grievances of uprooted villagers and incorporated them into a wider political insurrection against the national government. Whether or not they had the gift of charisma, such leaders emerged from the shadows of earlier leaderless movements as instruments, rather than guiding forces, of the growing conflicts that accompanied the pervasive changes in the Mexican countryside during the nineteenth century. Some regional leaders, such as Manuel Lozada, maintained an impressive hold over their bands of country people clamoring for land and village autonomy. Most would-be leaders, like Miguel Hidalgo in the independence movement in the Bajío in 1810 and Colonel José Cetina in Yucatán in the 1840s, unleashed forces of hatred and despair they could not control. Among leaders of rural insurrections, Emiliano Zapata stands out as uniquely successful—a leader who gained the fellowship of campesinos in Morelos, not because of charisma or personal ambition, but because he understood their cause and was true to it.

The challenge to village boundaries and to the psychic territory of daily and seasonal routine that derived from government support of private estates and new opportunities for commercial agriculture grew in intensity in the last decades of the nineteenth century. But under a strong personalist national government there were few serious insurrections. Rural unrest became a regional and national force once again in 1910, when the legitimacy of the aged Díaz government was challenged by urban and provincial people outside of the government who sought the aid of rural groups that shared their perception of worsening conditions. [Francisco] Madero found potential allies in the rural communities of Morelos that were rapidly losing their lands and their very existence under the Porfirian political system and the expansion of the sugar plantations. But even in Morelos in 1910–11, the village leaders were demanding little more than the right to exist alongside the big estates and the return of the lands that had been taken from them. The rural movement in Morelos spread and became truly revolutionary in goals and methods under the leadership of Emiliano Zapata and less powerful but still independent chieftains; but as Octavio Paz says, "Zapata would have been an obscure figure lost in the solitudes of the south if his insurgency had not coincided with the nation's general insurrection and the fall of the Díaz regime in the capital."[54]

By comparing them with the eighteenth-century peasant rebellions, the nineteenth-century regional insurrections shed some additional light on the earlier uprisings. Regional movements after independence were more frequent and less scattered than the colonial insurrections. Since peasant subordination and perceived abuses of power by district authorities were sources of local conflict and violence in both periods, we should look to changing conditions in the nineteenth century for explanation. The nineteenth-century revolts seem to have occurred in areas of major new economic incursions during periods of ineffectual national and state government. The national crisis was crucial to rural insurrection in 1910, just as it had been in 1810 and 1846. Such crises at the top were lacking in the eighteenth century. A coincidence of regional peasant movements and national political crises suggests a rupture of trust between villages and the remote high authorities, which began with the overthrow of the Spanish monarchy by Napoleon in 1808. Furthermore, the eighteenth-century villages of central Mexico and Oaxaca were more secure, integrated units in comparison to their late-nineteenth-century counterparts, which apparently were experiencing more factionalism, outmigration, and loss of lands. New taxes on land, the laws against communal property, the pressure of expanding cash crop enterprises, and the spread of debt peonage threatened the very existence of some nineteenth-century villages and were perceived as terminal threats by others, raising the latent potential for revolt. Late colonial villages suffered material distress, but it was not the kind of pervasive, dislocating threat to their existence that might have promoted a concept of struggle between classes or orders and united villages in regional insurrections.

Notes

Abbreviations for works frequently cited:

AEO	Archivo del Estado de Oaxaca.
AGI	Archivo General de las Indias.
AGN	Archivo General de la Nación, Mexico.
CDCh	Centro de Documentación del Museo Nacional, Chapultepec Park, Mexico City, Serie Oaxaca.
UT	University of Texas, Austin, Latin American Collection.

1. Charles Tilly, "The Changing Place of Collective Violence," *Essays in Theory and History: An Approach to the Social Sciences*, ed. Melvin Richter (Cambridge, MA, 1970), 140; Gerrit Huizer, " 'Resistance to Change' and Radical Peasant Mobilization: Foster and Erasmus Reconsidered," *Human Organization* 29 (1970), 303–13, and *The Revolutionary Potential of Peasants in Latin America* (Lexington, MA, 1972); Gerrit Huizer and Rodolfo Stavenhagen, "Peasant Movements and Land Reform in Latin America: Mexico and Bolivia," *Rural Protest, Peasant*

Movements and Social Change, ed. Henry A. Landsberger (London, 1974), 378–409; Eric J. Hobsbawm, "Peasant Land Occupations," *Past and Present*, no. 62 (1974), 120–52; Nelson Reed, *The Caste War of Yucatán* (Stanford, CA, 1964); John H. Rowe, "Movimiento Nacional Inca del siglo XVIII," *Revista Universitaria del Cuzco*, no. 107, 2d semester (1954), 17–47.

2. Henri Favre, *Cambio y continuidad entre los Mayas de México* (Mexico, 1973), 269ff.

3. AGN *Criminal* 123 exp. 21, 180 fols. 361–430, 430–75, 155 fol. 111–, 169 fols. 103–43, 210 fols. 189–, 229 fols. 263–, 232 exp. 2, 284 exp. 5, 304 fols. 1–4; *Civil* 865 exp. 9; José Antonio Calderón Quijano et al., *Los virreyes de Nueva España* (1759–1808), 4 vols. (Seville, 1967–72), I:306–8.

4. Calderón Quijano, I:306–38; AGI *Audiencia de Mexico* 1934 (Papantla 1767); AGN *Criminal* 54 exp. 14, 57 exp. 1, 75 exps. 3–4, 90 (November 1773), 104 fol. 452r, 117 exp. 7, 123 exp. 21, 180 fols 361–430 and 430–75, 203 exp. 4, 155 fols. 111–; *Civil* 241 exp. 1, 1599 exp. 9, 865 exp. 9, 2292 exp. 10, 1505 exp. 7.

5. AGN *Criminal* 283 exp. 3.

6. See Robert F. Wasserstrom, "White Fathers and Red Souls: Indian-Ladino Relations in Highland Chiapas, 1528–1973," (Ph.D. diss., Harvard University, 1976), 134, for a critique of the view that the Tzeltal revolt of 1712 was led by members of the Indian cabildo.

7. AGN *Inquisición* 746 exp. 18 fols. 337–56.

8. Wasserstrom, 69, 75.

9. Natalie Z. Davis, *Society and Culture in Early Modern France* (Stanford, CA, 1975), 169–70, makes this distinction.

10. AEO *Juzgados* bundle for 1612–83; "Como los indios se crían en el campo, verse enjaulados lo tienen por mayor pena que la muerte."

11. Teodomiro Manzano, *Anales del Estado de Hidalgo desde los tiempos más remotos hasta nuestros días* (Ixmiquilpan, 1677), 3 vols. (Pachuca, Mex., 1922–27), I:13; AGN *Criminal* 243 exp. 1, 92 exp. 5, 218 fols. 1–19, 229 exp. 231, 107 exp. 1, 307 exp. 2, 202 exp. 1, 151 exp. 1, 306 exps. 1 and 6, 308 (August 31, 1769), 507 exp. 17; *Civil* 241 exp. 1, 865 exps. 8 and 9; AGI *Audiencia de México* 2588 report of Dr. Joseph Ruiz, fol. 4v; CDCh *Oaxaca*, roll 6, exp. 209; roll 8, exp. 286; roll 9, exp. 529; roll 15, exp. 430.

12. AGN *Criminal* 304 exp. 1 fols. 1–4.

13. AGN *Criminal* 79 exp. 1 fol. 6r.

14. AGN *Criminal* 57 exp. 1, 232 exp. 2, 243 exp. 1.

15. AGN *Criminal* 55 fols. 122–, 79 exp. 1 fol. 62v, 304 exp. 1; Calderón Quijano, II:163–75; AEO *Juzgados* bundle for 1806.

16. AGN *Criminal* 304 fol. 366r.

17. AGN *Criminal* 283 exp. 1, 218 fols. 1–19, 54 exp. 14, 230 exp. 15, 203 exp. 4, 166 fols. 185–272, 75 exp. 3, 202 exp. 1, 241 exp. 1, 162 fols. 187–306 exp. 5; *Indios* 54 exp. 85, 70 exp. 69; *Tierras* 381 exp. 5.

18. AGN *Criminal* 306 exp. 6; *Historia* 335 exp. 1.

19. Report on the parish of Tlacochahuaya submitted by Lic. Juan José de Echarri, April 29, 1803, typescript in the possession of Lic. Luis Castañeda Guzmán, Oaxaca, Oaxaca.

20. Herbert I. Priestley, *José de Gálvez, Visitor-General of New Spain (1765–1771)* (Berkeley, CA, 1916), 213–20; AGN *Criminal* 306 exp. 6.

21. AGN *Criminal* 138 exp. 2; R. Contreras, and J. Daniel, *Una rebelión indígena en el partido de Totonicapán en 1820: El indio y la independencia* (Guatemala, 1968), 32.

22. AGN *Criminal* 306 exp. 5.

23. AGN *Criminal* 79 exp. 8 (March 6, 1777).

24. AGN *Criminal* 79 exp. 1 fol. 6r.

25. AGN *Criminal* 308.

26. AGN *Civil* 241.

27. AGN *Criminal* 123 exp. 21.

28. AGN *Criminal* 54 exp. 14, 241 exp. 1.

29. Roland Mousnier, *Peasant Uprisings in Seventeenth-Century France, Russia, and China*, trans. Brian Pearce (New York, 1970), 306; Barrington Moore, Jr., *Social Origins of Dictatorship: Lord and Peasant in the Making of the Modern World* (Boston, 1966), 256–57, 380; Emmanuel Le Roy Ladurie, *The Peasants of Languedoc*, trans. John Day (Urbana, IL, 1974), 265, 269; C. S. L. Davies, "Révoltes populaires en Angleterre (1500–1700)," *Annales: Economies, sociétés, civilisations* 24 (1969), 53, explains the fewer peasant uprisings in England than in France on the basis of lower taxes.

30. AGN *Criminal* 210 fols. 189–205.

31. For example, AGN *Criminal* 166 fols. 354bis–.

32. For example, Calderón Quijano, II:163–75.

33. AGN *Criminal* 166 fols. 320–, 54 exp. 14, 55 fols. 122–, 181 fols. 201–, 163 fols. 295–; *Civil* 865 exp. 8; *Historia* 334 exp. 5; *Indios* 70 exp. 69; CDCh *Oaxaca*, roll 10, exp. 551.

34. AGN *Hospital de Jesús* 307 exp. 4 fol. 5r.

35. AGN *Tierras* 381 exp. 5 fol. 1r–v.

36. AGN *Epidemias* 15 exps. 2, 8, 9, 10 exps. 1, 3, 4, 12 exp. 6.

37. AGN *Tierras* 148 exp. 3, 2384 exp. 1.

38. AGN *Indios* 3 exp. 241; *Criminal* 92 exp. 5; CDCh *Oaxaca*, roll. 21 legajo 2.

39. AGN *Criminal* 180 fols. 361–430.

40. AGN *Criminal* 104 fols. 380–, 123 exp. 21, 180 fols. 430–75, 202 exp. 1, 157 fols. 93–, 507 exp. 17, 55 fols. 122–, 92 exp. 5, 210 fols. 189–, 226 fols. 401–, 229 fols. 263–, 283 exp. 3, 284 exp. 5; *Civil* 241 exp. 1, 2166 exp. 6.

41. For example, AGN *Criminal* 284 exp. 5.

42. AGN *Civil* 241 exp. 1; Manzano, I:13. The 1642 Ixmiquilpan rebellion was surprisingly early and centered in an area of Indian villages. The potential for insurrection there was evident again in 1677 and was momentarily realized in a millenarian movement more than one hundred years later.

43. AGI *Audiencia de Mexico* 2588, report by Dr. Joseph Ruiz, fols. 4v; Bancroft Library, Mexican MS 435 p. 21; UT Mexican MS G-205; AGN *Criminal* 54 exp. 14, 283 exp. 3, 75 exps. 3–4, 306 exp. 5.

44. For example, José Miguel Guridi y Alcocer, *Apuntes de la vida de D. José Miguel Guridi y Alcocer, formados por él mismo en fines de 1801 y principios del siguiente de 1802* (Mexico, 1906), 72–73.

45. AEO *Juzgados* bundle for 1807, January 7, 1744, Santiago Amatepec, jurisdiction of Villa Alta, complaint against Br. Santiago Mariano Villanueva.

46. AGN *Hospital de Jesús* 307 exp. 4; *Criminal* 180 fols. 361–; *Tierras* 318 exp. 5.

47. AGN *Criminal* 306 exp. 5A, 151 fols. 140–, 210 fols. 189–.

48. Moore, 208.

49. The extremely localized nature of rebellion in these two regions is particularly evident when it is compared to the character of peasant uprisings in southern France in the late-sixteenth and seventeenth centuries, many of which were true insurrections with far-reaching objectives. Le Roy Ladurie, 192–202.

50. Moisés González Navarro, "Tenencia de la tierra y población agrícola (1877–1960)," *Historia Mexicana* 19 (1969), 63–86.

51. Reed, *Caste War*; Meyer, *Problemas campesinos*, 11–13, 62–66.

52. Jean Meyer, *Problemas campesinos, y Revueltas Agrarias (1821–1920)* (Mexico City, 1973), 10–13.

53. Paul Friedrich, "Political Homicide in Rural Mexico," *Anger, Violence, and Politics: Theories and Research*, ed. Ivo and Rosalind Feierabeno and Ted R. Gurr (Englewood Cliffs, NJ, 1972), 269–82.

54. Octavio Paz, *The Other Mexico: Critique of the Pyramid*, trans. Lysander Kemp (New York, 1972), 60.

7

Yaqui Resistance to Mexican Expansion

Evelyn Hu-DeHart

The Yaqui people of northwest Mexico have maintained a remarkable record of ethnic solidarity and resistance to the unwanted demands and incursions of the colonial and national governments of Mexico. Like the Araucanians of Chile described in Chapter 4, the Yaquis accepted some cultural modifications in order to retain their political autonomy.

This selection describes the measures the Yaquis took to combat the unprecedented onslaught on their lands, strongly supported by the dictator Profirio Díaz, in the late nineteenth century. This struggle resembles a number of others by native peoples in the eighteenth and nineteenth centuries. Often the leaders of these movements were acculturated individuals—like Cajeme of the Yaqui—who renounced their affiliation with the European sector of society in favor of reinvigorating the autonomy and traditions of their natal peoples.

Many native societies were subordinated by strong national governments that emerged in Latin America in the late nineteenth century. The entrepreneurs of that prosperous era coveted the lands and labor that the natives controlled, and the governments sought to bring all national territory under their effective jurisdictions. Although Cajeme's movement was defeated, the Yaquis continued to resist. Ultimately, through their military participation on the winning side in the Mexican Revolution, the Yaquis attained government recognition of their sovereignty over their lands, some political autonomy, and protection of their traditional cultural and religious practices.

When Vice-Governor José T. Otero addressed the Seventh Constitutional Congress of Sonora in September 1879, he cried out angrily that "there is in this state an anomaly whose existence is shameful for Sonora." He used these words to denounce the Yaquis' "separate nation within the state" and called upon the federal government to give financial and military assistance to destroy such a dangerous situation.[1] Having always considered themselves a separate nation in name and spirit, the Yaquis had made this concept a formal political reality as well. Credit for it belonged primarily to Cajeme, the most extraordinary leader in Yaqui history.

Unusual for the broad experiences he had had outside the Yaqui River before assuming leadership of his people, Cajeme restructured Yaqui society, introduced new methods of waging warfare, and disciplined the Yaquis to rely on their own resources and initiative in confronting the hostile Mexican world. Never since the days of the Jesuit missions were the Yaquis more tightly organized, more secure economically, more prepared militarily, than they were under Cajeme. His goal was not to extend Yaqui hegemony beyond its traditional boundaries, but to strengthen and preserve that autonomy which his people had always claimed was rightfully theirs. That is why his position was essentially a defensive one. His Mexican adversaries unanimously acknowledged their great respect for the man, his intellect and accomplishments, even as they put their heads and resources together to crush his regime.

Born José María Leyva in Hermosillo in 1837, the son of Yaquis Francisco Leyva and Juana Pérez, Cajeme spent the first years of his life in the Yaqui pueblo of Ráum. In 1849, while just a lad of twelve, José María went with his father to California for the gold rush.[2] Not finding the pot of gold that they had dreamed about, father and son returned home after a few years, dejected and disillusioned. But Francisco and Juana Leyva still wanted a better life for their son, so they sent him to school in Guaymas, entrusting him to the guardianship of Prefect Cayetano Navarro. At the age of eighteen, having learned the rudiments of reading and writing in Spanish, José María joined the Guaymas defense forces against the French filibuster, the Count de Raousset Boulbon. Then he drifted south to Sinaloa, where he was briefly apprenticed to a blacksmith before he was drafted into the army. Unwilling to tolerate the harsh life of a lowly recruit, José María escaped to work in a nearby mine. During the wars of the reform (1859–1861), José María volunteered for a Sonoran battalion commanded by Ignacio Pesqueira, who was then defending Liberalism in Sinaloa. After Pesqueira recaptured the crucial port of Mazatlán from the Conservatives, José María returned to Sonora with the governor.

When they arrived in Sonora, the Yaquis were in rebellion; José María immediately signed up for the expeditionary forces sent against the rebels, his own people but with whom he had had practically no contact during his adolescence. Afterwards, he also fought for Governor Pesqueira against the Gandaristas. During these years, when not serving in the military, José María drifted around the state with no stable occupation. In 1867, he again volunteered for the Yaqui campaign, then commanded by Próspero S.

Bustamante, and probably witnessed the infamous Bácum massacre of that year. Until mid-1868, José María fought in the Yaqui against his own people and distinguished himself so valiantly in combat that he was elevated to the rank of captain with his own company of one hundred. By the time of the Carlos Conant revolt in 1873, José María Leyva had become a dependable volunteer for the state forces whenever there was a crisis. In recognition of his many services, Governor Pesqueira awarded him the post of alcalde mayor of the Yaqui River, undoubtedly with the hope that he would help the government pacify his indomitable people and obtain their total and permanent submission. There is no indication that the Yaqui manipulated himself into this position of authority.

Soon after he became alcalde mayor, however, José María Leyva betrayed Pesqueira's trust in him and abruptly changed his entire attitude towards the Mexican government. Shocked and dismayed, state officials suggested that Leyva, after returning to the Yaqui River, became "conquered by the Yaquis' imperishable tendency to maintain themselves independent."[3] This brief but insightful observation probably explained the whole story of how José María Leyva became the great Yaqui leader Cajeme, which means in the Yaqui language "He who does not drink."

Cajeme first made himself heard as leader of the Yaquis in the middle of 1875, when Sonora was in the throes of a hotly contested election between Ignacio Pesqueira's puppet José Pesqueira and the caudillo's former protégé Jesús García Morales. Threatening to rebel if his message was not heeded, Cajeme announced he would not recognize the government unless the Yaquis were granted total freedom to govern themselves, because they were the "natural owners" of the Yaqui River. At first the authorities did not view Cajeme with much alarm, because Yaquis had not caused great trouble since 1868. "The Yaquis are not as terrible as they used to be," officials comforted themselves. But they must have had an inkling of what was taking place in the Yaqui, for they also warned that the Yaquis must not be allowed to form "a separate republic."[4]

Granted extraordinary powers of the treasury and war to suppress the insolent Yaquis, Governor Pesqueira immediately raised a forced loan of thirty-five thousand pesos. Before he could proceed to the Yaqui, however, Francisco Serna pronounced against him and José Pesqueira, who was about to take office as the new governor. This delay allowed the Yaqui rebellion to gain momentum, as rebel bands raided and pillaged ranchos and haciendas. Following the orders of Cajeme, they burned to the ground Cócorit, the pueblo which colonists had most infiltrated. Many white families had already fled the Yaqui in fear; traders who customarily did business in the river were afraid to reenter. To make matters worse for the government,

Mayos also rose up in rebellion, burning in their turn Santa Cruz, an important port for the Alamos merchants.[5]

Since the rebellion coincided with the Sernista movement, Governor José Pesqueira feared another of the formidable alliances and deemed it imperative to suppress the rebels first. In fact, he had already received reports that Sernista agent Gabriel Monteverde was seen trying to persuade the Yaquis to join the cause. On November 26, Pesqueira marched into the Yaqui with five hundred men, reinforced shortly by a "company of natives" from Hufrivis.[6] On December 1, Colonel Eleazar B. Muñoz led three battalions, a cavalry force, and the Hufrivis company on the first foray. Hoping to conclude the campaign rapidly and avoid violent, open confrontation, he offered Cajeme the chance to negotiate a settlement. Cajeme scoffed at the attempt to make peace with the curt message that he would be waiting for the Mexicans.

At the first battle, government troops engaged Cajeme's five hundred-man force in forty-five minutes of hard fighting. When the rebels dispersed, they left behind fifty-six dead bodies strewn over the field, according to government reports.[7] Colonel Muñoz stayed in the Yaqui until the last day of December, advancing as far as the middle of the river territory. Although he did not encounter Cajeme again, he had several skirmishes with smaller bands of rebels. In reconnoitering the entire territory, his men found only a few deserted camps and several wandering families, although they did manage to round up several hundred head of cattle, horses, and sheep. The results after a month of the campaign were clearly not encouraging.[8]

With Cajeme deliberately elusive and unwilling to negotiate, and with the Sernista revolt gathering strength throughout the state, José Pesqueira was forced to call off the Yaqui campaign and concentrate his energies on the Sernistas instead. With all the bad news, the governor was perhaps heartened by Cajeme's decision, despite the advice of some of his subordinates, not to join the Sernistas. Nor did Cajeme ally with any subsequent opposition to the Pesqueiras.[9] Because the Yaquis remained uncommitted to any outside political faction, they called little attention to themselves during the next three years, which saw Pesqueira deposed and a new regime come into office. Yaquis spent the interlude quietly but methodically reorganizing their society according to Cajeme's novel ideas.

Cajeme did not shut off the Yaqui River entirely from the outside world, which he needed as much as it needed the Yaqui. He allowed non-Yaquis to enter the river, by foot or by water, for certain legitimate businesses. Ship captains, for example, continued to ply between the port of Guaymas and El Médano, the entrance to the Yaqui River, trading clothes and cheap trinkets for firewood, straw mats, and other products Yaquis manufactured. Individual traders also came by land, mainly to buy the salt Yaquis mined on the coast.

On the basis of this trade, Cajeme instituted a tax system, probably the first one in Yaqui history. He charged a duty on imports brought in by ships and exacted a toll from traders and all other travelers. In addition to the money collected in this manner, he imposed another form of taxation: ship captains had to deliver a certain quantity of guns and ammunition on each trip from Guaymas. Moreover, individual travelers who carried firearms had to contribute them to the Yaqui arsenal. Later Cajeme extended this obligation to deserters from the state or federal armies who sought refuge in the Yaqui.

At first Cajeme did not restrict the mobility of Yaquis themselves to and from the river, although his presence most likely attracted many Yaquis on the outside back to their homeland. Individuals or families continued to move about the state, either to trade or to work in the customary places. When they returned, they often brought back guns and ammunition, purchased or obtained through other means from the towns and Mexican communities.[10]

To increase the revenues internally, Cajeme revived a practice that was most effective in the old mission days—the community plots. Each pueblo in the Yaqui had to plant a field of a certain size and maintain a rotation of workers to cultivate these fields. Some of the harvest might have been traded, but most of it was stored. Another ingenious and rather devious source of revenue was the demand of ransoms from hacendados and ranchers who wanted their stolen cattle back.[11]

In addition to the production and storage of grains, Cajeme also laid great emphasis on the buildup of war materials. Although he did not mobilize Yaquis to fight offensively for their independence, he clearly foresaw the day when they would have to defend it. Besides the guns which were confiscated and brought in by the ships, Cajeme called up those war supplies which Yaquis had stashed away from past rebellions. Besides cleaning and repairing the old guns, Yaquis further stocked their arsenal with their own freshly manufactured gunpowder.

As the chief civil, judicial, and military authorities within their pueblos, the *gobernadores* became Cajeme's administrative assistants. Subordinate to them were the captains of war, who were responsible for the mobilization of men in the pueblos: each had to maintain a certain number of men who could be armed and equipped on short notice. Another official role, which had not been noted since the mission days but which received new attention at this time, was that of the *temastian*, or sacristan. As the most important cultural officer, he was in charge of sustaining religious practices and organizing fiestas and ceremonies. Since the Yaqui River did not have permanent resident ministers at this time, the *temastianes* became in effect the chief guardians of religion and culture.[12]

Even though Cajeme was the obvious brain and motivating force behind the new organization and unchallenged as captain general, he chose to stay in the background. Instead, he pushed into the forefront another ancient Yaqui custom—the popular council, in which every Yaqui man and woman had equal participation. Although these assemblies had been convened spontaneously or on an ad hoc basis in the past, Cajeme institutionalized the council as the major decision-making body and professed to abide by its consensus.

With little difficulty, Cajeme also won the allegiance of some of the Mayos, although he did not reorganize them as thoroughly as he did his own people. He was considerably impeded by the Mexicans' much deeper penetration of the Mayo River. Four of the traditional Mayo pueblos—Navojoa, Tesia, Camoa, and San Pedro—had already been converted into regular municipalities. The other four—Echojoa, Masiaca, Cuirimpo, and Santa Cruz—swore fealty to Cajeme and obeyed his orders to store up weapons and cultivate community plots. To ensure their allegiance, Cajeme himself occasionally traveled to the Mayo to meet with his supporters there.[13]

As Cajeme took control, the state and nation which he confronted also became more organized, more powerful than ever before. For the first time since independence, Mexico attained political unity and stability under President Porfirio Díaz, whose strong, centralized rule destroyed the power of regional caudillos such as Pesqueira of Sonora. In the minds of Díaz and his henchmen, national economic development had to become the country's first priority, given its proverbially abundant natural resources and the anxious foreigners waiting to invest their surplus capital in Mexico. In the particular case of Sonora, its development program entailed Apache pacification, revitalization of the mines, construction of a vast communication and transportation network to improve the state's infrastructure, stimulation of agriculture, industry, and commerce, and finally, colonization and fruitful exploitation of the rich river lands of the Yaqui and Mayo.

Porfirian governor Luis Torres wasted no time in initiating such a program for Sonora. After repeated delays since its original conception in 1860, construction of the Sonoran Railroad finally got under way; by 1881, the American company was hiring some six hundred workers and indicated it could easily employ more.[14] New mining laws and relaxed restrictions brought about a boom in both gold and silver mining in almost every district, with North Americans bringing in most of the capital and technology.[15] Railroads and mines in turn stimulated greater commercial activities. In 1881, Governor Torres approved the establishment of the Bank of the

State of Sonora, a joint American-Mexican enterprise.[16] Those interested in agricultural development successfully pushed for the breakup of more indigenous community lands. Pima, Pápago, and Opata pueblos became easy targets as they outlived their usefulness for frontier defense when U.S. and Mexican authorities finally succeeded in neutralizing the Apaches.[17]

Not surprising, colonization of Yaqui land presented the greatest difficulties. Ignacio Pesqueira, who initiated the effort, had made little headway. In fact, many of the colonists who had settled in the Yaqui between 1868 and 1875 fled when Cajeme came to power; those who had been granted land and water concessions found it nearly impossible to take possession of their newly acquired property or to begin work on development projects.[18] In 1879, speaking for the new state government, Vice-Governor Otero reiterated its strong belief in colonization:

> The government under my charge has decided to appeal to that of the Union, requesting its help in organizing these tribes civilly, reducing them to the obedience of the authorities, dividing the land of their pueblos in a manner convenient to the support of life by means of work and forcing them to enter at once onto the road of civilization.
>
> For this objective the Executive hopes that the Congress would lend its efficient and strong support, because a successful colonization of those rivers would result immediately in a great increase of the civilized population and a bountiful production in all the various branches of wealth.[19]

To local developmentalists, colonization became a much broader concept that went beyond Pesqueira's original idea of planting a few agricultural colonies along the Yaqui River. It would include, for example, such a proposal as the "bifurcation of the Río Yaqui with the object of bringing its waters to the valley situated to the northeast of the city of Guaymas."[20] An even more immediate benefit expected from colonization would be to increase the state's labor supply. As Governor Luis Torres explained, by forcing the Yaquis onto "the road of civilization," those displaced from the land would then "provide all the labor necessary for the railroad enterprise and others established in the state, such as agriculture, mining and many others."[21] This would be especially convenient, he continued, since the Yaqui workers could be paid a lower wage than what the other Mexican workers demanded.[22]

The Díaz government, of course, concurred fully with this policy of colonization and development. As early as February 1879, the secretary of development, colonization, industry and commerce granted Wenceslao Iberri, a leading merchant of Guaymas and one of Sonora's representatives to the national congress, a concession to colonize the island of Ciari in the middle of the Yaqui territory.[23] In February 1881, it approved a comprehensive, three-month contract to Manuel Castro to survey and colonize the *terrenos baldíos*, or unused lands, of the Yaqui and Mayo. The contract expired before any surveying was even begun, however, mainly because conditions in the Yaqui did not permit the entry of engineers.[24] The Mayo was more accessible, especially those pueblos which Mexicans had already substantially expropriated. Since 1880, the Geographic Exploratory Commission, headed by Colonel Augustín Díaz and staffed by army engineers, had been dividing land in some Mayo pueblos into private lots.[25]

Before 1881, however, the federal government was unwilling, or unable, to aid Sonora's efforts at colonization beyond the granting of concessions and contracts. Clearly little progress could be made in this direction if the Yaqui people continued to resist outside attempts to control their persons and land. Having little resources of its own to conduct a full-scale military campaign to crush Cajeme's regime, the state government repeatedly—in 1879, 1880, and 1881—requested soldiers, weapons, and provisions from the federal government.[26] Before Mexico City could promise any substantial aid, an internal power struggle in Sonora precipitated a local crisis, which in turn provoked the Yaquis into armed action.

In July 1881, Luis Torres turned over the reins of government to the newly elected governor, Carlos R. Ortiz, a rich merchant and hacendado from Alamos. This action paralleled a similar peaceful transference of power by President Díaz to his son-in-law and the president-elect, Manuel Gonzáles. Such gestures were deemed politically necessary, since the Porfiristas had overthrown the old Liberals on the principle of "no re-election." In fact, of course, they merely turned over power to one of their own.

Carlos Ortiz, however, who had been active in the inner circle of Torres, soon broke with the other Porfiristas. At odds was the primacy of state sovereignty, which Ortiz emphasized, and the solidification of a close working relationship between the state government and the federal Díaz regime, which Torres projected. Six months into office, Governor Ortiz suddenly recalled the state of Sonora's National Guards from General Bernardo Reyes's Apache campaign at the frontier, citing the urgent need to defend the state government against an imminent coup by Ramón Corral, Luis Torres, and federal general José G. Carbó. When this unsubstantiated story gained little credibility, Ortiz changed his line. This time he declared a state of emergency, charging that the Yaquis and Mayos were on the verge of open rebellion.[27] In early September, the governor's brother, Agustín Ortiz, led several squadrons of National Guards, totaling some one thousand men, into various Mayo pueblos, purportedly for the reason of gathering information on the alleged rebellion. Actually, there was no disturbance in the Mayo, but the sudden presence of unpopular government troops aroused much resentment. On the nineteenth, Ortiz reported a skirmish between his men and thirteen hundred *indios* led by Jesús Moroyoqui and his sons.[28] Then he spread rumors that Cajeme was preparing the Yaquis to enter the Mayo. When Cajeme still had not appeared by the twenty-seventh, Ortiz extemporized an explanation that Cajeme was delayed because Yaquis were still waiting for more ammunition from Guaymas.[29] His numerous reports during this period were full of alarming news about large gatherings of Mayos in different pueblos, or instructions and promises they had received from Cajeme, and of projected attacks on Baroyeca and other Mexican communities in the vicinity.[30]

General Bernardo Reyes, who had reluctantly released the guards to Governor Ortiz because he had no final authority over them, steadfastly refused to believe that the Yaquis and Mayos were in a state of rebellion. On the contrary, he denounced the movement of troops into the Mayo as a provocation, warning that a full-scale rebellion at this time would be a most undesirable consequence when Apaches were still posing a serious threat to the state.[31] Having apparently seen through Ortiz's scheme of fomenting a Yaqui-Mayo uprising in order to rally statewide support behind himself against his real or imaginary enemies, Reyes instructed his subordinates under no circumstances to lend federal support to Ortiz.[32] This so enraged the governor that he turned around and accused Reyes of being the main instigator of the alleged plot against him.[33]

By this time, if Ortiz had any second thoughts about his scheme, it was too late. Cajeme had indeed arrived in the Mayo with over two thousand Yaquis to take on Agustín Ortiz. On the night of October 15, Cajeme moved his men from their camp at Echojoa to Capetemaya, where they had better access to ranches which could provide food. Thinking that Cajeme had merely divided his forces, and that he could not possibly have more than one thousand men at Capetemaya, Ortiz launched a surprise attack on them, confident of a quick victory. He took with him only a small force of 130 cavalrymen and 150 infantrymen. Instead of one thousand men, Ortiz encountered closer to three thousand, according to his first report. After two-and-a-half hours of hard fighting, the Yaquis and Mayos dispersed towards the Yaqui River, leaving eighty dead comrades, again according to Ortiz's first report.[34] Later, as the Ortiz government unabashedly claimed total victory over Cajeme, it inflated the Yaqui-Mayo forces to four thousand and their casualties to two hundred. It further accused Cajeme and his men of having destroyed and pillaged all the haciendas and ranches within a seven-league radius between the Mayo port of Agiabampo and the city of Alamos. In the same breath, Carlos Ortiz attempted to implicate his political enemies with Cajeme, supplying as evidence that among the dead in

Capetemaya were several Mexicans. He accused the federal forces in Sonora, although without specifically naming General Reyes, of having made an accord with Cajeme "to produce a complete disturbance of the public order in the state and force the disappearance of its constitutional powers."[35]

Governor Ortiz's machinations and accusations had so little credibility that, by the end of October, the citizens of Hermosillo and Guaymas, as well as the National Guards, had begun to disavow his authority. Seconding the original analysis by Reyes, they accused Carlos Ortiz and his brother, Agustín, of having "penetrated the territory of the Indians" to provoke them deliberately into a defensive war. To allow Ortiz a graceful exit from what was clearly a political defeat, Reyes provided federal troops to escort him safely into exile in the United States and into political oblivion. Filling out Ortiz's term, Vice-Governor Antonio Escalante immediately ordered that no further action be taken against the Yaquis and Mayos.[36] With Luis Torres returning as governor in March 1883, the Porfirista clique never again relinquished control of the state until it was ultimately overthrown during the Mexican Revolution of 1910.

Besides these general political consequences, the Ortiz incident brought much attention to the Yaquis and Mayos. The confrontation of 1882 demonstrated to the Mexican public the high level of preparedness on the part of Cajeme and his followers in both river territories. When provoked, they were able to mobilize at short notice at least two thousand well-armed, well-trained men, certainly the largest fighting force amassed since Banderas. The maneuvers at Capetemaya had shown Cajeme to be a good strategist; he had learned his lessons well from past experiences as soldier and officer in state and federal armies. No doubt he had been training his men in new techniques of combat and in the use of the modern weapons which they had assiduously collected. Moreover, as their first testing round, the battle gave the Yaquis and Mayos a definite taste of their new strength. It also deepened their mistrust of the Mexicans. It is significant to note that under Cajeme's leadership, the Yaquis and their Mayo allies would rarely venture outside their own territories to take the offensive against the Mexicans. The key to Cajeme's strategy lay in training and preparing his people for the defense of their land and autonomy.

The Ortiz incident had another unforeseen effect: it encouraged the Mayos of Cuirimpo, Navojoa, and Tesia, recently converted into Mexican municipalities, to attempt to regain control of their pueblos. As José Zarapero, *gobernador* of Navojoa and suspected leader of the movement, explained, the Mayos wanted permission "to name their own authorities and to remove the municipal governments."[37] Throughout 1883 and 1884, rumors abounded of plans to attack the municipality of Navojoa and of the imminent arrival of large contingents of Yaqui auxiliaries. But these attacks never took place, nor did the arrival of Yaqui armies.[38] While Cajeme never openly discouraged the Mayos, he was hesitant about sending Yaquis to aid their cause. On one occasion, he reportedly called off a planned attack on Navojoa at the last moment. Another time, a revolt apparently fizzled when Cajeme reneged on earlier promises to send help.[39] The reluctance to become involved suggested a Cajeme policy not to initiate hostilities as long as the government left the Yaquis alone. During these two years, except for the usual complaints of depredations on nearby haciendas and ranches—Yaquis continued to demand ransom from owners for stolen cattle—they directed relatively little attention to themselves. Some of the thirteen thousand residents in the area, however, still felt unsafe and [they] departed.[40]

While the state enjoyed a rare period of uncharacteristic peace, interest in Sonora and its resources grew, especially on the part of North Americans. The *Los Angeles Times* of February 23, 1883, carried a feature story entitled "Seductive Sonora." It recounted the trip to Sonora taken by Mr. John Lowe of California, who was in the "agricultural implement and hardware business." Lowe spoke "in glowing terms of the bright prospects and rapid development" of the state and how Americanized it was fast becoming, observing further that the people are progressive and gladly welcome Americans to their midst, and peace and order are preserved to an extent hardly believed by Americans." With eight hundred to one thousand Americans already living there, Lowe concluded that he expected "to see Sonora an American state within five years if the present influx of Americans continues."[41]

Stories about the real or alleged wealth of the Yaqui territory were particularly attractive. Americans were interested in the carbon fields, salt pits, and oyster beds of the Yaqui.[42] In November 1882, the Mexican secretary of development granted a contract to the American Robert Symon to build a short railroad "from the carboniferous fields of the Río Yaqui to a point called El Morrito on the Bay of Guaymas."[43] Moreover, Mexicans and foreigners alike were obsessed with the thought of discovering large mines in Yaqui-controlled land. Rumors circulated of fabulously rich silver mines in the Sierra de Bacatete, jealously guarded by Yaquis who could not be persuaded to divulge their exact locations; nor would Cajeme permit his people to exploit these mines themselves.[44] There was also the unsubstantiated item carried by the *Arizona Daily Star* of February 14, 1883, on a Mr. Huller of New York selling Yaqui mines to English speculators.[45]

Such growing interest in the Yaqui prompted the state to renew its own efforts to wrest control of the territory from Cajeme. Sonora continued to hound the federal government for cooperation in launching the long-projected campaign. Finally, after an investigation of the Yaqui and Mayo, General José G. Carbó rendered a preliminary report to the secretary of war in October 1884. In it he noted that Cajeme always had three to four hundred armed men around him, but could easily mobilize three to four thousand. He estimated that the Yaquis had two hundred metallic weapons between rifles and carbines, two hundred pistols, and four hundred percussion rifles, all up-to-date war matériel. A fair man, General Carbó offered a personal assessment of Cajeme which agreed with the Yaqui leader's recent conduct: "The character of the jefe Cajeme is very little warlike and his main tendency is not to extend his domain, conquering all the pueblos civilly organized [that is, the Mexican towns] and subject them to the obedience of the government which is found between the two rivers . . . but it is to conserve the independence of the territory which they now possess."[46]

For the moment, Carbó concluded in his report, there were only fifty men of the Sixth Battalion guarding both rivers. They had instructions only to defend their position, since they were hardly capable of attacking the much larger Yaqui and Mayo forces.

As the federal government still bided its time in coming to a decision, the more impatient state government searched for other ways to destroy Cajeme. Ramón Corral, secretary of the state government, received the intelligence from Prefect J. A. Rivera of Guaymas of growing discontent among Cajeme's followers. Reportedly, Cajeme was dealing severely with those Yaquis and Mayos who dared oppose him. One of the victims was Loreto Molino, a Yaqui captain expelled from the river [territory] for insubordination. Hoping to take advantage of the schism, Corral directed Rivera "to try to foment diplomatically the divisions in the Río."[47] Accordingly, Rivera successfully persuaded Molino to avenge his ouster from the Yaqui.

One night in January 1885, Molino surreptitiously entered the Yaqui from Guaymas with twenty-nine other men, armed with a plan to assassinate Cajeme at his home at Los Guamúchiles. When they arrived, much to their dismay, they found that Cajeme had departed that very night for the Mayo. In their frustration, Molino and [his] cohorts burned Cajeme's house, terrorized his family members and neighbors, [and] then fled as quietly as they had come.[48]

Immediately notified of Molino's heinous acts, Cajeme rushed back to the Yaqui. His own intelligence network had supplied him with a good inkling of the conspiracy between the renegade Yaqui and the government. Cajeme's first act was to detain all the ships docked at El Médano as hostages, imposing fines of fifty to two hundred pesos on each one. Then he informed the captain of the port of Guaymas that this seizure was necessary because the state had sent Molino to assassinate him and create a crisis in the Yaqui. Finally he demanded the prefect of Guaymas to give him a full explanation of the plot and to remit the Yaqui conspirators to him for punishment.[49]

At this tense moment Governor Torres himself communicated with Cajeme to assure the irate Yaqui leader that justice would be done once proper guilt had been ascertained, but not according to Cajeme's methods.[50] Totally unappeased by this answer, Cajeme ordered his followers to begin massive assaults on haciendas, ranches, and stations of the Sonoran railroad in the Guaymas and Alamos districts. Then, by burning the twenty-one ships detained at El Médano, he signaled the beginning of full-scale rebellion.[51]

The government's plot to foment a civil war inside the Yaqui, whereby the people would mercilessly kill each other off, had obviously backfired. Utterly disorganized and unprepared to meet the fury unleashed by Cajeme, it sent all available state and federal troops in the Guaymas and Alamos districts against the rebels, while instructing hacendados to organize their own private forces to defend their properties.[52] The raids, fires, and killings had become so serious that several major mines in Alamos closed down. Mexican residents in the area fled in droves. Soon Mayos joined the Yaqui rebellion, burning the port of Agiabampo. Reports on the size of Yaqui and Mayo rebel bands ranged from five or six hundred to as large as one thousand.[53] The most exposed and raided area was the Guaymas Valley to the northwest of the Yaqui River, between the Sonoran railroad and the Sierra de Bacatete. There were quite a few ranches and haciendas in the valley, engaged primarily in cattle and horse raising and the cultivation of maize, beans, wheat, and cotton. Between twenty-five hundred and three thousand persons lived in that area, some of whom undoubtedly were Yaqui workers.[54]

Only in view of this grave situation did the federal government begin to pay attention to Sonora, much to the relief of local authorities. The secretary of war authorized all available federal forces in Sonora and Sinaloa to engage in the suppression of the rebels.[55] The state government itself began mobilizing its National Guards, as well as raising money in the form of forced loans from merchants and mine owners in Alamos and Guaymas.[56] Finally, on March 31, President Porfirio Díaz authorized his secretary of war to open a formal campaign against the rebels, designating General Carbó, commander of the First Military Zone, to direct it.[57]

By May, General Carbó had gathered in the Guaymas Valley a substantial force of 801 National Guardsmen and 868 federals, with another 500 to join them shortly. General Otero commanded an additional four hundred men to watch over the Mayo while Carbó conducted the campaign in the Yaqui. Many prominent Sonorans from across the state, including Secretary Ramón

Corral and Deputy Rafael Izábal, as well as several foreign residents, volunteered for the campaign. As the first expedition taken against the Yaquis in many years, it obviously had great popular appeal.[58] The military rosters read like the Sonoran social register.

The campaign formally began on May 8, 1885. Dividing his forces into two columns, General Carbó led one into the Yaqui from La Pitahaya and the pueblo of Belém at the mouth of the Yaqui River, while General [Fausto] Topete went around it to enter from upriver, through Buenavista and Cócorit. They planned to meet in the pueblo of Tórin, located in the middle of Yaqui territory. Carbó also armed a two hundred-man Yaqui auxiliary force, commanded by the turncoat Loreto Molino, to serve as explorers, for they alone knew the Yaqui terrain well.[59]

The general arrived at El Médano on the twelfth to set up his campaign headquarters there, choosing this site because it was on an elevation and hence safe from the rains, had easy communication with Guaymas and the coast, and was a port to which small ships could sail with provisions and other necessities. The small number of Yaquis who usually resided there had all fled. The area near the mouth of the river, from La Pitahaya to El Médano and including the first three pueblos of Belém, Ráum, and Huírivis, was rather bare of vegetation. Except for a few families, Yaquis had also deserted this area, leaving their unharvested crops for the troops to gather.

The rebel stronghold really began with Pótam, situated about two kilometers upriver in a thickly wooded terrain. On the left bank an impenetrable forest stretched towards the Mayo. In its densest part, somewhere between Pótam and Vícam, Cajeme had build a huge fort, which he named El Añil. The trees around it were so thick that it took Carbó's scouts a full day to reconnoitre forty meters of the parapet. They reported that the fort was surrounded by an immense moat in front of which was a sturdy palisade. From the fort to the river, the Yaquis had constructed a covered path so that they could travel with some protection to bring in water.

The government located its base of operations in Tórin, which was considered an excellent military vantage because of its position on top of a small hill. As with all the other pueblos, it too was deserted. General Carbó ordered the construction of a small reduct, where he stationed five hundred men under Colonel Lorenzo Torres to watch over the entire river territory. Scout reports revealed that near Tórin, on the Cerro de Onteme, the Yaquis had built several smaller fortifications. On the left bank facing Tórin, they had dug trenches, which they abandoned when the soldiers arrived. One league downriver was another fortification surrounded by a moat and trenches, and defended by some eight hundred Yaquis. As the scouts continued their explorations, they constantly reported the discovery of still more forts and trenches inside the forests, such as the one near Bácum, five leagues from Tórin and two kilometers inland. Cócorit, the last pueblo, marked the limit of Yaqui territory; beyond it lay Buenavista, the nearest Mexican community.

General Carbó estimated there were twenty-five thousand Yaquis in the river [territory], with another ten thousand Mayos. He calculated that five to six thousand men could be easily mobilized to fight, although not all with firearms.[60] The descriptions of the forts and trenches confirmed that Cajeme had indeed introduced elements of the Mexican or European art of warfare.

With four hundred infantrymen between federals and National Guards, and another two hundred cavalrymen, General Topete marched downriver toward the headquarters at El Médano. On May 16, he engaged in the first battle with Cajeme's forces at El Añil fort. Fixing their only cannon on the fort, Topete ordered his men to attack. Within two hours, the Yaquis successfully repelled the soldiers, causing them twenty dead and fifty-seven wounded. The rebels also recovered the cannon which the troops had abandoned in beating their hasty retreat.[61]

Even though the Yaquis did not totally rout the attackers, they were much encouraged by the results. They celebrated Cajeme as a great military tactician and acclaimed the advantages of the fortifications. With most of the Yaquis barricaded within one of the many forts, only about two hundred of them, armed with firearms, and another three hundred with bows and arrows, moved outside to gather intelligence on the opposition. Consequently the soldiers encountered very few Yaquis in their forays and explorations. Although General Carbó spread the word from the outset of the campaign that any peaceful Indian who went to El Médano headquarters would be well received and pardoned with mercy, few accepted his offers.[62]

In June, several skirmishes and another major battle at El Añil fort took place. This time, General Caamaño and his fourteen hundred men attacked from the Cerro de Onteme facing the fort. Again, they failed to force out the Yaquis or penetrate the well-protected fort.[63]

Obtaining no measurable results militarily, Colonel Lorenzo Torres tried to negotiate a settlement with three Cajeme representatives at Tórin. The rebels offered to end the rebellion if all troops would retreat from the river [territory], but the government considered these demands unacceptable. It in turn offered the rebels guarantees of life and property if they would lay down their guns and submit to the government. The Yaquis deemed these conditions unreasonable. It became clear to Colonel Torres that the rebels, knowing that imminent rains would hinder further troop movements along the swollen river and in the drenched forests, were merely stalling for time.[64] As anticipated, the rains came in July, forcing General Carbó to retire all his men to El Médano, thereby temporarily suspending the campaign.[65]

General Carbó decided not to launch a major attack before the withdrawal, because he was not confident enough that his men could take Cajeme at El Añil. He had discovered from a Yaqui lad who had come from among the rebels that the fort actually had two sections: inside the visible one behind the moat was another. Cajeme and his people were thus double-barricaded within the second wall. Moreover, the lad informed Carbó, the Yaquis planned to fight to the bitter end and never surrender. They even had many of their families with them, along with cattle, horses, and other beasts. Although they were out of ammunition, they had sent for more gunpowder and lead from the Mayo.[66]

Knowing they were coming back, Cajeme nevertheless interpreted the government retreat as a victory for the Yaquis. The temporary letup of the campaign gave him breathing space and a chance to resupply and recuperate from the months of hard fighting. He ordered the Yaquis to return to their fields and prepare seeds for the new planting. He even allowed the resumption of some trade with Guaymas.[67]

Of the troops that had retreated from the Yaqui, the state contingents from Arizpe and Moctezuma went home to help fight the Apaches, who had lately increased their depredations. One section of troops covered designated spots in the Guaymas Valley to prevent raids on haciendas and ranches. Garrisons posted at critical points around the Yaqui and Mayo rivers attempted to block rebels from leaving the area.[68]

Conditions in the Yaqui and Mayo were actually quite miserable, for the months spent holed up inside the forts had depleted their supplies of food, while the new planting could not be immediately harvested. More and more Yaquis and Mayos wanted either to have peace or to leave the river lands. To add to their hardships the yellow fever epidemic, which had been spreading in Sonora since 1883, finally reached the Yaqui in September.[69] In order to affirm his authority in the Mayo, Cajeme went to the extreme of personally executing the leader of a growing peace faction, Andrés Capusari.[70] To prevent the flight of Yaquis, he ordered some of the roads out of the river closed. Only those whom he trusted could go to Guaymas, Alamos, Hermosillo, and Ures to buy guns and ammunition.[71]

In December, a group of citizens from Guaymas, Father Tomás G. de Galdeano, Nicanor Ortiz, and Nieves E. Acosta, entered the Yaqui to try to negotiate a peace with the *gobernadores* and people of the eight pueblos. The only condition they presented to the Yaquis assembled in Pótam was their submission to the Mexican government. Although Cajeme called the meeting, he deliberately remained at an inconspicuous distance, aloof from the actual parleys. When it came time to sign the surrender, the Mexican negotiators asked for Cajeme's signature. Emerging quietly from the background, the Yaqui leader expressed his agreement with the surrender, since it appeared to be the will of the people. But he adamantly refused to sign anything, maintaining simply, "My word is worth as much as my signature and the people have always made peace without signing any piece of paper."[72] Immediately sensing that they had failed in their mission, the three men, dejected, returned to Guaymas. The Mayos refused a similar peace offer that General Otero extended them.[73]

In March 1886, the campaign was reopened. General Angel Martínez, the new commander of the First Military Zone, replaced General Carbó, who had died in October. More federal troops reinforced those already in Sonora. Residents and property owners of the state organized an additional eight hundred auxiliaries to send against the Mayos. This time the campaign was fought on two fronts: General Martínez marched with two thousand men to the Mayo, while General Marcos Carrillo took the remaining two thousand men to the Yaqui.[74]

On May 5, General Carrillo stormed El Añil fort, which Cajeme with just eight hundred Yaquis valiantly but unsuccessfully defended. The rebels had clearly lost much of their morale and vigor from the previous year. As rebels spilled out of El Añil, they fled towards their last refuge, a newly built fort in Buatachive, high in the Sierra de Bacatete.[75] Enclosed by natural protective barriers, Buatachive was thought to be impregnable. Cajeme ordered his men, their families, and all available food and cattle behind its walls. Some religious objects and ornaments stripped from the pueblo churches were also stashed inside for safekeeping.

Noting that Cajeme had in effect entrapped himself with all his people and resources inside Buatachive, General Martínez seized the opportunity to deal him the coup de grace. Leaving the Mayo, he rushed into the Yaqui and ordered the entire campaign force to lay siege to the fort. Four days later, on May 12, the soldiers attacked from all sides. Although the Yaquis defended themselves with their usual valor, there was really no contest. As they scrambled out and escaped into the sierra, the troops stormed inside, there to witness a scene of utmost misery: yellow fever had stricken about two thousand people, women, and children, the result of unsanitary and crowded conditions, insufficient food, and lack of fresh water. All of the fighting men, which Martínez estimated to have been two thousand, had managed to escape, except for the two hundred dead scattered over the battlegrounds outside the fort. Not a single piece of weaponry was in sight.[76]

After their disastrous defeats at El Añil and Buatachive, the Yaquis could not longer sustain the rebellion. General Martínez announced the conclusion of the campaign by offering amnesty to all Yaquis and Mayos who presented themselves with their weapons within twenty days of May 15. Hungry, sick, and demoralized, rebels drifted into the military camps established in Tórin, El Médano, Cócorit, and Pótam, as soldiers gathered the old men wandering around the battlefields.[77]

At the camp in Tórin, General Martínez informed the Yaquis who had surrendered that the government's magnanimous policy was to pacify them without destroying them, for they were "intelligent, vigorous and susceptible to civilization and would become a hardworking and useful people, contributing greatly to strengthen the national element on the frontier and develop the public wealth." They would be allowed to keep the land which "pertained honestly to them, according to the law." Furthermore, the *gobernadores* who had served under Cajeme would retain their offices, "because they had been chosen by the people."[78]

After sending blankets, food, and clothing to succor the suffering, Governor Luis Torres personally went to Tórin to accept the surrender. Then he put Colonel Lorenzo Torres in charge of reorganizing the administration of the pueblos.[79] Even though Cajeme was still at large and showed no signs of submission, General Martínez believed that the rebellion had been suppressed. He withdrew a large portion of his men from the Yaqui, leaving three strong detachments in El Médano, Tórin, and Cócorit. Next he marched to the Mayo to arrange the act of surrender there. Mexicans began moving back to the Yaqui to live; traders returned to conduct their usual businesses.[80]

Cajeme made one last major effort to save his faltering regime. He convinced some of the Yaquis who had surrendered in Tórin to rejoin him and those who had not capitulated. As in the past, the Yaquis had salvaged most of their weapons, for those who surrendered their persons seldom gave up their guns. Cajeme had also hoped that the approaching rains would again force the withdrawal of troops from the Yaqui River, as they had a year before. This time, however, the government was determined not to give him a second chance.

First, Cajeme reoccupied the fort of El Añil, but soldiers quickly dispersed his men. The Yaquis regrouped and with a force of twelve hundred tried to take El Médano from Colonel Lorenzo Torres on July 22. Again, they were defeated. Cajeme still did not give up. He divided his men into many small bands, which engaged government troops in minor skirmishes. By October, it became necessary to send more troops back into the Yaqui.

The rebels fled into the Sierra de Bacatete, and when the pursuit became too hot there, they slipped into the Guaymas Valley, where they raided and terrorized the haciendas and ranches. During this whole period, no soldier actually saw Cajeme in person: "He seemed to be an imaginary being, invisible, a myth created by the fantasy of his people."[81] Although he no longer had the total and active support of all Yaquis and Mayos, he had enough loyal men to perpetuate an unstable situation in both river territories.

General Martínez finally concluded that only a war without quarter could force Cajeme into submission. He sent his men like hunters into the forests and the sierra, killing any moving person on sight, confiscating all cattle and food materials. Cajeme was still nowhere to be seen. Many times a soldier thought he had spotted the formidable Yaqui leader, only to find upon approach that the form had simply "vanished like a shadow." Even with all the hardships and intense persecution, Cajeme still had about eight hundred followers, who sustained themselves by the traditional plunder in the Guaymas Valley.[82]

At this time Cajeme made an effort to end the hostilities, perhaps again to buy time. He wrote General Juan Hernández, commander of El Médano garrison, offering to surrender if all government troops were withdrawn from the Yaqui territory immediately. Otherwise, he warned ominously, he would fight to the bitter end. The government obviously could not accept these terms, which contradicted its intention to break the Yaqui autonomy. As General Hernández explained it to Cajeme in his reply, the Yaqui was part of the Mexican republic and the republic had a right and obligation to send forces to wherever it deemed necessary. With this answer Cajeme withdrew the olive branch.

Not letting up for one moment, General Martínez ordered his men to increase their search expeditions into the Sierra de Bacatete, into the Guaymas Valley, and into the Mayo, where Cajeme still had some supporters. At first these searches netted only more women, children, and old disabled Yaqui men. But as the persecution intensified, with troops relentlessly chasing after the rebels in their circular flight from the river to the sierras, from the sierra to the valley, and from the valley back to the river, more and more of them surrendered. At the end of the year, the military conducted one last major expedition to the Sierra de Bacatete, along the margins of the Yaqui River, and to the other favorite hideouts of the rebels.[83]

In the final tally, four thousand had surrendered in the Yaqui and another two thousand in the Mayo, but Cajeme was not among them. Despite the insistence of the commanders, only 140 firearms were recovered.[84] The people in the two river territories had not been able to plant any crops during the year of rebellion; their animals had either been consumed or confiscated. To alleviate their misery, the government sent in food and clothing. Although Cajeme was still at large, General Martínez formally terminated the campaign.

Sonora had spent much of its revenues to pacify the Yaquis. Deputy Rafael Izábal reported that the campaign had cost the state eighty thousand pesos in 1885, and another seventy-four thousand in 1886.[85] Many of the funds were raised through forced contributions. The merchants of Alamos, for example, regularly advanced six to ten thousand pesos a month during 1885.[86]

General Martínez experienced considerable frustration in his first encounter with the Yaquis. During the difficult period of trying to trap the elusive Cajeme and the hardcore rebels, he actually proposed to President Díaz that all Yaqui prisoners be deported out of the state of Sonora. Díaz vetoed the idea because it would "initiate a war of extermination." He demonstrated a sensitive understanding of the Yaqui mentality in explaining: "The Indian prefers death to exile, and before the prospect of being removed from his home, he would fight until he perishes." In view of this, Díaz proposed an alternative, suggesting that once pacification was assured, the leaders of the rebellion be remitted to Mexico to be drafted into the military.[87] Although leaders had been occasionally deported in the past, this was the first time that Mexican authorities seriously considered deportation as a possible solution to the Yaqui problem. While the idea was set aside for the time being, deportation would be discussed again and eventually adopted on a large scale within the next decade.

With peace seemingly assured for the Yaqui River, Mexicans from neighboring communities rushed in. They came mainly from Baroyeca, Quiriego, Rosario, Batacosa, Buenavista, and Cumuripa, to trade, to take up land for cultivation, or to raise cattle. This time, three permanent garrisons were posted along the river territory: at El Médano at the entrance, Tórin in the middle, and Cócorit at the end. In addition to the surveillance of the Yaquis, they also supervised the establishment of the first permanent colonies in the Yaqui.[88]

Yet no one felt really safe as long as Cajeme remained free. General Hernández presented to Secretary Ramón Corral a list of thirteen known rebel leaders still at large, headed by the name of José María Leyva Cajeme. Corral circulated this list to all the prefects so that "the greatest vigilance is exercised, for it is not difficult [to see] that some of these Indians, attempting to flee from the forces which pursue them, find refuge in some pueblo or rancho in your jurisdiction, or touch these points during their flight."[89] He included a description of Cajeme: "regular height, rather fat, big eyes, thick lips, beardless, much black hair. Special markings: missing half the index finger on the right hand. Speaks good Spanish and his speech is measured."[90]

It seemed that Cajeme had simply vanished; not even a hint of his presence was detected anywhere. Then one day in April 1887, someone finally spotted the "most wanted man" in Sonora: an Indian who recognized him hiding in a private home near Guaymas. The Indian immediately informed Salvador Armenta, a state official in Guaymas. Before Armenta could ascertain the identity of the suspect, and being afraid that a precipitous move on his part would alert the suspect to escape, he contacted Governor Torres in Nogales by telegraph. The governor in turn notified General Angel Martínez to take the next express train to Guaymas. On the morning of the twelfth, Martínez went with a small escort to the house near Guaymas, confirmed that the man hiding there was indeed Cajeme, and apprehended him. The famous fugitive put up no resistance, seemingly relieved that his long ordeal of flight was over.

General Martínez treated Cajeme with the utmost courtesy, lodging him in his own home like an honored guest, permitting Cajeme's family to visit, and allowing the general public, filled with curiosity or respect, to meet with him. Cajeme received everyone cordially, always with a faint smile on his face. Yaquis especially crowded around General Martínez's house, knowing it would be their last chance to see their fallen leader. Among those who met Cajeme for the first time was Ramón Corral, who interviewed him for a biography and recorded a favorable first impression: "I thought I was going to meet a corpulent Indian, silent and with a ferocious expression on his face. I was never so surprised to see a man of medium height, slim but not skinny, with an astute smile on his wide mouth, friendly and good-natured and communicative as few Indians are."[91]

Cajeme readily answered all of Corral's queries regarding his personal life. With total recollection of dates and details, he also proudly recounted how he had built the separate state in the Yaqui River and how he led his people to defend their independence. But according to biographer Corral, Cajeme had realized since their defeat that the Yaquis must learn to live a new existence, to submit to the government: "Before we were enemies and we fought; now all this is over and we are all friends."[92] To Corral, the Yaqui maintained that he had always been a "patriotic Mexican," recalling how once, when a North American had asked for his cooperation in building a railroad to the Yaqui to facilitate the exploitation of the carbon fields, he had replied: "We Mexicans do not need foreigners to come and take us by the hand and bless us."[93]

Cajeme was the most excited when he talked about the skill and valor of his people. In describing the first battle at El Añil with General Topete, Cajeme told Corral that he had no more than three hundred Yaquis inside the fort. When Corral reminded him that all accounts of the battle would contradict this excessively small number, Cajeme replied with a mysterious smile, "That is because when the Indians are behind a weapon, they become many."[94] When he left the Yaqui prisoner, Corral concluded in his biography, "I was filled with a profound sense of liking for this Indian, so intelligent and so brave. . . . "

On April 21, Cajeme was taken by ship to the Yaqui River. When his guard assured him that nothing was going to happen to him, Cajeme chided him, "Do not waste your jokes on a man who is about to die."[95] He had no illusions about his destiny, as he was marched through all the pueblos, arriving at Cócorit on the twenty-fifth. On that day, Cajeme was executed by a firing squad. His own people then solemnly buried him in a quiet ceremony.

An Obituary for Cajeme

Ramón Corral, Sonoran statesman, Cajeme's official biographer, and leading Porfirista spokesman for progress, wrote the words of an appropriate Mexican obituary to the fallen Yaqui leader: "The sacrifice of Cajeme was very painful, but it would give the effect of securing the peace in the [Yaqui and Mayo] rivers, the basis and beginning of a period of civilization for the tribes." In the same optimistic vein, he expressed a personal conviction that Cajeme would be the last Yaqui rebel leader.[96] Corral could not have been more wrong in forecasting the future. Within only a few months of Cajeme's execution, the Yaquis had chosen new leaders and reactivated their armed struggle for their own sovereignty, against a government more powerful and more determined than any previous regime to dispossess and integrate them.

Had Cajeme been able to pen his own obituary, he would have written a more fitting one. He might have provided an inkling of why and how, having spent his early life outside the Yaqui River, apart from the Yaqui people and way of life, in the company largely of Mexicans, his life took such a drastic turn when he finally returned to be among his people. He might have suggested that the brutality of the Mexican military campaigns, some of which he observed and might even have participated in, including the Bácum massacre of 1868, and the compelling persistence of the Yaquis, which he finally came to appreciate, convinced him of the justness of the Yaqui cause. He might have sensed that as a Yaqui—an "Indian"—in Mexican society, he could never have attained great social mobility, so his proper place was with his own kind. He certainly would have lamented the profound suffering his people experienced under his failed leadership in attempting to create a separate Yaqui republic, but he was proud of the fight they had put up against an immense adversary. Finally, he might not have been as contrite at the end as Corral made him out to be. He might have noted that the course of past Yaqui history assured the rise of a new leader and a new form of resistance from the smoulder of the last defeat.

Despite its crushing demise, the Cajeme regime was in many ways the high point of Yaqui history in the nineteenth century. A creative, charismatic leader, Cajeme assumed power at a time when the Yaquis, after a long period of costly alliances, were demoralized, unorganized, leaderless, and unsure about their future. Heeding Cajeme's call, Yaquis who had been living outside the [Yaqui] returned in droves to their traditional pueblos, eager to revitalize their weakened communities. With the goals of autonomy, self-reliance, and self-sufficiency in mind, Cajeme strengthened the Yaquis' economic base by combining innovations, such as the tax system, with traditional practices, such as the community plots. These insured revenues and surpluses that allowed for the purchase of arms and the stockpiling of food. He sharpened the Yaquis' skills with the white man's war methods, thinking this would enhance their ability to fend off *yori* aggression. Unfortunately, despite initial victories, in the end Yaqui forts, trenches, and maneuvers were an insufficient match for the more experienced, better equipped, and better provisioned Mexican armies which invaded their territory. This was Cajeme's biggest miscalculation.

In spite of, or perhaps because of, his long early absence from the Yaqui River, Cajeme's attention to the revival of traditional Yaqui political and religious institutions was significant. In conjunction with the recall of the dispersed Yaqui population to their traditional pueblos, Cajeme seemed intent to revitalize what he might have perceived to be a sagging commitment to Yaqui culture. While he was indisputably the supreme commander, and brooked no challenge to his authority, on public occasions he deferred to the traditional council of *gobernadores* and elders, who represented the will of the people. He emphasized the important role of sacristans, or *temastianes*, and other native religious personnel. Although there is very little information on their precise functions and activities, they were apparently responsible for the upkeep of the village churches and the safeguard of religious objects. In the best days under Cajeme, Yaqui society probably conformed most closely to its traditional form since the beginning of Mexican independence.

A strong initial unity began to weaken under factional disputes, a problem in part created by deliberate Mexican attempts to foment dissension among the Yaquis and their Mayo allies. Cajeme also had difficulty maintaining high morale, strict discipline, and firm commitment when the regime came under constant Mexican attack. After each military setback, less resolved Yaquis could be seen leaving the river. Yet Cajeme, by force of his personality if nothing else, managed to hold a large portion of his people together until the final rout.

For the larger Mexican state, Cajeme's audacious experiment could not be allowed to succeed, because the state could not tolerate the viable existence of an autonomous Indian state within its boundaries. A strong central government lent massive military assistance to Sonora in crushing what was considered a dangerous anomaly. This marked the beginning of serious federal cooperation in the pacification of the rebellious Yaquis. Beginning as only a local problem, the Yaquis had finally generated national concern, as a potential embarrassment to President Díaz's program of national social integration and a troublesome obstacle to his vision of national economic development.

When the Díaz government finally recognized the gravity of the Yaqui question, it also inherited the dilemma that had plagued local authorities since independence: how to force the Yaquis into submission without having to resort to outright extermination. The government rejected the direct military solution of all-out destructive war, because the Yaquis were not just another Indian group on the frontier, a menace with no redeeming social value. On the contrary, while no Mexican disputed the expediency of killing off the landless, useless, marauding Apaches, all agreed that the Yaquis constituted a potential asset for Sonora's progress and prosperity. Sturdy, hardworking, and talented, they would make valuable laborers for the expanding rural economy or even desirable colonists on their contested homeland. The task facing the Díaz regime was to find some way to change the Yanquis' attitude regarding their integration into Mexican society.

As always, the Yaquis' perception of their condition was markedly different from that of the Mexicans. Cajeme's defeat forced them once again to reassess their position and form of resistance, but certainly not to capitulate. Already in the waning days of Cajeme, they had begun to relearn the effectiveness of small, mobile bands in harassing large contingents of regular army troops. These bands soon grew into a widespread guerrilla movement, hallmark of the next phase of the long Yaqui struggle.

Notes

Abbreviations for works frequently cited:

INAH   Son Instituto Nacional de Antropologia e Historia. Fondo de Micropeliculas. Sonora. Mexico, D.F.
PHS   Patronato de la Historia de Sonora. Archivo de la Revolución Mexicana. Mexico, D.F.

1. José T. Otero, Address to the First Session of the Seventh Constitutional Congress, *La Constitución* (official organ of state government), September 18, 1879, INAH Son 7.
2. Ramón Corral, "Biografía de José María Leyva Cajeme," *Obras Históricas*, vol. 1 (Hermosillo: Biblioteca Sonorense de Geografía e Historia, 1959). This

biography, first published in 1886, is perhaps the most authoritative and accurate on Cajeme. Corral, a leading member of the new ruling elite, interviewed Cajeme just before Cajeme's execution in 1886 and obtained from him most of the known details on the Yaqui leader's life. Though Corral called Cajeme "el terrible Cajeme," he did not disguise his own respect and admiration for the man, nor deny him recognition for his accomplishments.

3. Corral, "Cajeme," 149–55.

4. *Estrella de Occidente*, May 7, 1875, INAH Son 6.

5. Prefect of Alamos to governor, Alamos, April 29, 1875, INAH Son 6.

6. *Estrella de Occidente*, November 5, 1875, INAH Son 6; José V. Pesqueira, Report, Hacienda del Aguila, November 27, 1875, *Estrella de Occidente*, December 3, 1875, INAH Son 6.

7. Eleazar B. Muñoz, Report on battle at La Pitahaya on December 1 and 3, 1875, El Médano, *Estrella de Occidente*, December 10, 1875, INAH Son 6.

8. Muñoz, Diary of operations in the Yaqui, November 28 to December 31, 1875, Tórin, December 31, 1875, *Estrella de Occidente*, February 4, 1875, INAH Son 6.

9. General José Montijo, Report on failure of Sernistas to win support of Cajeme, *Estrella de Occidente*, January 21, 1876, INAH Son 6. Carlos Conant, who pronounced against Pesqueira in 1873, also reportedly tried to enlist Yaqui support, but apparently failed, because Yaquis were not known to have fought for his cause; see Report on Conant movement, *Estrella de Occidente*, October 10, 1873, INAH Son 6.

10. Corral, "Cajeme," 156; State legislature to Secretary of War, October 12, 1881, in Francisco P. Troncoso, *Las guerras con las tribus Yaqui y Mayo del Estado de Sonora* (Mexico: Tip. Dpto. Estado Mayor, 1905), 70–71. This is an extremely important source, covering the period from Cajeme to the beginning of the twentieth century, since it is essentially a collection of key military documents.

11. Corral, "Cajeme," 155–56.

12. Ibid., 157; Troncoso, *Guerras*, 71.

13. Troncoso, *Guerras*, 70; Agustín Ortiz, Report to prefect of Alamos, May 24, 1881, PHS 2:174.

14. Report on the progress of the railroads, *La Constitución*, February 17, 1881, INAH Son 7.

15. Report on the mining boom, *La Constitución*, June 1881, INAH Son 7.

16. State of Sonora. Decree no. 107, Hermosillo, July 7, 1881, *La Constitución*, July 21, 1881, INAH Son 7.

17. Several examples illustrate how Pimas and Pápagos were unable to prevent the alienation of their community lands. In early 1880, the Pimas of Onavas complained to the government that, contrary to the law, they were not even given their due share of land. They accused the prefect of Ures of indiscriminately selling off their land to hacendados and speculators. Municipality of Onavas, Petition to governor, Ures, March 20, 1880, PHS 2:140.

In 1881, the Pápagos of Pozo Verde lost their land to hacendado Fernando Ortiz when they could not show a clear title of ownership. Prefect of Altar to governor, Report on Pápago complaints, Altar, August 17, 1881, PHS 2:190–91; another complaint lodged by Pápago captain general Jesús Parra to prefect of Altar on a piece of land usurped by an Italian, Altar, August 31, 1881, PHS 2:193–94.

18. "La pacificación del Yaqui," *La Constitución*, February 24, 1881, INAH Son 7.

19. José T. Otero, Address to the First Session of the Seventh Constitutional Congress, *La Constitución*, September 18, 1879, INAH Son 7.

20. Luis Torres to state Congress, submitting the project proposal which had been submitted to him earlier, Guaymas, April 21, 1879, *La Constitución*, June 3, 1880, INAH Son 7.

21. Governor to federal government on pacification of Yaquis, Hermosillo, January 19, 1881, PHS 2:167–68.

22. Pedro Monteverde, prefect of Hermosillo, Report on mines in his district, Hermosillo, February 12, 1886, INAH Son 8.

23. Secretary of Development to Wenceslao F. Iberri, Mexico, February 4, 1879, *La Constitución*, April 11, 1879, INAH Son 7.

24. "Colonización del Yaqui y Mayo," *La Constitución*, June 16, 1881, INAH Son 7.

25. Claudio Dabdoub, *Historia de El Valle del Yaqui* (Mexico: Lib. de Manuel Porrúa, 1964), 125, 252.

26. José T. Otero, Address to the First Session of the Seventh Constitutional Congress, *La Constitución*, September 18, 1879, INAH Son 7; Bernardo Reyes, Report to secretary of war on the Yaqui-Mayo situation, May 28, 1881, in Troncoso, *Guerras*, 64–67; Luis Torres, Report to Secretary of War, Hermosillo, November 30, 1881, in Troncoso, *Guerras*, 67–68; Carlos R. Ortiz, Report to Secretary of War, October 12, 1881, in Troncoso, *Guerras*, 72–73; Secretary of war to Bernardo Reyes, July 19, 1881, in Troncoso, *Guerras*, 72; Secretary of War to congress of Sonora, in Troncoso, *Guerras*, 74.

27. It has been difficult to verify the Corral-Torres conspiracy alleged by Ortiz. Torres, Corral, and General José G. Carbó, then commander of the First Military Zone, held a secret meeting in San Francisco, California. When Ortiz learned of this, he immediately declared that the state government was threatened by "enemies"; see Dabdoub, *El Valle del Yaqui*, 125. Ramón Corral, in his otherwise meticulously constructed work on Cajeme, was evasive on the reasons for Ortiz's mobilization of forces against the Yaquis and Mayos and the consequences of these seemingly, inexplicable actions; see Corral, "Cajeme," 158. For the exchanges between Reyes and Ortiz regarding release of state troops, see Troncoso, *Guerras*, 75–78.

28. J. S. Quirós, prefect of Alamos, to governor, Alamos, September 19, 1882, PHS 3:182–84.

29. Agustín Ortiz, Report from Navojoa, September 27, 1882, PHS 3:197–98.

30. Agustín Ortiz to prefect of Alamos, Navojoa, September 19, 1882, PHS 3:180–81; Ortiz to prefect of Alamos, Navojóa, September 22, 1882, PHS 3:191–92; Ortiz to prefect of Alamos, Navojoa, September 27, 1882, PHS 3:194–96.

31. Bernardo Reyes to José Carbó, Hermosillo, September 22, 1882, in Troncoso, *Guerras*, 79.

32. Reyes, Circular to his colonels, Hermosillo, September 20, 1882, in Troncoso, *Guerras*, 81.

33. Carlos Ortiz, Report to state congress, accusing Reyes, Hermosillo, October 10, 1882, in Troncoso, *Guerras*, 86; Reyes to President of the republic, answering accusations against him, Hermosillo, October 15, 1882, in Troncoso, *Guerras*, 88.

According to Carleton Beals, the Yaquis rebelled in 1882 because Governor Ortiz "was extending the boundaries of his Navarro hacienda," presumably into Yaqui-held land. Beals however does not cite his source for such an allegation, and no other evidence has been found to support it. None of Ortiz's contemporary critics, such as Reyes or Corral, made such a charge in their documents. See Carleton Beals, *Porfirio Díaz, Dictator of Mexico* (Philadelphia: J. B. Lippincott Co., 1932), 310.

34. J. S. Quirós, on Ortiz's report of the Battle of Capetemaya, Alamos, October 17, 1882, PHS 3:214–15.

35. *La Constitución*, October 21, 1882, PHS 3:239–46.

36. Bernardo Reyes to Secretary of War, Hermosillo, November 3, 1882, in Troncoso, *Guerras*, 103–4; Vice-governor to Agustín Ortiz, ordering him to discharge his men, Hermosillo, November 2, 1882, PHS 3:271.

37. E. F. Díaz to prefect of Alamos, Navojoa, January 3, 1883, PHS 4:3–4.

38. C. Gregorio Cháves of Baroyeca, Report on rumors of seven hundred armed Yaquis moving to the Mayo, Baroyeca, June 27, 1883, PHS 4:33; J. de Jesús Salida, prefect of Alamos, Report on rumors of planned attack on Navojoa, Alamos, November 3, 1883, PHS 4:39; General Carbó to governor, on Mayo plans to attack Navojoa on August 7, Mazatlán, August 25, 1884, PHS 4:83.

39. Municipal president of Navojoa, Report to prefect of Alamos on an attack called off by Cajeme, Alamos, August 15, 1883, PHS 4:81; "Sublevación de los indios de Río Mayo," *La Constitución*, August 8, 1884, INAH Son 7.

40. Police commissioner of Batamotal, Report to prefect of Guaymas on Yaqui depredations in his area, Guaymas, August 7, 1883, PHS 4:34; Prefect of Alamos, Report on depredations in the Alamos and Guaymas districts, Hermosillo, April 23, 1883, PHS 4:31; Leonides Hamilton, *Border States of Mexico: Sonora, Sinaloa, Chihuahua and Durango. A Complete Guide for Travelers and Emigrants*, 3d ed. (Chicago: n.p., 1882), 47.

41. *Los Angeles Times*, February 23, 1883, PHS 4:23.

42. Hamilton, *Border States*, 43–47.

43. *La Constitución*, January 19, 1883, INAH Son 7.

44. C. Monteverde, prefect of Guaymas, Report on mines in his district, Guaymas, January 1, 1886, INAH Son 8.

45. *Arizona Daily Star*, February 14, 1883, PHS 4:12–14.

46. José Carbó to Secretary of War, Guaymas, October 6, 1884, PHS 4:89–92.

47. Ramón Corral to J. A. Rivera, prefect of Guaymas, January 7, 1884, PHS 4:68–69.

48. Loreto Molino, Report to J. A. Rivera on his abortive attempt at Cajeme's life, Guaymas, January 30, 1885, PHS 4:110–11; *La Constitución*, February 13, 1885, INAH Son 7; Cajeme's version of the assault, reported to the captain of the port of Guaymas, El Médano, February 3, 1885, in Troncoso, *Guerras*, 111.

49. Cajeme to captain of port of Guaymas, El Médano, February 3, 1885, in Troncoso, *Guerras*, 111.

50. Ibid., 112–13; Corral, "Cajeme," 161.

51. Reports on Yaqui and Mayo assaults in the Guaymas and Alamos districts, *La Constitución*, February 20 and 27, 1885, INAH Son 7; J. A. Rivera, Report on Yaquis in open rebellion, Guaymas, February 16, 1886, PHS 4:117; J. de J. Salida, prefect of Alamos, Report on Cajeme's instructions to the Mayos to mobilize, Alamos, February 17, 1885, PHS 4:120; *La Constitución*, February 22, 1885, PHS 4:132 (this article reports that Cajeme detained twenty-one ships and burned them all, but a Yaqui sailor claimed that only sixteen were detained and fourteen burned).

52. *La Constitución*, February 27 and March 6, 1885, INAH Son 7; J. A. Rivera to Corral, Guaymas, February 22, 1885, PHS 4:131.

53. J. de J. Salida, prefect of Alamos, to governor, March 5, 1885, PHS 4:140; "Los sublevados," *La Constitución*, March 20, 1885, INAH Son 7; J. H. Salazar, prefect of Hermosillo, Report on rebels in his district, Hermosillo, April 4, 1884, PHS 4:184.

54. General Carbó to president of the republic, July 25, 1885, PHS 4:71–84. Haciendas such as La Misa employed about 800 laborers, Noria del Valle 300, San Antonio 200, Santa Rosa 150, and Santa María 100.

55. Secretary of War to General Carbó, Telegram, Mexico, February 28, 1885, in Troncoso, *Guerras*, 113.

56. Lists of contributors to the campaign, March–May 1885, PHS 4:160–62 (almost all the contributors were merchants, including foreign merchants); Corral to José T. Otero, Orders to mobilize National Guards, Hermosillo, March 27, 1885, PHS 4:170.

57. Secretary of War to governor, Mexico, March 31, 1885, PHS 44:178.

58. Description of campaign forces, *La Constitución*, May 1, 1885, INAH Son 7; *La Constitución*, May 8, 1885, INAH Son 7.

59. Corral, "Cajeme," 162; Reports in *La Constitución*, May 15 and 29, 1885, INAH Son 7.

60. General Carbó to president of the republic, July 24, 1885, PHS 4:71–84; Description of Yaqui fortifications, *La Constitución*, July 3, 1885, INAH Son 7.

61. Report on the Battle of El Añil, *La Constitución*, May 29, 1885, INAH Son 7; Corral, "Cajeme," 163.

62. Reports in *La Constitución*, May 8 and July 3, 1885, INAH Son 7.

63. *La Constitución*, July 3, 1885, INAH Son 7.

64. Corral, "Cajeme," 164; *La Constitución*, June 12, 1885, INAH Son 7.

65. *La Constitución*, July 24, 1885, INAH Son 7.

66. *La Constitución*, July 3, 1885, INAH Son 7.

67. Municipal president to Guaymas, remitting testimonies taken from Yaquis who had come from the Yaqui River, September 16, 1885, PHS 5:134–39.

68. *La Constitución*, July 24 and 28, 1885, INAH Son 7.

69. Corral, "Cajeme," 165; Prefect of Guaymas to Corral, Report on epidemic in Yaqui, September 21, 1885, PHS 5: 143; Testimonies of Yaquis on conditions in the Yaqui River, October 16, 1885, PHS 5:168–70.

70. Testimony of a Mayo on execution of Capusari, November 5, 1885, PHS 5:185.

71. Testimonies of Yaquis outside the Yaqui River, Guaymas, October 3, 1885, PHS 5:159–62; October 23, 1885, PHS 5:175–77.

72. Tomás G. de Galdeano, Nicanor Ortiz, and Nieves E. Acosta, Report on their mission, Guaymas, December 21, 1885, PHS 5:202; Corral, "Cajeme," 166.

73. *La Constitución*, March 26, 1886, INAH Son 8.

74. *La Constitución*, February 19, March 26, and April 2, 1886, INAH Son 8.

75. General Angel Martínez to Secretary of War, May 6, 1886, in Troncoso, *Guerras*, 124–25.

76. Angel Martínez to Secretary of War, Report on the Battle of Buatachive, May 9, 12, and 13, 1886, in Troncoso, *Guerras*, 125–29; Corral, "Cajeme," 167–70.

77. Angel Martínez, Report, Tórin, May 15, 1886, *La Constitución*, May 21, 1886, INAH Son 8; *La Constitución*, June 25, July 2, 6, and 9, 1886 (covering the period May 12 to May 30), INAH Son 8.

78. *La Constitución*, July 6, 1886, INAH Son 8.

79. *La Constitución*, May 21 and 23, July 9, 1886, INAH Son 8.

80. *La Constitución*, June 18, 1886, INAH Son 8.

81. Corral, "Cajeme," 171–72.

82. Corral, "Cajeme," 171–80. (For some reason, neither INAH nor PHS contains any documents for this period; similar gaps occur for other short periods.)

83. Corral, "Cajeme," 180–85.

84. List of Yaquis and Mayos who surrendered and the guns that were turned in, in Troncoso, *Guerras*, 148–49.

85. Rafael Izábal, Report on cost of campaign in 1885–86, *La Constitución*, October 14, 1887, INAH Son 8.

86. Many lists of contributors from Alamos, in PHS 4 and 5, for example, for May–April 1885, PHS 4:264, for a total sum of 9,722 pesos.

87. President Porfirio Díaz to General Martínez, Mexico, November 18, 1886, PHS 6:139–40.

88. Corral, "Cajeme," 189.

89. General Juan Hernández, Report, El Médano, January 13, 1887, PHS 6:159; Corral, Circular to all the prefects, Hermosillo, January 18, 1887, PHS 6:160.

90. General Martínez to Corral, Guaymas, December 30, 1886, PHS 6:147.

91. Corral, "Cajeme," 190.

92. Ibid., 190–91.

93. Ibid.

94. Ibid.

95. Ibid.

96. Ibid.

8

Native Cultural Retention and the Struggle for Land in Early Twentieth-Century Bolivia

In his study of a failed uprising by the Chayanta of southern Bolivia in the 1920s, Erick Langer illustrates how native peoples endeavored to use distinct practices on the one hand to invoke their traditional cultural unity and on the other to appeal effectively for help from the national authorities. Throughout Latin America, indigenous societies, even those that enjoyed considerable autonomy, appreciated the importance of national governments and their officials in determining the outcome of native efforts to retain their lands and customary leaders.

For years the Chayanta had engaged in boundary disputes with surrounding haciendas. When they finally rebelled, they believed that they had simultaneously to assert their ethnic identity—to demonstrate their legitimate claims to the contested lands in terms both they and neighboring native groups would recognize—and to follow legal formulas that they recognized government officials would insist upon before acknowledging a claim as rightful. The Chayanta thereby accepted the authority of certain non-Indian procedures even to ratify their seizure of a hacienda during a revolt.

*The author wishes to acknowledge the helpful comments of members of the Mentalities Seminar of the Pittsburgh Center for Social History, to whom this article was first presented; his thanks go particularly to Donald Sutton and Daniel Resnick for their suggestions. This article also benefited from the comments of James Lockhart and two anonymous readers and from discussions with Philip M. Keyes. Financial support for the research was provided by a Maurice Falk Semester Leave Grant, a Fulbright-Hays Faculty Research Grant (CIES), an American Philosophical Society Research Grant, and an Albert J. Beveridge Grant for Research in the History of the Western Hemisphere.

It is inherently difficult to uncover the motivations of peasants in revolt. Many of the sources available to the historian are quite removed from the thought processes of the protagonists. In the case of the Andes, most interpretations of the motives of rebelling peasants (who were usually monolingual Aymara—or Quechua-speaking Indians) come from newspaper accounts written by Spanish urban dwellers, reports by government officials, trial records, or, in the most exceptional cases, documents written by or for the rebels themselves. While all of these sources are to a certain extent helpful, they reveal only small fragments of the motivations and consciousness of the peasants when used in conventional ways.

The inherent difficulties of revealing the mental constructs and assumptions of an overwhelmingly nonliterate people can in part be overcome by analyzing the rituals that were an integral part of the revolts. For rituals, as actions endowed with special symbolic meaning, organize perceived reality in certain ways. These often repetitive actions express ideal social and political arrangements as well as relationships with the supernatural. As David Kertzer suggests, "Ritual helps give meaning to our world in part by linking the past to the present and the present to the future."[1] Thus, not only the motivations of revolt but also the kind of world the peasants see around them and the world they want to construct can be revealed through the rituals in which the rebels try to deal with and make sense of this time of momentous stress in their society. In this article, two rituals from the 1927 Indian rebellion in southern Bolivia are compared and contrasted to arrive at a more profound understanding of how peasants perceived their world and how they thought it should be changed.

The 1927 rebellion can be seen as the culmination of a number of long-term trends and tendencies in the region. In the southern Bolivian highlands, the twin institutions of Indian communities and haciendas (large landed estates) predominated, although there were also a significant, albeit much smaller, number of individual smallholdings, owned largely by mestizo town dwellers. The peasant communities, called ayllus in the Andes, were the remnants of preconquest ethnic groups. Although the Spanish colonial government had reorganized the communities in an effort to control and evangelize the conquered population, provide for efficient tribute collection, and make possible the extraction of labor resources (in this region, primarily for the silver mines), the ayllus maintained most of their aboriginal organization and culture. The communities continued to control much of the region's land, especially in the uplands of the department of Potosí. In turn, owners of the haciendas were typically members of the elite, descendants of the Spanish. Haciendas were generally concentrated in the valleys, where the warmer climate and access to irrigation made land more productive and valuable. The estate's resident labor force was for the most part indistinguishable from the population of the surrounding communities. Thus, the vast majority of the southern Bolivian highland population (even on the haciendas) was Indian and, in one sense or another, imbued with Andean rather than European culture.[2]

The patterns of land ownership changed rapidly in the half century prior to the revolt, and this can be seen as one of the prime reasons for the 1927 uprising. As a result of legislation introduced in the 1870s that abolished Indian communities, the haciendas expanded dramatically at the expense of the former communities. Despite the abolition of the communities' legal status, the Indians of southern Bolivia attempted to keep their communal organization and authority structures intact, often locally resisting the measurement and later the acquisition of their lands by outsiders. They succeeded to a larger extent here than in northern Bolivia, for the decline in silver mining, the region's economic mainstay, weakened the southern Bolivian landlords and precluded their wholesale usurpation of complete communities. Thus the assault on community lands took on a piecemeal character; nevertheless, in certain areas, such as northern Chuquisaca, it severely weakened some communities. In northern Potosí, on the other hand, the loss of Indian lands, through hacienda expansion and acquisition by mestizo townspeople, was relatively slight and did not completely disrupt the traditional predominance of the Indian communities. One observer noted in 1921 that in Potosí the better part of the aboriginal population continued to live in Indian communities, whereas in Chuquisaca most of the land and the rural population were under the direct control of the white landlords.[3]

Although their effects were greater in certain areas than in others, the laws abolishing the indigenous communities clearly worked to the detriment of the Indian peasants of southern Bolivia. The principal legislative bills, adopted in 1874 and the early 1880s, anticipated that the Indians, through their participation in a free land market and through the abolition of the archaic institution of the community imposed by colonial circumstances, would become full citizens of the nation. The reality was rather different from the legislators' ideal of turning the Indians into yeoman farmers. Not only did land purchasers and government officials often use fraudulent means to acquire land very cheaply, but in no other way were the community members enfranchised to participate in national life and utilize the opportunities that the liberal laws gave them in theory. In southern Bolivia most Indians continued to pay the traditional tribute. Although the name of the tax had been changed to *contribución territorial* and was collected by departmental rather than national authorities, the reality of a discriminatory tribute exacted on one ethnic group because of its earlier conquest by the Spanish remained.[4] In other ways community members remained outside national society as well; they could not speak Spanish, the official language of Bolivia; received no schooling; did not vote; were generally the poorest members of society; and were disdained by all other groups within the country.

On July 25, 1927, one of the largest peasant rebellions of the twentieth century erupted in Chayanta province, in northern Potosí. The Indians attacked a number of estates there and elsewhere, sacking hacienda houses, killing cattle, and destroying gardens and orchards. Peasants in four of the country's nine departments rose in revolt, but in only a month troops armed with machine guns were able to suffocate the rebellion. All told, about ten thousand peasants participated in the revolt; hundreds were killed. Although the revolt was suppressed, it effectively halted the expansion of the hacienda onto Indian community lands and prompted the government to replace corrupt local officials.[5]

On July 27, 1927, in the midst of the rebellion, a revealing ritual took place. On the recently conquered Hacienda Peaña, in the presence of all the members of Jaiguari allyu, the *ilacata*, or community official, solemnly took declarations from a number of witnesses about the abuses committed by the owner of Peaña and Hacienda Murifaya. Taking a transcription of the proceedings in the correct legal form was the corregidor (highest political authority), Néstor Sotomayor, recently captured by the Indians. After declarations had been taken, Sotomayor and another minor official, the *juez parroquial* J. Villalta, drew up a document giving Peaña and Murifaya to the "surrounding community members" from Macha and Pocoata. They were forced to copy this document four times onto other sheets, as well as a paper signed by another landowner that gave all his land to the Indians.[6]

Two days later, the Indian rebels stormed Hacienda Guadalupe. A very different ritual took place there. The attackers captured the owner of the estate, Julio Berdeja, who had valiantly fought them off with a pistol and even managed to kill one Indian. The Indians took Berdeja to the river and killed him. Marcelino Burgos, one of the leaders of Jaiguari ayllu, ate portions of the dead man; according to court testimony, other Indians from that community joined Burgos in the act. Afterwards, the rest of Berdeja's body was sacrificed to the god residing in the mountain known as Condor Nasa by interment at the mountain.[7]

The Meaning of Judicial Ritual

What can these rituals tell us about the Indians and their motivations and about the world they wanted to construct? Let us first examine the first incident, which resulted in the officials' signing over Hacienda Peaña and Murifaya to the rebels. The format of this "judicial ritual" was a trial, but without the usual European authorities presiding. The Indians did not usually imitate European forms to resolve their disputes, but in this case they minutely observed the various legal formalities of a regular court. The papers that document this incident look almost exactly like the record of the Indians' later trial for subversion, in which these documents served as some of the authorities' prime inculpatory pieces of evidence. Other than the lack of stamped, official paper, the documents are the same as those from the subsequent trial. The Indians reproduced the same phrases that one would hear in the criminal cases in even the most backward village court; witnesses were called, and all those testifying against the landowner were asked the same questions, just as in regular court proceedings. Unfortunately, other than the documents inserted into the later trial to back the charge against the rebels of subversion, we have no other source for this ritual. This means that we cannot decipher from the records exactly how the trial was set up, the position of the accusers, the Indian judge, and the captured officials, nor the ceremonies surrounding this event. Nevertheless, the extant documents are sufficiently rich to provide important insights into key aspects of the rebels' mindset.

In certain ways, this trial was very different from those that occurred daily in the many small town courts throughout the country. Perhaps most obvious was the fact that an Indian community official presided as judge, unlike the normal hierarchy, in which the judge was always a city-bred member of the elite and any lawyers were of the same ethnic heritage or were small-town mestizos. Nevertheless, the presence of local officials to take down the proceedings and sign documents points to the Indians' continued acknowledgment of Europeans as legal specialists (and the only ones who could speak and write Spanish, the official language of all court documents).

The use of legal forms even during rebellions and uprisings is much more common than might be supposed. Witness, for example, E. P. Thompson's discovery that crowds in eighteenth-century English bread riots acted in a legalistic manner when attacking price gougers and setting what they considered to be fair prices.[8] There are numerous Andean examples as well, particularly in the much-studied case of the Tupac Katari/ Tupac Amaru rebellions in the late eighteenth century. In 1780, one of the first acts of Tupac Amaru's rebellion had been the public trial and execution of the hated corregidor Antonio Juan de Arriaga. Likewise, Sergio Serulnikov has recently argued that the Indian rebel leaders of the 1780s in northern Potosí (the same area where the 1927 rebellion occurred) were only trying to enforce the edicts of the Buenos Aires courts, at least as the Indians interpreted them.[9] Certainly, the Indians in early twentieth-century southern Bolivia were also familiar with the trial setting and the legal forms, as the multitude of cases in the local courts that dealt with community members shows.

What was innovative, however, was the content of the legal proceedings themselves, namely, the reasons for the expropriation of the haciendas. One would have expected, after the tremendous expansion of the Bolivian hacienda just prior to the rebellion, that the Indians would assert that the land had simply been theirs to begin with. In fact, direct evidence from many sources confirms that one of the main tenets of the rebel leaders was that all land belonged to the Indians and the haciendas should all be turned back into community land.[10]

Despite these precedents, this was not the reason cited for expropriation. Instead, the community Indians based their claims to the haciendas on the abusive treatment that the hacienda peons, or *colonos*, had received at the hands of [Andrés] Garnica, the hacendado. The eleven *colonos* who testified at the trial described three basic abuses. The most common complaint was that the landlord treated his laborers unfairly. Garnica "abusively entered the sheep corrals and takes one and does not pay a fair price"; "the cost of taking a [loaded] donkey costs us one Boliviano, and he pays [only] forty *centavos*."[11] The second complaint was the rapid rise in rental costs for the land that the peons occupied. According to one *colono*, "Garnica charges for my plot what once cost five *pesos febles* [debased coins worth 80 percent of the Boliviano] today charges 40 Bolivianos."[12] The last major complaint was that he "was accustomed to raping the married and single women" of the estate, both in the hacienda house and in the fields, where he "committed abuses to those women and girls who went to pasture the cattle or sheep." In fact, rape of women and girls who watched the family livestock in the hills alone was (and still is) rather common (moreover, courtship rites among Indians were frequently accompanied by violence). However, Garnica's position as outsider and the impunity with which he allegedly committed these crimes were reprehensible enough to merit inclusion among the abuses that led to the forfeiture of his properties.[13]

It is remarkable that throughout the trial the only reason given for the hacienda expropriations was the abuse of the *colonos*. Why did the Indians not even mention the Spanish conquest and that the hacendados had abusively taken the land in the past forty years? There are a number of possible answers. For one, witnesses in the government trial against the rebels asserted that Manuel Michel, the self-styled "Casique [Chief] General de Chuquisaca" and the prime mover of the revolt, claimed that there were "only three properties or estates and the others were all Indian lands."[14] Perhaps Peaña and Murifaya were those non-Indian lands that Michel referred to, and so another reason than aboriginal rights had to be adduced. This is unlikely, however, given the fact that the properties were handed over to the Macha and Pocoata communities and were not kept by Michel himself, as others alleged. The other possibility is that these estates had been part of the Indian lands so long ago that they were not considered community lands anymore. This possibility, however, argues against much of the thrust of the rebels' apparent call for the abolition of all haciendas and their return to Indian ownership.

What is interesting is that despite the *colonos'* collaboration in this judicial ritual, it seems that Peaña and Murifaya were turned over not to them but to the Indians of the nearby communities of Macha and Pocoata who had stormed the properties. Moreover, instead of burning the hacienda books, as the rebels did on other estates, the Indians preserved them. Perhaps the books were seen as icons (given the almost universal illiteracy of the rebel leadership and its army), which could also prove the claims of possession by communities. In any case, both of these facts suggest that the communities wanted merely to switch ownership of the estates and maintain the hacienda workers in some kind of dependent status. In fact, this was already occurring. Evidence from the early twentieth century in the region points to the creation or transformation of a group within the ayllus to *colonos* of other community members, mirroring the categories on the haciendas.[15]

Although analysis of the content of this judicial ritual by itself leaves important questions unanswered, an understanding of who the intended audience was can help determine why the rebels proceeded as they did. Ritual is frequently directed not only at those present but at audiences elsewhere, and the ending is certainly preordained. The ending in this case probably reflected quite accurately how the community members felt when they entered the official court system in Bolivia.

The rebels undoubtedly used a trial format to assert legitimacy of their actions. As Steve Stern has shown, Andeans soon after the Spanish conquest had accepted the colonial legal system, though at first they used it to play various factions within European society against one another and mitigate their condition.[16] By the late colonial period, as mentioned above, the Indian rebels of the 1780s had also utilized the public trial to legitimate the execution of a hated official. The Indians' use of the court system to settle disputes accelerated after the 1874 laws abolishing the Indian communities. Once ayllu officers lost their officially sanctioned roles as arbiters within the communities, the courts increasingly became involved in the myriad intra-ayllu disputes, particularly over land rights. Thus the courts—and, by extension, the legal procedures themselves—became the standard for settling these types of matters even among the Indian population.

The legitimacy of this particular proceeding was also confirmed through the presence of the two officials who had been captured. As those arrested during the rebellion testified, rebel leaders emphasized that they had "through the corregidor and the juez parroquial made them give us the above-mentioned properties [Peaña and Murifaya], driving out the landlords" in meetings, and they brandished the carefully preserved hacienda account books to prove it.[17] Although these officials did not participate voluntarily, they were important legitimating agents not only because of their presence but also because they produced the documents used to extend this air of legitimacy.

The procedures the rebels used suggest that the trial was directed at three principal parties. First of all, it was directed at fellow rebels, to show that the movement had made significant gains. It was the first time since 1871 that the Indians had gained rather than lost land.[18] Interestingly enough, one of the copies of the documents transferring the properties to the Indians (the only one bearing the seal of Manuel Michel, the leader of the rebellion) contains a curious addition. After the certification by the two captured officials, it states that "now there is news here so that all the community members of the Copavilque Valley know of this."[19] This phrase was put there either to strengthen the Macha and Pocoata ayllus' claim to these properties, to the exclusion of the other major groups that participated in the uprising in the area, such as the members of the Condo ayllu who had lands in the Copavilque valley, or simply to indicate to whom the copy of the document should be sent. In either case, it is clear that the ritual—and its end result, the certificate transferring property rights—was directed internally.

The trial ritual was also directed at the larger society, in particular at the hacendado whose properties were expropriated; by using the formulas which the landowners themselves accepted when they fought their legal battles with the communities, the rebel leaders appealed to the legitimacy that the judicial ritual implied. There even remained an implication that there was some room for negotiation of the terms of this transfer, since the document promised that the community members "will make formal arrangements with the *patrón* Andres Garnica."[20]

The Indians considered the papers of the trial and the certificates themselves powerful artifacts. As James Lockhart has found for central Mexico in the late seventeenth and eighteenth centuries, villagers created their own "primordial titles" to assert their rights to land, though these titles were not accepted by colonial society as legitimate documents. By the early twentieth century, the Zapatista peasants were still preserving these types of titles and attributing the same values to them.[21] Similarly, in the agitation prior to 1927, the Indians engaged in a kind of "paper war," using "official" documents to assert their rights to land and causing real consternation among the hacendados. One of the tactics was the pasting of fliers, which mimicked some broadly worded governmental resolutions in favor of Indian rights, on the walls of landlords' hacienda houses.[22] This tactic of psychological warfare was certainly effective, for it greatly upset the landowners. As the overwhelmingly illiterate Indians thought, these relatively meaningless fliers possessed a certain efficacy as pieces of paper; though crudely written, they invaded the very center of the landlord's power and symbolically challenged the legitimacy of his rule. They also suggested that the national government identified with the Indians' cause, emboldening the peasants to take matters into their own hands.

The trial and the documents written during this ritual also aimed at reaching some kind of understanding with the national government, perhaps the most important audience inasmuch as its army controlled the forces of repression. For this reason, the transfer document stated that the change of ownership was provisional until ratified by petition to "higher authorities."[23] Further indicating that this ritual was directed at the larger society and at the government in particular was the fact that the documents were written in Spanish, not Quechua or Aymara. It is clear from the trial records of the Indian rebels that few of their leaders even spoke Spanish. That their accusations were translated into a foreign tongue, a troublesome procedure, implies that the rebels were addressing the national government, composed exclusively of members of the urban, Europe-oriented elite.

Imitating the legal forms of a trial, in which witnesses brought charges against a defendant, also provided a basis for legal action by the government on behalf of the Indians. Perhaps the rebels felt that claims based on aboriginal rights to the land would be rejected because in the past fifty years the state had sanctioned the sale of Indian land to outsiders and was dedicated to the preservation of private property. In this fashion, the rebels were trying to gain the high moral ground and impress upon the government the justice of their cause. Only a year earlier the government had supported a failed effort by the Catholic church to prevent abuse against the Indians.[24] By making the abuse of the hacienda labor force the crux of the communities' right to take over the hacienda land, the rebels put the whole governmental reform effort to the test as well.

Why were the Indians so anxious to legitimate their actions in front of the national government in this ritual, when they in fact were breaking the law? After all, the rebels had taken two government officials prisoner and threatened them, attacked the private property that the government was sworn to protect, and expropriated land from local elites. One possible answer is that the rebels conceived of the country's political organization differently than the Europeanized members of Bolivian society. The national government, and the president in particular, were seen to be distinct from corrupt local officials and the urban-based European society. Frank Salomon has recently asserted that the Indians in late eighteenth-century Arequipa

(Peru) considered society to be divided into two human groups, the Spanish and the Indians. The Indians' segmentary view of society, in which kin groups were divided into moieties and other discrete units, corresponded rather closely to the organization of the early Spanish colonial state. Thus, according to Salomon, the Indians felt that they were part of the "Indian republic" (*república de indios*) overseen by the Spanish king, who was above both Europeans and Indians.[25] The argument can be made that these conceptions of society remained in force into the twentieth century because they dovetailed very nicely with Andean ideas of social organization. For example, Catherine Allen has shown recently how the quintessentially Andean idea of complementary but opposing pairs, such as the Indians and non-Indians, is still evident in the present-day Andean peasants' conception of society.[26]

There is considerable evidence that the Indians conserved a conception of the Bolivian state that echoed colonial rather than early twentieth-century political realities. For example, even after the de facto capital had moved to La Paz, Indians went to Sucre, the colonial administrative capital, to petition the national government. Manuel Michel's self-styled title, "Casique General de Chuquisaca," had these colonial resonances, as Indians still saw Chuquisaca, with Sucre as its capital, as the center of legitimacy in the national political system.[27] Thus, the conceptions of social and political organization remained filtered through the prism of Andean standards (in which the three centuries of colonial experience naturally loomed large), which helps us to understand why so much care was taken in this judicial ritual to follow procedures used by the national court system.

The issues of this ritual's audience and the need for legitimacy, primarily among fellow Indians and the national government, inform an understanding of the goals and motivations of the rebels. The trial is very suggestive about the kind of society the Indians had in mind after the uprising. The trial probably reflected not only the ideas of the rebel leaders but, to a certain extent, those of their followers, who, after all, participated or at least acquiesced in this ritual. Moreover, the leadership had been winnowed during the numerous smaller incidents that had taken place in the previous two or three years. Thus, those who led and those who followed probably had roughly congruent goals, hammered out during the lengthy phase of rebellion leading up to 1927.

Quite clearly, the trial showed that the Indian did not conceive of a world without non-Indian elites. The rebels' scrupulous regard for the forms of judicial procedure shows that they were willing, in some way, to accept the legitimacy of the national government. Their incessant petitions and requests for legal relief both in La Paz and in Sucre also suggest that the communities accepted the government's prerogative to dispense justice, one of the primary functions of any government.

A common cry among many revolutionaries, at least in the beginning, was that only the local representatives were corrupt; if only the president (earlier, the king) heard of these matters, they would be straightened out.[28] In fact, the national government's actions had encouraged this belief; virtually every time the Indians had petitioned the higher levels of government on some matter, they had received a favorable *resolución* (which in practical terms was so vague as to be useless). Thus, the rebels saw the national government as on their side; the problem was that local authorities refused to carry out the national authorities' orders. This ambivalence towards government was common among peasants throughout the Spanish empire and, in fact, among peasant populations throughout the world—it amounted to a modified version of "Long live the king but down with the local officials."[29] In the Spanish American case this propensity had much to do with the colonial administrative structure (and its republican successors), where ordinary countryfolk had little access to high officials. The judicial ritual, in which local authorities were forced to accept the Indians' verdict, confirms this.

Implicit in the judicial ritual, and its insistence on maintaining many legal forms, was an appeal by the rebels for the support of the national government. The rebels were quite aware of the power the state could muster. The many incidents prior to the 1927 rebellion (most notably the siege of the town of Tarabuco during carnival in 1925) showed the repressive power of the state, when it mobilized police forces and soldiers armed with machine guns and cannons, arms which the Indians could never hope to match.[30] By keeping to legal forms even within a potentially revolutionary setting and recording these acts, the rebels undoubtedly were aiming at an eventual accommodation with the state. That they thought these legal forms and these papers could help achieve this goal, or at least keep this possibility open, shows the power that the judicial ritual was thought to possess.

In the Andean case, this apparently contradictory behavior—accommodation within a revolutionary setting—was amplified by the Indians' perceptions of two divergent societies, one European and the other Indian, ruled over by a common sovereign.[31] Of course, the perception of dual societies was based on many concrete realities which the liberal reforms of the nineteenth century had done little to change. Indians still paid tribute in many cases (although it was now called something else), were treated as second-class citizens by non-Indians, and spoke a different language. On the other hand, the division of the world into Indian and non-Indian spheres did not necessarily mean that the Indians accepted contemporary roles within society. With their actions, the rebels clearly showed that they felt that hacendados were illegitimate usurpers of Indian land and should lose their land if they mistreated their laborers.

These *colonos'* complaints and the verdict of the trial, which gave the land to the communities, also suggest a certain hierarchical conception of society. Clearly, the community members knew of the abuses the hacienda peons had suffered under their landlord. This, however, was insufficient for the abolition of *colono* status. Rather, as mentioned above, the mistreatment justified the hacendados' loss of authority over the *colonos* and the territory they worked to the presumably more benevolent Indian community members. Equality for all was not one of the rebels' goals; the invading community Indians were content to maintain a hierarchical society with the *colonos* as their inferiors, even though they shared virtually the same ethnic heritage. This attitude manifested itself in the structure of the trial, in which an official from the Macha ayllus, not one of the *colonos*, acted as ritual leader. Furthermore, many of the hacienda workers suffered abuse at the hands of the community Indians during the hacienda takeovers.[32] This situation was a far cry from the accusations hurled by the landowners and certain officials, who claimed that the Indians were inspired by communist ideas and wanted to wipe out all distinctions between the wealthy and the poor.[33]

Human Sacrifice, Mountain Gods, and Ritual Limits

Prior to the rebellion, Julio Berdeja, owner of Hacienda Guadalupe, who also happened to be the corregidor of *canton* (county) Guadalupe, had apparently harassed the Indians from Tinguipaya who traveled to the valleys to take care of the fields they owned there. He made them work without pay on his hacienda by taking their pack animals and tools until they had finished the tasks that he assigned them. In addition, the hacendado had acquired some Indian lands. Using a common strategy, Berdeja apparently had lent some money to an Indian and later had taken over his property, claiming that he had not been paid back. The hacendado also disputed water rights over an irrigation ditch with the Indian residents of the Guadalupe Valley.[34]

As the rebellion spilled into Gaudalupe on July 29, Berdeja killed an Indian and cabled for help from Sucre to contain the revolt. However, before the government could mobilize its troops, three hundred Indians attacked Berdeja's hacienda with clubs and sticks, took him to the small stream in the middle of the valley, and killed him. His fingers were cut off and put in the rebels' coca bags. Marcelino Burgos, one of the rebel leaders, began to eat the body; according to one witness, "all of Burgos's ayllu ate the cadaver." Another witness testified that Burgos had asserted afterwards "that Berdeja's flesh had been stringy." The Indians then buried the bones at Condor Nasa, on the border between Antora and Pitantora counties, offering him to the mountain god who dwelled there.[35]

For this set of rituals we unfortunately have no records written as they happened. Most of the information about the human sacrifice comes from police records, which only contain answers to leading questions. Moreover, none of the accused was willing to admit that he had participated in this ritual, though many claimed that they had heard of it from a third person and were quite sure of the names of the instigators. The other source of information is the accounts of anthropologists who have worked in the northern Potosí area and tapped into the apparently rich oral traditions that record this event.[36]

What can we tell from this ritual? Certainly, the few details that we have suggest an affair very different from the first ritual described. Most striking is the violence displayed; there apparently was no attempt to employ the forms of the national justice system. An obvious explanation of the ritual, compared to the previous one, might be that the Indians by now realized that their actions would bring about violent repression from the government and thus were willing to leave aside legal niceties. This, however, is not borne out by the facts. A group of the revolt's leaders was not captured until the night of August 3, fully five days after the murder. Among the captured leaders were Manuel Michel and members of the Jaiguari, Janina, Condo, Quilaquila, Copavilque, and Pitantora ayllus. The main purpose of the meeting at which the leaders were captured, from what we can gather from the interrogations, had been to show off the success of the revolt by asserting that the rebels had gained legal ownership of Haciendas Murifaya and Peaña. Thus, the leaders were still trying to insist on the legitimacy of their actions, since all those who confessed to having been at the meeting asserted that the rebel leaders had displayed the papers transferring the estates to the communities as well as the hacienda records at that time. The police in fact found these documents in the possession of their prisoners, and they thus entered the record of the proceedings against the Indians involved in the rebellion. Moreover, the Indian leaders held the meeting in the suburbs of Sucre (where they were captured), far beyond any territory controlled by rebel bands. The choice of location suggests that they were hoping for some kind of support from high government authorities.[37]

There are reports that episodes of cannibalism also occurred in earlier revolts, such as the great Tupac Katari/Tupac Amaru rebellion, which engulfed what is now southern Peru and Bolivia at the end of the colonial period, and the most important Indian rebellion in republican Bolivia before the 1927 rebellion, which occurred in 1899 at the end of the Federalist War. The latter episode of cannibalism occurred during the massacre of a troop of

soldiers in the church at Mohoza in the Bolivian altiplano. During the trial
of the Indians involved at Mohoza, the Indian leader's attorney, Bautista
Saavedra, asserted that the rebels

> ripped out the [soldiers'] eyes, cut the tongues off and mutilated the
> testicles, to eat them with undefinable pleasure . . . inclined face down-
> ward, over the puddles and rivulets of blood [the Indians] drank it. . . .
> This type of cannibalism is very common among the Aymaras, because it
> is based on the superstitious belief that drinking the blood of the enemy
> gives one great courage and satisfies fully [their desire for] revenge.[38]

Saavedra sensationalized the incident in the courtroom and, to help make
his case, claimed a greater frequency for ritual cannibalism among Aymaras
than probably existed. It is probably more useful to think of cannibalism as
an "occasional" ritual associated with rebellion and violence. What was
apparently new in the 1927 ritual was, as we shall see, the association of
ritual cannibalism and human sacrifice to indigenous deities with claims to
land rights and ethnic identity.

The most likely explanation is that this ritual was directed primarily
toward the Andean sacred sphere, although there were also a number of very
concrete intentions and consequences directed toward outsiders. Fernando
Montes Ruiz has postulated that during rebellions after the Spanish conquest,
the Aymara frequently renounced Christianity and sacked churches and
other Catholic religious shrines. This in fact occurred during the 1927
rebellion, for the rebels sacked the pilgrimage site of Pumpuri. Rejection of
Catholicism and its representations provided a symbolic means of rejecting
Spanish conquerors and promoting a specifically Andean ethnic identity.[39]

Anthropologists have documented that an Andean belief system has
persisted among the Aymara peasantry, despite the efforts of Christianization,
since the Spanish conquest. Although the Indians consider themselves
Catholic, their world is inhabited by a hierarchy of aboriginal gods and
spirits closely associated with geographical locations and natural phenomena.
The most important spirits live in high mountains, streams, lakes, and the
like; the next order of spirits are place spirits; the least important are house
guardians. Some of these spirits are wholly good or bad, whereas others can
be benevolent or evil, depending upon their treatment by the Indians.
Lightning is also greatly feared, since it is a source of supernatural power.[40]
It was to these most powerful supernatural beings that the rebels were
primarily addressing themselves when they sacrificed Berdeja.

To understand this event, it is necessary to examine both the act of
cannibalism and the act of sacrifice to the mountain god of Condor Nasa.
Fernando Montes Ruiz, in a generally lucid analysis, postulates that the
Indians ate Berdeja because they were afraid that the victim and other

hacendados might bewitch them and punish them for the murder. Thus, according to Montes, the hacendado was treated like a malignant witch whose power (and perhaps symbolically that of other hacendados, the Indians' declared enemies?) could be nullified through ritual cannibalism. In addition, as also in the 1899 episode noted above, it gave the rebels the courage to fight against superior forces.[41]

The sacrifice of the hapless hacendado's bones is related to cannibalism but, according to Montes, had a different purpose. Condor Nasa is one of the highest peaks in the region and thus possesses extraordinary powers. Moreover, this mountain was traditionally associated with lightning, the ancient Aymara god of war. After the Spanish conquest, however, the European invaders appropriated lightning as a symbol of Santiago, the saint who led the Christians against the Moors during the long *reconquista* in Iberia. Even today lightning is associated with Santiago, who is sometimes described as wearing a silver revolver (much like some of the hacendados of the period), killing anyone he pleases. Montes asserts that the sacrifice of Berdeja's bones was a propitiation of the mountain god and so of the lightning deity. This rite thus served as a way of reappropriating an Aymara god and ensuring success against the Europeans.[42]

While this interpretation makes some sense, Montes ignores other elements which give the episode a much wider significance and show that both the cannibalism and the human sacrifice combine to make a powerful symbolic statement for the rebels. According to Tristan Platt, who complements but also expands upon Montes's analysis, the Indians of northern Potosí equated the act of cannibalism with the doctrine of transubstantiation, which the Franciscans imported into the region. The eating of the host was thus reinterpreted in terms of the Andean solar cult, in which the consumption of the human body was related to the propitiation of the sun. In turn, the burying of the bones at the base of Condor Nasa (significantly, the mountain bases are called *saphis*, or "roots," in the region) also nourished the other part of the world under the earth; it was part of the characteristic effort by Andeans to maintain a natural balance at all times.[43]

More importantly for our purposes, both rites incorporated powerful assertions of territorial rights, and closely related ethnic identity, against the European society that had been insinuating itself into the northern Potosí countryside. To understand how these are related, it is necessary to examine *tinkus*, ritual battles between different kinship groups, because it is during the *tinku* that cannibalism probably occurs most frequently in the northern Potosí. In these battles, drunken community members from different ayllus or from the two moieties within an ayllu fight against each other, men against men and women against women. Tristan Platt has interpreted the *tinkus*, in which outright "winners" are never declared, as representing the affirmation of boundaries between the various levels of ethnic group organization and rights to land. According to Platt, *tinkus* can occur between different kinship-based subgroups, also called ayllus, within the larger ethnic unit, which he calls the Great Ayllu. However, if the members of one Great Ayllu attack members of another, then the various subgroups unite behind their Great Ayllu to fight against the others, who are even more different. Verb forms with the root *tinku* also mean "to fit together." (The *tinku* has sexual connotations and is a fertility rite as well.)[44]

Tinkus are also closely related to *ch'axwas*, or battles between ethnic groups over land. In fact, at times the *tinku* and the *ch'axwa* can scarcely be distinguished, for both types of battles relate to struggles over the control of land, are highly ritualized, and put into play essentially the same underlying ideologies. In both, cannibalism occurs. The *ch'axwa*, however, is usually even more ferocious and is engaged in only with those defined to be outside the larger segmentary organizations (the Great Ayllus) and thus outsiders far removed in human society from the particular ethnic group. In many ways, of course, the 1927 rebellion can be defined as a *ch'axwa*, since the dispute was over land and involved, as we have seen, an ethnic group (Europeans and perhaps also mestizos) seen as outsiders in the northern Potosí countryside.[45]

It has generally been assumed that people engage in cannibalism because it appropriates the victim's strengths and emasculates him.[46] This, to a certain extent, is the case in northern Potosí, where only those who fight well during the *tinku* are sacrificed; the cannibals want to imbibe the victim's fighting abilities.[47] In the case of Berdeja, the hacendado undoubtedly earned a reputation as a powerful man and a good fighter from his desperate resistance, during which he managed to kill one of his attackers. But the powers of the victim were only a minor consideration. More importantly, the rites served to distinguish the cannibals from their victims. Jan Szemiński asserts that the rebels during the Tupac Amaru rebellion of the late eighteenth century only killed and mutilated Spaniards because they were identified as *nak'aq* (devilish and evil hominoids), but this interpretation is too limited. Berdeja might have been considered an evil creature, but in the Andean case many different types of outsiders, witches, members of other ayllus, and Europeans, are consumed.[48]

The act of cannibalism, an extraordinary rite that is taboo during "normal" times, serves to bring this group together. Thus, the fact that "all of Burgos's ayllu ate the cadaver" helped unite the rebels (and probably even those who until then had participated only halfheartedly) in a powerful common bond, or, at the very least, in a shared guilt. On the other hand, the consuming of a hacendado, as Tristan Platt has asserted, showed the enmity of the Indians toward those whom they considered the usurpers of their land and, as in the case of Berdeja, toward the abusers of power (both as local officials and as hacendados), the representatives of European society who penetrated into the countryside. Thus, I disagree, at least in part, with Szemiński, who believes that "Andean tradition condemns cannibalism." Andean tradition permits cannibalism of powerful but evil individuals under special circumstances of war or in ritual battles.[49]

As Olivia Harris and Xavier Albó have pointed out, the subsequent sacrifice to the mountain god served essentially the same purpose. They suggest that the location of the burial, along the boundaries of two counties, "underlined symbolically the ancestral right of the ayllus over land usurped by landlords."[50] Of the two *cantones* in question, Pitantora was the one in which the hacienda predominated; in Antora, it did not. Harris and Albó suggest that perhaps the boundaries of the two counties were also based on territorial divisions among local elite groups. Thus, the ayllus asserted the predominance of the communities over both types of *cantones* and also perhaps reaffirmed the territorial coherence of the region divided among the different ethnic groups. As we have already seen in the *tinkus* and the *ch'axwa*, land rights and ethnic identity were closely interwoven, as is natural in a peasant society. The Indians in a sense restricted the landlords, members of the urban elite, to their own sphere in the cities, thus liberating the countryside in favor of the autochthonous population. This the landlords undoubtedly also understood, though perhaps on a different symbolic level. The killing of one of their compatriots combined with the Indian "savagery," almost certainly made the estate owners think twice about venturing out into the countryside, which the Indians now claimed for themselves.

Conclusion

A comparison between these two rituals can help us understand the motivations of the Indian rebels and how they conceived of the world around them. In a sense, rituals describe how participants perceive the world or how they would like the world to be. Each ritual also creates a rich symbolic language that speaks not only to participants but to observers and outsiders alike. Certainly, it is likely that to each group these rituals mean different things, but they are nevertheless important for understanding the discourse between groups within a society. The revolutionary politics of peasants, especially that of a nonliterate population that does not even communicate in the language in which records are kept, is difficult to disentangle without recourse to extralingual behavior. A look at rituals and how certain forms were utilized to make radical demands can help overcome this problem.

The rituals examined above, especially when taken as different expressions of the same political program, reveal many aspects of the rebels' goals shorn of the interpretations which outsiders attempted to impose on them during and after the uprising. The judicial ritual, with its almost slavish imitation of legal forms, showed that the peasants were concerned about the legitimacy of their actions and attempted to enlist the national government on their side or at least to co-opt it into not repressing the movement. By emphasizing the abuse of workers, a political issue on which the government had already declared itself on the side of the peasants, the rebels hoped to justify their radical expropriation of the haciendas. The abduction of local officials and their forced participation in the trial do not contradict this intent, since the Indians considered these individuals part of a different "republic"; in any case, only in this fashion could the Indians force the landlords to follow what they interpreted as the intentions of the government all along. Even the murder, consumption, and sacrifice of a hacendado did not, in the Indians' view, negate the efficacy of the judicial ritual, since the sacrifice of Berdeja was directed primarily towards the supernatural sphere. One issue which connected the two rituals and provided the rationale for both was the abuse of Andeans, though in the case of Berdeja the shooting of a rebel probably triggered the murder and sacrifice of the hacendado.

Both the expropriation of the haciendas and the rituals surrounding the killing of Berdeja were intimately tied to the issue of land ownership and ethnic identity. It is difficult, in fact, to make distinctions between these issues, because in the Indians' cognitive framework land and ethnic identity were two sides of the same coin. As the connections between ritual cannibalism and the *tinku* (and by extension, the *ch'axwa*), as well as the location of the landlord's sacrifice, indicate, the Indians were symbolically delineating the boundaries between (to use sixteenth-century terminology) the "república de españoles" and the "república de indios." This ritual and other pronouncements indicate that the Indians were asserting their rights to the countryside. After all, one of their slogans was that all haciendas, whether they had in recent memory been ayllu property or not, be turned into *terrenos de origen* (community lands). Non-Indians were presumably restricted to the towns and cities.

What is interesting to note is that the trial showed no efforts toward revolutionary egalitarianism, as urban elites, alarmed over the rebels' ties with the Socialist party and the spread of communism, claimed. Rather, the rebels' actions reflected an ideology in which the communities asserted the right to a determined place within the larger social and political hierarchy.

The Macha ayllu's *ilacata*, or community official, who presided as judge, resumed a sense of superiority, in particular in reference to the haciendas' *colonos*, who appeared only as witnesses and (at best) indirect beneficiaries of the hacienda expropriation procedure. The *ilacata*'s authority rested ultimately on the consent of the community members and the prestige accumulated through reciprocal (and, to a certain extent, redistributive) ties to the other members, ties maintained by progressing through a series of ritual offices and their abundant festival expenses. Few such links existed with the *colonos* from the haciendas, who were only peripherally involved in the communities' moral and material economy. Thus, the *colonos* remained outside the communities' networks, in an inferior position. Whether or not they spoke the same language or had originally come from the same ethnic groups mattered little. While other evidence suggests that many hacienda workers joined the conspiracies preceding the 1927 rebellion and initially welcomed the rebels with open arms, the actions that the community members took made it clear that the *colonos* were to remain in more or less the same inferior position even if the Indians permanently occupied the haciendas.[51] The judicial ritual confirms this view. In effect, in the eyes of the *colonos*, the rebels were reproducing the old hierarchical society. But now their masters were to be the community members, the new owners of the haciendas.

The *ilacata*'s judgeship also implied a certain competence and equality with judges in the European world. At the same time, the imitations of national legal forms and the promise to negotiate with the national government to make the expropriation documents effective show that the Indians were willing to work within the larger society's legal framework, which the communities had utilized since the early colonial period. Perhaps this can be subsumed into the framework of Aymara political thought, which Tristan Platt has tried to develop. Aymara "justice" involves two parts that maintain a state of equilibrium; one side, however, is also superior.[52] Accepting the national state as the superior member, the rebels at the same time tried to reestablish a new equilibrium between both "republics." This did not imply that high national authorities ultimately were not in some sense superior to Andean ethnic authorities.

The episode of cannibalism and its attendant rituals were in the main internally oriented. Unlike the trial, put on for the benefit of the national government (and perhaps for other ethnic groups as well), this episode of cannibalism was oriented primarily towards the Indians' own supernatural sphere. Again, it is difficult to separate the concern for the supernatural from the issue of ethnic identity, for if Fernando Montes Ruiz is correct, the reappropriation of the supreme lightning god by the Indians and the repudiation of Christian symbols were attempts to reconstitute the Aymara cultural sphere independently of European intrusion. Thus, as in the land question, the Indians attempted to assert their own autonomy and delimit their world from that of their oppressors. In this fashion they tried to reverse the penetration of the hacienda into the northern Potosí countryside that had taken place in the previous forty-odd years and the exploitation that followed. To do this, the rebels utilized a new combination of rituals to assert their dominion over the land and the outsiders who had abused them and to revive their own gods. Their goal was to bring about a new equilibrium, in which old wrongs were righted and each portion of human society remained within what the rebels considered its proper boundaries.

Concurrently, the act of cannibalism might be interpreted as an act of psychological warfare as well. It is unclear whether the rebels had publicized this incident or, for that matter, wanted to do so. Nor is it evident, though it is certainly possible, that the community members and their leaders had heard or thought of the implications of the well-publicized trial of the Mohoza massacre a few decades earlier. In their dealings with national society, community members frequently used their status as Indians to their advantage; might they not have used this incident, which proved them "savages," to strike fear into the hearts of hacendados and mestizo smallholders? It is difficult to ascertain whether this had been an intention of the rebels, because the leadership was captured before it made public its motivations.

There are a number of apparent contradictions in the messages contained within these two rituals. Most obvious is the contrast between the scrupulous abandonment of them in the second. However, as I have argued, this might not have appeared contradictory to the rebels, for their conceptions of the Bolivian political and social systems were quite coherent and in many ways reflected the realities of life. Catholicism and its symbols had penetrated into the countryside but had achieved meaning for the peasants only through the prism of Andean ideology. Ethnic identity was still framed within the crucibles of links with fellow community members, territory, and the reciprocal relationship with the earth, mountains, sky, and weather. Local officials exploited the Indians according to their own interests. Hacendados were abusive in their relations with community members and even with their own workers and thus merited punishment as evil, though very powerful, personages. In a real sense, Indian and non-Indian societies were two different worlds held together only by the unequal relationships between mestizos and hacendados (who also were the local officials) on one side and the Indians on the other, in combination with the very tenuous hold of the government on the countryside. The rebels saw the national government as a distant but potentially benevolent institution, to which they appealed in the judicial ritual. No such effort could be made for the hacendados, who had to be eliminated from the rural setting (symbolically and concretely) so that the community members could achieve their rightful ownership over the land.

These rituals reflected, in many ways very accurately, the historical movement in which the southern Bolivian community members found themselves. The Indians had what might be considered "archaic" conceptions of society, in that they presumed a social and political order not far removed from the colonial period. Ironically, as we have seen, these conceptions were quite true to the way in which Bolivian society treated the Indian population. Even after decades of liberal reforms by the state, in which (at least in theory) the Indians were to be integrated into society as equal members and full citizens, this important segment of the nation's inhabitants remained alienated and largely disenfranchised. The Indians countered the forces of hacienda expansion and exploitation by outsiders with rebellion, which included these types of rituals. In many ways, the rebels reacted in this fashion because they were conditioned to do so through their relationship with the other parts of Bolivian society.

Nevertheless, the rebels failed to bring the national government over to their side in their fight against the hacendados. Although some groups within the larger society were willing to support the Indians' demands, such as the small Socialist party and certain reformist politicians, once the Indians had committed themselves to a violent course of action against the hacendados, the national government, inevitably, repressed the movement. While the panic-stricken government misunderstood the rebels' actions and demands, the Indians themselves possibly misunderstood the revolutionary implications of their actions. Thus, the leaders of the rebellion were easily captured, and hundreds of Indians lost their lives when the government troops began a concerted campaign against them, bringing the revolt to an end by late August. Nevertheless, the Indians achieved some success; the bloody uprising did bring to a halt the wholesale usurpation of community lands by outsiders.

Notes

1. David I. Kertzer, *Ritual, Politics, and Power* (New Haven, CT, 1988), 9–10. There is a vast literature on defining ritual; most of it deals with the connection between ritual and the supernatural. For an introduction to "secular ritual" and its meanings, see also Sally Falk Moore and Barbara G. Myerhoff, eds., *Secular Ritual* (Assen, 1977), passim.

2. For an overview of nineteenth- and twentieth-century southern Bolivian social and economic history, see Tristan Platt, *Estado boliviano y ayllu andino: Tierra y tributo en el Norte de Potosí* (Lima, 1982); Erick D. Langer, *Economic Change and Rural Resistance in Southern Bolivia, 1880–1930* (Stanford, CA, 1989). For the purposes of this article, I have defined the southern Bolivian highlands as comprising

Yamparaez province in Chuquisaca, the old province of Chayanta in Potosí, and the region between Lake Poopó and northern Potosí in Oruro.

3. George McCutchen McBride, *The Agrarian Indian Communities of Highland Bolivia* (New York, 1921), 19–25. For maps of ethnic boundaries, see Tristan Platt, "Mapas coloniales de la provincia de Chayanta: Dos visiones conflictivas de un solo paisaje," in *Estudios bolivianos en homenaje a Gunnar Mendoza L.*, comp. Martha Vrioste de Aguirre (La Paz, 1978), 113; Erick D. Langer, "Persistence and Change in Southern Bolivian Indian Communities in the Nineteenth Century," paper delivered at the Ninth International Symposium of CLACSO, "Las comunidades campesinas en los Andes del siglo 19," Quito, Ecuador, July 27, 1989, 6.

4. Nicolas Sánchez Albornoz, *Indios y tributos en el Alto Perú* (Lima, 1978), 187–218; Tristan Platt, "Liberalism and Ethnocide in the Southern Andes," *History Workshop* 17 (1984), 3–18; Erick D. Langer, "El liberalismo y la abolición de la comunidad indígena en el siglo 19," *Historia y cultura* 14 (1988), 59–95.

5. For an overview of the ramifications of the 1927 revolt for Potosí, see René Danilo Arze Aguirre, *Guerra y conflictos sociales: El caso rural boliviano durante la campaña del Chaco* (La Paz, 1987), 11–25; Olivia Harris and Xavier Albó, *Monteras y guardatojos: Campesinos y mineros en el Norte de Potosí*, rev. ed. (La Paz, 1984), 59–71; Fernando Montes Ruiz, *La máscara de piedra: Simbolismo y personalidad aymaras en la historia* (La Paz, 1986), 339–42. For a discussion of its impact primarily in Chuquisaca, see Erick D. Langer, "The Great Southern Bolivian Rebellion of 1927: A Microanalysis," paper delivered at the symposium "Peasant Resistance and Rebellion: New Perspectives," Forty-sixth International Congress of Americanists, Amsterdam, July 7, 1988. Philip M. Keyes is presently working on an important analysis of the rebellion.

6. "Sublevación Indigenal" (1927), vol. 2, Criminal, Corte Superior de Chuquisaca (Sucre), fols. 100–104. My thanks to Philip Keyes, who found and made available this important document.

7. Although it is clear from the trial records and newspaper accounts that Berdeja was killed and parts of his body eaten (see ibid., fols. 19, 2; Claudio Andrade P., "Sublevación Provincia Chayanta 1927," unpublished manuscript in the author's possession, 1985, 3), the actual sequence of events is provided only in oral traditions uncovered by anthropologists Olivia Harris and Tristan Platt, who have worked extensively in the northern Potosí area. See Harris and Albó, *Monteras y guardatojos*, 61–62; Platt, *Estado boliviano*, 145–47.

8. E. P. Thompson, "The Moral Economy of the English Crowd in the Eighteenth Century," *Past and Present* 50 (1971), 76–136.

9. For standard, though somewhat dated, accounts of the Tupac Amaru rebellion, see Lillian E. Fisher, *The Last Inca Revolt, 1780–1783* (Norman, OK, 1966); Boleslao Lewin, *Túpac Amaru: Su época, su lucha, su hado* (Buenos Aires, 1973); Sergio Serulnikov, *Tomás Catari y la producción de justicia* (Buenos Aires, 1988); Serulnikov, *Revindicaciones indígenas y legalidad colonial: La rebelión de Chayanta (1777–1781)* (Buenos Aires, 1989).

10. This tenet is mentioned throughout the trial, both by suspects interviewed and by the landowners bringing suit. For the development of this radical idea, see Langer, "The Great Southern Bolivian Indian Rebellion," passim.

11. "Sublevación Indigenal," vol. 2, fois. 101, 103.

12. Ibid., fol. 101v.

13. Ibid., fols. 101v–102. For the courtship and sexual practices of the peasants in the region under discussion, see the pathbreaking work of Javier Isko, "Condores y mast'akus: Vida y muerte en los valles nortepotosinos," in *Tiempo y muerte: Estudio de caso en dos contextos andinos de Bolivia*, by Javier Isko, Ramiro Molina, and René Pereira (Cochabamba, 1986), 11–168.

14. "Sublevación Indigenal," vol. 2, fol. 56v.

15. See Erick D. Langer, "La comercialización del siglo 20," in *La participación indigena en los mercados surandinos*, ed. Olivia Harris, Brooke Larson, and Enrique Tandeter (La Paz, 1987), 583–601. The community Indians' neglect of the hacienda peons' demands that they be given the hacienda lands in northern Potosí and elsewhere led to the dissolution of the temporary alliance that both groups had formed prior to 1927 and was one of the main reasons for the movement's disintegration into local units. See Langer, "The Great Southern Bolivian Indian Rebellion."

16. Steven J. Stern, "The Social Significance of Judicial Institutions in an Exploitative Society: Huamanga, Peru, 1570–1640," in *The Inca and Aztec States, 1400–1800: Anthropology and History*, ed. George A. Collier, Renato J. Rosaldo, and John D. Wirth (New York, 1982), 289–320; Stern, *Peru's Indian Peoples and the Challenges of Spanish Conquest: Huamanga to 1640* (Madison, WI, 1982), esp. chap. 5.

17. "Sublevación Indigenal," vol. 2, fols. 1–13v. The quote is from fol. 13v.

18. For the retaking of Indian lands from the haciendas during the revolution against the Melgarejo regime in 1870–71, see Langer, "El liberalismo," 72–73.

19. "Sublevación Indigenal," vol. 2, fol. 104.

20. Ibid., fol. 100.

21. James Lockhart, "Views of Corporate Self and History in Some Valley of Mexico Towns: Late Seventeenth and Eighteenth Centuries," in *The Inca and Aztec States*, ed. Collier et al., 367–93. For the Zapatista experience, see John Womack, Jr., *Zapata and the Mexican Revolution* (New York, 1970), 371–72.

22. For a discussion of this point, see Langer, "The Great Southern Bolivian Indian Rebellion," 20.

23. "Sublevación Indigenal," vol. 2, fol. 100.

24. The "Great National Pro-Indian Crusade" by the Bolivian Catholic church in 1926 and its failure are chronicled in Herbert S. Klein, *Parties and Political Change in Bolivia, 1880–1952* (Cambridge, 1971), 90–91.

25. Frank Salomon, "Ancestor Cults and Resistance to the State in Arequipa, ca. 1748–1754," *Resistance, Rebellion, and Consciousness in the Andean Peasant World, Eighteenth to Twentieth Centuries*, ed. Steve J. Stern (Madison, WI, 1987), 148–65. For another, albeit flawed, attempt at explaining the apparently contradictory actions of Andean rebels, see Jan Szemiński, "Why Kill the Spaniard? New Perspectives on Andean Insurrectionary Ideology in the Eighteenth Century," ibid., 166–92.

26. Catherine J. Allen, *The Hold Life Has: Coca and Cultural Identity in an Andean Community* (Washington, DC, 1988), 107–12. Part of this analysis is based upon Tristan Platt's seminal study of a northern Potosí community, "Symétries en miroir: Le concept *yanantin* chez les Macha de Bolivie," *Annales: Economies, sociétés, civilisations* 33 (1978), 1082–84.

27. Michel undoubtedly selected this title in large part for these connotations. In fact, he lived in the neighboring department of Potosí and could claim adherence to an ethnic group whose residential center lay in that department. Moreover, even

today many Indians refer to Sucre as Chuquisaca, the aboriginal name of the city's location.

28. Soon after the Spanish conquest the colonial government had used its monopoly on the dispensation of justice to make various ethnic groups rely on non-Andean authorities to ensure the smooth functioning of society, thus fatally dividing the Andeans. See n. 16 for references.

29. For the Mexican case, see William B. Taylor, *Drinking, Homicide and Rebellion in Colonial Mexican Villages* (Stanford, CA, 1979), 133–34. See also John L. Phelan, *The People and the King: The Comunero Revolution in Columbia, 1781* (Madison, WI, 1978). Of course, this was also a common sentiment during the early phases of the wars for independence throughout Spanish America.

30. Langer, "The Great Southern Bolivian Indian Rebellion," 16–20.

31. The substitution of the president of the nation for the Spanish king is also documented for the Ayacucho region in Peru and probably was common elsewhere in the Andean region as well. See, for example, John Earls, "La organización del poder en la mitología quechua," in *Ideología mesiánica del mundo andino*, ed. Juan M. Ossio (Lima, 1973), 393–414.

32. Langer, "The Great Southern Bolivian Indian Rebellion," passim. In fact, after 1927 the quite substantial support the rebel community members garnered from the *colonos* evaporated.

33. The Socialist party had attempted to integrate the peasant movement into its struggle and had invited many rebel leaders to its 1927 convention in Oruro, where the Indians gave speeches and in return received certificates of attendance and other paraphernalia from the Socialists. It is clear, however, that the Socialists had a very different agenda, according to which they attempted to subordinate the peasants to their labor movement. Despite the scare tactics of the right wing and the landowners, who tried to tar both with the same brush, all evidence points to the Socialists' failure to integrate the Indians effectively by 1927.

34. See Andrade, "Sublevación Provincia," 3–4; Harris and Albó, *Monteras y guardatojos*, 61.

35. This account, which comes largely from oral traditions, is contained in Harris and Albó, *Monteras y guardatojos*, 61–62; Platt, *Estado boliviano*, 145–46. The quotations come from "Sublevación Indigenal," vol. 2, fols. 19, 21.

36. See in particular Harris and Albó, *Monteras y guardatojos*; Montes, *La máscara de piedra*; and Platt, *Estado boliviano*. Both written and oral sources must be treated with caution; however, they are generally consistent internally and with each other. Other than the caveats expressed in the text, I feel that the information can be given credence. On another level, of course, what the Indians imagined this ritual to have been is as important as the actual sequence of events, which is impossible to reconstruct in detail in any case.

37. In fact, as Philip Keyes has found, the rebel leaders earlier had received support from the president of the university in Sucre, as well as from the other prominent members of the southern Bolivian society, for building schools in the countryside.

38. Bautista Saavedra, *El ayllu* (La Paz, 1903), 185. Saavedra later became president of Bolivia (1921–1925). Curiously, Ramiro Condarco Morales, in *Zárate, el "temible" Willka: Historia de una rebelión indígena de 1899* (La Paz, 1966), the standard account of this rebellion, makes no mention of cannibalism. Incidents of cannibalism during the 1780 rebellion are summarized in Leon G. Campbell,

"Ideology and Factionalism during the Great Rebellion, 1780–1782," in *Resistance*, ed. Stern, 124–26.

39. Montes, *La máscara de piedra*, 356–84. The sacking of Pumpuri is mentioned in Harris and Albó, *Monteras y guardatojos*, 61. An interesting view of shrines and the roles they play in Andean society is contained in Michael J. Sallnow, *Pilgrims of the Andes: Regional Cults in Cusco* (Washington, DC, 1987). Unfortunately, we lack the information on Pumpuri necessary to analyze the burning of the shrine based on Sallnow's hypotheses. Was Pumpuri considered a "mestizo shrine" and so open to attack?

40. Harry Tshopik, Jr., "The Aymara," in *Handbook of South American Indians*, vol. 2, ed. Julian H. Steward (Washington, DC, 1946), 558–60. Also see Tristan Platt, "The Andean Soldiers of Christ; Confraternity Organization, the Mass of the Sun, and Regenerative Warfare in Rural Potosí (Eighteenth–Twentieth Centuries)," *Journal de la société des américanistes* 73 (1987), 139–92.

41. Montes, *La máscara de piedra*, 378–79. The need to consume part of the witch's body to render it harmless is confirmed by another incident during the 1927 rebellion. An accused witch who had earlier aided hacendados in acquiring land from the Indians was imprisoned by rebels. According to witnesses, the Indians threatened to kill her and drink her blood. See Criminal Juzgado de Instrucción (Tarabuco), 1927, vol. 1, fol. 16v.

42. Montes, *La máscara de piedra*, 236–38, 379–80. For the most detailed analysis of the mountain gods, see Gabriel Martínez, "Los dioses de los cerros en los Andes," *Journal de la société des américanistes* 69 (1983), 85–115.

43. Platt, "The Andean Soldiers of Christ."

44. Tristan Platt, *Espejos y maíz: Temas de la estructura simbólica andina* (La Paz, 1976), 17–18; Platt, "The Andean Soldiers of Christ"; Thérèse Bouysse-Cassagne and Olivia Harris, "Pacha: En torno al pensamiento aymara," in *Tres reflexiones sobre el pensamiento aymara*, ed. Thérèse Bouysse-Cassagne, Olivia Harris, Tristan Platt, and Verónica Cereceda (La Paz, 1987), 29–31; Platt, "Entre Ch'axwa y Muxsa: Para una historia del pensamiento político aymara," ibid., 82–93. Ludovico Bertonio, *Vocabulario dela lengua aymara* (Cochabamba, 1984 [1612]), 350, in addition to the various meanings related to meeting in battle, interprets *tincusitha*, for example, as "conformarse una cosa con otra; venir bien, ajustarse."

45. For an explanation of the *ch'axwa*, see Platt, "Entre Ch'axwa y Muxsa."

46. See Montes, *La máscara de piedra*, 376–77; Fritz John Porter Poole, "Cannibals, Tricksters, and Witches: Anthropophagic Images among Bimin-Kuskusmin," in *The Ethnography of Cannibalism*, ed. Paula Brown and Donald Tuzin (Washington, DC, 1983), 6–32; Gillian Gillison, "Cannibalism among Women in the Eastern Highlands of Papua New Guinea," ibid., 34–50; I. M. Lewis, *Religion in Context: Cults and Charisma* (Cambridge, 1986), 63–77.

47. Javier Isko, pers. comm. March 29, 1989.

48. This line of reasoning, of course, stands William Arens's argument, that cannibalism does not exist, on its head. See Arens, *The Man-Eating Myth: Anthropology and Anthropophagy* (New York, 1979); see also Lewis, *Religion in Context*, 63–72. I am not implying that cannibalism functions in this way everywhere; see, for example, Gillison, "Cannibalism among Women." Moreover, in some religions within the Andes foreigners are seen as vampires and cannibals. This occurs even today in places such as Ayacucho province, Peru. See Szemiński,

"Why Kill the Spaniard?" 170–71; Jean-Marie Ansion, *Demons de Andes: La pensée mythique dans une région des Andes péruviennes (Ayacucho)* (Louvain-la-Neuve, 1984). For the Cuzco region, see Allen, *The Hold Life Has*, III.

49. The quote is from "Sublevación Indigenal," vol. 2, fol. 19. Platt, *Estado boliviano*, 145–46; Szemiński, "Why Kill the Spaniard?" 169.

50. Harris and Albó, *Monteras y guardatojos*, 62.

51. See n. 32.

52. Platt, "Entre Ch'axwa y Muxsa."

9

Ethnic Identity and Land Tenure Disputes in Modern Mexico

Frans J. Schryer

So many Spaniards and mestizos (people of mixed European and Indian ancestry) have moved into the countryside over the centuries in countries such as Mexico, Guatemala, and Ecuador that it is often speculative to designate a particular community or region as being inhabited solely by people of indigenous origin. Furthermore, the business, social, and family relationships between natives and mestizos have been so intimate for so long that stipulating an individual's ethnic identity can be problematic. Among the natives and mestizos are many individuals who determine their social behavior and language (many are bilingual) by the company that they happen to be in and the role that they wish to play at the time. To some extent they can choose the ethnic identity they wish to assume in any particular situation.

The complexity of these rural societies—and the continued centrality of ethnic identity in them—are pointed out in this selection from Frans Schryer's detailed study of the ongoing (sometimes lethal) disputes over land tenure in the Huasteca region of central Mexico. Customarily, the Nahuas (natives who speak Nahuatl, the primary Indian language of Mexico) have been portrayed as impoverished peasants who wish to establish ejidos (village collectives) as the dominant landholding system against the mestizos who support ranchos (private family farms). But such distinctions make little sense—or at least seem mutable—in the case of contemporary Huasteca, as government agencies seek to carry out the land reform that the Mexican Revolution made a national imperative.

Despite the continuation of a culture of violence based on firearms, dating back to the Mexican Revolution, the patterns of violence and homicides have changed dramatically between the era of caciquismo of the first half of the twentieth century and the outbreak of a peasant revolt in the seventies. The analytical approach used by William Taylor in connection with colonial Mexican villages can be applied to Huejutla in the twentieth century.[1] In comparing the two time periods, one can examine how political violence reflects changes in social relations, and in this case in particular, class relations. Between 1910 and 1950, most homicides in Huejutla involved the murder of political opponents of the same class (the rancheros) in factional disputes or vendettas. Such homicides generally took place in bars, under the influence of alcohol. According to local folk theory, anyone who was not "brave" enough to avenge his opponents laid an ambush to kill their enemies along some deserted road. In contrast, although a variety of intimidation tactics were used against the population as a whole, poor peasants were generally not assassinated. Poor peasants and other "ordinary" people were much more likely to get wounded or killed in actual gun battles between private armies whose members were recruited from a variety of class backgrounds. Such political shoot-outs usually took place in village plazas or out in the open fields.

In the seventies, the number of assassinations of peasants went up dramatically while old-fashioned face-to-face shoot-outs between traditional rancheros occurred very rarely. Moreover, agrarian peasants were usually killed in small groups, while traveling together or while attending meetings in Huejutla. This change in the pattern of homicides reflects the changing function of violence: from a means of settling intraelite disputes to a direct method of conducting class war in the face of open opposition from economic subordinates. Assassinations of peasants became prevalent at a time when more subtle methods of class control (including intimidation) no longer worked. Also, the assailants responsible for such political assassinations were rarely identified or caught, which gave rise to a great deal of ambiguity. In the past, either most people knew who were murderers (there were usually lots of witnesses) or, in the case of ambushes, everyone could guess who was probably responsible. During the height of the agrarian revolt of the seventies, members of different classes often had different interpretations of who was responsible for political assassinations. Militant peasants usually blamed well-known "caciques" or rich landowners, while modern, educated rancheros often assumed that the government itself had ordered assassinations of peasant leaders if they "had gone too far" or become too independent.[2]

Another difference in the pattern of political violence between the [nineteen] thirties and the seventies is the complete absence of paramilitary forces in the latter period. Between 1974 and 1988, few military confrontations occurred either during electoral disputes or in the process of invading land. Both invading peasants and landowners (or their retainers) usually showed up with arms, but landowners could do little against the numerically more powerful agrarians. Instead, they chose to eliminate the leaders or small groups of representatives rather than risk open gun battles. Landowners also used their connections with the police and state officials to have peasant leaders arrested and jailed. Given the presence of a much stronger and more centralized Mexican state after 1950, it is unlikely that the government would have permitted open battles between the opposing sides, since the use of private armies would imply the usurpation of the right of the state to use force in such a public manner. Instead, the landowners would ask the army to dislodge agrarian peasants, who usually retreated only to return a few days later. On other occasions, the army or police even oversaw "land invasions" if such invasions had prior authorization through the mediation of peasant organizations (such as the CNC [Confederación Nacional de Campesinos] or the PST [Partido Socialista de los Trabajadores]). Despite the symbolic show of military power, most of the struggles for land involved a lot of backroom maneuvering and political negotiations. Given the lack of "real battles" (for the most part), one older peasant from Yahualica who had fought in the Mexican Revolution even told me glibly: "Before we old guys were real revolutionaries; nowadays, these young guys are little, make-believe revolutionaries."[3]

Another noticeable change in the pattern of violence is the eruption of machete fights and even shoot-outs within rural (especially Nahua) villages, something that had rarely occurred before. In the thirties or forties, the predominant pattern of factional in-fighting was among mestizo rancheros who lived in mestizo cabeceras or small ranchos, as has been seen. Such factionalism usually took quite violent forms. At that time there was not nearly as much overt violence within Nahua communities or villages inhabited mainly by poorer mestizo peasants. Whenever fights did break out (often in bars), they usually involved disagreements between individuals over personal matters. In contrast, in the seventies and eighties, huge fights (with machetes and fists) frequently broke out in larger Nahua communities between whole groups of people belonging to opposing factions, especially in the southern zone. Such group confrontation, usually between radical and conservative peasants, reflected completely opposing and irreconcilable interpretations about the status of land tenure and whether or not to join in the agrarian movement. In villages with such internal divisions, it became increasingly more difficult to hold the communal feasts that used to last for two or three days. Municipal as well as village authorities could no longer afford to allow such feasts, with their communal drinking bouts, because "too many people will attack each other under the influence of alcohol."[4] This eruption of internal violence is an indication that the level of internal differentiation, combined with an extremely ambiguous and contradictory land tenure situation, had reached a breaking point in such Nahua villages.

Another form of group violence that developed in Huejutla in the seventies was demonstration marches led by peasant leaders. Such marches usually involved not only a high level of verbal but occasional physical attacks by groups of agrarian peasants against local authorities or representatives of opposing political factions. Such groups of radical peasants often traveled from one village to another on foot, picking up supporters on the way. In each village they passed, local peasants would point out the houses of minor caciques or "the rich" for ridicule or vandalism. In some cases local militants even rounded up unpopular teachers, students, or government technicians whom they perceived to be too sympathetic to local landowners and then forced them to work in the fields to "teach them what it is like to be peasants." Such behavior was not that different from the mob scenes described by Edward Thompson for rural England in the eighteenth century.[5] In Huejutla, members from such mobs also painted slogans (for example, "death to" so-and-so) on public buildings or fences. These marches also involved minor looting from stores belonging to rich peasants or landowners considered to be "enemies of the peasants," although stores owned by politically neutral or sympathetic landowners or merchants were not touched. Such group violence became an opportunity to express past grievances against people who were perceived as having unfairly exploited the peasants in the past, although no doubt some people also took advantage of such situations to carry out acts of hooliganism.

Once agrarian peasants managed to win control over a particular village, coercion continued to be used against local opponents, especially in Nahua communities in the southern zone. Nahua villages that used to be Indian republics have long traditions of authoritarian rule and internal law enforcement (through the use of ropes to tie up offenders if their villages did not have special buildings used as jails).[6] In such communities, with their emphasis on the need to achieve unanimity, there was no precedent for a formal, institutionalized, political opposition. Rather, decisions were always reached on the basis of a long process of informal discussion, debate and consultation rather than open voting.[7] External political leaders and even government officials took advantage of this traditional system of consensus for their own political ends. For example, while very much in favor of more open elections and competing candidates in Mexico in general, the PST (just like the PRI [Partido Revolucionario Institucional—the dominant official party]) received bloc votes from Nahua villages like San Francisco where the majority of peasants were affiliated with their party. Indeed, a group of peasants there told me that they would not allow anyone to vote for or join any other party because "democracy is for the cities but not for the countryside."[8]

Class Conflict and Kinship

Both land invasions and the types of violent demonstration described above were frequently initiated by younger and partly acculturated peasants who had worked as migratory laborers in other regions. These young radicals challenged the authority of traditional village elites who were usually older and wealthier peasants.[9] In many cases, more conservative peasants (who also had more secure access to land) complained that land invasions and other radical actions were undertaken "only by boys" (that is, men less than twenty-five years old). While this generalization is not completely true (many older peasants also became agrarians), class conflicts in both Nahua and mestizo communities frequently coincided with divisions between older and younger members within the same family. For example, when the radical peasants affiliated with the OIPUH [Organización Independiente de los Pueblos Unidos de las Huastecas] took over the rancho of San Miguel, owned by a wealthy (and elderly) Nahua peasant, this old man fled to Tenexco. But some of his own sons and his many grandsons joined the radical agrarians who came from Tenexco and Cuatapa to set up their new homes in Emiliano Zapata.[10]

Such intrafamily splits, involving richer versus poorer relatives, also occurred in mestizo families. . . . Conflicts within the [Ramírez] family continued in the 1970s when several brothers joined the agrarians of Tenexco and then expelled a cousin, an older brother, and even their own grandfather (who had been a rural schoolteacher)! The Ramírezes who became agrarians had all worked as migratory laborers or had joined the army before returning home. Their more prosperous relatives (who did not want to join in the land invasions) were teachers or modern ranchers (sometimes both at the same time).[11] Such intrafamily splits continued in the 1980s, when members of the Ramírez family who remained in Cuatapa (that is, the agrarians) joined forces with El Chino of Huitzotlaco to attack even poorer and more radical (mainly Nahua) peasants who wanted a more equitable distribution of land within their ejido. At this point, however, at least one Ramírez, instead of supporting El Chino (the new conservative leader), sided with radical peasants who later moved to Emiliano Zapata.[12] Such class-based factional divisions among members of large, extended families (especially conflicts between people related as second or third cousins) were also found in other villages. For example, in the mestizo village of El Cojolite, many of the agrarian peasants (whose last name was Hidalgo) could trace their kinship connections to the same landowners whom they invaded in 1979.[13] However, unlike intrafamily disputes among mestizo ranchers in the past, which more often took the form of a competition between people of the same generation (first cousins or even brothers), those that took place in the seventies were more likely to involve conflicts between members of different generations. Such family splits often coincided with the traditional (uneducated) versus modern (educated) distinctions.

While class conflict took the form of both intrafamily and interfamily disputes, family connections between poor and rich peasants (or between landowners and day laborers) also inhibited class conflict because of strong patron-client bonds often established through kinship. This was especially true in the case of families where the majority of members continued to share the traditional culture of peasant communities. In such families, poor peasants did not want to attack members of their own extended families precisely because of the powerful norm of kinship solidarity. Another cultural norm that influenced political behavior was that of harmony among people connected to each other through the institution of compadrazgo (fictive kinship), an institution that plays such an important role in Latin American society. The very fact that people lamented that compadres sometimes became bitter enemies during the peak of the agrarian struggle indicates that the norm of solidarity among fictive kin basically remained intact. In most (but not all) cases, ties of compadrazgo between people who belonged to different social classes (what the literature calls vertical compadrazgo) continued to reinforce the class structure.[14] At the same time horizontal compadrazgo (fictive kin ties among equally poor peasants) created greater loyalty and solidarity in a common struggle for land. Ongoing patterns of social relationships, inherited from the past, thus shaped the form of class conflicts that developed in the seventies and eighties.

Class Conflict and Ethnicity: Image and Reality

Most scholars who have written about the peasant movement in Huejutla on the regional level have commented on the role played by the ethnic factor. For example, Agustín Avila argues that, in the seventies, formerly captive Nahua communities took charge of their own cultural values and forms of government necessary to maintain a unique way of life.[15] Avila also equates the class struggle in the Huasteca with ethnic strife involving the revival of ethnic pride on the part of the Indian peasants. This dichotomous view is also apparent in newspaper articles written by left-wing journalists who either ignore or gloss over any facts that contradict the equation of class and ethnicity. For example, in dealing with the conflicts in the ejido of Tenexco, nowhere does anyone mention that the infamous cacique and pistolero El Chino is a native Nahuatl speaker of Huitzotlaco, a village which has preserved the Nahuatl language and many of its traditions better than most other (and sometimes more radical) Indian communities. Nor is there any mention that the radical peasants who formed the new Nahua village of Emiliano Zapata also took over a rancho that belonged to a wealthy Nahua peasant. Similarly, when journalists want to quote an "Indian" opinion, they often cite Crisóstomos Arenas of Huautla, who was appointed president of the Consejo Supremo Nahuatl [Supreme Nahua Council] in 1984. The fact that he is an Nahua Indian (as well as an official representative of the Nahua nation), however, is conveniently omitted when other writers accuse him of being one of the caciques affiliated with the CNC.

This equation of class and ethnicity is part of a broader set of assumptions that includes the image of a classless Indian society.[16] Most writers, especially popular writers and journalists, portray the Nahua community as the survival of a pre-Hispanic commune (albeit impoverished and exploited).[17] This simplified and idyllic image of the Indian community is widely shared by the Mexican public, including most politicians. Both academics and journalists also tend to use the terms "Indian" and "peasant" interchangeably. In many accounts, after a general introductory statement about the importance of ethnicity, any further references to the ethnic factor are omitted—the readers presumably already know that all the militant peasants are Indians, and that their opponents (the landowners and caciques) are mestizos. This dichotomy between Indians (who are always good and poor) and mestizos (mainly rich, even if not always bad) also appears in the book written by Ildefonso Maya, the subdirector of the INI [National Indigenous Institute] center in Huejutla. In this book, in referring to two important peasant leaders who were mestizos (Pedro Beltrán and Humberta Hernández), Maya says that they were "Indians in their hearts."[18] This educated Indian author, the press, and most social scientists who have written about the region also give the impression that all Indian villages throughout the region have the same cultural norms and share a common social organization (albeit in different stages of "purity").

My description of the peasant movement in Huejutla and the various case studies already presented give a very different picture. Class struggles in Huejutla not only saw Indian villages pitted against absentee, Spanish-speaking landlords, but also involved class conflicts within Nahua communities. During such internal class conflicts, ethnic labels were not widely used although members of opposite sides did use other types of dichotomous terms. For example, most conservative peasants portrayed militant agrarian peasants as being rebellious, disrespectful "troublemakers" (the Spanish term *revoltosos* was also used by Nahuatl speakers). Radical peasants, in turn, called the more conservative, wealthier peasants "the rich" (*los ricos*) or used the Nahuatl expression, "*tlakuajkejya*" (they have already eaten). In some cases militant peasants also used the pejorative label *coyomej* for somewhat more acculturated, wealthier villagers who were also better educated (including Nahua schoolteachers who owned land), although the latter still portrayed themselves as "authentic Indians" to outsiders.

Even when ethnic labels were used, the characteristics of Nahua communities or individual Nahua peasants involved in class struggles often bore little resemblance to what anthropologists would consider typical Indian versus Mestizo cultural traits. For example, poor Nahua peasants who became militant agrarians were more likely to wear Western dress and speak a mixture of Spanish and Nahuatl, while many conservative and wealthy peasants continued to use the traditional manta and spoke a "purer" form of Nahuatl. A few of these more prosperous Nahua peasants were even ceremonial specialists or traditional healers; yet, in at least one case, in Paajtla, poor Indian peasants invaded land owned by such a healer. On the other hand, from the viewpoint of their notions about community membership and equal access to land, younger, more acculturated day laborers were more "typically Indian" than their wealthier neighbors. This lack of fit between ethnic labels and the distribution of cultural traits does not mean, however, that ethnic differences can be ignored. We have already seen how the struggle for access to land and political power was conducted in a different manner in Nahua as opposed to mestizo communities located in the southern zone. Ethnic labels and ethnic identities were also employed in quite different ways by peasants involved in land invasions in the different subregions of Huejutla, especially in the north versus the south.

The Use of Ethnic Labels in Agrarian Conflicts

It has been seen how the struggle for access to land in Nahua communities in the southern zone was associated with legal disputes over whether or not such communities should become real (as opposed to fictitious) ejidos or whether or not such communities should retain their status as *comunidades*. However, although Nahuatl-speaking communities in the southern zone would be considered by ethnographers as "more typically Indian" (because of their unique communal institutions, including special toponyms), most of the land invasions involving the Indian peasants of such southern villages were not couched in ethnic terms. Rather, the fight for access to more land was generally couched in terms of a struggle against "all outsiders" (both Nahua and Mestizo). This absence of ethnic labels during agrarian disputes in most of the southern zone can be explained by the lower level of association between class and ethnicity. Here the struggle for land was generally conducted against both wealthy Nahua peasants and bilingual mestizo rancheros who frequently shared a similar lifestyle with their Indian neighbors.

The only exceptions were a few cases where conflicts over land in the southern zone did take the form of disputes between neighboring Nahua and mestizo villages. These conflicts, which were simultaneously class struggles and conflicts between neighboring villages of different ethnic status, involved a fight of poor Nahua peasants against Spanish-speaking landowners and merchants who lived in small commercial centers. The Spanish-speaking inhabitants of such centers had treated the Indian peasants of surrounding hamlets particularly harshly in the past. For example, throughout the seventies and eighties, the mestizo village of El Arenal was involved in vehement disputes with the Nahua village of Santa Teresa in the municipio of Yahualica. After invading most of the pastures belonging to the inhabitants of this mestizo *anexo* in 1978, radical Indian leaders from Santa Teresa wanted to take over the town itself and expel all of its inhabitants, whom they called *coyomej*. Such attempts resulted in an armed clash in 1985 that required the intervention of the army. Similar conflicts between neighboring Nahua and mestizo villages also took place in Huejutla (Tehuetlán versus Ixcatlan). In both cases, ethnic opposition coincided with an ideological battle about whether or not mestizo landowners should be allowed to own and operate ranchos within the communal boundaries of Nahua villages.

Unlike their counterparts in most of the southern zone, Nahua peasants in the northern zone more clearly expressed their disputes with local landowners in ethnic terms because of a closer correspondence between class and ethnicity on the local level. Not only were the vast majority of landowners mestizos, but these landowners usually lived in the predominantly Spanish-speaking towns of Huejutla or San Felipe Orizatlán. Such mestizos included the descendants of the original hacienda owners (mostly of direct European extraction) as well as rancheros from the southern zone who had moved to Huejutla after buying ranchos in the northern zone. Many of these larger landowners were no longer bilingual at the time of the eruption of a peasant revolt. Militant agrarian peasants in the north not only saw their class struggle in terms of ethnic opposition, but they also emphasized the exploitative nature of the hacienda system (especially the institution of serving as *semaneros*) to which their parents or grandparents had been subjected prior to 1940.[19] Yet, from the perspective of many anthropologists, such ethnically conscious northern Indian villages were less "typically Indian" insofar as they did not have communal administrative boundaries or such institutions as the civil-religious hierarchy. The equation of class conflict with ethnic opposition between Nahua day laborers and Spanish-speaking landowners could also be observed in the intermediate zone of Huejutla, which had been dominated by landowners from the mestizo villages of Vinasco and Huichapa. This area, which was also characterized by a continuation of marked ethnic discrimination by mestizo (or "white") rancheros, resembles the northern zone in terms of a strong correlation between class and ethnicity, although the landowners who lived in Vinasco and Huichapa continued to speak Nahuatl as a second language and tried to maintain paternalistic relations with their workers and tenants to a greater extent.

Although agrarian struggles in the northern zone and intermediate zones were generally expressed in terms of ethnic opposition, there were actually very few confrontations between Nahua and mestizo peasants from neighboring villages. For example, in Los Humos (Orizatlán), mestizo cowhands and Nahua field laborers undertook joint land invasions.[20] Indeed, throughout the seventies, militant peasants from both mestizo and Nahua peasant communities invaded lands together. Likewise, agrarian peasants from the completely mestizo ejidos of La Coneja and Las Piedras joined forces with their Nahua neighbors, and these two Spanish-speaking ejidos subsequently became part of the rural development and resettlement project that brought together several mestizo and Nahua ejidos. Even in Vincaso, poor mestizo peasants and recent Nahua newcomers to this mestizo village joined forces.

As in the southern zone, ethnic labels also did not always "fit" reality (as defined by anthropologists) because such labels were often used in an extremely ambiguous manner. For example, when various ejidos joined together to form a common association (a producers' union) in the eighties, their mestizo leader from the Spanish-speaking town of Las Piedras insisted that this political association be designated as a union of Indian communities.[21] However, the Nahua community of Los Coyoles referred to the "*coyomej* of Las Piedras" when a mestizo gunman from that village was suspected of killing their more radical mestizo *comisariado*, who was the leader of the "Indian" peasant union. The wealthier and more conservative mestizo peasants from places like Las Piedras and La Coneja in turn more frequently used the pejorative label of *indios* to refer to militant agrarian Indians.

The great variation found in the use of ethnic labels, and the lack of fit between class and ethnicity in the region as a whole, does not mean that ethnic distinctions (which are part of a system of ethnic stratification in Mexico as a whole) can be ignored in the analysis of local class conflicts. A strong correlation between class membership and ethnic affiliation probably facilitated the earlier development of class consciousness (and hence class conflict) in places like La Corrala. Such communities, characterized by greater polarization of class as well as a strong correlation between class and ethnicity, were also less likely to be disrupted by internal divisions and internecine fighting (as happened in Tenexco). However, the influence of ethnicity on class conflict can be examined even when the correlation between class and ethnicity was not very strong. A distinctive lifestyle and common membership in a stigmatized minority provided poor Nahua peasants throughout the region with a stronger sense of identity and cohesion than their mestizo counterparts. This distinctiveness gave Nahua peasants a competitive edge when they had to organize themselves to undertake conflicts with non-Indian landowners (once their ties of dependence on local patrons had weakened due to greater contact with the outside world and increasing access to the national language). Moreover, the fact that they could speak Nahuatl among themselves was of great tactical value when they did not want outside politicians, police spies from the state capital, or even members of the increasingly monolingual Spanish-speaking local elite to understand what they were saying to one another. We should also take into account the use of ethnic symbols by people who operate in the national arena and the impact of their actions on the local level.

An Interactive Analysis of Ethnicity and Politics

The historian Serge Gruzinski has shown how an Indian self-identity emerged during the colonial period, especially among former native rulers and noblemen, despite the ongoing process of Westernization.[22] This Indian identity developed as the only way of coping with and manipulating the political world created by the Spanish conquerors. Because land rights were vested in the name of Indian pueblos, the representatives of such pueblos came to be Indians, rather than members of specific ethnic enclaves. Historians have shown that toward the end of the eighteenth century, which saw increasing demographic pressure and a rash of legal battles over land in rural Mexico, many wealthy, partly acculturated Indian caciques again started to stress their Indian identity and even sent petitions in Nahuatl, although they could easily converse in Spanish.[23] Such revivals of an ethnic identity among members of Indian elites are not only a response to continued ethnic discrimination, but also a useful political strategy whenever the central government of Mexico gives special legal recognition to Indians as members of rural ethnic minorities. This recognition became more explicit in the twentieth century, especially after the Mexican Revolution. The politics of ethnicity on the local level must therefore be seen in this broader context of national policy. The use of ethnic symbols by national-level politicians affects the ethnic identity and the use of ethnic labels by people on the local level, which in turn affects government policy.

The renewed emphasis on native rights by the government of Mexico under [Lázaro] Cárdenas can explain why it was necessary for mestizo politicians in Huejutla, including Nochebuena, to present themselves as pro-*indigenista*. To gain political merit and to show that they were good defenders of Mexico's native population, these mestizo politicians had to provide land to the Indians. This was easily done in the case of the northern zone where most peasants who had previously worked for hacendados spoke Nahuatl. These same politicians managed to give the impression that they had helped even more Indians by reviving the original communal boundaries in the southern zone. These mestizo politicians thus fulfilled the expectations of the central government by utilizing the appropriate ethnic symbols. Such an emphasis on ethnic labels by mestizo ranchero politicians happened to coincide with their own economic class interests since a land reform ostensibly designed for Indian peasants did not affect their own class interests.

Thirty years later, President Luís Echeverría resurrected a policy of radical *indigenismo* in an era of renewed social tensions in the countryside caused by great regional disparities and a crisis in agricultural production because of two decades of rapid but lopsided economic development.[24] The rural districts hardest hit by this economic recession included many of the predominantly indigenous regions, like Huejutla. Echeverría's program included support for the setting up of a supreme council representing different indigenous regions of Mexico, including Nahuas. Now, however, it was radical peasant leaders, engaged in a struggle for land, who had to take into account (and, if possible, take advantage of) new ethnic images and ethnically defined institutions on the national level. For this reason, peasant leaders from both the southern and northern zones couched the general agrarian struggle on the regional level in terms of an opposition between *masehualmej* and *coyomej*.

The first president of the Consejo Supremo Nahuatl, Pedro Amador Hernández, was a radical Indian peasant from the village of Huextetitla (Orizatlán). After his death, he was succeeded by Agustín Castillo, one of the agrarian leaders from Chililico. This man not only had taken part in land invasions but also wanted his village to be an ejido instead of a *comunidad*. When Castillo was officially elected president, forty-six Nahua *comisariados* still showed up at a meeting held in the local offices of the official government party, the PRI.[25] However, Castillo's term of office was less controversial than that of his predecessor. Although he was subjected to at least one possible attempt on his life, he maintained close contact with state officials and became one of the principal collaborators to Gabriela Rojo, the niece of [Jorge] Rojo Lugo, who supported but also tried to control local peasants. After Castillo stepped down, the Consejo Nahuatl became even more subject to control by mestizo politicians who realized the need to keep tight control over this potentially powerful organization because of its symbolic importance. For example, state officials used all of their influence to ensure that members of the regional committee were not too radical; they included, among others, Feliciano Sánchez (El Chino, the conservative

CNC representative and the owner of a de facto private property) and a young man from Yahualica who worked as a government employee. With such blatant manipulation by the government, and the presence of conservative Nahua politicians, it is not surprising that many radical Nahua peasants became less interested in this organization. According to Agustín Castillo, only ten community representatives showed up at the 1980 elections, and the committee became less and less involved in agrarian politics.

Although the Consejo Nahuatl became almost totally divorced from the struggle for land, its presence is one indication of a new trend: the tendency of better-off, more educated Nahua men to stress their Indian identity vis-à-vis the central government and its representatives. For example, the new president of the Consejo for the period 1980 to 1985 was Ramón Sagahún, a Nahua merchant from Jaltocan. This man had actually been opposed to land invasions in his home region, although he later became quite willing to collaborate with agrarian leaders to further his own political career. Throughout the eighties, wealthy Nahua peasants and even some mestizos were to develop an Indian identity as a way not to achieve a more equitable distribution of land, but to consolidate their position as small landowners and members of the village elite. Identification with the label "*indio*" was now used more and more with officials in the Office of Land Reform, state politicians and technicians in charge of a new program of rural development. Peasants who continued to struggle for land also learned the necessity of stressing their Indianness with political agitators and more politicians on the state level who might be able to provide them with assistance. This is why it is important also to take into consideration the perception of ethnicity and ethnic relations of the mestizo outsiders who worked in the government bureaucracy.

The manner in which ethnic relations in the Huasteca were perceived by people from other parts of Mexico not only influenced the way agrarian conflicts were presented to outsiders, but often determined their outcomes as well. Government officials and political agitators from other regions (including professionals who considered themselves to be Indians) saw all Nahua communities as classless, but they also were oblivious to the differences in agrarian politics between north and south. They were also unaware that some of the formerly Nahua communities had become completely acculturated (to the extent that their inhabitants had lost both their Nahuatl language and their identity) and that there were very poor peasants who lived in communities that have always been mestizo. These outsiders perceived the struggle for land throughout the whole region as one pitting Indian peasants against the direct descendants of European landlords. This image was reinforced through their initial contact with places like La Corrala and Lemontitla. However, the combination of communal structures and ethnic/class polarization characteristic of places like La Corrala and Lemontitla was not representative of most of Huejutla. Land conflicts that received a great deal of publicity in the seventies, such as those in Tenexco and Pepeyocatitla, were directed against wealthy Indian peasants or bilingual rancheros. However, these subsequent events were filtered through a set of perceptual glasses that did not allow outside observers to see the intra-ethnic dimensions of such conflicts.

The cultural perception of outsiders explains why the struggle of peasants in ethnically diverse regions received more press coverage (and government attention) than [it did in] more homogenous mestizo areas. Nahua villages in the Huasteca initially received more visits from sympathetic outsiders than their non-Indian counterparts, until members of mestizo villages, especially those that had once been Indian pueblos, learned to portray themselves as "Indians" to outsiders. This happened in the case of Tecolotitla. This strategy was used by both poor and wealthy Nahua peasants, and even by people who technically were not peasants. Thus, in Macuxtepetla, a schoolteacher and part-time rancher, who was the son of a mestizo ranchero, recovered several plots of his previously privately owned land by defending his rights as a full-fledged member of an Indian ejido. Although this man had been attacked as a *coyotl* by fellow villages, he still represented himself to outsiders as an Indian (he was, from his mother's side) and a member of a Nahua community with a long history of heroic struggle to maintain its own land and its own identity!

Nahua professionals who did not own rural property or engage in commercial activities occupied an even more ambiguous and more contradictory position in the social structure of Huejutla in the seventies. A good example is Ildefonso Maya, the founder and current director of a Nahua cultural center in the city of Huejutla who was quoted at the beginning of this chapter. His life history and subsequent career can be used to illustrate the role of educated, urbanized Indians as mediators, or brokers, between a predominantly Nahua-speaking peasantry and the national state committed to the ideals of *indigenismo*.

The Case of Ildefonso Maya: A Nahua Intellectual

Ildefonso Maya was born in 1936 in the *municipio* of Ilamatlán (Veracruz), which borders on the region of Huejutla. His father, a Nahua merchant, sent him to primary school where he learned Spanish. The young Ildefonso continued his studies in Mexico City where he took classical Nahuatl and art.[26] He was also exposed to the intellectual and artistic world of Mexico City, including some of the famous muralists whom he got to know working part-time as a servant in their houses.[27] In 1954 he returned to Huejutla to accept a position as art instructor in a recently established private high school, and he also gave private lessons. He married a mestiza woman who was a member of a prominent mestizo ranchero family from Atlapexco. Maya was thus incorporated into the social network of upper- and middle-class families in Huejutla to whom he served as an example of the talented, educated people in the city of Huejutla. He also made many trips to Nahua villages to collect samples of folklore and local history from which he drew inspiration for his paintings. One of these paintings, depicting traditional pre-Hispanic themes and the struggle of native peoples against the evil and corruption of Western civilization, can be seen in the lobby of the main hotel of downtown Huejutla, the Hotel Fayad—a hotel owned by one of the most successful capitalists of Huejutla.

During the agrarian turmoil of the seventies, Ildefonso Maya sympathized with the peasants' struggle for land and often acted as a spokesman for the Nahua peasantry. For example, he chided more racist mestizos for their opposition to the inevitable implementation of a long overdue land reform and for their use of violent tactics. However, his role in class conflicts within Nahua communities was more ambiguous. For example, he helped the peasants of Toltitlan (Jaltocan) in their attempts to set up a sandle-making workshop and to become more independent vis-à-vis their cabecera. He also defended these peasants when they were unjustly accused of leading land invasions. In other cases, however, Maya's interest in promoting local crafts put him at odds with more radical agrarian peasants. In Chililico he organized a display of ceramics in collaboration with a group of peasants who belonged to a faction of wealthier, more conservative peasants. As a result, he was perceived as an enemy by the more militant peasants who were engaged in a class struggle. For this reason members of this conservative faction, who sided with local landowners and who were later expelled from Chililico, were referred to by their opponents as *mayamej* (a pun on Maya's surname, which in Nahuatl can also be made to sound like the plural of the word *mayatl*, a type of string bag).[28]

While often criticizing the cultural imperialism of the Western world (including the Mexican state), Ildefonso Maya nevertheless collaborated with various state governments whose leaders tried to contain peasant unrest or channel it into an officially approved direction. . . . Maya became a close collaborator of Gabriela Rojo (the niece of Governor Rojo Lugo), who was appointed to several local administrative posts, including that of director of the INI. Gabriela Rojo appointed Maya as her subdirector of the INI, which made him the chief administrator in charge of the regional coordinating office located in Huejutla. In this capacity, he was in charge of setting up small community projects as well as acting as a consultant for the program of indigenous education. Maya, the first and only Nahua subdirector of this center, tried to introduce some changes, such as making its mestizo employees learn at least some Nahuatl. However, not only did he fail to make local INI personnel more sensitive to cultural issues, but he soon realized that the coordinating center of the INI in Huejutla actually had little autonomy and a very small budget.[29] After stepping down from his position at the INI, Maya opened up a small museum of Nahua art and pursued his career in painting and teaching. He also continued to act as a consultant and expert on Nahua culture for the mestizo intelligentsia of Huejutla, some of whom had gone to live in Mexico City. Ildefonso Maya, a kind of unofficial spokesperson for the Nahua population of the Huasteca, again entered politics in the eighties.

Ildefonso Maya is an example of what often happens in Mexico when an Indian intellectual becomes involved in regional politics or takes up a post in the government bureaucracy. Maya is both a beneficiary and a critic of the *indigenismo* establishment; a member of a still stigmatized minority, yet one who also belongs to a privileged stratum of professionals; a believer in the noble, egalitarian Indian community, yet the son of a prosperous Indian small town merchant; a radical and a critic vis-à-vis the mestizo elite of Huejutla, but at the same time criticized and rejected by at least one group of poor, Nahuatl-speaking peasants engaged in internal class conflicts.

Conclusion

The politics of ethnicity has many facets. Ethnic stereotypes and their opposite—the acclamation of a positive ethnic identity—form part of a set of cultural symbols used by a wide variety of actors belonging to different classes. For example, the preservation of Nahua culture has become part of a set of political demands [made by] the intellectual spokesmen of the OIPUH. This radical independent peasant organization usually includes at least a couple of lines of Nahuatl in its public bulletins to give them a special Indian flavor. Its members or supporters have also organized Nahua cultural events (song and dance) in conjunction with solidarity meetings for Nicaragua and the rebels of El Salvador. However, this same emphasis on the value of maintaining a separate ethnic identity is also characteristic of various government departments that are portrayed as the enemy by the OIPUH. Appeals to Indianness or demands for ethnic survival in such ethnically diverse regions as Huejutla are neither inherently reactionary nor inevitably revolutionary, as rival scholars would like to argue. In each case, it is necessary to examine the relationship between belief and behavior, between the official ideology and the actions of state representatives, between the rhetoric used by agrarian politicians and their personal interests and real intentions.

Notes

1. William B. Taylor, *Drinking, Homicide and Rebellion in Colonial Mexican Villages* (Stanford, 1979).

2. Apart from the fact that the Mexican government does not have the resources to conduct thorough investigations into all of these assassinations, it could be argued that the failure to establish clearly who is responsible contributes to some level of political stability by keeping everyone guessing and allowing opposing sides of the political spectrum each to keep believing their own version of what really happened.

3. Conversation with Porfirio Ontiveros, Yahualica, May 12, 1981.

4. I often heard this type of statement from both village and municipal authorities and also saw the aftermaths of some of these fights as the wounded were carried to the nearest available clinic or hospital.

5. Edward P. Thompson, "The Moral Economy of the English Crowd in the Eighteenth Century," *Past and Present* 50 (1971), 76–136.

6. This authoritarian tradition is consistent with the norms of conformity and loyalty that probably go back to colonial or even pre-Hispanic times.

7. In the context of a small community, such a discussion and consensus system is probably more democratic than one based on competing slates of candidates.

8. Interview (in Nahuatl) with village authorities, San Francisco, June 7, 1985. This village also evicted a group of peasants who had joined an even more radical peasant organization.

9. Agustín Avila and Alma E. Cervantes, *Procesos de organización campesina en las huastecas* (Mexico, 1986), 19.

10. Interview with Anacleto Mendoza, Huejutla, May 12, 1985.

11. Interview with Manuel Ramírez, Chalma (Veracruz), June 11, 1984.

12. Interviews with Claudio Ramírez, Audiencia Pública, May 17, 1985; wife of Braulio Pérez, rancho la Reforma, May 21, 1985.

13. Interviews with Odilón Hidalgo, El Cojolite, June 13, 1984.

14. Sidney Mintz and Eric R. Wolf, "An Analysis of Ritual Coparenthood (Compadrazgo)," *Southwest Journal of Anthropology* 6 (1950), 341–68.

15. Avila and Cervantes, *Procesos de organización*, 34–35.

16. Frans J. Schryer, "Class Conflict and the Corporate Peasant Community: Disputes over Land in Nahuatl Villages," *Journal of Anthropological Research* 43 (1987), 99.

17. Julio Ortega, "Gobernadores Indígenas," *El Sol de Hidalgo*, Nov. 25, 1978; idem, "Un Calpulli Huasteco," *El Sol de Hidalgo*, March 2, 1979.

18. Ildefonso N. d. Maya, *Kenke: Que han hecho de mi pueblo?* (Huasteca, 1986), 41.

19. For example, when the radical peasants from Chalahuiyapan established their own chapel after invading a private property in 1985, they emphasized the fact that they would have been unable to do so in the past "when our fathers were still slaves of the hacienda owners." Interview (in Nahuatl) with a group of peasants during a fiesta, June 10, 1985.

20. Several years later, however, a dispute between these two ethnic groups did arise when the Nahua peasants received a larger share of land. Interview with Nicanor Rebolledo and Carlos Robles, Mexico City, January 6, 1987.

21. Interview with Nicanor Rebolledo, Mexico City, January 4, 1987.

22. Serge Gruzinski, "La red agujerada. Identidades étnicas y occidentalización en el México colonial (Siglos XVI–XIX)," *América Indígena* 46 (1986), 411–34.

23. Arij Ouweneel, "Onderbroken Groei in Anáhuac: De ecologische achtergrond van ontwikkeling en armoede in Central-Mexico, 1730–1810," Latin American Studies Series no. 50 (Amsterdam: CEDLA, 1988), 179.

24. Judy Hellman, *Mexico in Crisis* (New York, 1983); Frans J. Schryer, "From Rancheros to Pequeños Propietarios: Agriculture, Class Structure and Politics in the Sierra de Jacala, Mexico," *Boletín de Estudios Latino-americanos y del Cáribe* 34 (1983), 41–42.

25. Interview with Agustín Castillo, Huejutla, May 14, 1985.

26. Part of this life history is recounted on the inside cover and in a preface (written by Roberto Garrido Gutiérrez) of a book by Maya (1986, 11–14). The book's title, in translation, is *Why: What Have They Done to My People?*

27. These aspects of this life history were based on various interviews or conversations with Ildefonso Maya in Huejutla between 1983 and 1986. I was not able to verify through other sources all of what he told me.

28. Conversation (in Nahuatl) with a peasant from Chililico on a bus, April 27, 1985.

29. Apart from running a small clinic, the local INI center could do little more than distribute basketballs to Nahuatl communities and act in a kind of consultative capacity to a variety of other programs.

10

The Maintenance of Mayan Distinctiveness

Evon Z. Vogt

If some of the preceding selections have argued the difficulty of defining native peoples in many regions and situations in modern Latin America, this one, from a study of the Maya municipality of Zinacantan by Evon Vogt, demonstrates the resilience and vitality of the Maya's distinct ethnic identity and the beliefs and behavior that underlay it. Zinacantan itself is composed of a complex of communities organized into the classic head town–subject village relationship that was characteristic of pre-Hispanic times. Each community is subdivided further into a series of family house compounds. Strict gender and age hierarchies prevail. Despite more than four centuries of Catholic influence, the cosmology of the residents is dominated by ancient beliefs, and although modern medicine and improved hygiene have resulted recently in dramatic population growth, the natives still commonly look to local shamans to cure their ailments and troubles.

The question I am most frequently asked about Zinacantan concerns the extent to which the contemporary culture contains or reflects pre-Columbian patterns; or, phrased somewhat differently, what proportion or part of the culture is Ancient Mayan and what proportion is postconquest Spanish or ladino fashioned during the colonial period, then transformed in the last century by the forces of the modern world?

Anthropologists have discovered that no culture is totally static and unchanging. The changes may seem painfully slow, as they undoubtedly were in the Paleolithic, or they may proceed at a breakneck pace, as in the contemporary world. But we have also discovered that cultures display remarkable continuities that persist for hundreds or even thousands of years. The most impressive continuities are structural principles that evolved as the members of an ancestral culture coped with the natural environment, faced problems of order and disorder in their society, and wondered about the meaning of life and death and the movements of the sun, moon, and stars.

In other words, a culture is a complicated combination of structural continuities and constant changes, and Zinacantan in the final decade of the twentieth century is no exception, as will be evident as I look briefly at some important domains of Zinacanteco culture and delineate what we have discovered about its continuities and changes. The continuities are most evident in language, cosmology, and ritual life; the major changes have been demographic, technological, and economic.

Language and Cosmology

Perhaps the most impressive continuity in Zinacanteco culture is the persistence of the language. Although increasing numbers of Zinacantecos are learning Spanish, in school or in wage-work jobs for ladinos, all of them speak fluent Tzotzil, and speak it by preference when they are at home in Zinacantan. To be sure, the Tzotzil that is spoken today has an increasing number of loanwords from Spanish, but the grammar—which follows important structural principles or rules—and most of the vocabulary are Tzotzil Maya, not Spanish. Further, it is clear from our recent field research that Zinacantecos continue to think and dream in Tzotzil.

The implications of this basic persistence of the Tzotzil language are, of course, profound for their cosmology. The casual observer might think that contemporary schooling combined with radio listening, and some television viewing, would by now have altered significantly the Zinacanteco's view of the universe. But compared to the school learning, consider the intense experiences of Zinacanteco children in the family households with shamans arriving frequently to perform ceremonies and pray in Tzotzil to the Ancestral Gods, to Holy Father Sun, and to Holy Mother Moon, or with their parents on a visit in the ceremonial center observing the dancing and the ritual dramas of the cargo holders carrying on their witty dialogues in Tzotzil. It is not surprising that the Zinacanteco universe with its quadrilateral cosmos, its Ancestors in the mountains, its Earth Owner under the ground, and its Saints, Souls, and Crosses is intact and vital.

Family and Social Life

The family and social life of Zinacantan manifests considerably more ongoing change. The house compounds are still present, but the houses are rarely constructed of wattle and daub walls and thatched roofs. Instead, adobe (or cement block) walls with tile roofs (or, in some cases, even laminated roofs) have replaced the old-style houses in almost all of Zinacantan. The tiles, adobes, and cement blocks are a mixed blessing. While they provide a more permanent house, this type of construction is dangerous during the earthquakes that are frequent in southern Mexico. During the devastating earthquake of 1977 in Guatemala, just across the border from the land of the Zinacantecos, most Indians who were killed lived in houses with tile roofs and heavy adobe walls (an architectural style introduced by the Spaniards) that collapsed upon them; the families who still lived in the more traditional wattle-and-daub houses with thatched roofs were spared.

Since the electrification programs of the Mexican government have reached into every major hamlet, Zinacantecos now proudly turn on their electric lights after dark and play their radios and record players. There are also telephones in some of the larger hamlets, and a few families have purchased television sets.

There are a few multiroomed houses, but most are still single-room structures with the fire in the open hearth on the floor. There has been an increase in the use of factory-manufactured utensils in recent years, including pots and pans, enamel and plastic cups, bowls, and buckets. But the traditional "house cross" is still invariably found in the patio outside the principal house in the compound.

Zinacanteco clothing fashions have changed in style and color, especially in the appearance of much more red thread and elaborately embroidered flower designs in the woven shawls of the women and the *chamarras* of the men. Further, almost all the men now wear long trousers and many go bareheaded; the short pants and traditional hats, handwoven from palm strips and displaying flowing, multicolored ribbons, appear mainly on fiesta days in Zinacantan Center or when the men are performing in rituals at home.

There is a marked trend toward more single biological families living by themselves. This trend is due in large part to the recent experience of young Zinacantecos in wage work away from home where they did not have to depend upon the father for farming land and a plot for a house, and where they could also accumulate money to rapidly pay off the bride price without depending on the father for funds. In increasing numbers young men are also choosing to elope with a young woman, then pay off the bride price with money and ask her parents to pardon them in lieu of going through the traditionally long courtship and complex wedding ceremony.[1] Fewer extended patrilocal families also mean fewer *snas*, or patrilineages, of the traditional nature we observed a generation ago in Zinacantan. But since Zinacantecos are returning more to maize farming in the past few years following the bust of the oil boom in southern Mexico, it will be interesting to observe if extended patrilocal families and patrilineages increase again and long courtships and complicated marriage rites become more popular, or whether, as [George A.] Collier suggests, the structure of the family and lineage, and of courtship and marriage practices, are irrevocably changing.[2]

Meanwhile, the flow of daily life continues in the domestic group (whether this unit be an extended family or single biological family), with babies being born at home with the aid of a midwife and being nursed and carried on their mothers' backs, [and] with the customary sexual division of labor; emphasis upon age ranking; and precedence of males over females in bowing-and-releasing behavior, in seating order and the serving of food and liquor at ceremonial meals, and in marching order along trails and roads. All reflect ancient, traditional principles of Mayan social organization.

The Economic System

The economic life of Zinacantan has undergone more rapid and profound changes in the past two decades than any other domain of the culture. There has been a burst in population (from eight thousand to an estimated twenty thousand) as a result of a declining death rate that came with improved sanitary and medical conditions. The consequent scarcity of farming land, the attraction of wage work in the construction projects of the Mexican government, especially highways and hydroelectric dams, and the temporary oil boom in southern Mexico all combined to generate a significant shift from maize farming to other economic activities and to involve the Zinacantecos in the modern world to a greater extent than ever before.

Even traditional maize farming (which continues to be largely of the swidden type) has undergone important changes as Zinacantecos have adopted the use of petrochemicals, especially fertilizers and weed killers. The fertilizers allow some of the highland plots to be continuously farmed for longer periods; the weed killers reduce significantly the amount of labor and time needed for the summer weeding operations, and hence permit fewer men to weed more land. This means that the need for large farming groups, composed traditionally of patrilineal kinsmen and/or hired Chamula laborers, has been reduced, with important consequences for organization of large patrilineages. Enterprising Zinacanteco entrepreneurs who devoted their efforts to growing surplus maize a generation ago are now purchasing trucks and buses and becoming a new type of elite that provides transportation for people and goods.[3]

For the Zinacantecos who are not predominantly maize farmers or truck owners, several alternative economic activities have emerged. In agriculture, there is a new emphasis upon flowers and fruits grown on small

highland plots in or near the hamlets. Many more men have become primarily merchants, buying and selling the major products of Zinacanteco agriculture—corn, beans, fruit, and flowers—and retailing them in the major
urban markets throughout Chiapas.[4]

Still others who own no farming land at all have become essentially
proletarians who sell their labor. As [Frank] Cancian describes them, they
are of several types, reflecting the diversity of the changing regional economy
and the roles of Indians in the system:

> The unskilled laborers work mostly on construction outside Zinacantan.
> They represent continuity with earlier labor roles, and, as before, they are
> predominantly young men. The government employees, truck drivers, and
> artisans (mostly masons) are in new occupations. Most of the government
> employees work in new reforestation programs; many of the artisans
> learned their trades during the construction boom in the 1970s; and the
> truck drivers are part of the expanded Indian role in local transportation
> that resulted from new roads and subsidized gasoline prices. All of these
> new occupations are tied to state and/or capitalist development programs
> that blossomed in the last ten or fifteen years.[5]

The Zinacanteco Cargo System

Unlike the rapid, ongoing changes in the economic and social domains, the
ritual life of Zinacantan, including both the ceremonies of the cargo holders
and the rites of the shamans, has shown little basic change and is amazingly
intact. There have been predictions that the cargo system of Zinacantan
would disappear as an important institution, as it had in other Mesoamerican
Indian communities, when the rate of population growth outstripped the
increase in cargo positions and surplus wealth began to be used in other
ways.[6]

As of 1990, the cargo system is intact, with sixty-one positions, and the
cargo ceremonies are being performed much as they were twenty years ago.
The major changes we note are matters of elaboration or enrichment of the
basic patterns (such as the addition of more coins, ribbons, and mirrors on
the images of the saints, or the addition of electric singing bird ornaments on
the branches of trees surrounding the crèche erected in the Church of San
Lorenzo for the Christmas season), rather than changes in ritual sequence or
structure.

On the other hand, the role of the cargo system in the local social
structure has been diminished as the Zinacanteco population has nearly
tripled while the number of cargos has remained virtually constant. There
was a temporary increase from sixty-one to sixty-five cargos for a few years
in the 1980s that came with the addition of four positions from outlying
hamlets, but these were dropped in 1987.

With the vast increase in population, a smaller proportion of Zinacantecos is participating in the cargo system. This change was reflected in the waiting lists for cargos, which grew longer through the 1960s but became shorter in the late 1970s and early 1980s.[7] But significantly, when the oil boom ended and Zinacantecos returned home from wage work away, the cargo lists grew longer once more.

The other adjustments to greater population pressure on the cargo system are that rigid adherence to the rules of progress through the four levels of the hierarchy has begun to break down, and three-cargo careers have become an accepted alternative to the traditional four-cargo careers. But, perhaps the greatest factor diminishing the importance of the cargo system is the large number of civil cargos produced by the state modernization programs. Instead of the traditional cargo service, many Zinacantecos are, for example, now serving as secretary of the School Committee or as electric light commissioner. Still others find a significant alternative in serving as officers for political parties.

History and Functions of the Cargo System

The history and functions of the cargo system as a crucial institution in Mayan society have been the subject of spirited controversy in the past twenty years. The debate rages around three basic questions:

(1) Does the cargo system of the type we observe in Zinacantan have some pre-Columbian roots in Mayan prehistory, and can the system be useful in illuminating the probable sociopolitical organization of the Ancient Maya ceremonial centers? Or was the system introduced by the Spanish conquerors and/or developed during the colonial period? Since the names of the cargos and the saints are entirely derived from Spanish, it is evident that much of the content of the system was indeed introduced after the conquest. Some scholars maintain that many of the principles of organization have precedents among the Ancient Maya[8] while others argue that the cargo system was a new development during the colonial and modern periods in southern Mexico.[9] Bricker has recently demonstrated that some of the cargo rituals performed in contemporary Chamula have been performed by the Maya since the Classic Period 1,500 years ago.[10] The historian Nancy Farriss concludes that: "Most of the formal elements of the contemporary cargo system are colonial adaptations of earlier practices. Its underlying rationale, in which prestige and authority are based on material support of the corporate deity-saint, also has deep roots in the Maya past."[11] Recent summaries of the present state of the controversy may be found in [Gordon R.] Willey and [Evon Z.] Vogt.[12]

(2) Does the cargo system serve as a leveling mechanism that helps to erase differentials in wealth within the Maya communities and consequently to contribute to the social integration of the communities? [Manning] Nash and [Eric R.] Wolf maintained that the expenditure of funds by cargo holders did indeed serve as a leveling mechanism (like a graduated income tax) and help maintain social equilibrium within the closed corporate communities of the Indians.[13] Cancian discovered that the Zinacanteco cargo system is ineffectual as a leveling mechanism and does not keep the community homogeneous.[14] He suggests, rather, that service in the cargo system legitimizes the wealth differences and thus prevents disruptive envy. An illuminating review of this controversial point has been provided by [James B.] Greenberg.[15]

(3) Can cargo systems only be understood by studying them in the larger context of a regional market system and political structure? This question has been addressed by two types of theorists. On the one hand, there is the "dualist" argument that Indian communities are in a separate economic sector that is poorly integrated with the developed capitalist sector. In this separate section the cargo hierarchies maintain a system of reciprocity and redistributive exchange that serves to keep a portion of the surplus from entering the outside market and thus lessens the Indians' dependence on and exploitation by the market.[16] On the other hand, the "dependence" theorists maintain that the cargo system and its fiesta rituals were essentially a colonial instrument designed to reduce the costs of direct administration and to pump wealth and labor out of Indian communities. This position is argued especially by Harris, who views the effect of fiestas as one of raising consumption standards of the Indians and involving them in commercial transactions with ladinos who control the commodities they have come to crave.[17] Involvement in the market requires cash, which must be earned by producing and selling a surplus or by seeking outside wage work. [B. R.] DeWalt, [Waldemar R.] Smith, and Greenberg provide analyses of this controversy and show how knowledge of contemporary cargo systems of Mexico and Guatemala can be deepened by examining their operations in the context of the economic and political structure of the region and nation.[18] Cancian and Collier have clearly shown this to be true in Chiapas with their examinations of the intricate connections between Zinacantan and the regional political economy.[19]

Shamanistic Ceremonies

The rituals of the shamans are also carried on with great vigor and vitality. A new shelter has been constructed over the top of *Kalvaryo*, where the

Ancestral Gods meet on the hill at the edge of Zinacantan Center. But the new shelter is to keep the shamans from getting cold and wet during storms; it has not altered the structure and sequence of their rituals carried on at the old, traditional cross shrine under the new roof.

I estimate that there are now at least two hundred fifty shamans in Zinacantan, and they are still actively performing all of the types of ceremonies. On my last hike to the top of the Senior Large Mountain to visit the sacred shrine in the summer of 1987, I met three curing groups with their shamans in a single morning. They were all leading their patients and ritual assistants up the steep trail to reach the ancestral mountain shrine that lies over 2,000 feet above the valley of Zinacantan. Each was performing the "Great Vision" ceremony, the longest and most complex of the rituals of the shamans.

To be sure, more modern medicine is reaching the Zinacantecos via the government clinics and hospitals, as well as through the pharmacies of San Cristóbal and Tuxtla Gutiérrez. And the Zinacantecos have learned to be very pragmatic about trying out these medicines for their ailments. They readily seek dental work for toothaches, casts for broken bones, and aspirin for minor headaches. But if a Zinacanteco has a lingering illness, or if it is suspected that the trouble may be loss of parts of the soul, or, worse, that one's animal spirit companion has been turned out of its protective corral, or if an enemy is engaged in some type of witchcraft, a shaman is summoned with dispatch to perform divination and a proper curing ceremony.

Further, new houses must be ritually blessed and the Earth Owner properly compensated for the materials used in the construction; maize fields need ceremonies, as do the ancestors of lineages and waterhole groups; rainmaking rites are necessary in drought years. And who would think it even possible to dispense with the annual Year Renewal ceremonies that are performed so that the year may pass in happiness and contentment, without sickness or death?[20]

Politics and the Larger World

As Zinacantan has been enmeshed more deeply into the modern world, the past twenty years have been especially turbulent in the political sphere. Influence has passed from caciques (political bosses) whose power base was control of the distribution of ejido land to caciques that emerged either from ownership of trucks and buses that now provide the basic transport for Zinacantecos and their goods, or from control of new key economic positions, such as soft drink distributors. Twenty years ago the *presidentes* were mainly selected from the ranks of men who held key posts in the ejido committees; in recent years they have been truck owners, and the most recent *presidente* (as of January 1, 1989) is the Pepsi-Cola distributor.

The fissioning process that has long been evident in Zinacanteco communities also became more evident in the last two decades. Zinacanteco hamlets, especially those located along the Pan American Highway, have shown greater tendencies to become more autonomous. These hamlets have created local "*agencias*" (agencies) with civil officials who sit on benches and settle disputes. If the litigants accept the resolution of the case, then they do not have the extra expense and travel time involved in going to the *presidente* in Zinacantan Center. To date, no hamlet has achieved *municipio* status, but the pressures are there, and one wonders if we are witnessing the kind of fissioning process that must have characterized Maya culture over the centuries as outlying communities flourished in population growth and political power and separated from their parent communities.

The role of factions both within Zinacantan Center and within the hamlets also has become exacerbated in recent years. These factions, often originating in disputes over land, have been present throughout the decades we have observed Zinacantan, but in the early 1980s the major fission became hooked onto national Mexican political parties for the first time. The most dramatic conflict emerged in 1982 when a new *presidente* was to be chosen. As Frank Cancian succinctly describes the events:

> The dominant PRI [the Partido Revolucionario Institucional] party split into factions that were soon labeled *campesinos* (farmers) and *camioneros* (truckers). In an unusually contested public nomination meeting, the "truckers" succeeded in naming their candidate as the official PRI nominee—which is tantamount to nomination in most parts of Mexico. The "farmers" faction rebelled and voted for the candidate of the very small opposition (PAN, i.e., the Partido de Acción Nacional) party, and he was elected. PRI officials blocked his access to the town hall and the records he needed to function as mayor, and official delegations travelled to the state capital to try to resolve the dispute.[21]

In this factional dispute the number of "truckers" far exceeded those directly involved in trucking, indicating that the political party affiliation was a label for a preexisting faction. The dispute wrecked the 1983 to 1985 term of office of this *presidente*. By the next term, PRI had installed its candidate for *presidente*, and continued to hold the office in the 1988 election. In spite of the fact that Zinacantecos have very little knowledge of the national programs and ideologies of the two parties, the PRI and PAN labels continue to designate quarreling factions in most Zinacanteco hamlets. And it is clear that this line of fission between "farmers" and "truckers" symbolically represents an opposition between older, more traditional patterns and new patterns of Zinacanteco life that have come with their increasing involvement with the industrialized world.

Even deeper factional pressures have recently resulted from increasing activity of Protestant missionaries in the highlands of Chiapas.[22] Most Zinacantecos continue to be Catholics, in the sense that they have been baptized by a Catholic priest, and if you ask them directly about their religion they will tell you they are *Católicos*, even though, as we have seen, their knowledge of Catholic theology and practice may be slight. But in the past decade the first inroads into Zinacantan were made by a Presbyterian missionary who worked for a few years in the hamlet of Nabenchauk. When he was forced to leave the hamlet by the Indian authorities, a number of Zinacanteco families moved with him to a settlement called Nuevo Zinacantan located just off the Pan American Highway some fifteen miles east of San Cristóbal. Here the newly converted Presbyterian Zinacantecos farm plots of land provided them by the mission and attend Sunday church services that are an ingenious combination of their traditional customs and new ritual procedures. As I observed one of these services in 1987, I noted that there was no liquor, incense, or candles—these items being considered either too traditional or too Catholic to be included. But the fresh pine needles were on the floor of the church; the Indian participants as well as the Presbyterian missionary wore traditional Zinacanteco clothes; the prayers to the sick pronounced by members of the congregation kneeling on the pine needles on the floor followed the cadence and style of the prayers of the traditional shamans; and the Protestant hymns, translated into Tzotzil, were sung to the playing of guitars, violins, and trumpets, with tunes taken directly from various Mexican *ranchera* songs—such as *El Rancho Grande*—which the Zinacantecos have been hearing on their radios for the past thirty years.

Meanwhile, the Catholics have not been idle in the face of this Protestant threat. For the first time Zinacantan has a resident Catholic priest, and he is making every effort to relate significantly to the traditional customs. He is learning Tzotzil, he wears items of Zinacanteco clothing, and he encourages the traditional ritual dances to take place inside the Church of San Lorenzo, even when it competes with the Mass.

Whither Zinacantan?

At first glance, Zinacantan now seems completely caught up in the modern world: trucks, buses, and cars roar along the Pan American Highway and in and out of the ceremonial center on a paved road that has reduced the travel time to the market in San Cristóbal from over two hours (on foot carrying maize with a tumpline) to less than fifteen minutes by motor vehicle. Corn-grinding mills have replaced the laborious work of grinding the maize for tortillas on manos and metates. Electric lights and flashlights instead of pine torches illuminate the houses, churches, and streets at night. The scribes, who keep records for the cargo holders of their communitywide collections to pay the expenses of fiestas, now add up the totals with calculators rather than with grains of corn. Tourists arrive, often in tour groups by the busload, and must check in at the cabildo to purchase a permit to visit the churches.

But a longer visit, especially during early morning hours or at night during the times when important annual ceremonies are being performed, soon alters and deepens these first superficial impressions. In the summer of 1987 and the winter of 1988 I returned to Zinacantan, especially to observe the crucial summer (San Lorenzo) and winter (Christmas and San Sebastián) ceremonies. Comparing my recent field notes with my observations of these fiestas thirty years ago, I discovered there had been no changes in either the overall structure or in the sequence of ritual episodes in these ceremonies. Further, the attendance of people from the hamlets was impressive, and the ceremonies were performed with even greater vitality and enthusiasm than in earlier years.

Even more impressive was the general lack of drunkenness in these fiestas compared to earlier decades, when the scene was one of intoxicated Zinacantecos by the hundreds. In the last two large fiestas I attended, with over five thousand Indians present, I did not encounter more than six heavily intoxicated Zinacantecos. This is an extraordinary development; in fact, it may be one of the few cases in the New World in which a large native American population has managed to bring the excessive consumption of alcohol under control.

The crucial reason for this change is most probably an improvement in the morale of the Zinacantecos. During the last three decades I have personally witnessed a vast improvement in the morale of the highland Chiapas Indians. When I began field research in Chiapas in the 1950s the economic, political, and social oppression of the Indians was notable, and the consequent morale of the Indian communities was at a low ebb. One index of this morale was the excessive consumption of alcohol in the form of aguardiente (the cheap sugarcane rum which is called *posh* in Tzotzil).

In the 1950s the Instituto Nacional Indígenista, founded by Mexico's foremost anthropologist, the late Dr. Alfonso Caso, began to work in the highlands of Chiapas. In subsequent years, other federal and state agencies also began to institute programs to aid oppressed Indian communities. The programs that were introduced included a spectrum of development projects, ranging from improved breeds of chickens to the training of bilingual Indian teachers (called "Cultural Promoters") for schools. There has been much debate in Mexico and elsewhere about the success or failure of these programs. In perspective, it is clear that although many of the programs failed, or were of only limited success, the long-range effect of the Instituto Nacional Indígenista and its successors has been a vast improvement in Indian morale. The important thing is that for the first time in over four hundred years of oppression an *official* agency of the Mexican government appeared, saying, "We are here to help Indians." As a result, Indians slowly began to acquire a sense of pride in their own identity; they have also slowly learned during the past thirty years how to be politically effective with government officials, how to borrow money from banks for economic enterprises, and how to purchase trucks and buses.[23]

Further, I discovered that for the first time large numbers of Highland Chiapas Indians are living in the principal market town of San Cristóbal de las Casas *as Indians*. In previous decades Indians came to the city, but upon arrival, immediately began the process of "ladinoization." They learned Spanish as rapidly as possible, changed clothing so as to be dressed like working-class ladinos, and abandoned most of their Indian customs. Now, with the attraction of wage work in San Cristóbal with its burgeoning population, and with the arrival of Indian Protestant converts who have been forced to leave their native communities, the Indians are locating plots of land and building or buying houses and maintaining their Indian clothing styles and many of their customs. The Protestant movement has had the effect of energizing the traditional Maya work ethic: get up early, work hard, and be punctual. One of the results is that the San Cristóbal market, which was previously dominated by ladinos, is slowly coming more and more under the control of Indian merchants and entrepreneurs. While this process has involved the large Chamula population more than it has the Zinacantecos, the latter are beginning to participate as well.

While we used to describe "the ladinoization of the Indians" as one of the basic processes of change in the highlands of Chiapas, we are now beginning to consider "the Indianization of San Cristóbal" as a crucial contemporary trend. As Zinacantan approaches the twenty-first century, it presents an overall image of reproductive success, cultural vitality, and a generally successful, if somewhat uneasy, adjustment to the modern world.

Notes

1. George A. Collier, "Changing Inequality in Zinacantan: The Generations of 1918 and 1942," *Ethnographic Encounters in Southern Mesoamerica: Essays in Honor of Evon Zartman Vogt, Jr.*, ed. Victoria R. Bricker and Gary H. Gossen (Austin, 1989), 111–124.

2. Ibid.

3. Frank Cancian, "Proletarianization of Zinacantan, 1960 to 1983," *Household Economies and Their Transformation*, ed. Morgan D. Machlaclan (Lanham, MD, 1987).

4. Ibid.

5. Ibid., 134.

6. For example, Frank Cancian, *Economics and Prestige in a Maya Community: A Study of the Religious Cargo System in Zinacantan, Chiapas, Mexico* (Stanford, 1965).

7. Frank Cancian, "Las Listas de Espera en el Sistema de Cargos de Zinacantan: Cambios Sociales, Politicos y Economicos (1952–1980)," *America Indigena* XLVI(3) (1986), 477–494.

8. For example, Evon Z. Vogt, "Ancient and Contemporary Maya Settlement Patterns: A New Look from the Chiapas Highlands," *Prehistoric Settlement Patterns: Essays in Honor of Gordon R. Willey*, ed. Evon Z. Vogt and Richard M. Leventhal (Albuquerque, 1983), 89–114.

9. For example, Jan Rus and Robert Wasserstrom, "Civil-Religious Hierarchies in Central Chiapas: A Critical Perspective," *American Ethnologist* 7 (1980), 466–478.

10. Victoria R. Bricker, "The Calendrical Meaning of Ritual among the Maya," *Ethnographic Encounters in Southern Mesoamerica*, 231–250.

11. Nancy M. Farriss, *Maya Society under Colonial Rule: The Collective Enterprise of Survival* (Princeton, 1984), 348.

12. Gordon R. Willey, "Vogt at Harvard," *Ethnographic Encounters in Southern Mesoamerica*, 21–32; Evon Z. Vogt, "On the Application of the Phylogenetic Model to the Maya," *The Social Anthropology and Ethnohistory of American Tribes: Essays in Honor of Fred Eggan*, ed. Raymond B. DeMallie and Alfonso Ortiz (Norman, 1989).

13. Manning Nash, "Political Relations in Guatemala," *Social and Economic Studies* 7 (1958), 65–75; Eric R. Wolf, *Sons of the Shaking Earth* (Chicago, 1959).

14. Frank Cancian, *Economics and Prestige.*

15. James B. Greenberg, "Social Change and Fiesta Systems in Mexican Indian Communities," *Latin American Digest* 15(2) (1981), 1–5.

16. James W. Dow, *Santos y Sobrevivencia: Funciones de la Religion en una Communidad Otomi, Mexico* (Mexico, 1974).

17. Marvin Harris, *Patterns of Race in the Americas* (New York, 1964).

18. B. R. DeWalt, "Changes in the Cargo System of Mesoamerica," *Anthropological Quarterly* 48 (1975), 87–105; Waldemar R. Smith, *The Fiesta System and Economic Change* (New York, 1977); Greenberg, "Social Change and Fiesta Systems," 1–5.

19. Cancian, "Proletarianization of Zinacantan, 1960 to 1983"; Collier, "Changing Inequality in Zinacantan."

20. Evon Z. Vogt, *Tortillas for the Gods: A Symbolic Analysis of Zinacanteco Rituals* (Cambridge, MA, 1976).

21. Cancian, "Proletarianization of Zinacantan, 1960 to 1983."

22. Gary H. Gossen, "Life, Death, and Apotheosis of a Chamula Protestant Leader: Biography as Social History," *Ethnographic Encounters in Southern Mesoamerica*, 217–230.

23. Evon Z. Vogt, "The Chiapas Writers' Cooperative," *Cultural Survival Quarterly* 9(3) (1985), 46–48.

Glossary

Aclla
Women assigned to religious centers under the Incas.

Alcaldía mayor
Mayoralty office.

Arcabuz
An early musket.

Ayllu
A Peruvian term for a kinship group and the land it controls.

Cabecera
The head town of an indigenous province.

Cacicazgo
The lands controlled by a native lord.

Cacique
A term the Spanish apply broadly to native rulers.

Caciquismo
Political bossism.

Cargo system
A common practice in rural communities whereby men attain prestige and power through sponsorship of religious festivals.

Cofradía
A confraternity.

Corregimiento
The colonial political jurisdiction for an Indian province.

Curaca
See **Kuraka**.

Ejido
A collective landholding in Mexico.

Escribano
A notary public.

Huaca
See **Wak'a.**

Jacal
A hut.

Juez (jueces, pl.)
A judge.

Kuraka (curaca)
A native ruler or lord in the Andes.

Ladino
A hispanized Indian or person of mixed blood.

Macehual
The native term in Mexico for an Indian commoner.

Mestizo
A person of mixed European and Indian ancestry.

Mit'a
The Andean term for required rotary labor service.

Mitaq (or mitmaq) (mitimae, pl.)
Colonists from different ethnic groups under the Incas.

Nahua
The people of the largest indigenous language group in Mexico.

Obraje
A large workshop, often producing textiles and utilizing forced laborers.

Panaqa
A royal lineage under the Incas.

Pardo
A person of mixed European and African ancestry.

Peninsular
An immigrant from Spain.

Principal
A native noble.

Puna
High mountain grasslands in the Andes.

Ranchero
The owner of a private farm or ranch.

Sujeto
A village or hamlet under the jurisdiction of a head town in an Indian province.

Swidden
Slash-and-burn agriculture.

Tepache
Crude fermented drink derived from the maguey cactus.

Tributario
A tribute payer.

Wak'a (or huaca)
A sacred site or object in the Andes.

Yana (or yanacona)
A personal retainer in the Andean region.

Yori
The Yaqui term for a European.

Suggested Readings

The cultural achievements of the Aztecs, Maya, and Incas, reinforced by the relative abundance of documentation that we have on their civilizations both before and after the arrival of the Spanish, have understandably drawn the attention of scholars more than have those of other peoples of the Americas with important but less majestic histories. Scholars have likewise devoted themselves mostly to the colonial period, largely for two reasons. First, many of the most dramatic events and developments transpired during this period. Second, Indians as corporate groups are more difficult to trace in most Latin American countries following independence, while they likewise have seemed to most investigators as rather peripheral to the primary trajectories and issues in these national histories. This view is currently being modified, and, as we shall see, several fine books have recently examined the role of native peoples in the modern period.

Abundant archaeological remains, a few surviving codices, and a diverse body of postconquest chronicles written by both indigenous intellectuals and interested Spaniards (mostly clerics) provide a rich repository of evidence that reaches deeply into the pre-Hispanic history of Mesoamerica and the Andean highlands. The best single volume that outlines the salient characteristics of the great civilizations that punctuated Mexican history for perhaps three thousand years before the coming of Cortés is Nigel Davies, *The Ancient Kingdoms of Mexico* (New York: Penguin Books, 1983). A thorough and persuasive study of patterns of Aztec warfare and the growth and structure of the Aztec empire is Ross Hassig, *Aztec Warfare: Imperial Expansion and Political Control* (Norman: University of Oklahoma Press, 1988).

Charles Gibson, *The Aztecs under Spanish Rule: A History of the Indians of the Valley of Mexico, 1519–1810* (Stanford: Stanford University Press, 1964), represents one of the abiding monuments in the history of the natives of Latin America. It examines the indigenous communities of central Mexico in the colonial period to portray how various external forces brought about important transformations and how certain crucial continuities and ethnic identity were maintained. Many of the concepts and relationships that were first enumerated in this lengthy work remain central to our vision of this advanced culture zone.

More recently, scholars, especially some who have learned to read documents in Nahuatl, the primary native language to this day in Mexico, have penetrated more deeply into cultural change at the local level and have probed adaptations inside the indigenous community and even within the family after the arrival of the Europeans. Louise M. Burkhart, *The Slippery Earth: Nahua-Christian Dialogue in Sixteenth-Century Mexico* (Tucson: University of Arizona Press, 1989), analyzes how Christian concepts were translated into Nahuatl and were understood by native converts. S. L. Cline, *Colonial Culhuacan, 1580–1600: A Social History of an Aztec Town* (Albuquerque: University of New Mexico Press, 1986), utilizes a set of wills generated just a few generations after the conquest in a community close to Mexico City to study change in such vital institutions as landholding, inheritance, and the position and activities of women.

The most comprehensive examination of the transformation of native life and culture within central Mexican communities during the colonial period is James Lockhart, *The Nahuas after the Conquest* (Stanford: Stanford University Press, 1992). It analyzes social, political, and family relationships and even explores changes in belief systems and language use.

Much acculturation and race mixture transpired in urban settings. John K. Chance, *Race and Class in Colonial Oaxaca* (Stanford: Stanford University Press, 1978), which examines social and ethnic change in a city in southern Mexico, represents the best systematic study of such phenomena over an extended period.

Of course, not all aspects of pre-Hispanic religious belief systems were eliminated over time. In isolated areas that avoided systematic Spanish social and economic penetration, earlier traditions were maintained. Serge Gruzinski, *Man-Gods in the Mexican Highlands: Indian Power and Colonial Society, 1520–1800* (Stanford: Stanford University Press, 1989), looks at four natives who declared themselves to be god incarnate, examining their beliefs and what their existence says about the kind of cultural transformation that took place.

Steve J. Stern, the author of one of the contributions in this collection, has composed a more fully rendered book on the social and cultural changes that took place among the Andean peoples during the first century of colonization, *Peru's Indian Peoples and the Challenge of Spanish Conquest: Huamanga to 1640* (Madison: University of Wisconsin Press, 1982). Karen W. Spalding, *Huarochirí: An Andean Society under Inca and Spanish Rule* (Stanford: Stanford University Press, 1984), is an equally distinguished study of a native province, this one located closer to Lima, the center of Spanish settlement. It also offers careful consideration of the impact of the Inca empire on this subjugated people in the century before the coming of the Europeans.

Sabine MacCormack, *Religion in the Andes: Vision and Imagination in Early Colonial Peru* (Princeton: Princeton University Press, 1991), constitutes a modern classic. In a careful and thorough manner, it depicts the penetration of Christian ideas into the Andean world of the sacred, showing how some major writers and common people reconciled the two belief systems, their symbols, and their shrines.

Ann M. Wightman, *Indigenous Migration and Social Change: The Forasteros of Cuzco, 1570–1720* (Durham: Duke University Press, 1989), addresses the issue of native migration into the important regional center of Cuzco. She considers which types of people moved to the city, for what reasons, and what impact they had both on the communities they left behind and on the city they moved to.

The Indian peoples of the Andes maintained a tradition of violent resistance to external rule that was even more vibrant than the case in Mexico. This endemic protest peaked in the massive Tupac Amaru revolt that broke out in 1780. Scarlett O'Phelan Godoy, *Rebellions and Revolts in Eighteenth-Century Peru and Upper Peru* (Cologne: Böhlau Verlag, 1985), carefully examines the larger tradition of resistance in which this great revolt occurred. Steve J. Stern, ed., *Resistance, Rebellion, and Consciousness in the Andean Peasant World, Eighteenth to Twentieth Centuries* (Madison: University of Wisconsin Press, 1987), offers a series of case studies of violent protests in this culture zone over the last three centuries.

The extended resistance of the various Maya peoples to Spanish colonization has recently attracted the attention of a new generation of scholars who have rendered sensitive depictions of the military and cultural conflict that took place in the Yucatán. Two of the very best of these are Inga Clendinnen, *Ambivalent Conquest: Maya and Spaniard in Yucatán, 1517–1570* (Cambridge, Eng.: Cambridge University Press, 1987), and Grant D. Jones, *Maya Resistance to Spanish Rule: Time and History on a Colonial Frontier* (Albuquerque: University of New Mexico Press, 1989).

The Spanish experienced a greatly different situation among the tribal societies and hunting-and-gathering peoples found throughout much of Latin America. Some of these societies were able to resist very resolutely. Philip Wayne Powell, *Soldiers, Indians, and Silver: The Northward Advance of New Spain, 1550–1600* (Berkeley: University of California Press, 1952), lays out the series of Spanish initiatives against the nomadic peoples of northern Mexico in the late sixteenth century and the reasons for the failure of so many of them and for the limited success that finally occurred. A very different trajectory in native-colonist relations is treated in Elman R. Service, *Spanish-Guaraní Relations in Early Colonial Paraguay* (Ann Arbor: Univerity of Michigan Press, 1954). Here the Guaraní and the Spaniards, both vulnerable to depradations from the warlike peoples who surrounded them in central Paraguay, entered into an understanding in which they intermarried and joined forces in mutual protection. Spanish colonists gained access to the Indian labor that could bring about prosperity only through their relationships with senior females of this ethnic group, the people who had privileged claims on labor service from their male relatives.

As previously noted, the volume and overall quality of books on Latin American Indians in the national period are distinctly inferior to those for the colonial period. Nonetheless, some very valuable work has appeared, particularly in the last decade or so. Mexico is heavily represented in both the colonial and the national periods. Nelson Reed, *The Caste War of Yucatán* (Stanford: Stanford University Press, 1964), is a sophisticated examination of the character of a massive Maya revolt against the provincial government that broke out in the late 1840s and persisted into the early twentieth century. Deep racial animosities and the sanction a new local religion gave to the revolt's leaders fueled this enduring uprising. Even after the Mexican Revolution of 1910 to 1920, Maya communities far in the interior of the peninsula aspired to gain munitions and international support to initiate a new insurrection. They even sought to draw American archaeologists into their struggle, a facet well explored in Paul Sullivan, *Unfinished Conversations: Mayas and Foreigners between Two Wars* (New York: Alfred A. Knopf, 1989).

The Mexican Revolution itself included Indian participation, perhaps no place more than in the Zapata movement. This key aspect of the larger revolution is beautifully described in John Womack, Jr., *Zapata and the Mexican Revolution* (New York: Alfred A. Knopf, 1970). The subsequent twentieth-century history of the native peoples in this same region is explored in Arturo Warman, *We Come to Object* (Baltimore: Johns Hopkins University Press, 1981). Paul Friedrich, *Agrarian Revolt in a Mexican Village* (Chicago: University of Chicago Press, 1970), offers a marvelously well-developed yet succinct examination of the struggle for agrarian reform in an Indian community in another region of Mexico in the decades following the revolution.

Two distinguished studies have appeared recently on the responses of indigenous peoples in the Andean highlands to the economic transformations brought to the region in the late nineteenth and early twentieth centuries. Florencia E. Mallon, *The Defense of Community in Peru's Central Highlands: Peasant Struggle and Capitalist Transition, 1860–1940* (Princeton: Princeton University Press, 1983), looks at changes that transpired within communities brought about first by a foreign invasion of the nation and later by the installation of a modern copper smelter. Erick D. Langer, *Economic Change and Rural Resistance in Southern Bolivia, 1880–1930* (Stanford: Stanford

University Press, 1989), treats the impact of the emergence of commercial agriculture on diverse communities of native peoples in southern Bolivia, a region previously long divorced from the market economy.

Suggested Films

Valuable fictional and documentary films about the history and culture of Latin American Indians have been produced over the years. One of several films that portrays the subjugation of various peoples, *The Conquest of Mexico* (1988) is a thirty-five-minute documentary that describes Cortés's conquest of Mexico and how it has been viewed by individuals in different eras. *Conflict of the Gods* (1992, program two in the series The Buried Mirror: Reflections of Spain and the New World), retraces in one hour the world of pre-Hispanic Mexico, the nature and impact of the conquest, and the transformed world of the Indians in the early colonial world. *Francisco Pizarro: Inca Nation, Peru, 1532* (1976) is a sixty-minute fictional recreation of Pizarro's expedition into Peru through the capture and execution of Atahualpa and the Spaniards' entrance into Cuzco, the Incas' capital city.

Aguirre: The Wrath of God* (1972), the acclaimed German director Werner Herzog's full-length fictional version of a sixteenth-century expedition into the headwaters of the Amazon, concentrates on the deterioration of the Spaniards as they ventured deep into a lush natural setting populated by elusive natives, neither of which they could understand, let alone subdue. In addition to the compelling story and quality acting and production, the movie is evocative of the most ill-fated Spanish undertakings against the tropical hunting-and-gathering societies. A Hollywood production company is currently filming *Cortés*, a high-budgeted treatment of the conquest of the Aztec empire that seeks a laudable level of historical accuracy.

Perhaps understandably, little of value has been produced on Latin American Indian history in the colonial period and the nineteenth century; these developments are not well known by the general public, and they often lack compelling dramatic interest. The significant exception is Roland Joffé's popular film *The Mission* (1986), which, although it possesses considerable pedagogical value, greatly overstates and romanticizes an episode from the Paraguayan region in the mid-eighteenth century.

Elia Kazan's *Zapata* (1952), from a screenplay by John Steinbeck, regards this central figure of the Mexican Revolution as a spokesperson for the nation's suffering peasantry. It does not fully appreciate that his revolt emerged from one of the most Indian regions of that country, but it remains useful for depicting the nature of the revolution and the social and racial attitudes of the time. Of note is the fine historical documentary *Martin Chambi and the Heirs of the Incas* (1990), which, in fifty minutes, examines the career and work of an Indian of Peru who ran a photography studio in Cuzco during the early part of this century and recorded the lives and rituals of both rural peoples and city dwellers.

Two one-half-hour productions in the series Faces of Culture significantly enhance our understanding of the position and values of Latin American Indians in the modern world. Number 14, *The Aymara: A Case Study in Social Stratification* (1983), depicts the lives of two interdependent communities in highland Bolivia, one a mestizo market town and the other an Indian peasant village. The marketplace, religion, education, labor systems, and health care are among the subjects covered. Number 16, *The Highland Maya: A Case Study in Economic Anthropology* (1983), studies the role of the cargo system and fiestas in a Guatemalan community, showing their economic impact and how individuals utilize them to attain higher social standing and authority in local society.

Sacred Games (1989) provides a rich treatment of an annual carnival in a Mayan community in southern Mexico. One hour in length, it displays the merger of Catholicism with traditional Mayan rites and focuses on the activities of one of the sponsors of the week-long festival.

A more multidimensional examination of a contemporary Mayan community is *Todos Santos Cuchumatan: Report from a Guatemalan Village* (1983). In forty minutes it treats local rituals and ways of life, and examines the impact of the seasonal migration of people from the community to cotton plantations in the lowlands.

The Earth Is Our Mother (1986, fifty-five minutes) compares two Indian tribes in modern Colombia and Venezuela as they respond to intensive missionary campaigns. In one case the people have become heavily dependent on the religious order and cannot maintain their traditional way of life. The other society eventually ran the missionaries off its land and continues to maintain a vibrant, autonomous culture and control over its own land.

Jaguar Books on Latin America

William H. Beezley and
Colin MacLachlan
Editors

Volumes Published

John E. Kicza, ed., *The Indian in Latin American History: Resistance, Resilience, and Acculturation* (1993). Cloth ISBN 0-8420-2421-2 Paper ISBN 0-8420-2425-5

Susan E. Place, ed., *Tropical Rainforests: Latin American Nature and Society in Transition* (1993). Cloth ISBN 0-8420-2423-9 Paper ISBN 0-8420-2427-1

About the Editor

John E. Kicza is a professor of Latin American history at Washington State University and received his doctoral training at the University of California, Los Angeles. His previous publications include *Colonial Entrepreneurs: Families and Business in Bourbon Mexico City* (1983), and he is currently working on a comparative study of patterns in Spanish warfare against non-Western peoples to 1600.

He has held a Fulbright Program—American Republics Research Grant in Mexico City, was the Paul W. McQuillen Fellow at the John Carter Brown Library, and was a National Endowment for the Humanities Resident Scholar at the School of American Research.